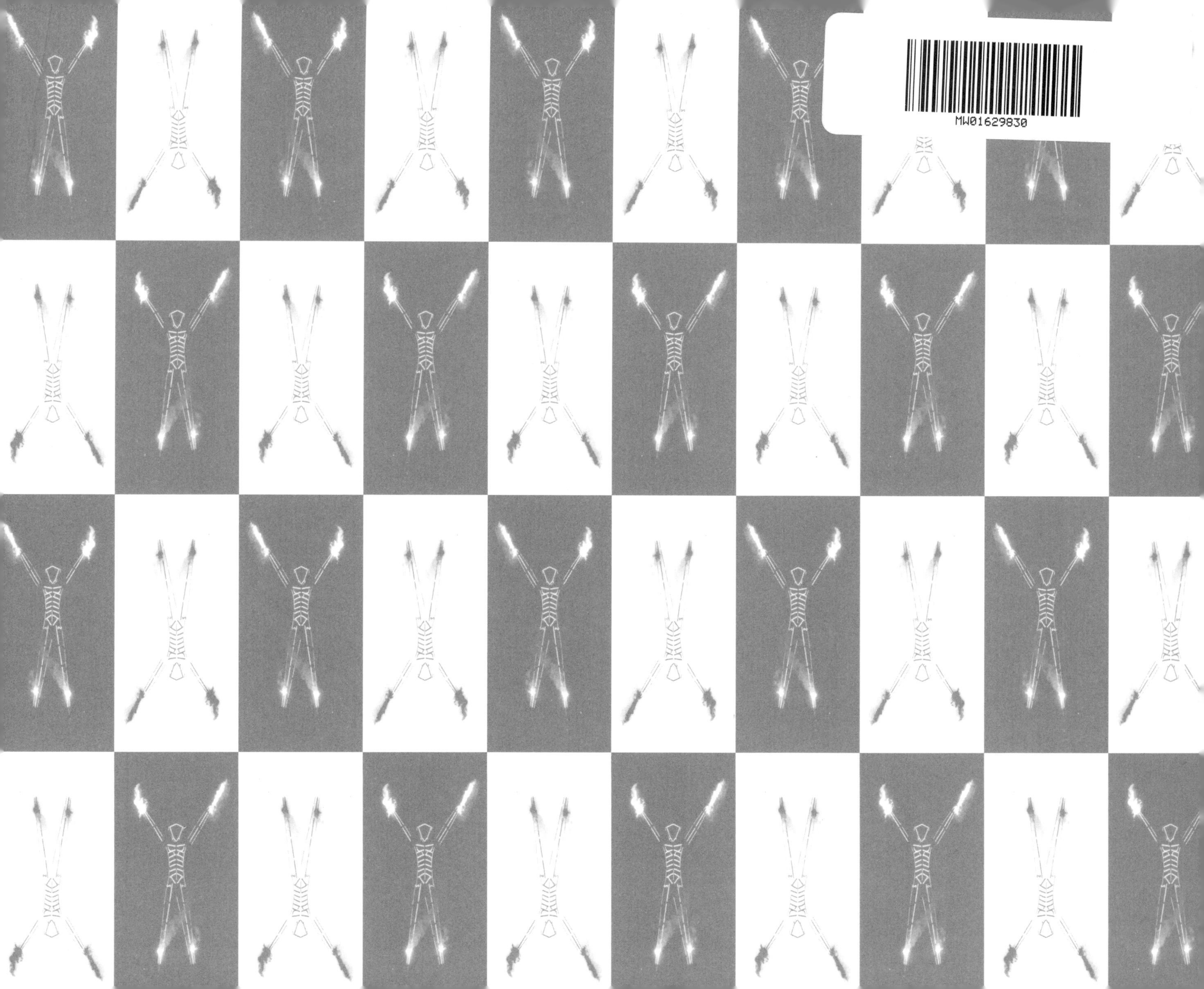

MW01629830

COMPASS OF THE EPHEMERAL
Aerial Photography of Black Rock City through the Lens of Will Roger

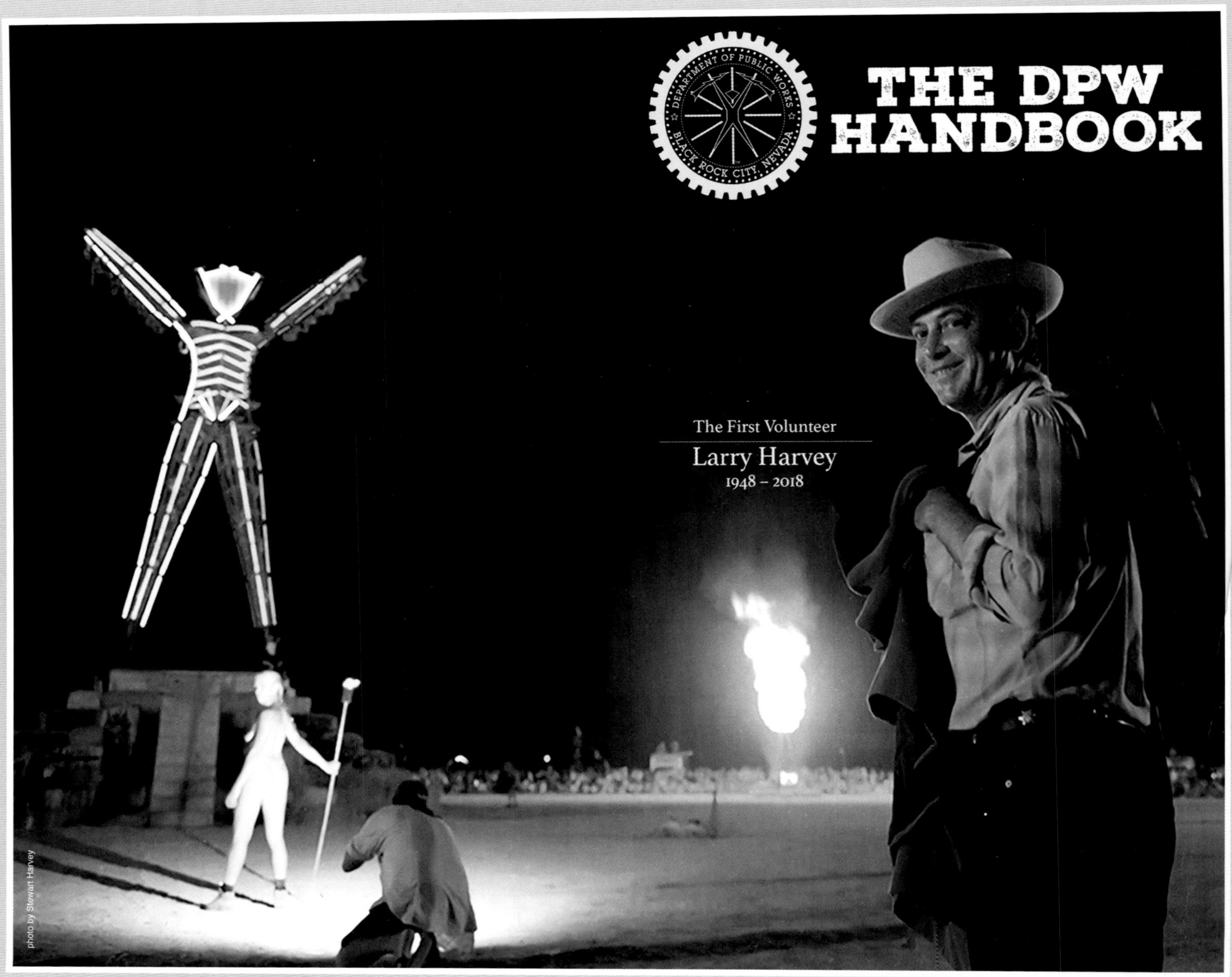

The 2018 DPW Handbook featuring Larry Harvey and Crimson Rose, photo (1998) by Stewart Harvey

I dedicate this book to the late Larry Harvey. He was a truly remarkable man who
believed in the virtue of humanity, the power of community, the creative spirit in everyone,
and the clarity of critical thinking. Larry's spirit and influence continue to grow.

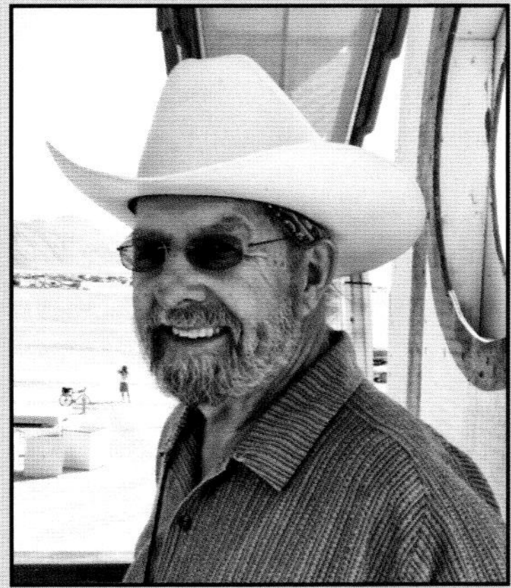

I also dedicate this book to the late Rod Garrett, a brilliant designer,
a true friend and mentor, and above all, a very interesting character
– one who believed in the magic in everything.

Rod Garrett photo (2006) by Heather Gallagher

I would like to thank Harley K. Dubois, William L. Fox, Tony Perez-Banuet,
Alexei Vranich, Rosa JH Berland and Crimson Rose for their fine essays,
Laura Henkel for motivating me to get this book to the publisher,
and Jim Stanford of Smallworks Press for having faith in me!

This book, like Black Rock City and the greater Burning Man Community is in fact
a synergistic sum of all its parts, all of the contributors. Burning Man Community Artists
including designers, photographers, sculptures, painters, musicians, poets, dancers,
characters, workers and participants have all contributed to this summary work in some
way over time. I would like to thank the amazing Burning Man Community in general
and especially those who contributed directly to this book by allowing the use of their art.
This book is special because all of us are a part of it.

Special thanks to Crimson Rose, my partner, my fire goddess, who has tirelessly
supported me through all the trials and tribulations of the last 25 years
and for introducing me to Burning Man.

—Will Roger

Front cover: *Aerial photo (2016) by Will Roger*
Back cover: *"Temple Galaxia" by architect Arthur Mamou-Mani, aerial photo (2018) by Will Roger*
End papers: *Burning man pattern by James Stanford, photo (1995) by Rick Egan*

Table of Contents

Aerial Photography of Black Rock City through the Lens of Will Roger

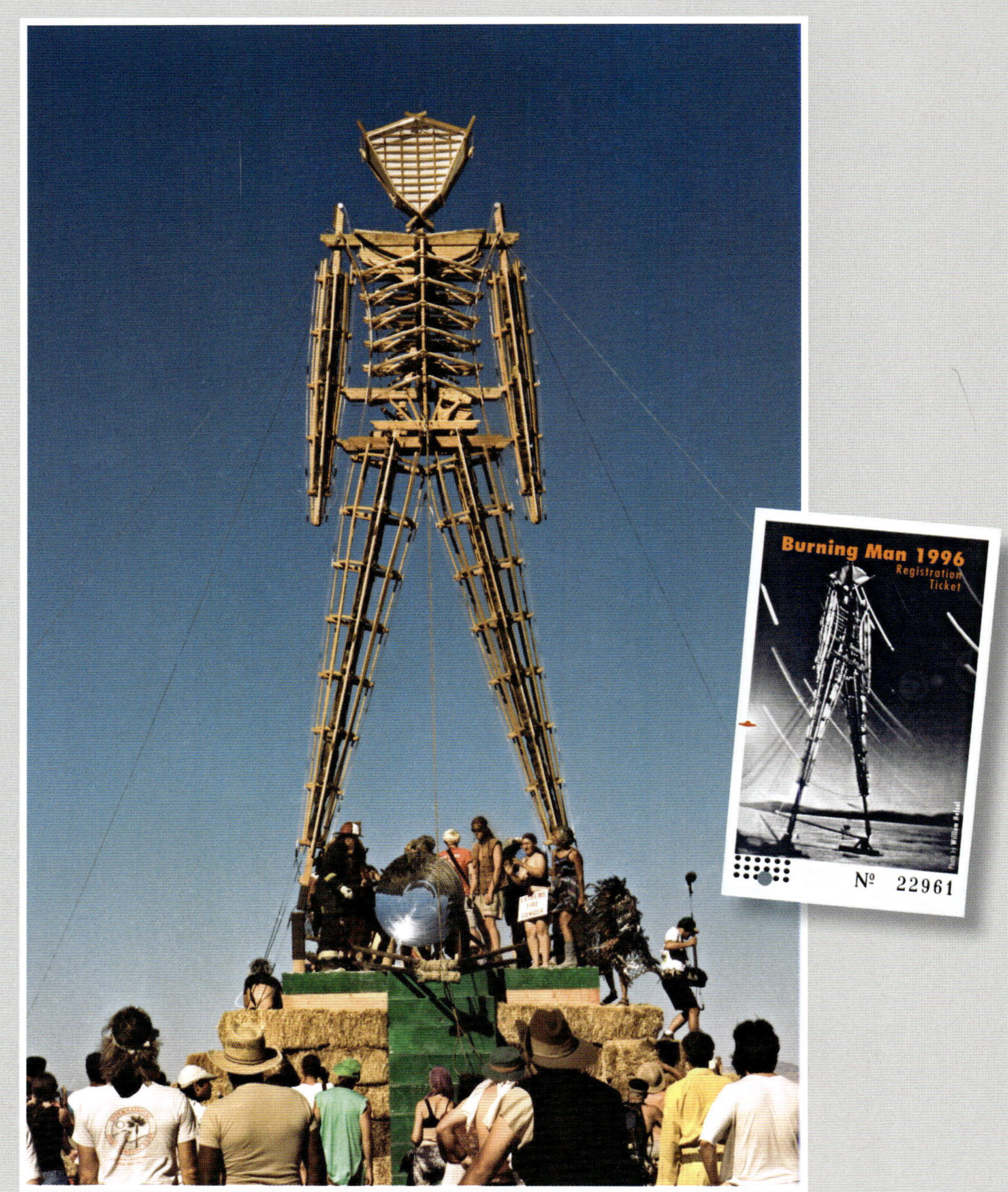

Burning Man 1996
Registration
Ticket
Nº 22961

Introduction: Creation of a Community

Harley K. Dubois, Co-Founder, Burning Man

Each year in late August, 75,000 people from around the world will gather beyond civilization for a week. Two hours north of the nearest urban center, a beautiful city will be made in the dust of a flat, ancient, dry, alkaline lake bed – the Black Rock Desert. For eight days, it will teem with creativity, experimentation, reunions, and celebration. Then it will disappear, leaving nothing behind. It is made of tents, recreational vehicles, creative temporary shelters, land/sea containers – in short, any kind of structures that can withstand high winds and harsh weather. The city is horseshoe-shaped, with radial streets that lead to the center, to the Burning Man edifice. Around it is art –large art – built to be played with and shared. Like any city, its hospital and fire department are ready to serve, its airport is the busiest in Northern Nevada for the one week it exists, but you will find no stores or anything to buy. People bring gifts to share, but no money. They will bring everything they need to survive and will take it all home again. Black Rock City is an experiment in temporary community.

In the beginning, Burning Man was just a weekend camping trip. Or was it? There was something special going on, but no one could name it. Burning Man more than doubled in size annually, and after 10 years, growing from 50 to nearly 10,000 people, it hit a tipping point. In 1996, there were too many campers for that amount of chaos. It got scary. It was clear that without more structure our favorite camping trip would not survive. The next year, a formal city grid was introduced, and with it the characteristics of a community began to emerge. I helped facilitate a ragtag group of weekend warriors who helped our staff cut the streets into the shoreline scrubs of the Hualapai Flat. Immediately, people began to gather in more intentional ways. I was able to place loud camps apart from quiet ones. Art was moved out in front of our camping areas. Driving was banned. The concept of a "village" was born with the Blue Light District. We produced a map. A camping trip transformed into a city.

People began to organize to do work as well. Our volunteer environmental arm, the Earth Guardians, was created. So was our Regional Network (which has now grown to hundreds of Regional Contacts in over 35 countries). I prototyped a greeting concept with our volunteer Ranger workforce. These were all precursors to a more organized future. It was intense and magical, and all very, very last minute.

Four people have been truly intimate with the inception and establishment of Black Rock City's design: Rod Garrett (1936-2011), its creator; Tony Perez, our City Superintendent; Will Roger Peterson (aka Will Roger), one of my Co-Founders; and me, Black Rock City manager emeritus. Rod saw the beauty of the design in every curve and angle. Tony surveyed it with accuracy down to the inch. Will delivered the final product on the desert floor in the middle of nowhere. I helped people live in it. I studied how the city was inhabited and how

"The Inferno" Ticket design by Michael Mikel; Ticket photo (1996) by William Helsel
People gathering on the Man base with the solar collector by Larry Breed.
Photo (1996) by J. Absinthia Vermut and Nevada Museum of Art, Center for Art
+ Environment Archive Collections

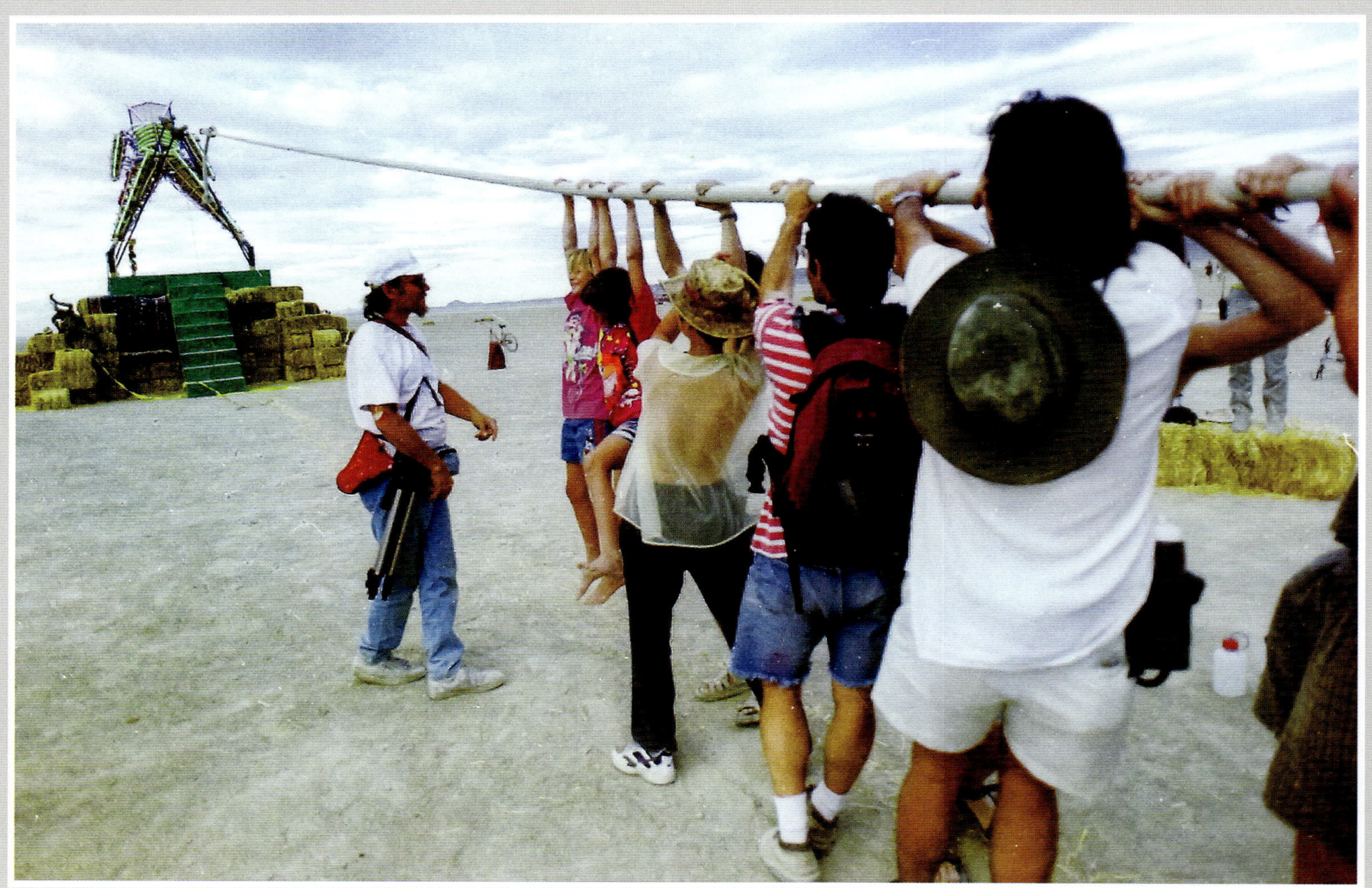

Volunteers assist in raising the Man, photo (1997) by Rick Egan

the design met the citizens' needs.

1998 was the year Will organized a team of people to build the city design Rod created. I continued to build the internal structures to support a burgeoning community. Placement of camps had begun in 1995 with me, a telephone, and a hot line messaging service. By 1998, Burning Man citizens were connecting year-round over the internet. Camps and villages were growing in size and complexity. With help from many amazing friends, I established key city services for our residents. A volunteer named General Direction created the first paper-based "Find Your Friend" index card system. It was the first year of a unifying disaster: rain storms that stranded hundreds of people in the mud, forging lifetime bonds and ultimately a wedding or two.

Soon, districts were evolving within Black Rock City. City design features began to develop around participants' increasing needs. Rod added plazas for more shared gathering space. The size and orientation of living spaces were experimented with. I had road widths adjusted for traffic flow and double-wide blocks added for growing camps and villages. I started Kids Camp on the hunch that people would fall in love and start families and need a different sort of camping experience.

From 2000 to 2010, our community deepened. Lives were being lived through the event, and identities were born from it. Our underground scene took hold in the real world; our Regional Network took root globally. In 2004, our guiding tenets, the Ten Principles, were written down, and then learning conferences were created for cross-cultural sharing. We began to name and own our identity as "Burners." A culture had been defined. We reached the mainstream, but we had not sold out; we simply had arrived.

What Burning Man offers is now needed more than ever: a place to create, unfettered by the opinion of others. A place to experiment, to fail and learn, to make better. A place to discover yourself and a place to plan a better future. We provide shelter from societal judgement, commodification, the pressures of the "norm," and proof that it is just a hoax. We provide a place to inspire, to heal, to explore.

It is not by accident that Burning Man's largest event happens on the Black Rock Desert. Black Rock City's intentionally temporary presence is fleeting in comparison to the 10,000-year history of this bleak, barren terrain. I discovered this mysterious place through Burning Man in 1991 and spent the next 10 years mesmerized–exploring every feature, soaking in all of the hot springs that would have me, learning the historic landmarks, and listening to the stories. It is exactly this sort of austere environment that pulls people together. Bill Fox, anthropologist and art historian, and Alexei Vranich, archaeologist, have added many additional layers of context to this book, *Compass of the Ephemeral.* Bill's expert essay on the Black Rock Desert and the phenomenon of Burning

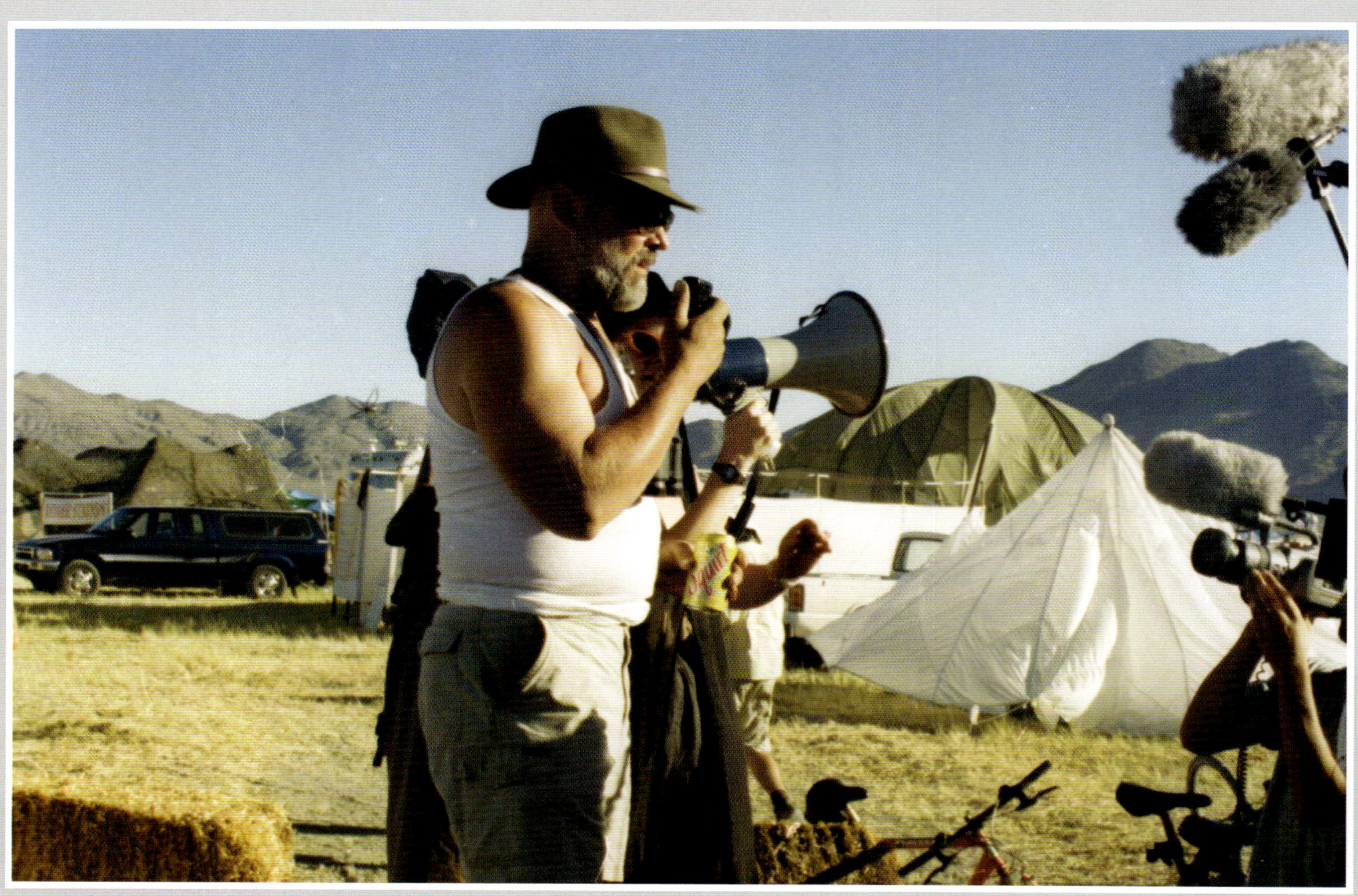

Will Roger speaking at Press Conference; On-site media included: CNN, ABC's Nightline, NBC, Time, Washington Post, a German television crew, and publications from England, France, Japan and Brazil. Photo (1997) by J. Absinthia Vermut, Nevada Museum of Art, Center for Art + Environment Archive Collections

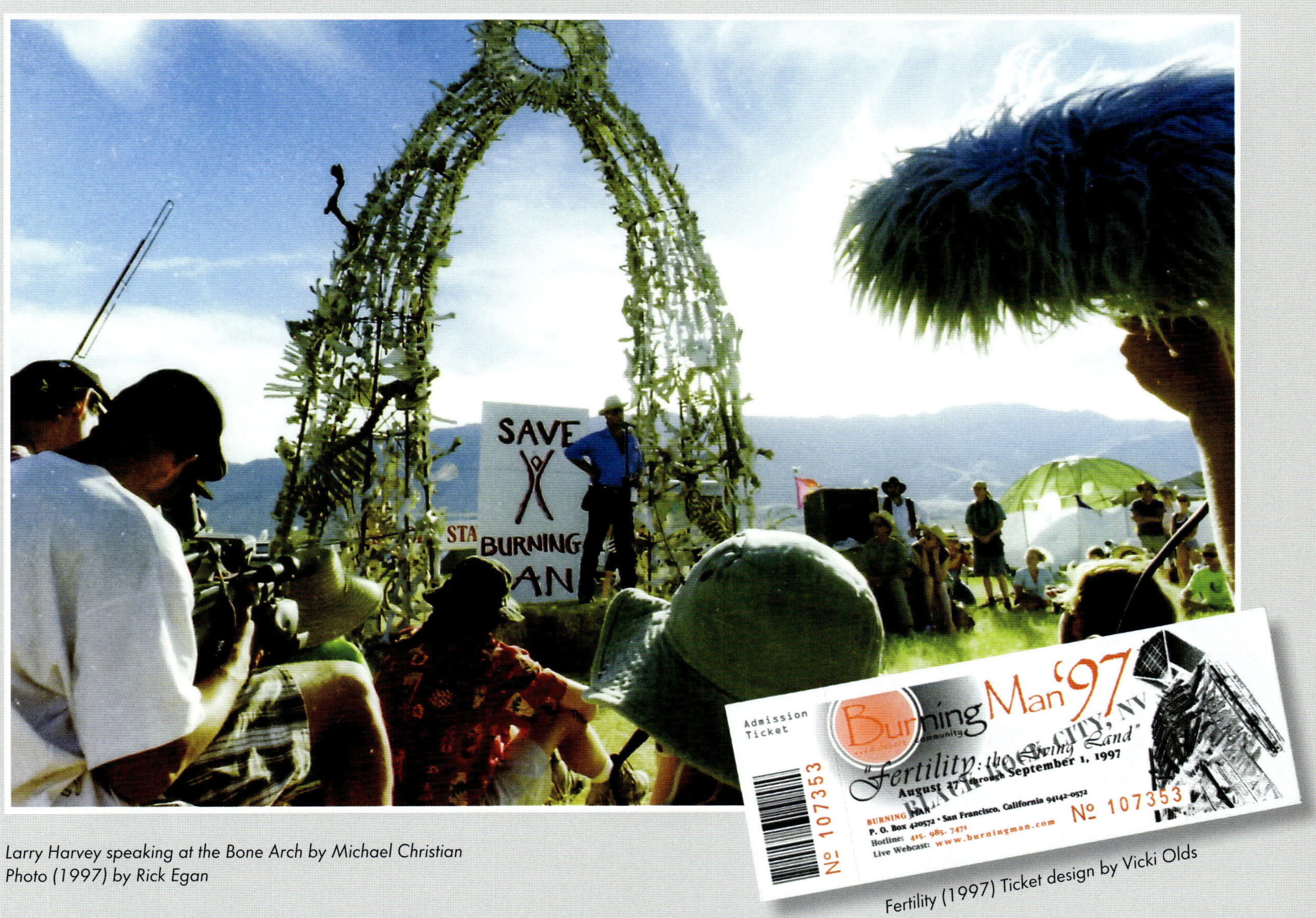

Larry Harvey speaking at the Bone Arch by Michael Christian
Photo (1997) by Rick Egan

Fertility (1997) Ticket design by Vicki Olds

Man describes how strange and special a pairing they are. Alexei's comparisons with similar ancient cities and the concept of sacred design show the connection to the human soul. Crimson Rose poignantly reflects upon the Art Spirit in the vastness of the Black Rock Desert. Their observations provide insight into why people resonate so profoundly with the Burning Man experience.

Compass of the Ephemeral is a wonderful look back at what has grown and what has been learned at Burning Man from the unique perspective of aerial photographs and early city design ideas. It tells the origin story of our now-global community. It also gives a glimpse into how the human psyche can be provoked into feeling a sense of belonging through sharing this particular physical space, of how a location and design can help unify people, creating an identity that can be shared across the globe.

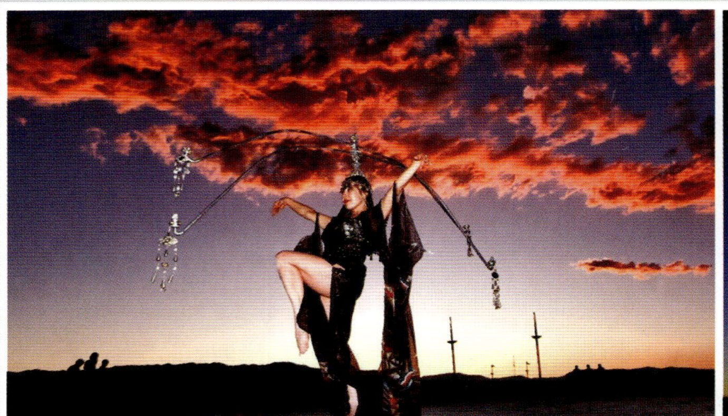
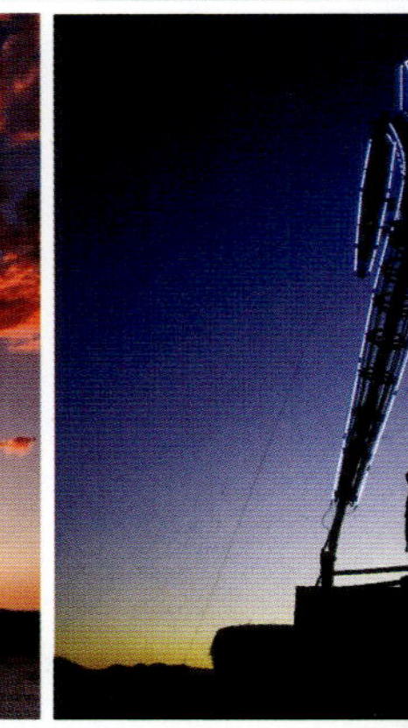
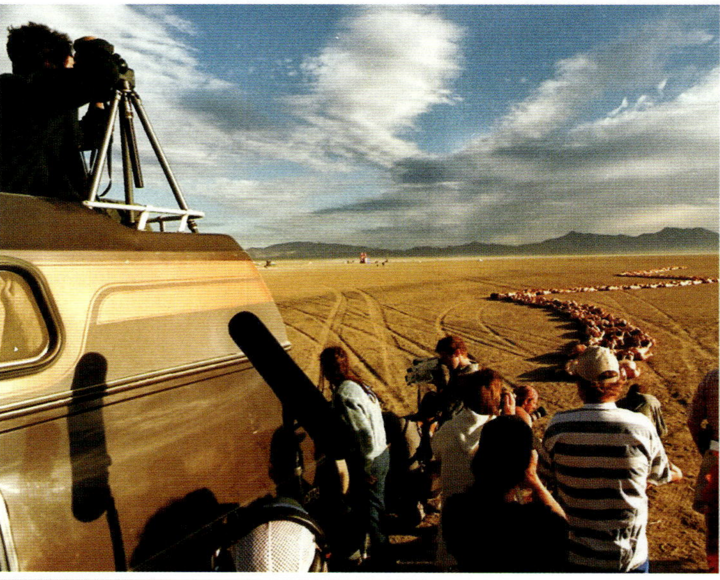

"Any art that we release by fire means that we're letting go of our ownership, because it doesn't belong to us. It really shows us this fleeting moment of life, that life is really very precious. Before you know it, it's gone. It's about taking advantage of what's happening right then, right there, and when thousands of people are watching the fire, it's this amazing part of the ceremony."

–Crimson Rose, The London School of Economics and Political Science, November 2017

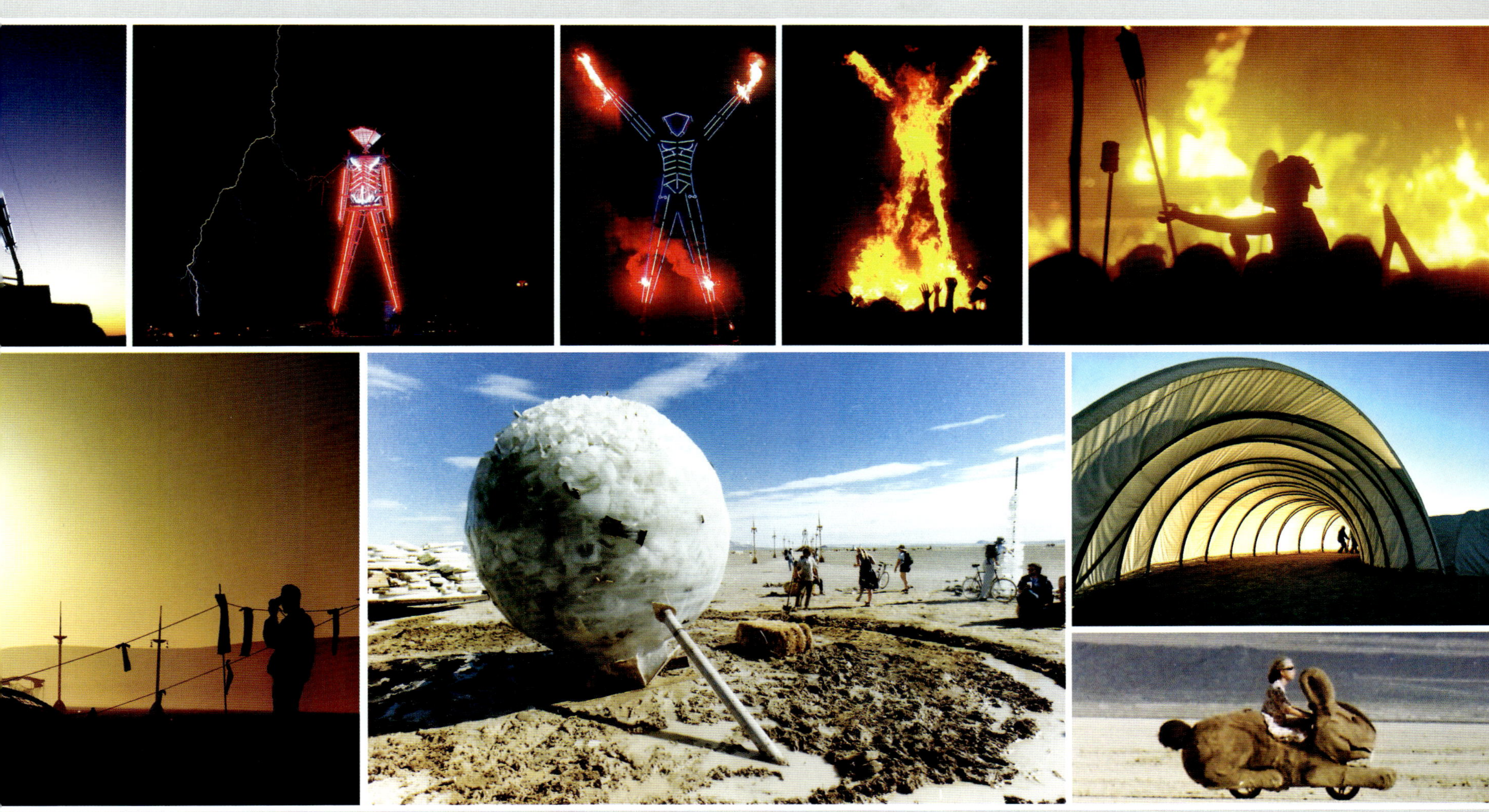

L-R, Top to Bottom: *Dancing at dusk, photo (1995) by Rick Egan; The Man at sunrise, photo (1997) by Rick Egan; Lighting and rain, photo (1995) by Rick Egan; Burn begins, photo (1995) by Rick Egan; Theme: Good and Evil, photo (1995) by Rick Egan; Burn celebration, photo (1995) by Rick Egan; "Nevada" by Spencer Tunick, photo (1997) by Rick Egan; "Future Primitive" by Steel Neal, photo (1997) by Rick Egan; "Temporal of Decomposition" by Jim Mason, photo (1997) by Rick Egan; "Das Ammouniten Projekt" by Henrik Hackl, photo (1997) by Rick Egan; "Rabbit Cycle," by Scott Dunlap, photo (1995) by Rick Egan*

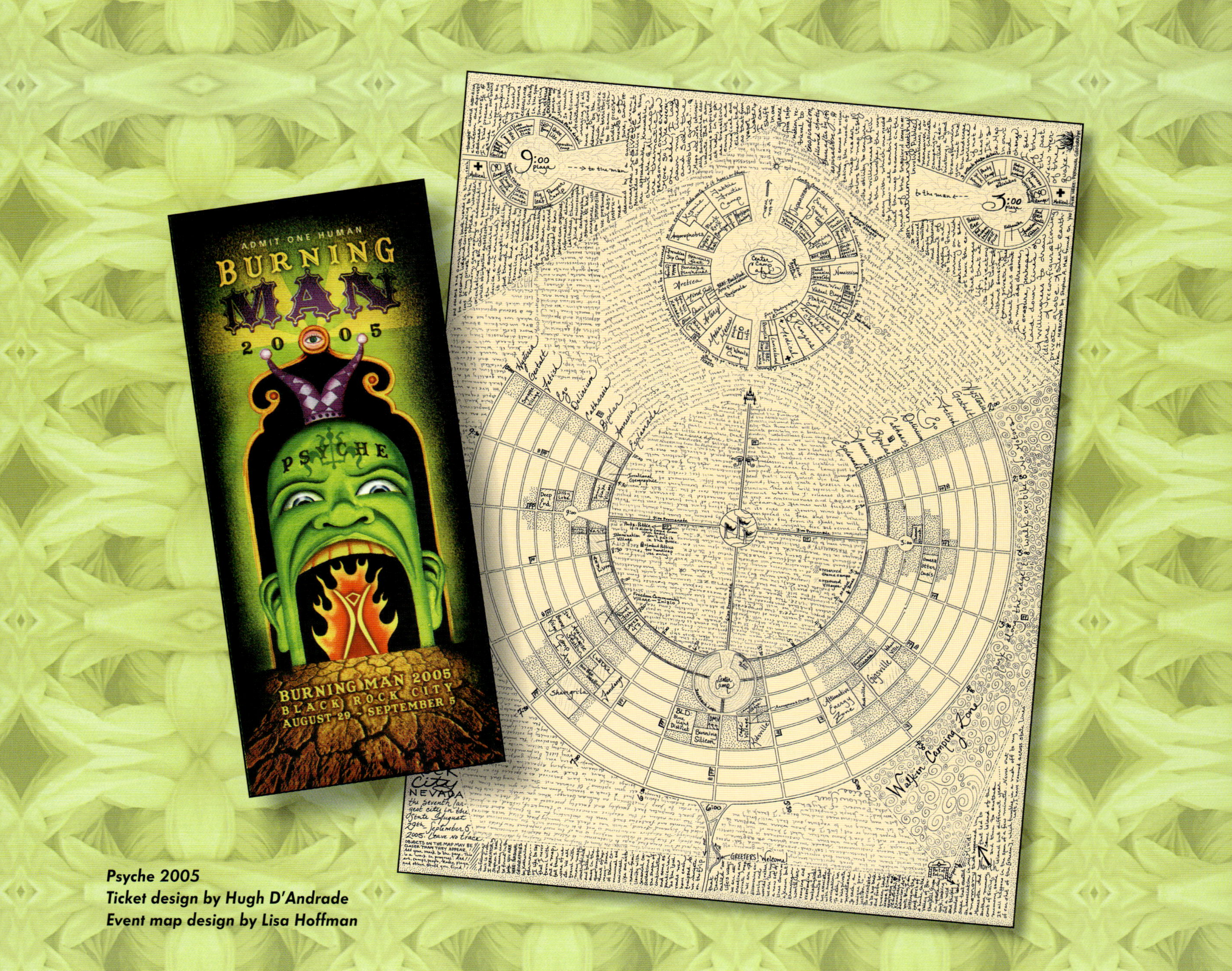

Psyche 2005
Ticket design by Hugh D'Andrade
Event map design by Lisa Hoffman

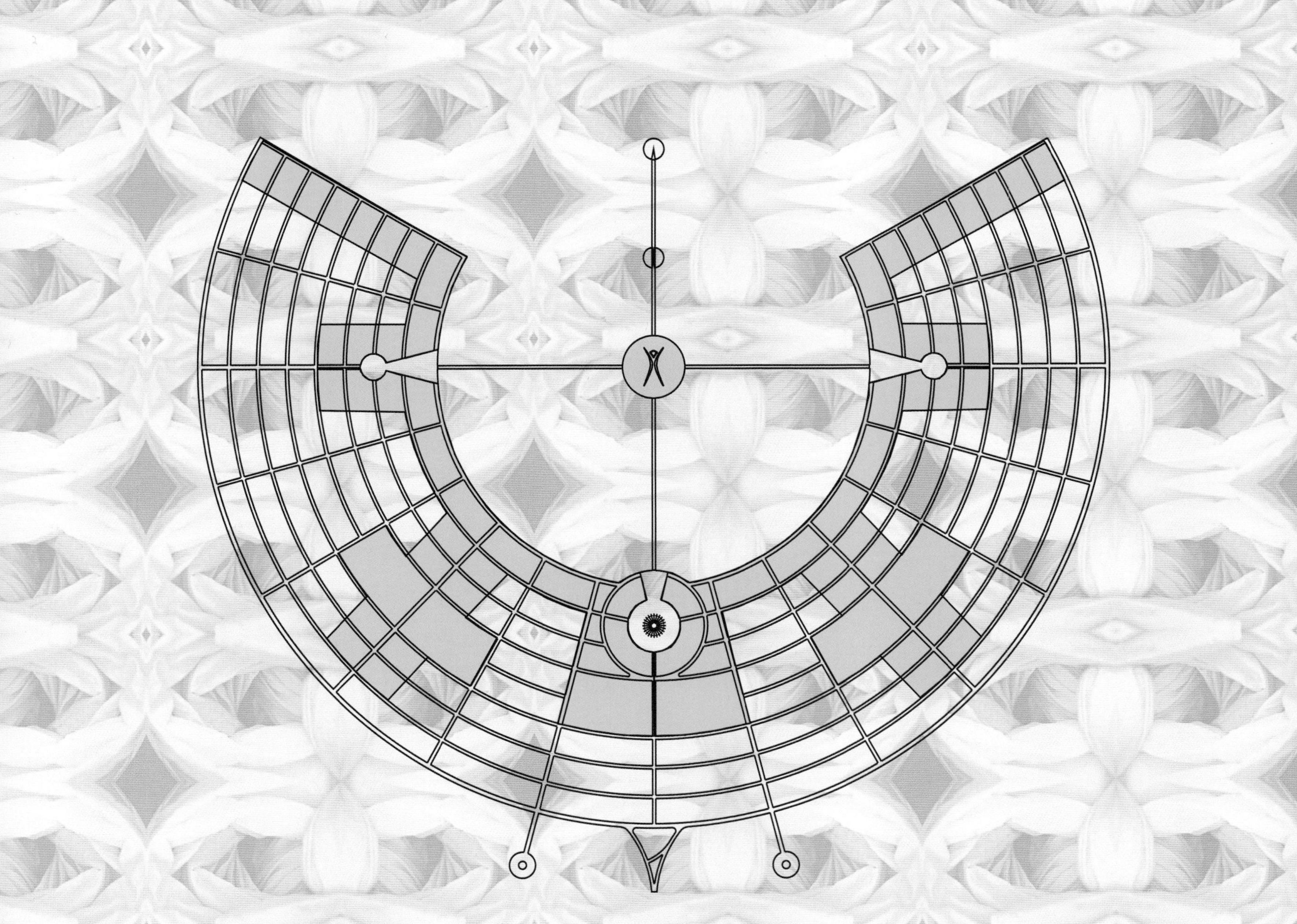

"Drape Fleur" photomontage by James Stanford

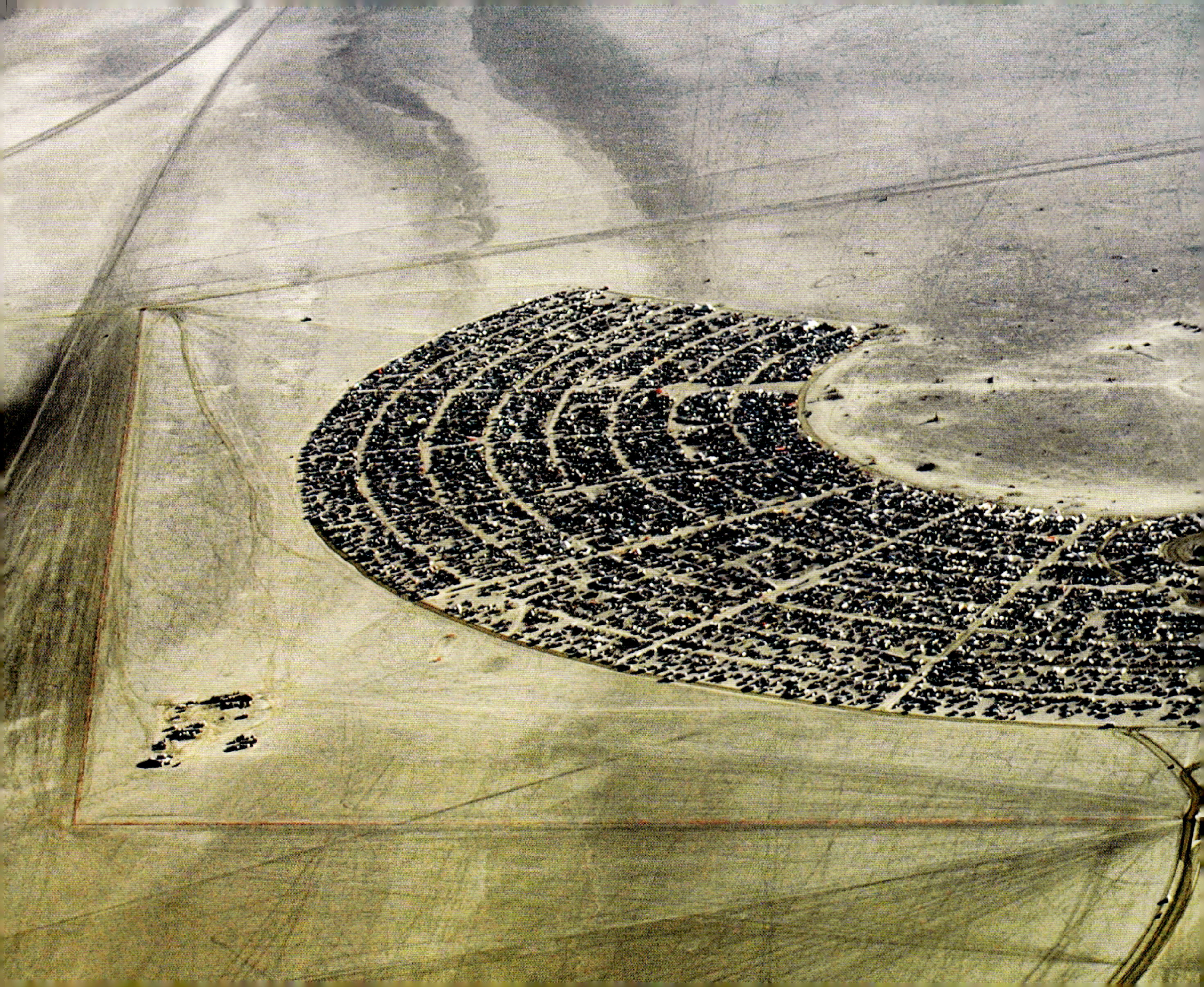

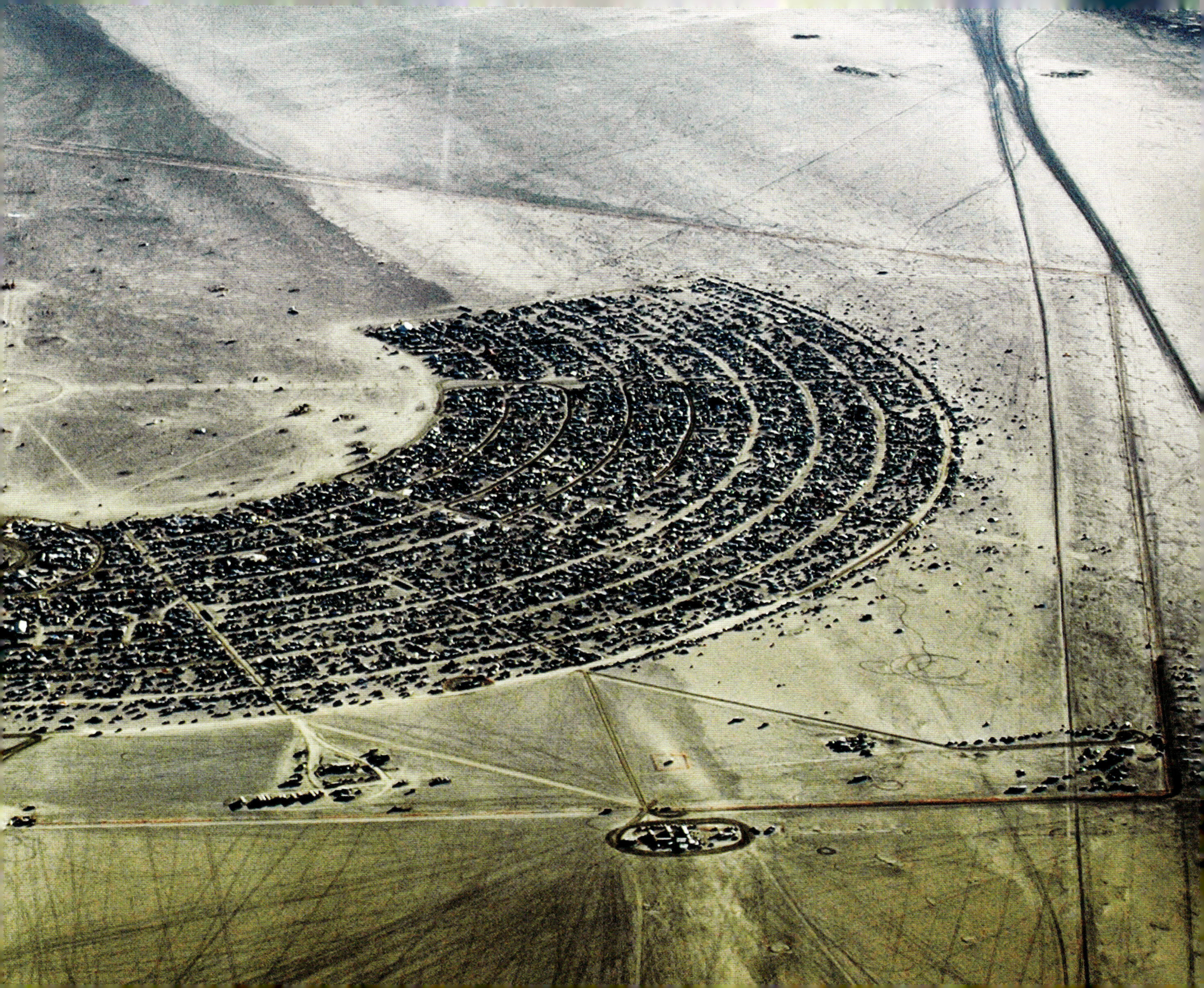

Looking up 5:30, foreground Greeters on left, DPW center, Fire Suppression on right. Population 35,567

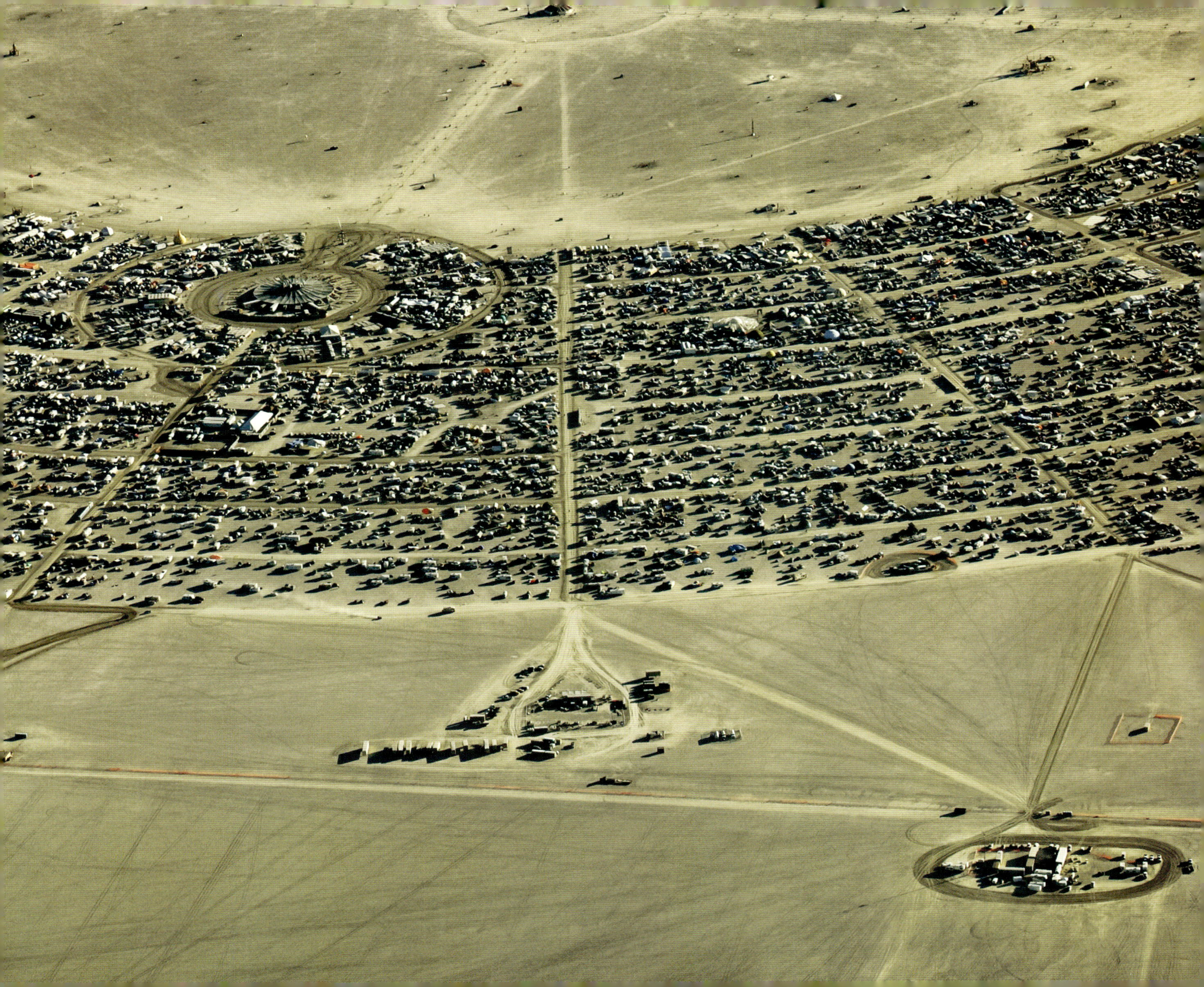

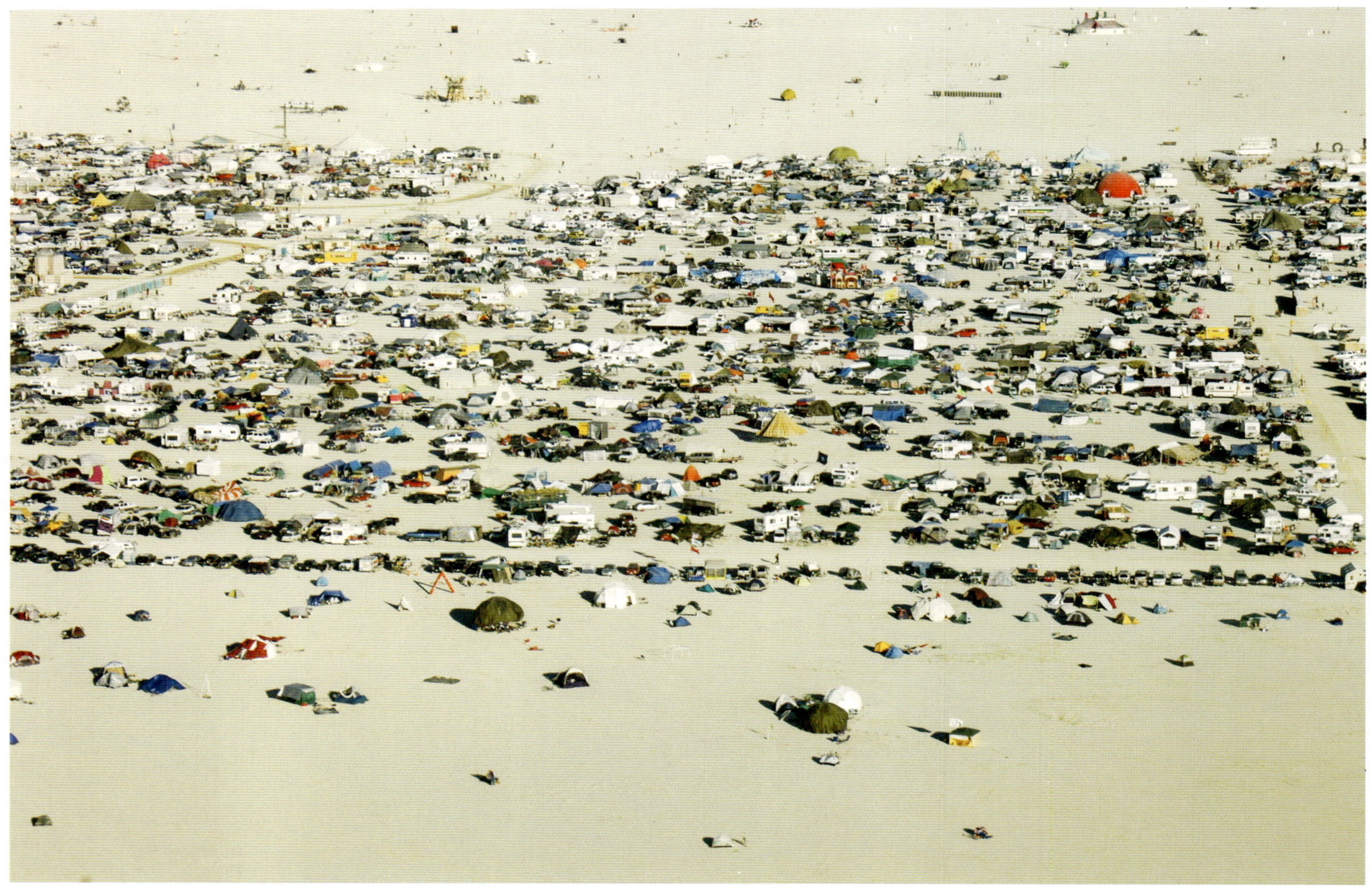

Above: *There were 485 theme camps that were placed in Black Rock City in 2005*
Right: *Black Rock City is the most populous settlement (albeit temporary) in Nevada's Pershing County and includes an FAA-approved airport, Black Rock City Municipal Airport (88NV)*

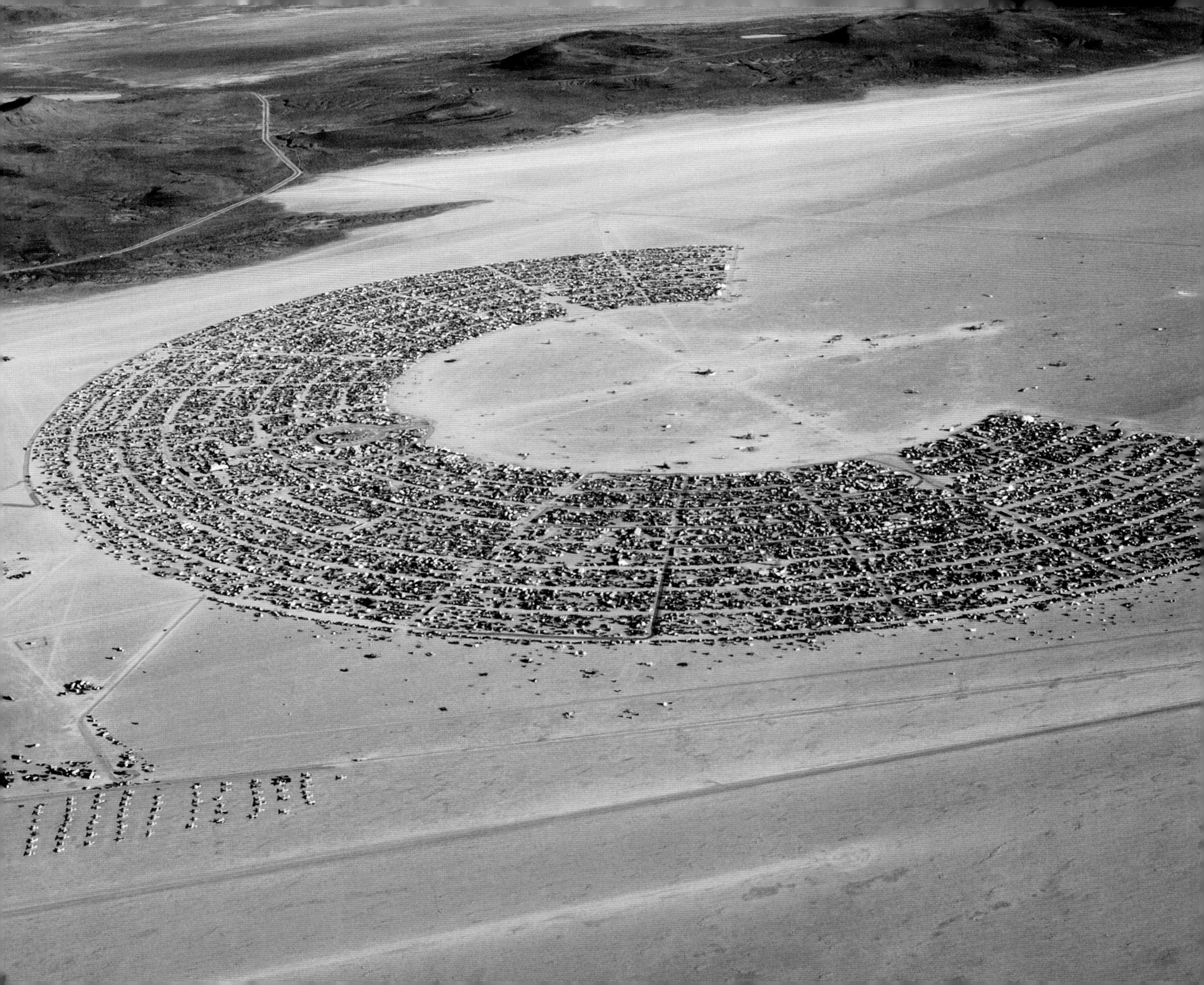

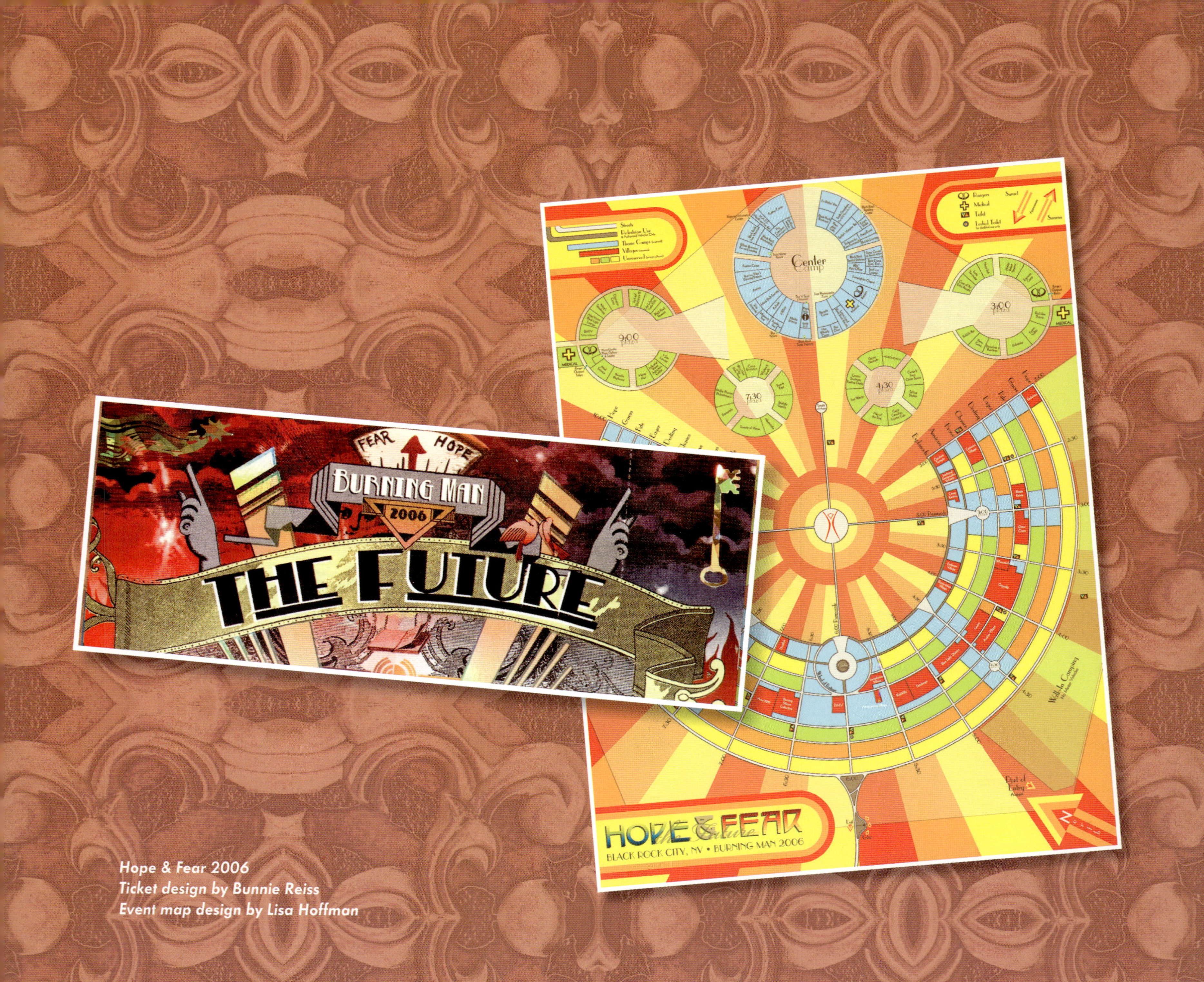

Hope & Fear 2006
Ticket design by Bunnie Reiss
Event map design by Lisa Hoffman

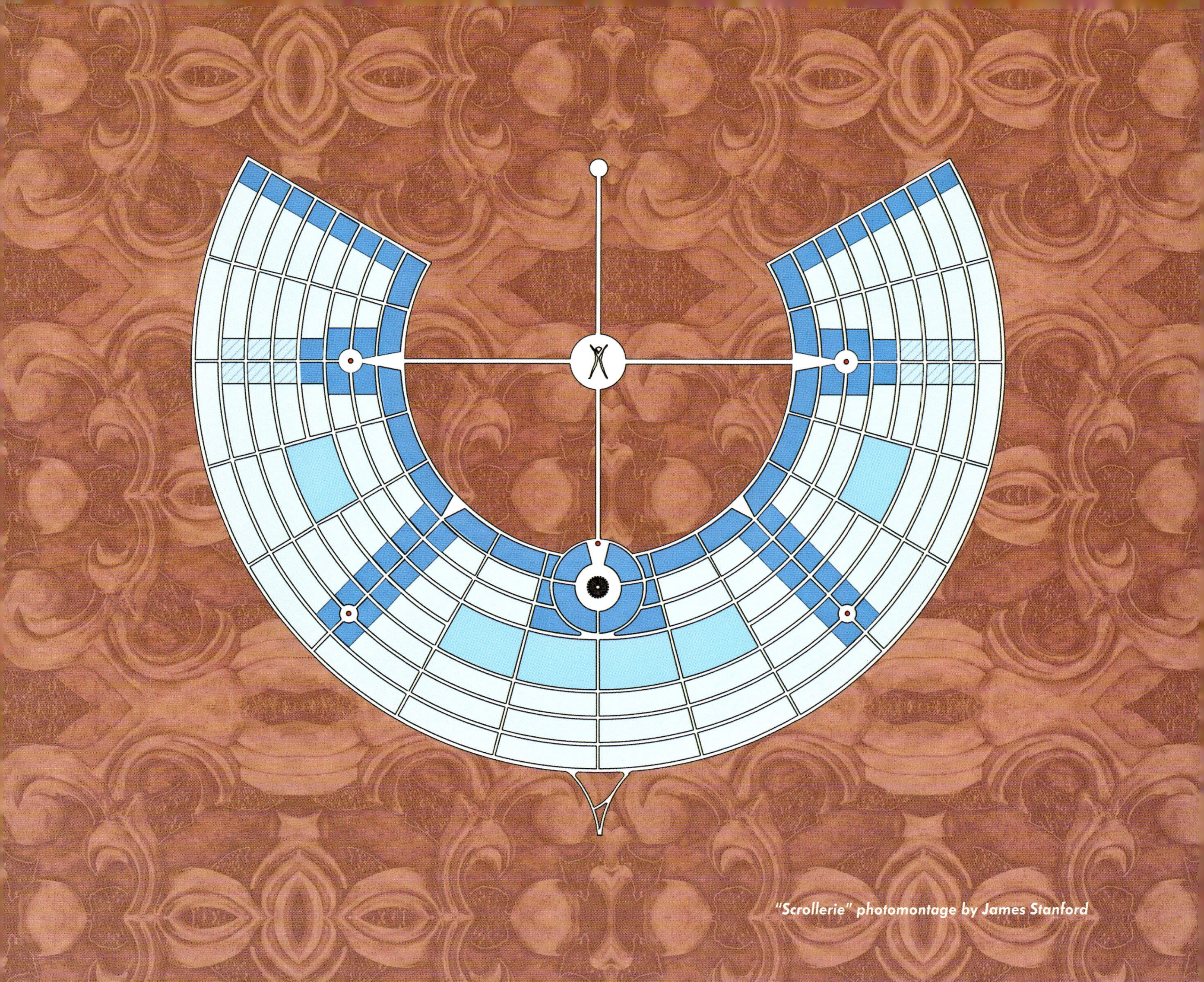

"Scrollerie" photomontage by James Stanford

For the first time since 2000, Black Rock City was relocated to a new site about one mile northeast of the previous site. Population 38,989

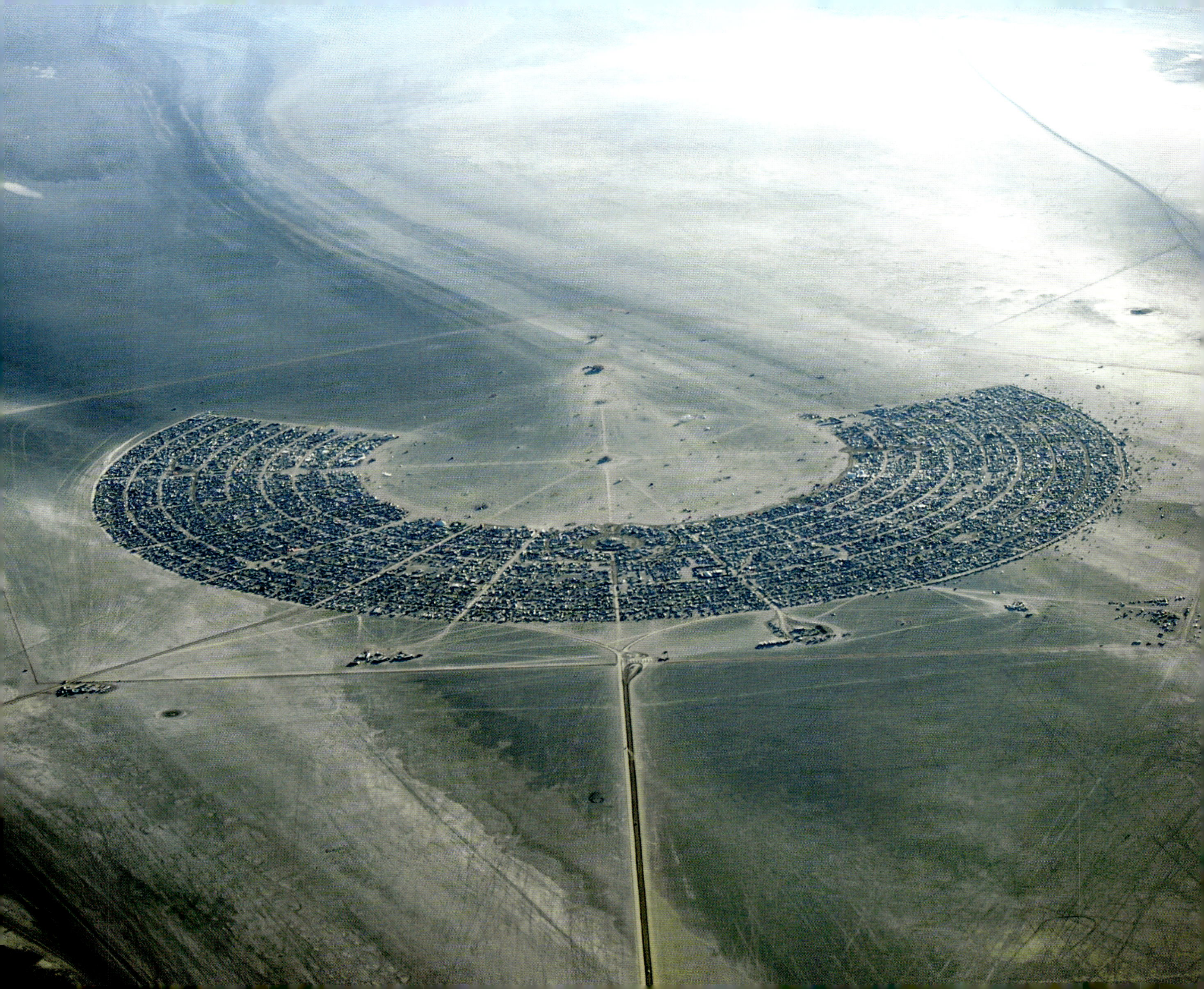

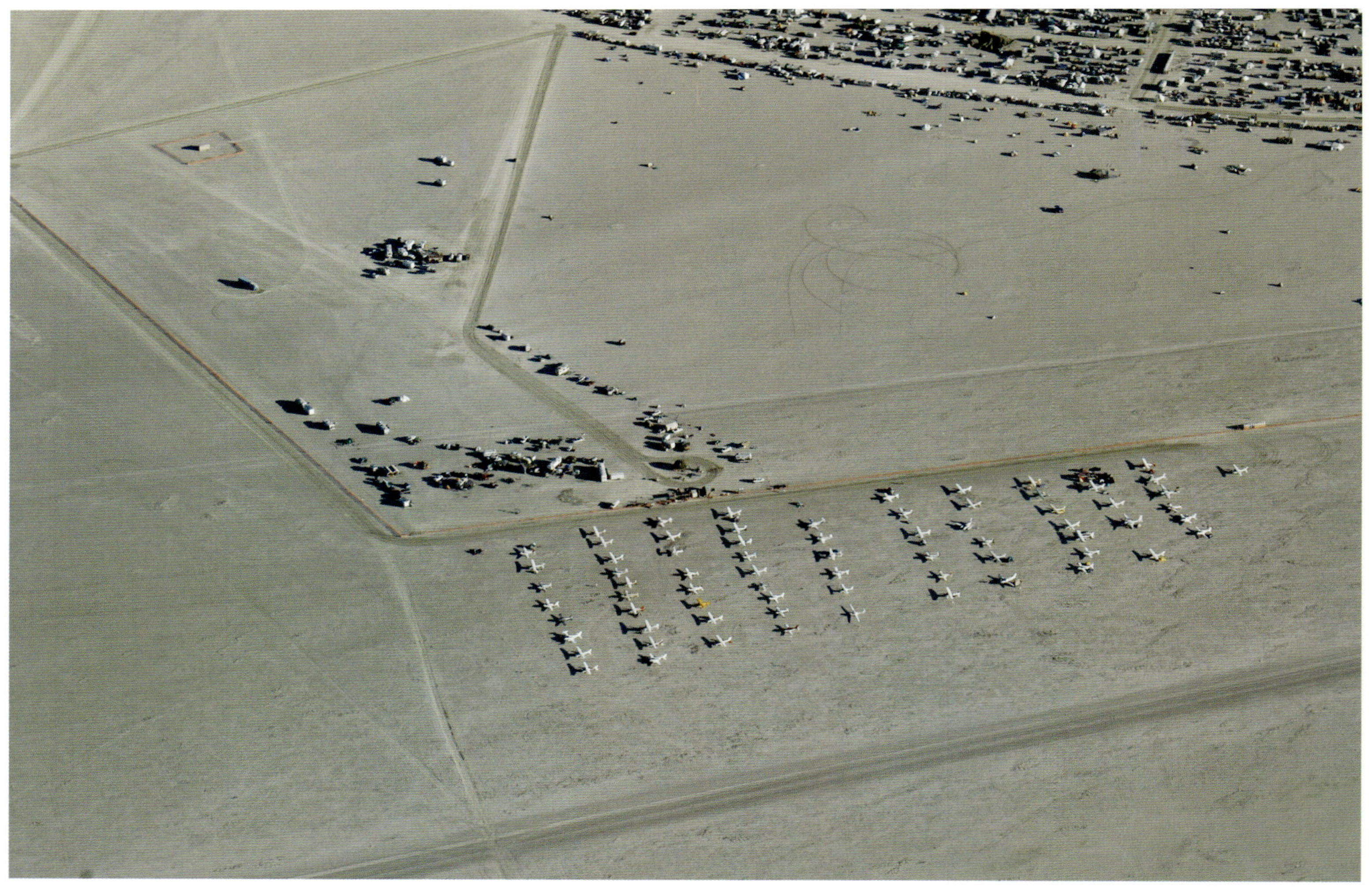

Above: Black Rock City Municipal Airport
Right: Center Camp Cafe, based from Rod Garrett's design, is the largest temporary freestanding tensile shade structure in the world

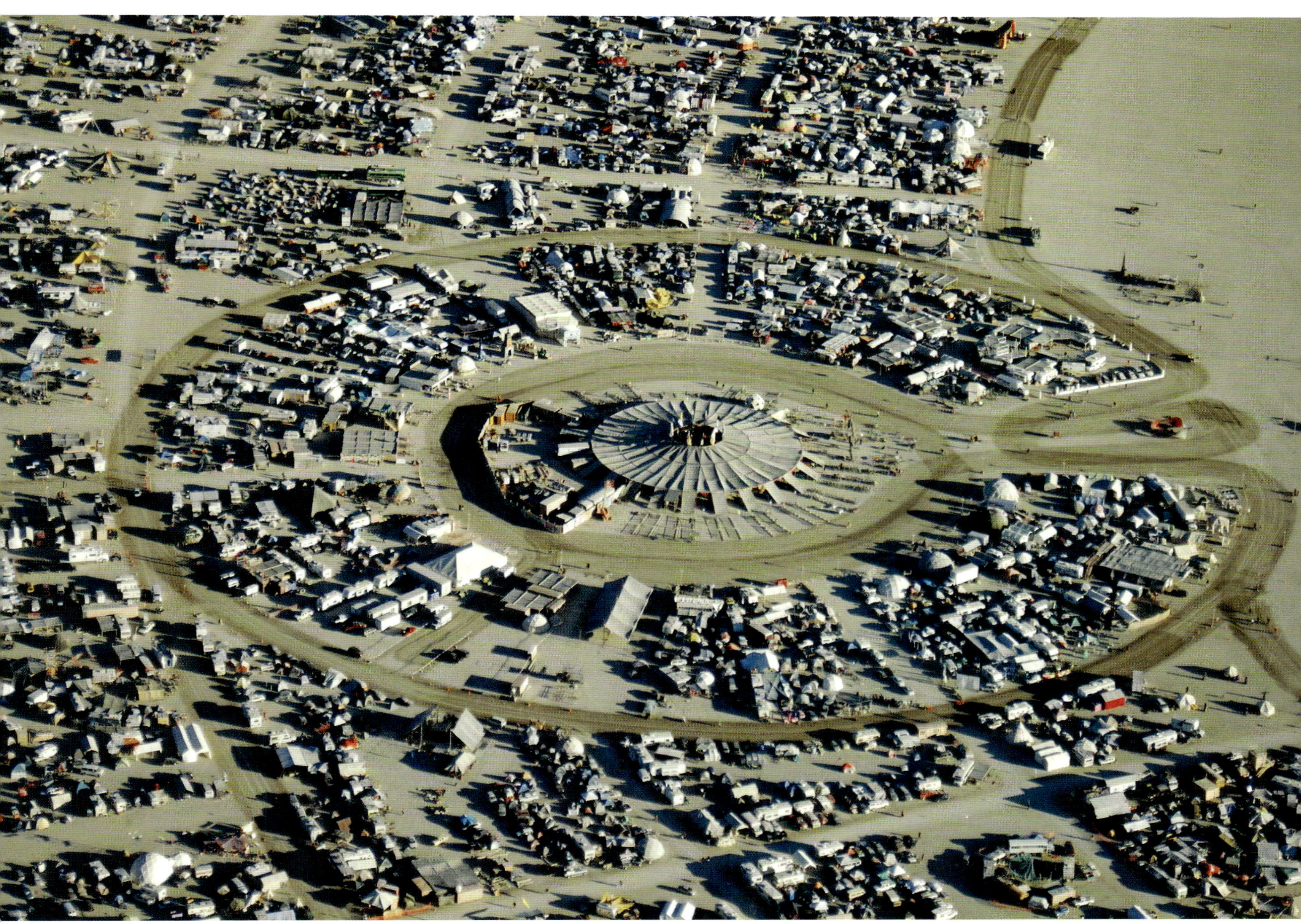

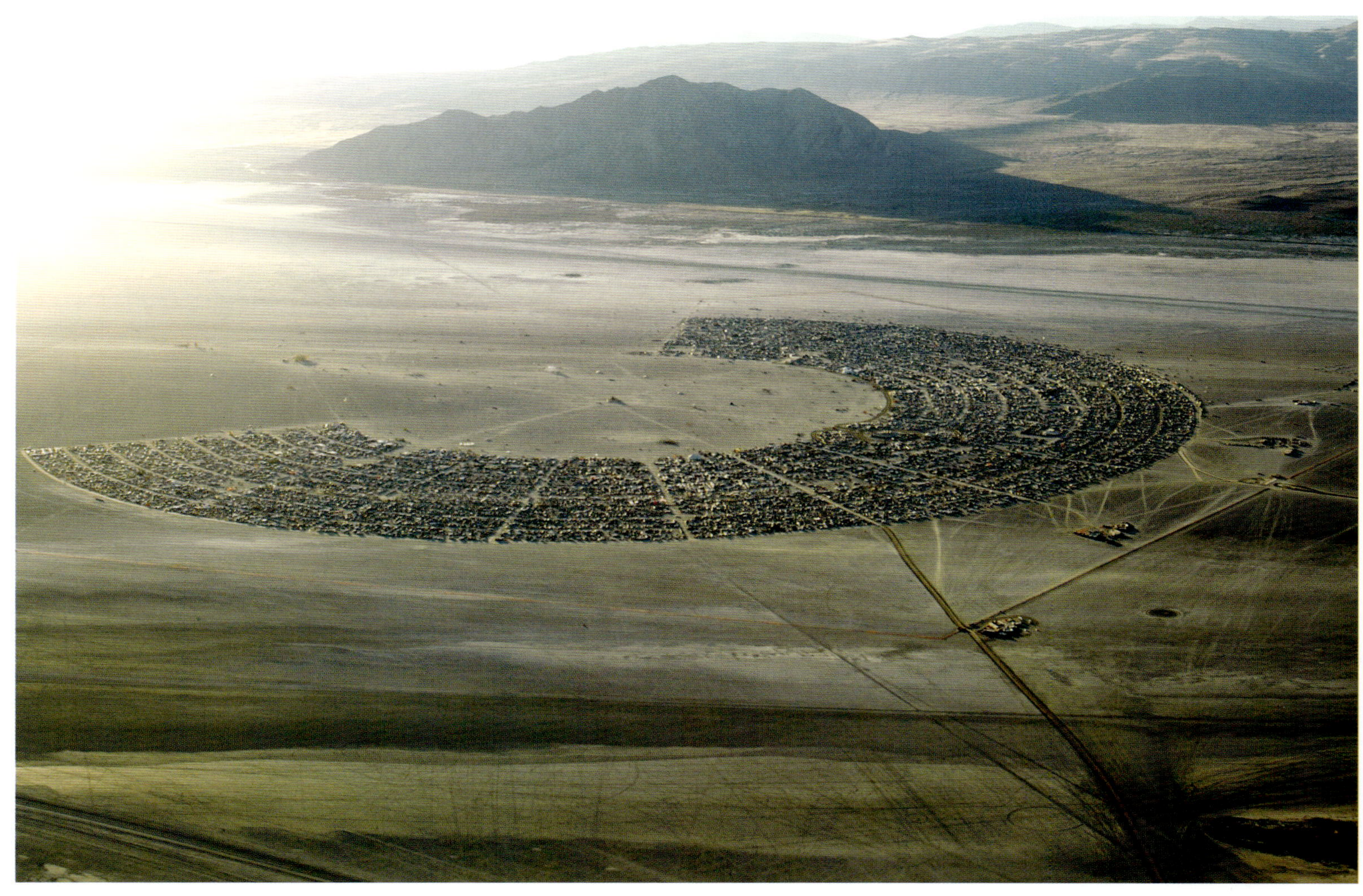

There were 300 art installations on playa, 240 of which had been pre-registered

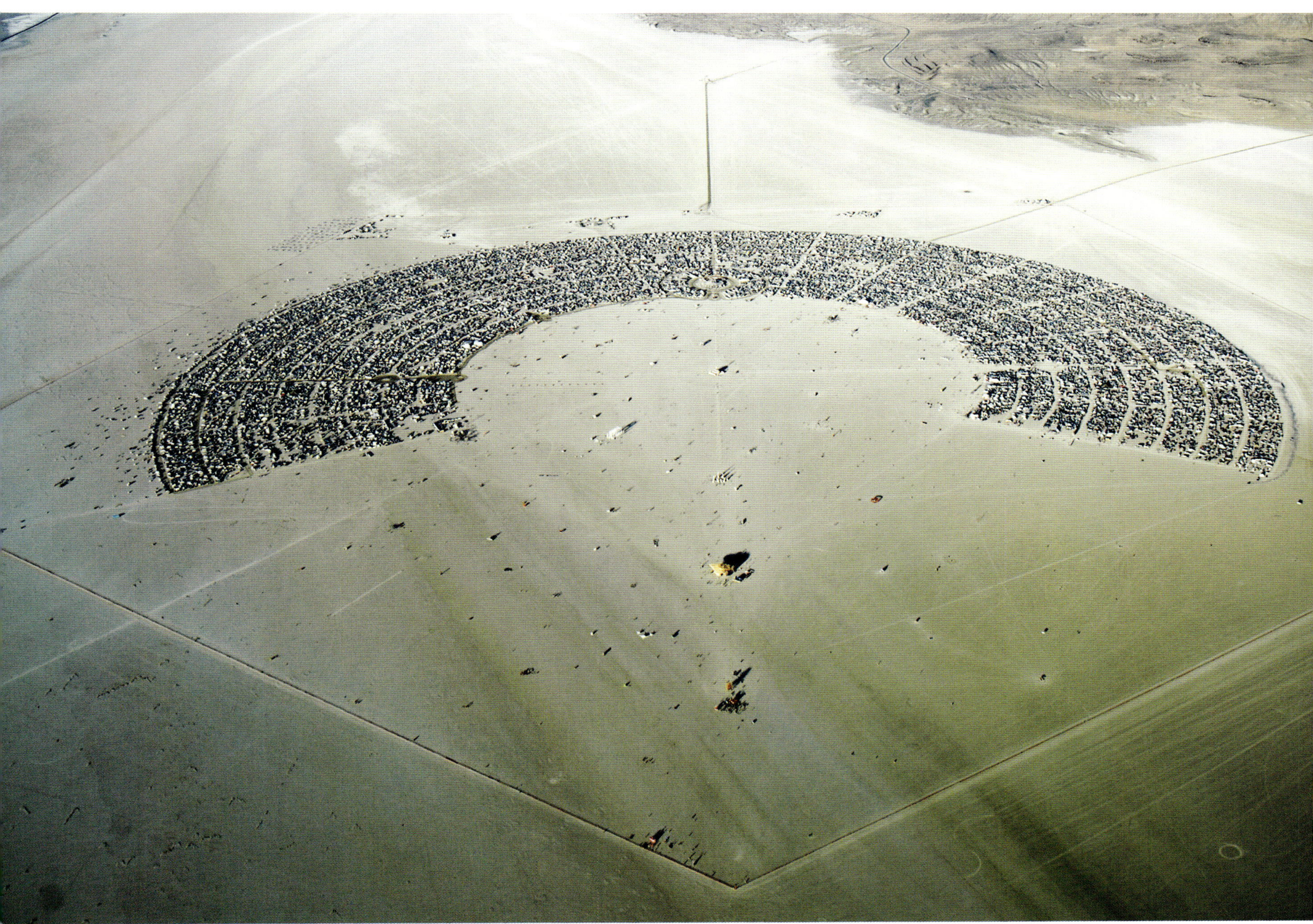

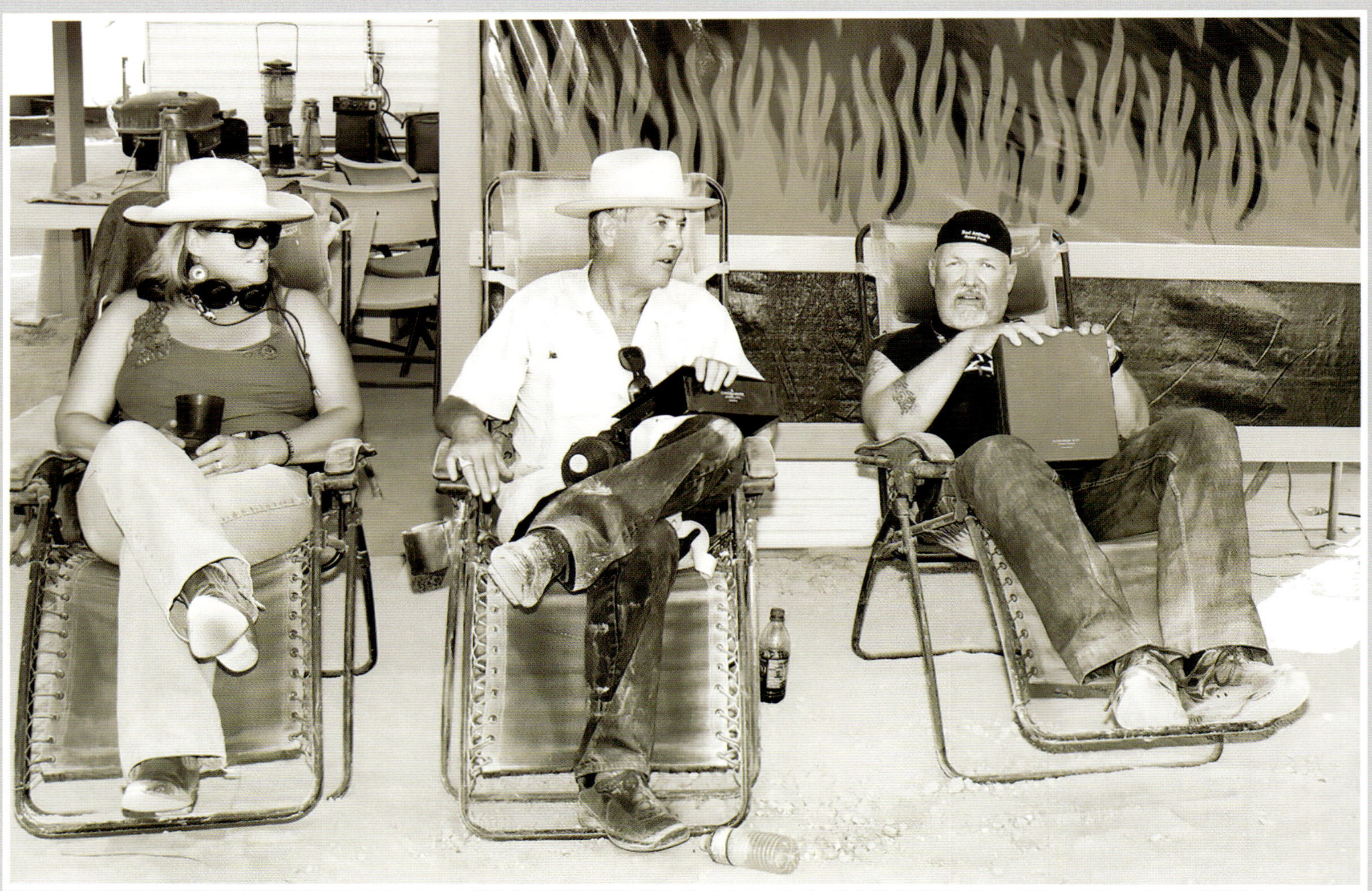

Harley K. Dubois, Larry Harvey and Will Roger at First Camp, photo (2011) by Garry Geer

Foreword: Compass of the Ephemeral

Will Roger, Co-Founder, Burning Man

I met Rod Garrett while on vacation visiting my sister in Marin County, California.

We immediately took a liking to each other. Our philosophy and views on the meaning of life, while very different, somehow meshed and resulted in 30 years of very interesting, compelling conversations.

While I was getting restless living in Rochester, New York, around 1987 Rod offered me a job working construction for his design company. I moved to California in 1990, and shortly thereafter I started working for Rod on an industrial building in Oakland that he had just bought. He would teach me the fine points of contract construction while we converted this 8,000-square-foot building into four artist live/work spaces. One of the spaces would become my live-in photography studio and processing lab, one would be his live-in design studio, and the other two he would lease to other artists. This project took 2½ years, a time where Rod became my mentor, and we grew to be close friends and work partners. Later, while establishing my studio, I did some side work building decks and pergolas around the Bay Area that Rod would design. Thus, began the trust and faith that are required between a designer and a builder.

My photography studio, called Provocative Portraits, began to attract business –mostly executives' portraits, couples' portraits, and some product and industrial photography. However, my main intention was to make art. I continued to create the series called Erotic Dance, which I had started in Rochester, New York. Through this work, in 1993, I met my life partner and muse, Crimson Rose. She brought me to the Burning Man event for the first time in 1994. We attended 1994-1996 as volunteers, becoming part of the loose-knit leadership headed by the Cacophony Society.

1996 was a crucial year in that many of the people who were part of the Cacophony Society organization at that point quit and said that Burning Man would never happen again. It had grown too big for them, so at the 1996 Bureau of Land Management meeting where they stated that Burning Man wouldn't happen again and quit, Larry Harvey turned to me, and he asked, "Would you do desert operations next year?" I said, "Sure." Desert operations to that point involved simply drawing a hundred-foot circle, putting the Man in the center, and then having a beer.

That's what it was. And so I thought, "Boy, yeah, I'll do desert operations. Cool." Little did I know at that point that we wouldn't get a permit for 1997 to do the event on the Black Rock Desert. We searched all of Nevada and found private land near the Black Rock Desert in Washoe County. We now needed to apply for a Washoe County permit. Those are affectionately known as the Anti-Woodstock Ordinances, and so they had 105 things that we needed to do. We had never dealt with any of this before, including numbered campsites, parking areas, flush toilets, streets

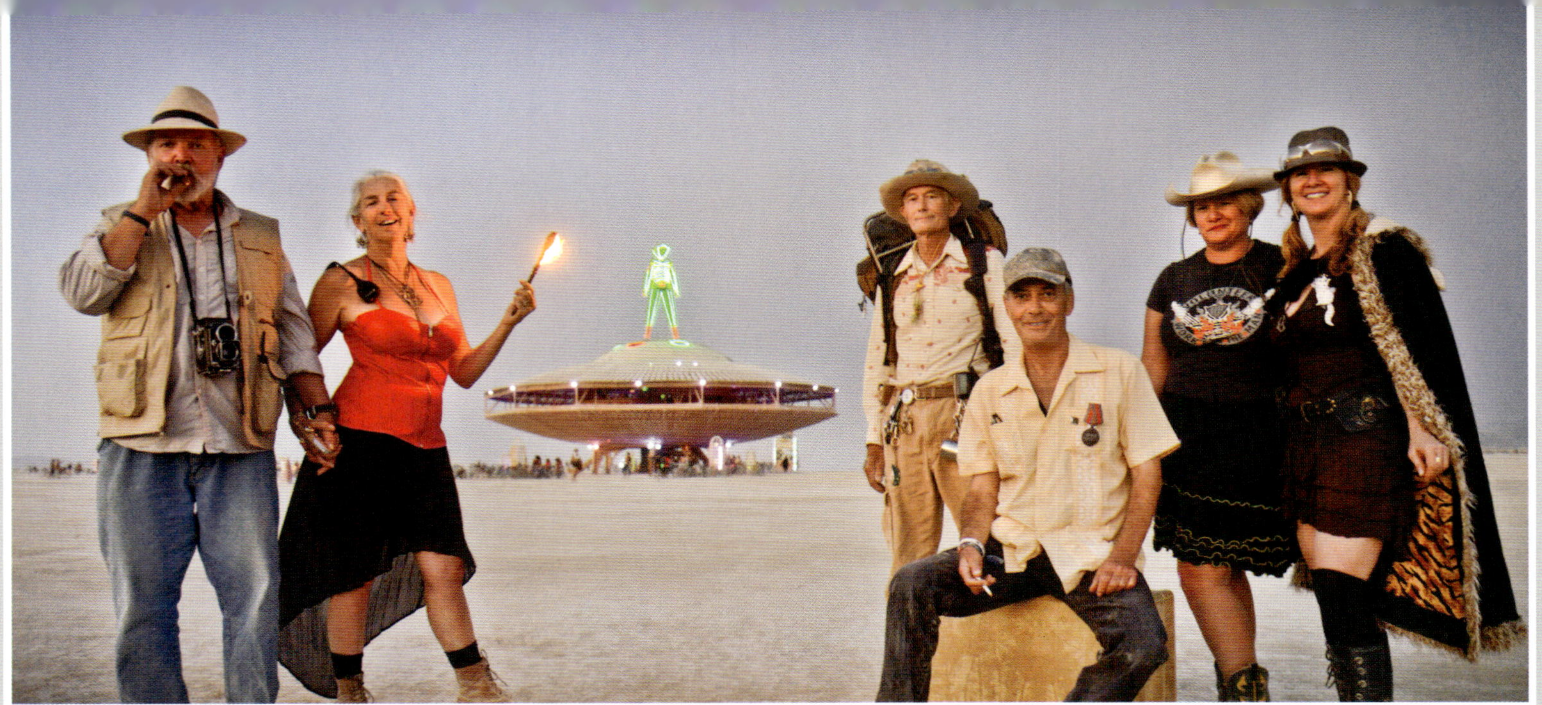

and avenues, lit street corners, street signs, and much, much more. I had to make all this stuff up as we went along. But it turned out that the compliance officer from Washoe County for the 1997 event, was a "Burner." And so when he said, "What about the flush toilets?" I pulled up in a pickup truck with a flush toilet and flushed it. And he said, "What about the lit street corners?" I pulled up in a pickup truck with a shop light and a generator, and I said, "Which corner do you want me to light?"

At some point, he said, "Okay, I understand. You're going to do this whether you comply with the event ordinance or not." And so we went ahead with our plan, which happened to be on the Fly Ranch, this remarkable, mythical place. We were making it up as we went along. It caused something–a synergism–to happen that was the most import-

ant step that Burning Man needed to take. Six people came together and founded the company, Black Rock City LLC. Larry Harvey, was the philosopher, the leader, the founder. Marian Goodell, started the Communications Department, and is currently the CEO of Burning Man Project. Harley K. Dubois ran the community services department. It was burgeoning, growing. Crimson Rose created and ran the art department. Michael Mikel was the Black Rock Ranger and emergency services lead. I had experience in camping and construction, although not in building a city. The other thing that happened that year that was really seminal in our growth, was bringing in an old friend, Rod Garrett.

The County required city designs, so I asked Rod. I had to drive 25 miles to use a phone in those days, and I called him and said, "Rod, design me a city," and hung up. Three

Rites of Passage: Will Roger, Crimson Rose, Michael Mikel, Larry Harvey, Harley K. Dubois and Marian Goodell; Photo (2011) by Karen Kuehn

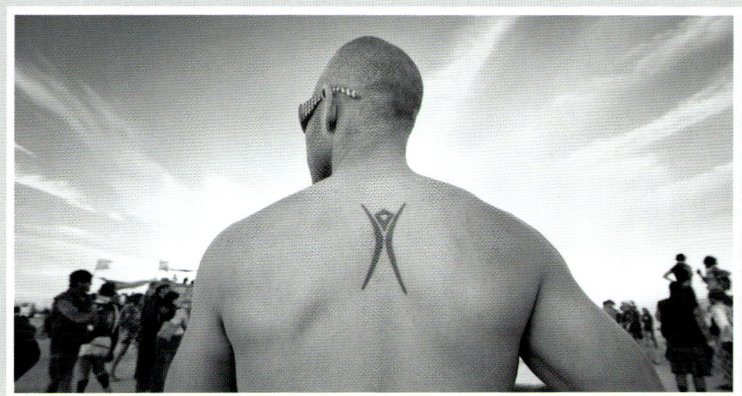

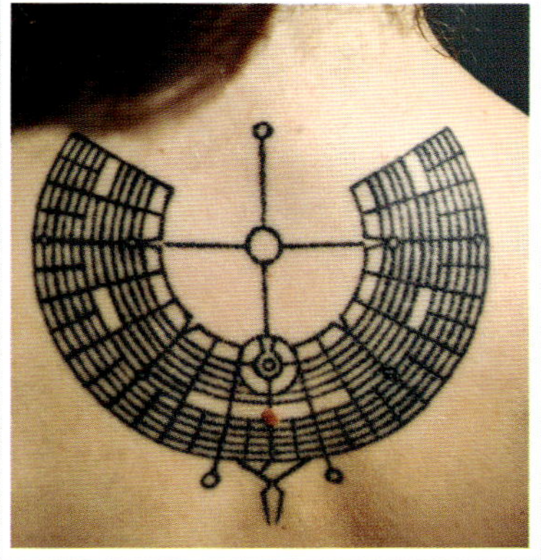

Tattoo Art
Left:
Photo (2011) by Bill Hornstein
Right:
Photo (2018) by Rachel Fee

days later, he called me back and he said, "Will, I haven't slept in three days. I don't know how to design a city. I've never designed one before." And so, I began to show him what the regulations were, what we needed for a city plan. We went back and forth rejecting some designs because they were too complex or relied on curved annular avenues that I didn't know how to lay out. Eventually, we came up with this beautiful rectilinear plan that is the 1997 site plan. Then the next year, he designed the beautiful serpentine city for the 1998 site. When I saw the 1998 Black Rock City plan, I knew that we were making land art. I expressed this to my desert operations staff, the BRC Department of Public Works. And then the rest is history. Rod's designs were not only beautiful and useful, they helped organize the campers into a community. The designs themselves became iconic:

they're part of artwork and jewelry, are in collections, and are even tattoos. So, the important thing in the transition was that we went from 1996, a cacophonous campout with friends, to 1997, an organized community called Black Rock City, based on Rod's designs.

We did it at Fly Ranch, which started my dream of having the Burning Man community be able to use Fly Ranch year-round. That was a 20-year dream that actually became a reality two years ago when BRC purchased the ranch. I'm really excited about that.

Two other people stepped up that year, Flynn Mauthe and Tony Perez-Banuet. Flynn is a musician, artist, builder, remarkable character, schooled by Survival Research Labs in the fire arts–unflappable, a genuine, engaging man. Flynn was my second-in-command. Tony, also a musician,

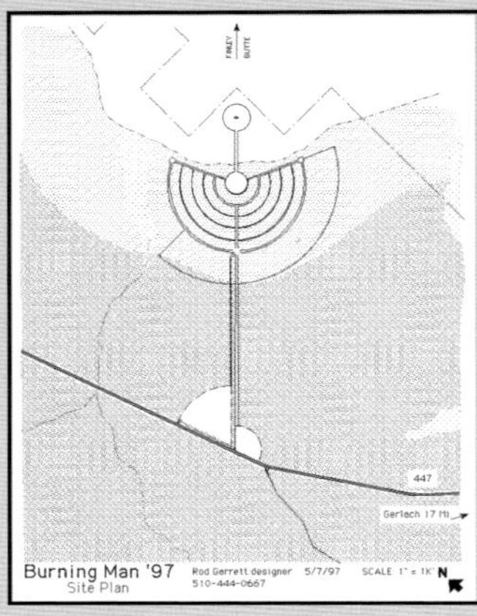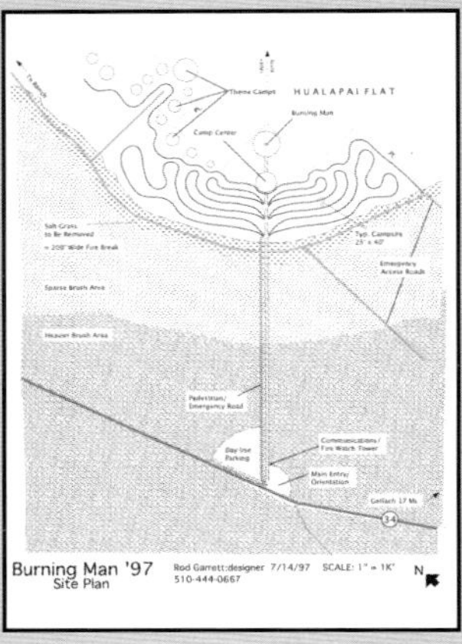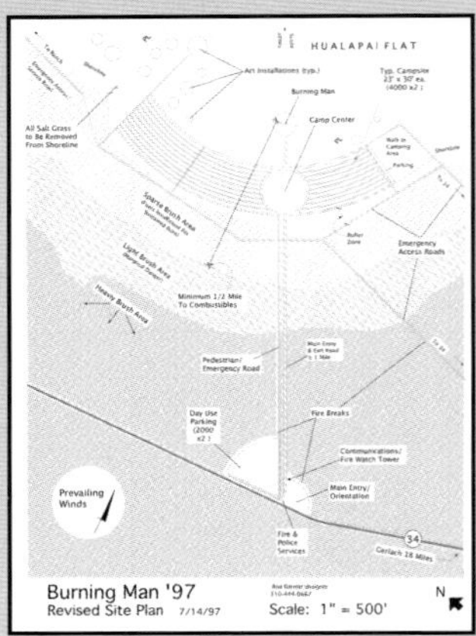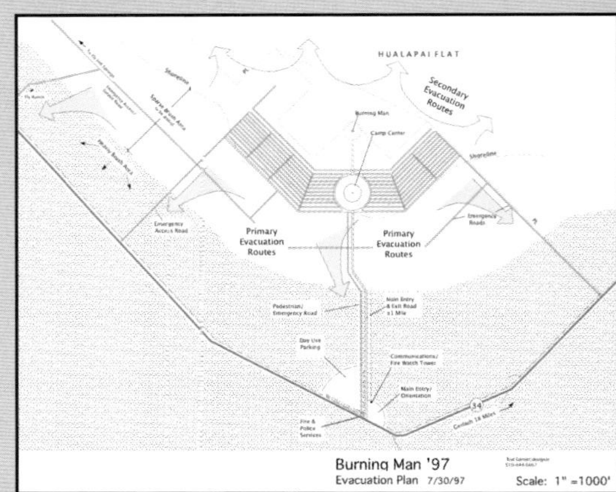

brought a can-do attitude to everything he did, a quality that working in the desert required. Tony became the surveyor, staff manager, and site superintendent. He is Black Rock City's Site Superintendent and Surveyor to this day.

After the 1997 Burning Man event, sitting around a campfire with Rod, Flynn, and Tony, in an effort to create an identity for the desert operations department so we might recruit better, I named the department Black Rock City Department of Public Works and asked Bill Moore, my life-long friend and artist, to design a symbol for it. As with Rod's early plans, Bill and I went back and forth, finally coming up with the appropriate symbol for the new department; the symbol is now also iconic, found in art works, jewelry, and tattoos. The qualities of hard work, reverie, comradery, and hard play of the BRC-DPW are legendary in the Burning Man community. I like to think that we started those attributes in 1997.

For the 1997 event, I included some early Rod Garrett renderings that I rejected for being too complex, my city-building skills being inadequate at the time. Also included is a Bureau of Land Management closure area map for the 2002 city to show how the Bureau of Land Management views the site. I make a distinction between a map and a plan. A map is a rendering of what exists; a plan is a rendering of what you are building. The difference is often field design, where the plan is altered based on conditions in the field. For 1997, I included the plan and the map that shows variations in the roads where we encountered sink holes and other obstacles. Rod and I had an understanding from the beginning that field design would be in play. Also included are photographs of the Fly Ranch, especially the geyser and the wetlands area. This ranch is over five square miles in size, has wind, solar, and geothermal energy potential, and is located in Hualapai Valley adjacent to the Black Rock Desert. The Fly Ranch holds the potential to actualize the experiment in community we call Burning Man.

Illustrations L-R: 1) A rejected site map for Black Rock City due to complexity or annular design. 2) An alternate site map that was rejected due to survey issues. 3) An annular site map for Black Rock City that was rejected due to design. 4) A rectilinear style rendering of the site map that was approved by the county and BLM, including escape routes. The design was later used to create the final rendering. City designs by Rod Garrett

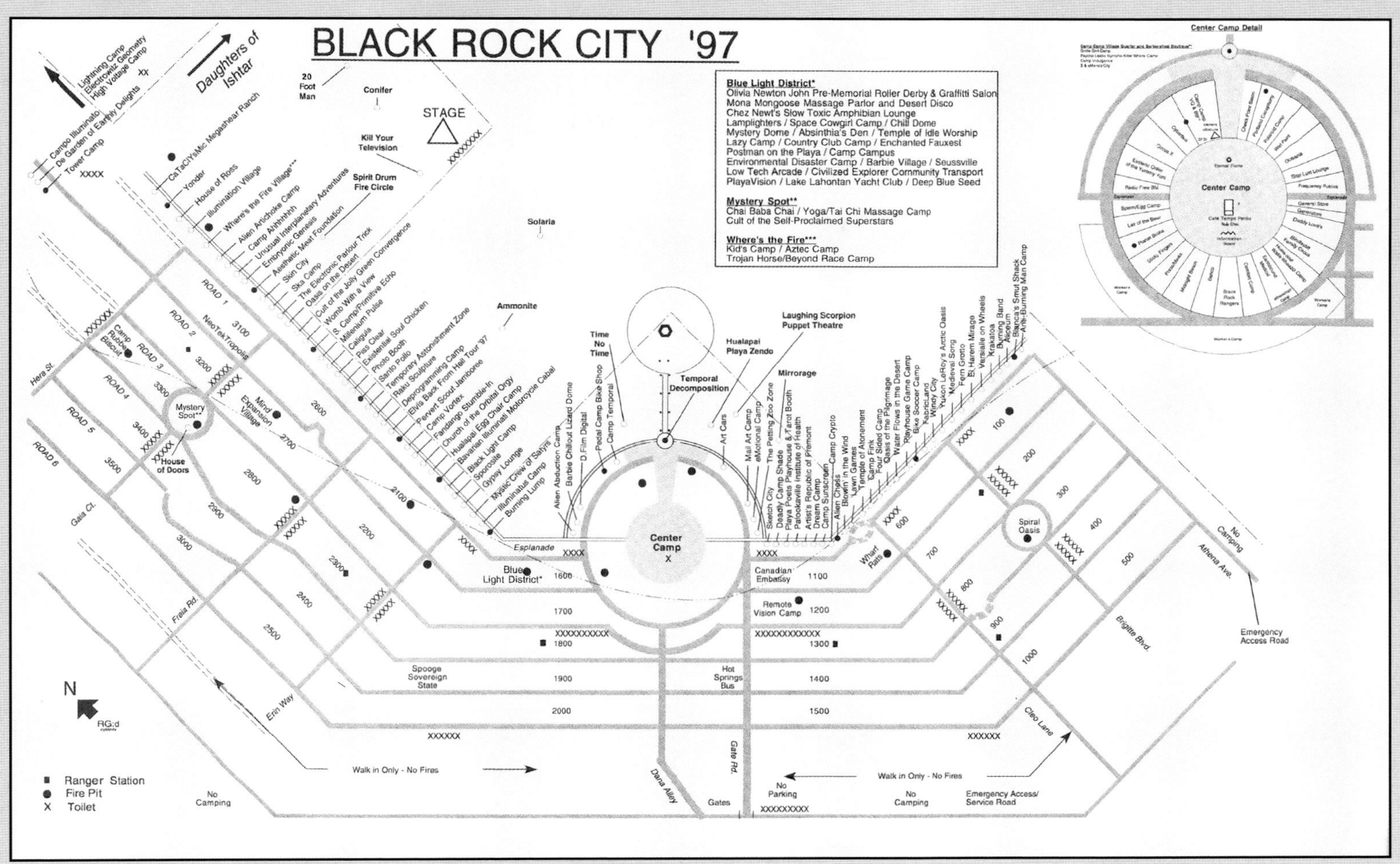

Harley K. Dubois was in charge of community services and theme camp placement. This is the site map that was made available for all camps

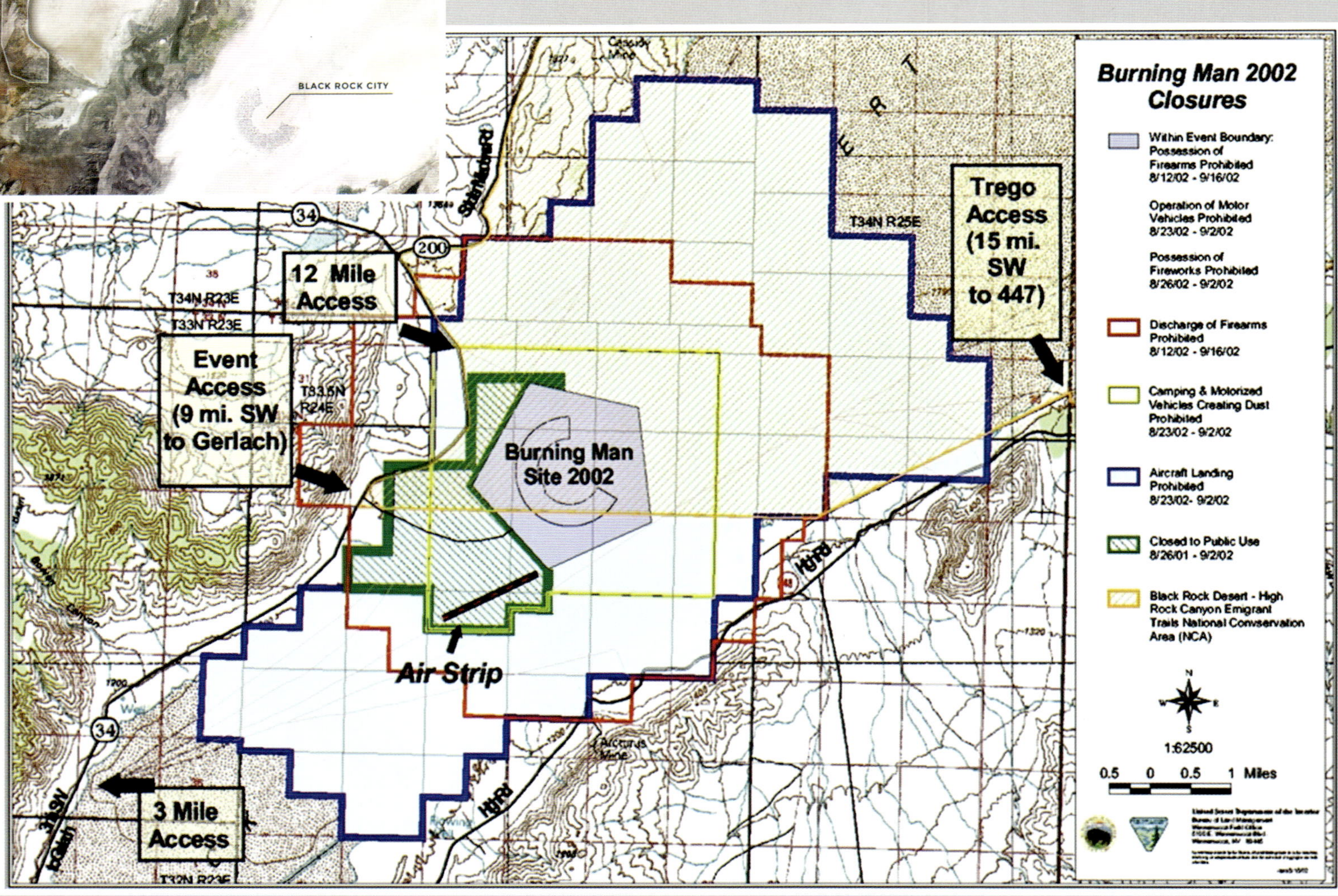

30

A topographic rendering that was submitted to the Federal Government's Bureau of Land Management in 2002.
The Burning Man closures as displayed show colored areas that have different federal guidelines which are date-specific

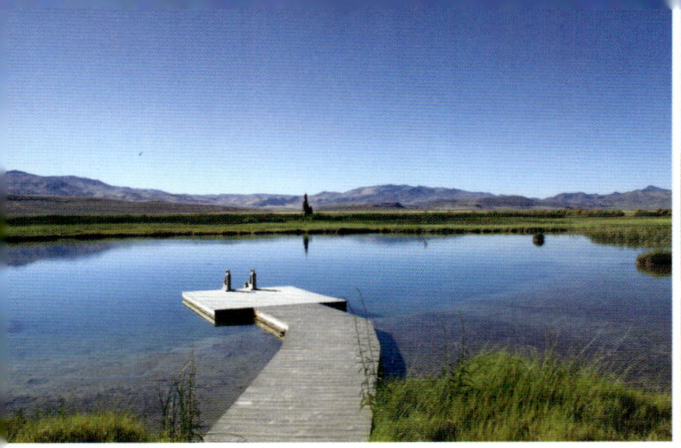

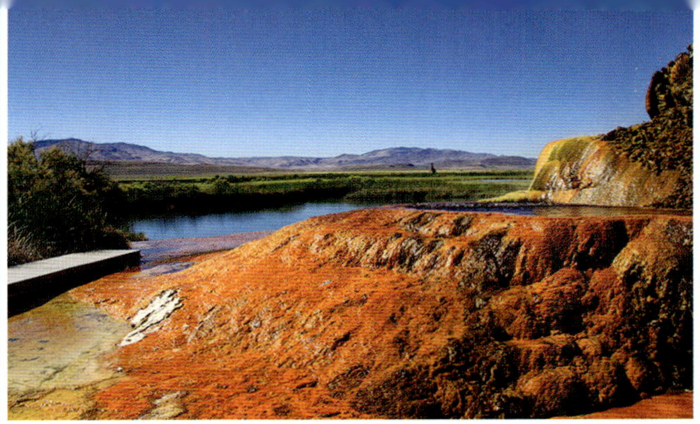

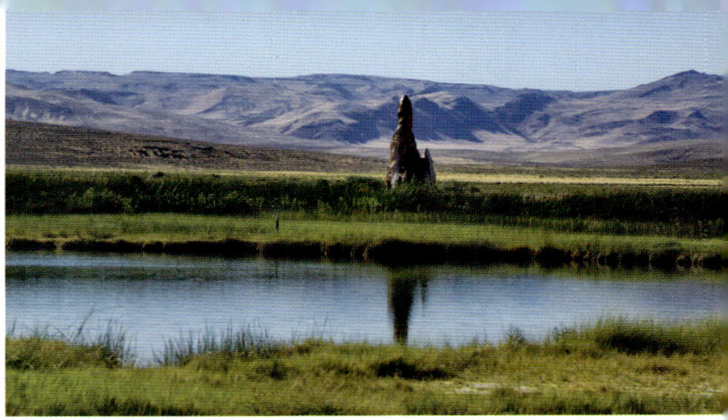

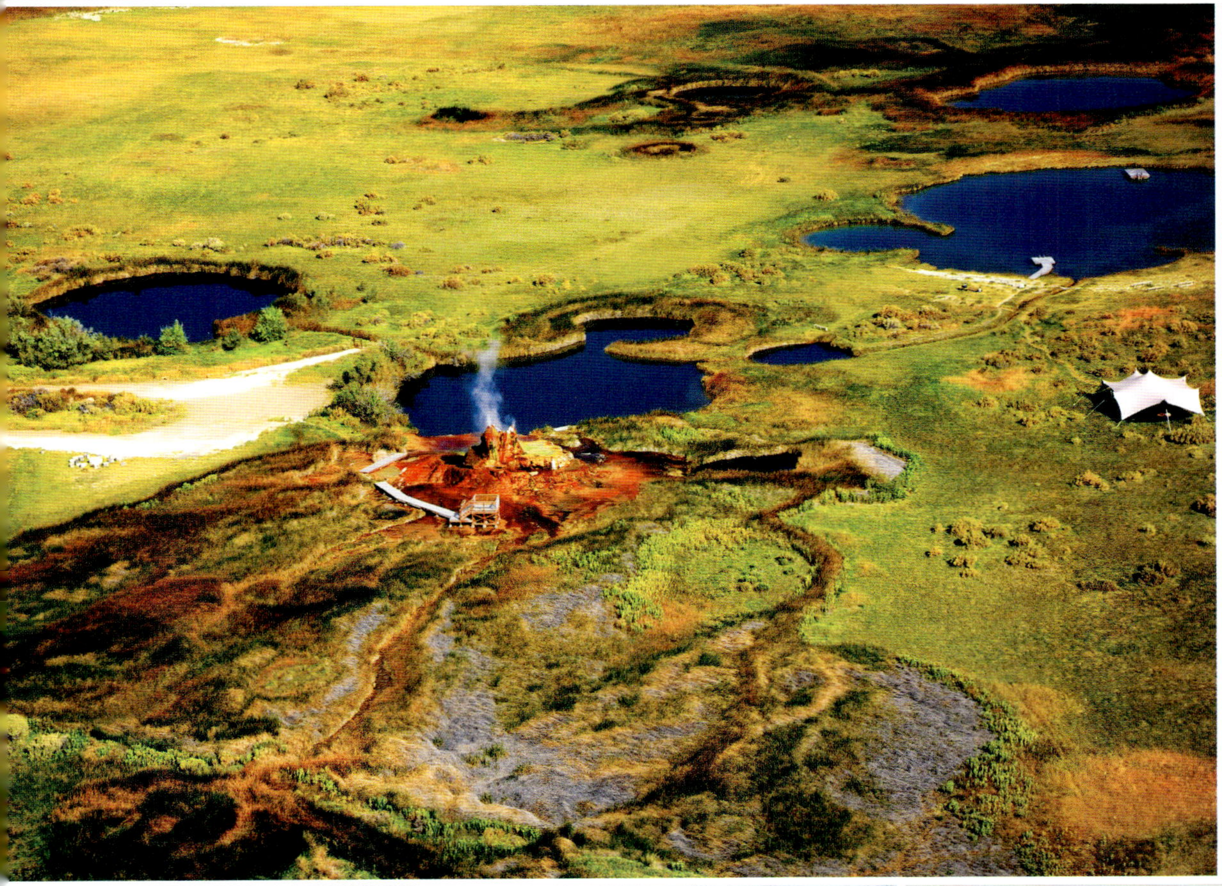

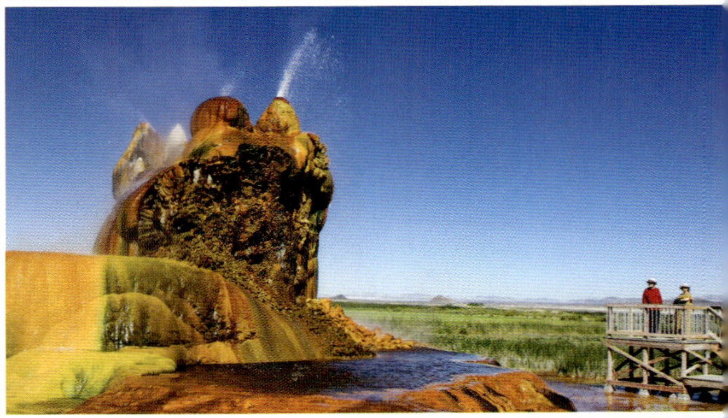

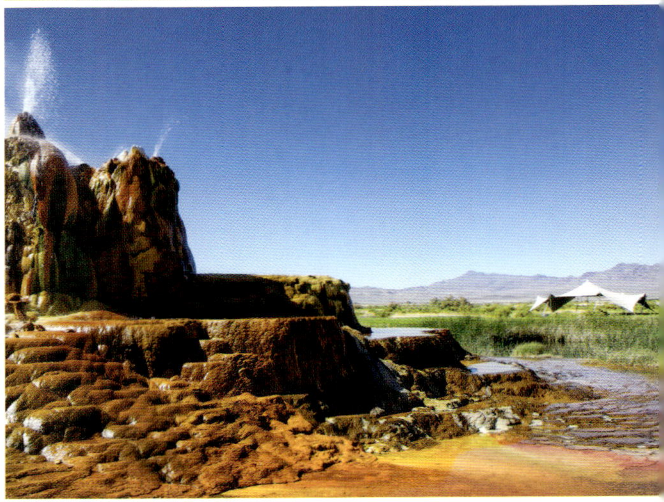

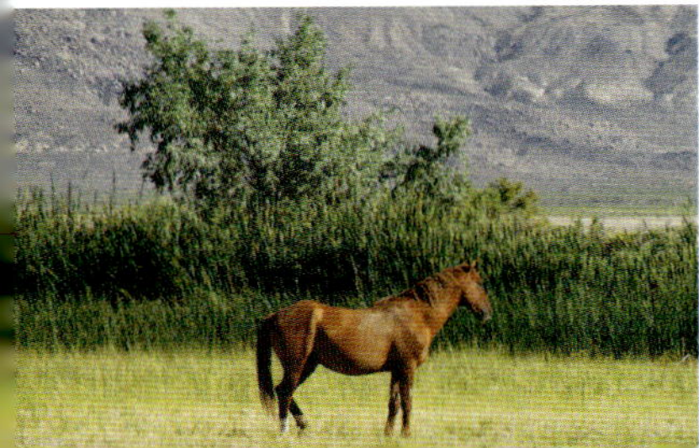
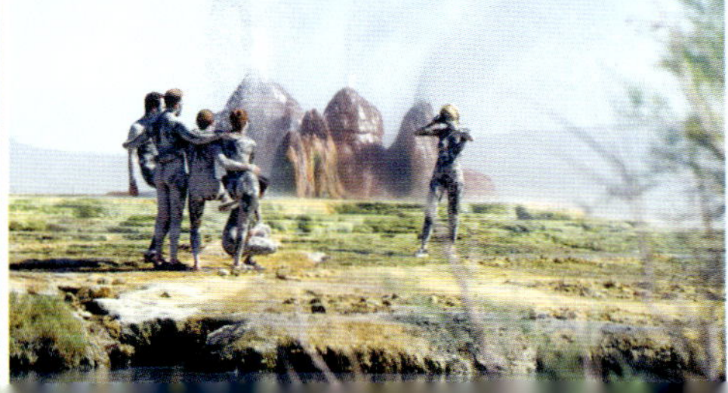

The Fly Ranch property has 640 acres of wetlands, dozens of natural spring-water pools ranging in temperature from hot to cold, sagebrush-grasslands, and a small area of playa that opens onto the Hualapai Flat. The land's most prominent feature is the stunning Fly Geyser, a unique and iconic geothermal geyser.

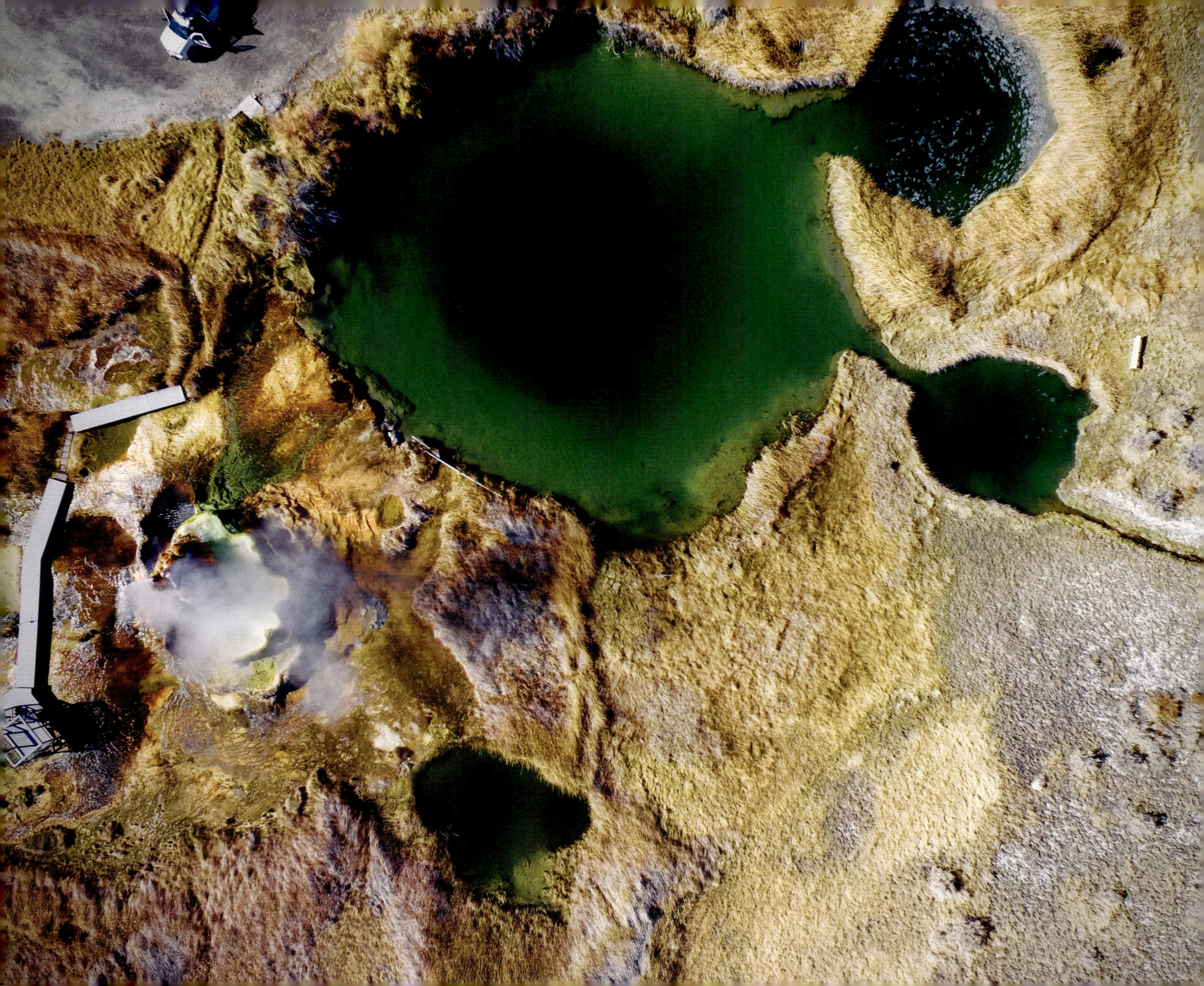

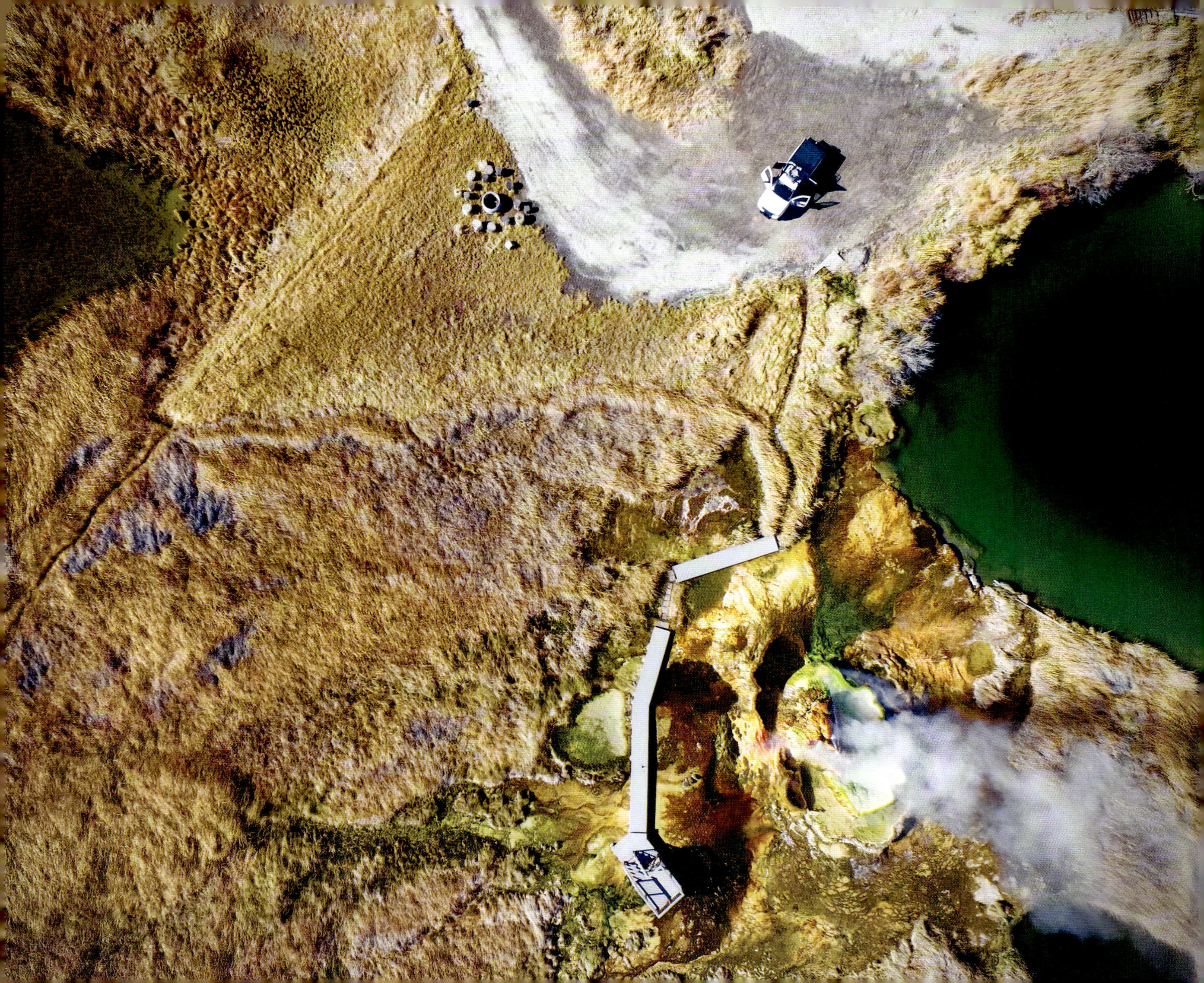

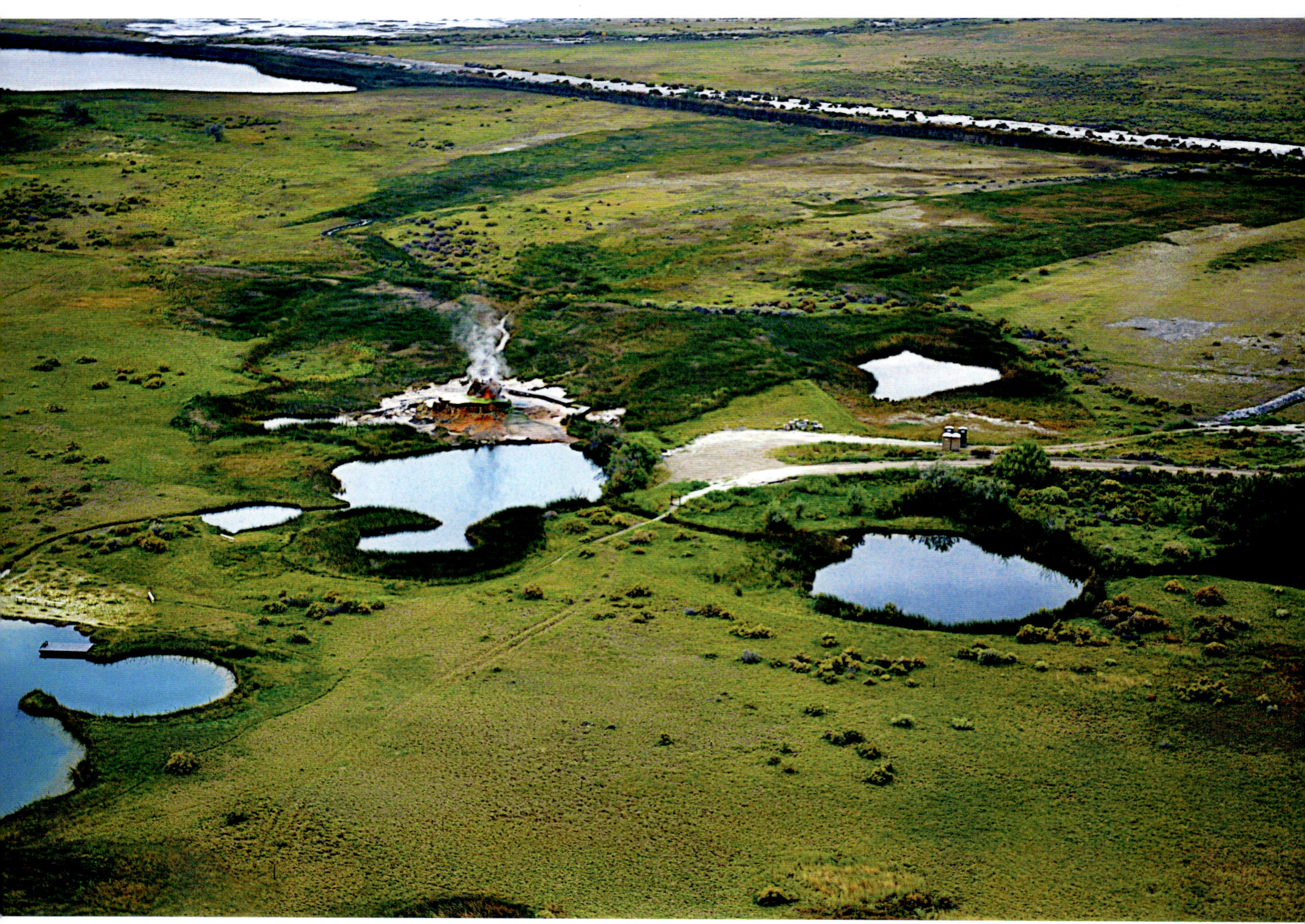

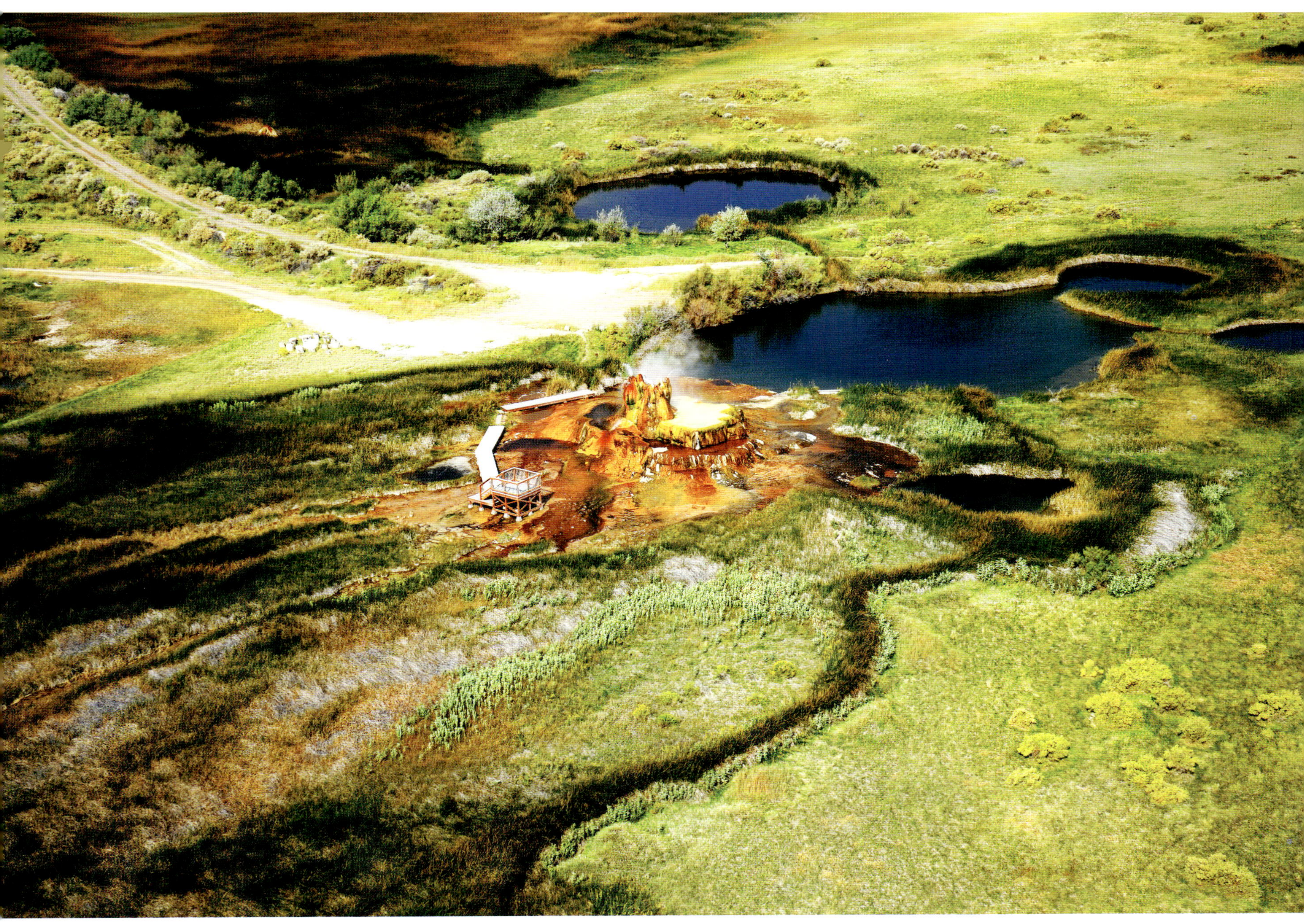

Botanist and Burning Man Project Land Fellow, Lisa Schile-Beers, (aka Scirpus) conducted a one-year environmental baseline study at Fly Ranch. Schile-Beers completed a list of all plants and animals observed on the property, an interactive map of all human-made objects, a map of botanical species, including a graph of those that are invasive, an analysis of weather data and sun activity, and documentation of hundreds of photographs of wildlife

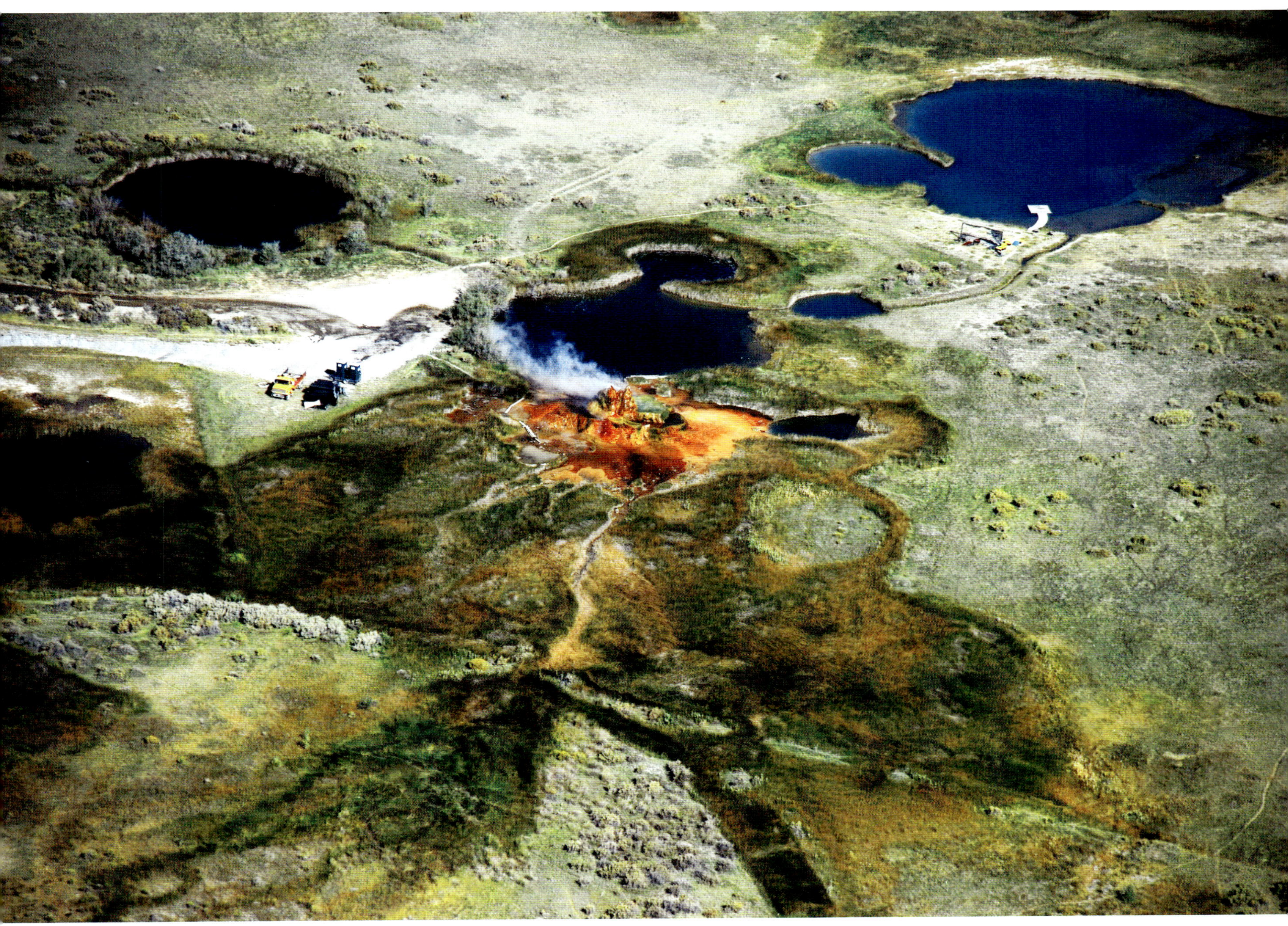

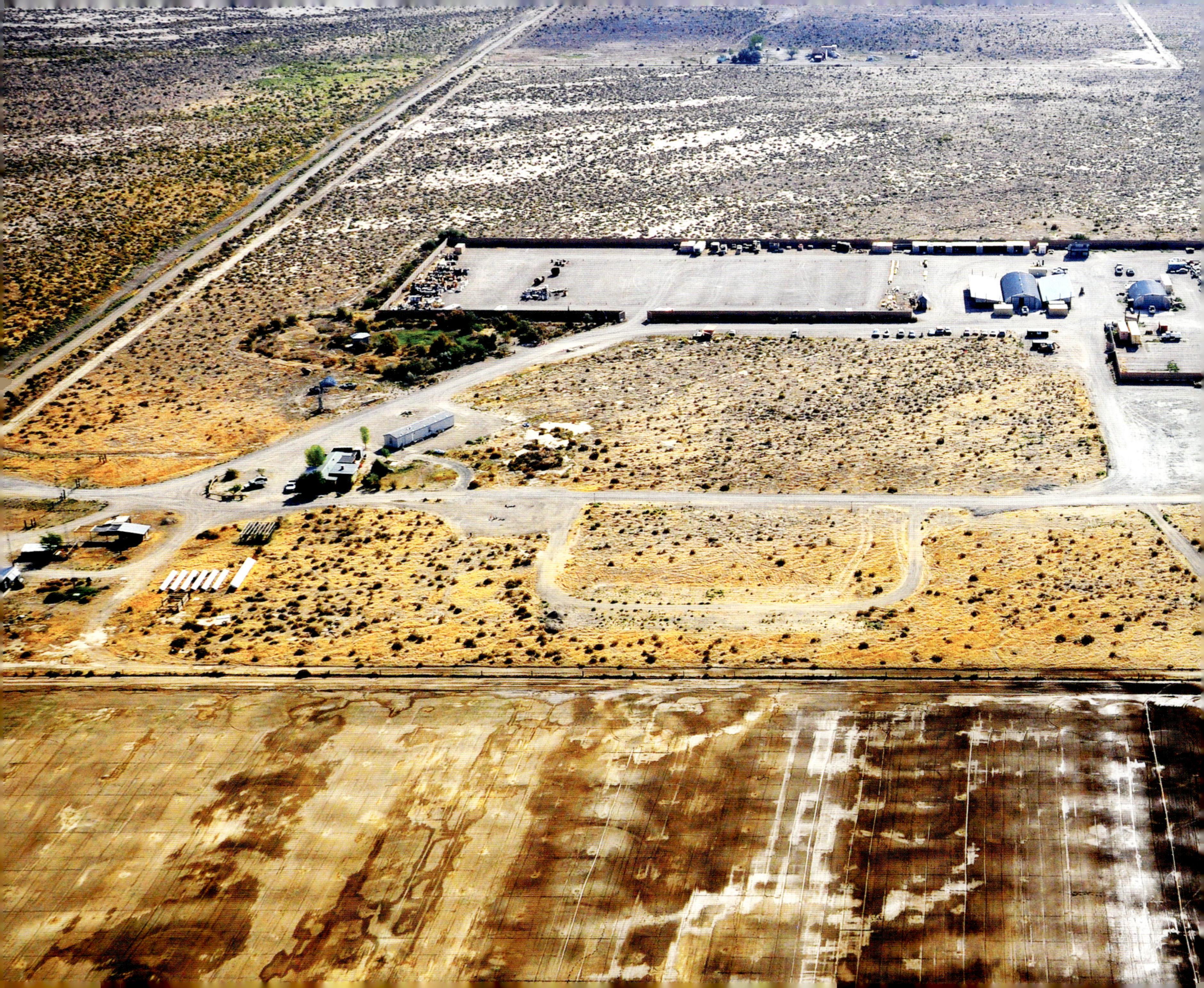

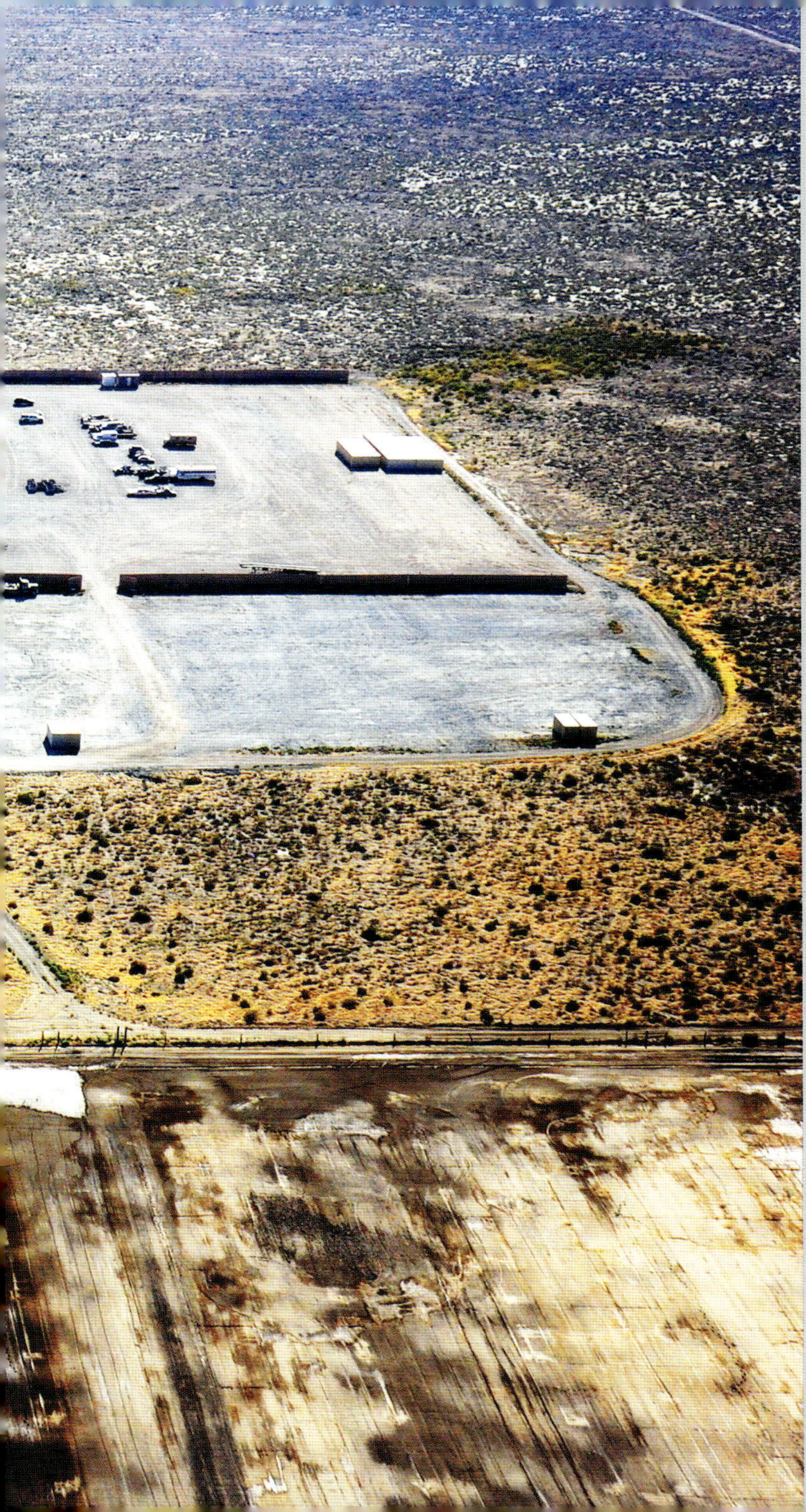

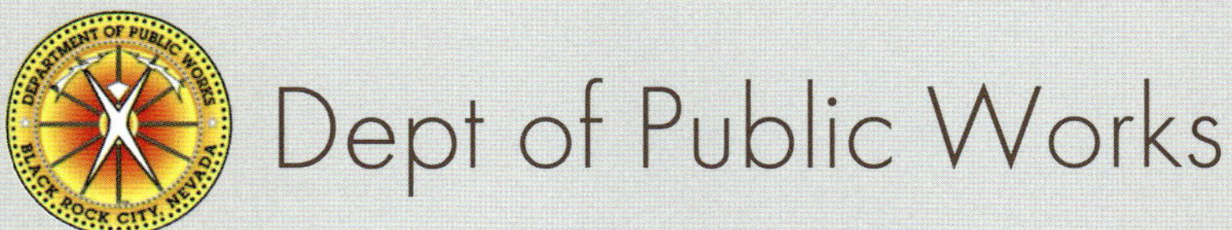

Dept of Public Works

The Black Rock City Department of Public Works (BRC DPW) is the group that plans, surveys, builds, and takes down the basic infrastructure of our temporary community in the desert. Since the 1997 event the DPW, hand-in-hand with other departments, has instituted the City Plan.

This includes:

    Building logical roads

    Creating and placing signage

    Establishing the gate

    Building and placing spires and city lighting

    Maintaining approved potable water systems

    Building functional/safe shade structures

    Maintaining a depot for material storage

    Building the Man, Center Camp, the lantern spires,
    the Gate and entrance to the city

    Surveying street alignments and city boundaries, theme camp
    and artwork locations, signage and border fencing

    Running the materials depot and mechanical shop

    Interfacing with staff and outside agency facilities

    Providing transportation

    Directing potty placement

    Providing portable and stationary electrical power

    Creating the welded steel fireplaces

    Assisting with major art projects

    Setting up small plane airport and runway

    Provide dust control on the roads via water trucks

After the event, the DPW strikes the set, stores gear for next year and makes sure that Black Rock City will truly Leave No Trace.

Black Rock Station 2009. Building and removing the city has evolved from a depository of materials toward becoming a professional facility for the production of Black Rock City and related arts projects

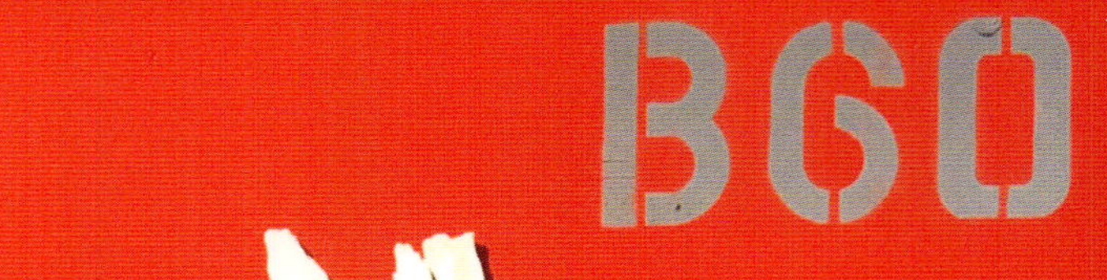

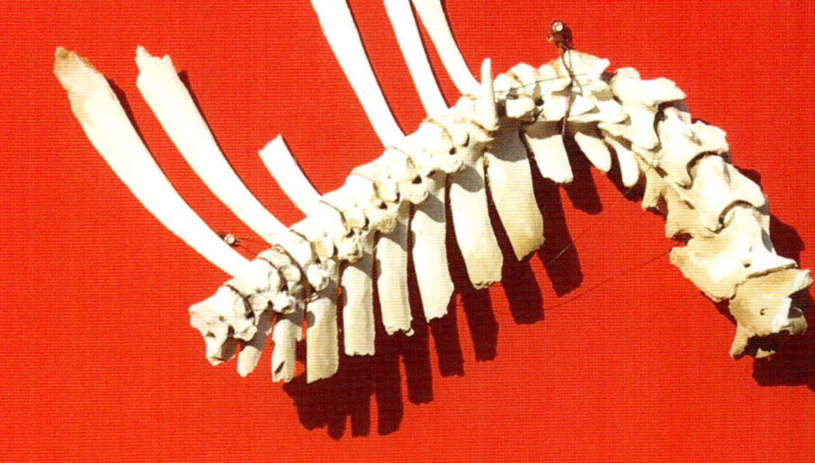

(2017) Photos by Laura Henkel
"Narwhal "mutant vehicle (2002) by Pepe Ozan
"Bone Tree" (1999) by Dana Albany from Nebulous Entity (1988) by Michael Christian
"Dragon Smelter," (2012) by Danny Macchiarini
Aerial of the Jackson Ranch house, photo (2013) by Will Roger

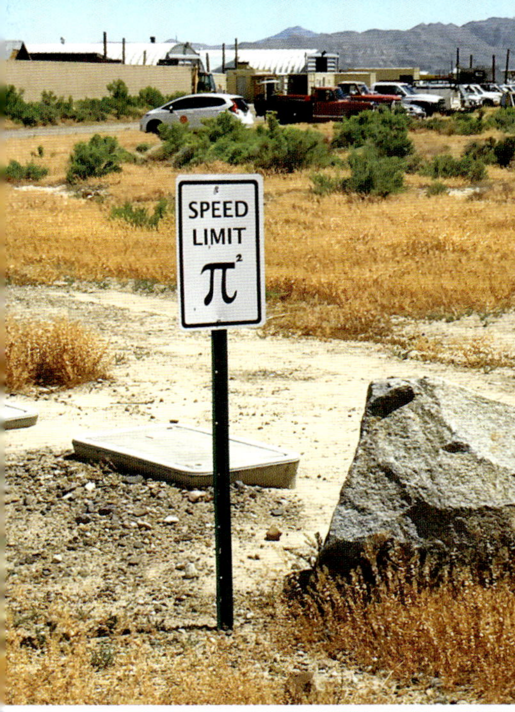
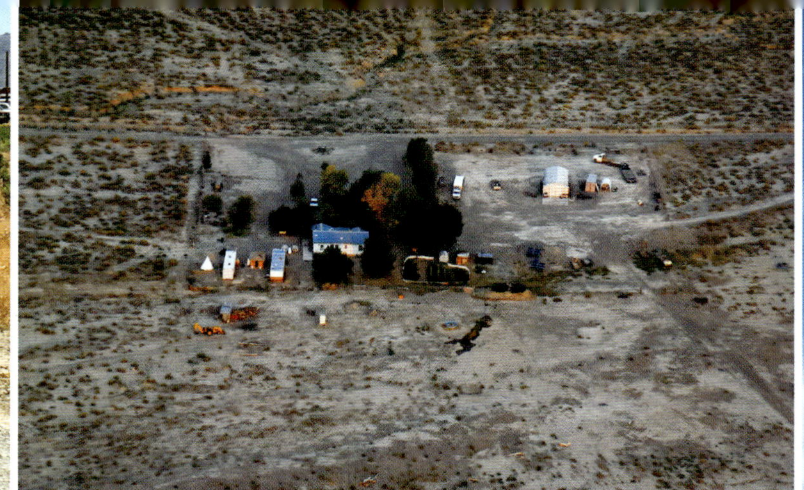
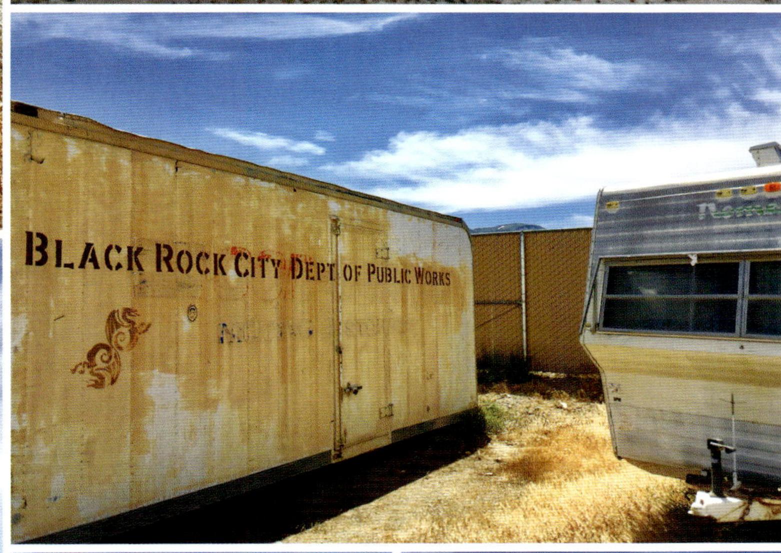
BLACK ROCK CITY DEPT OF PUBLIC WORKS
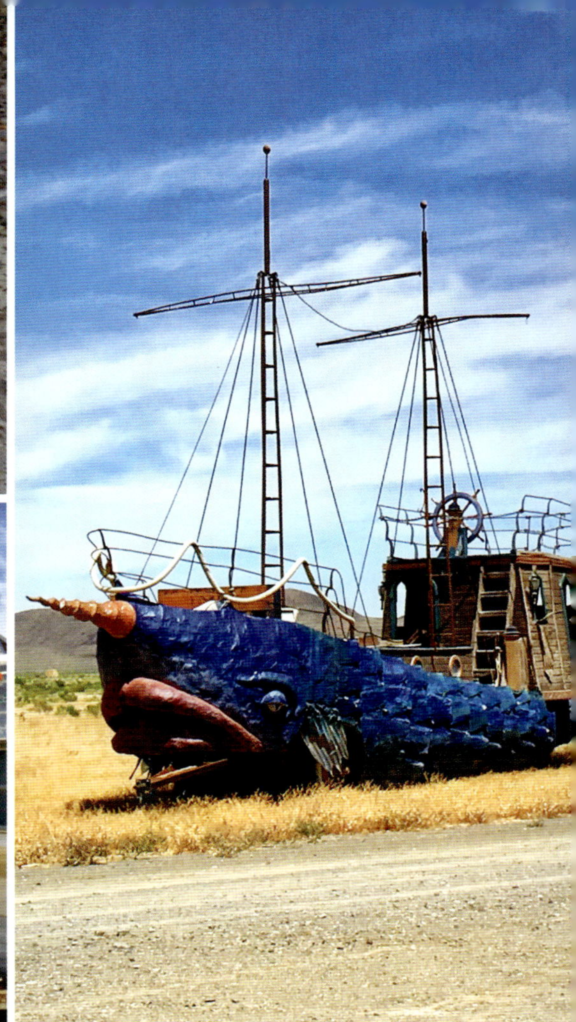
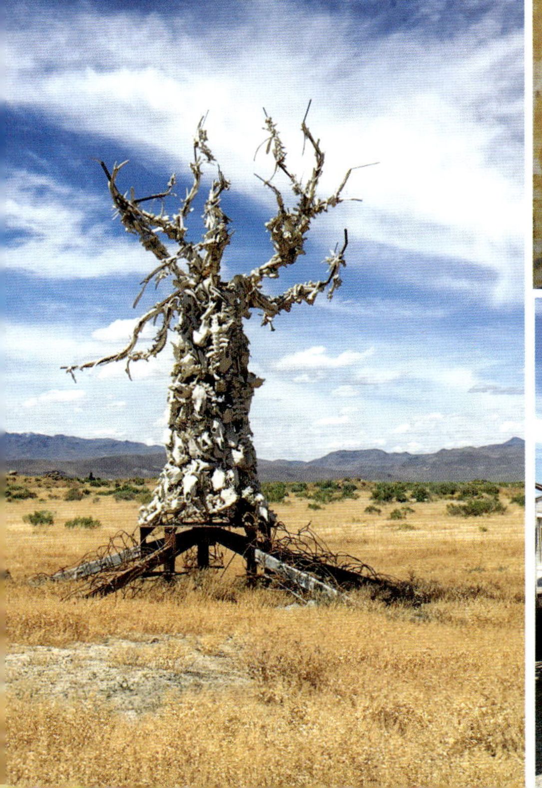
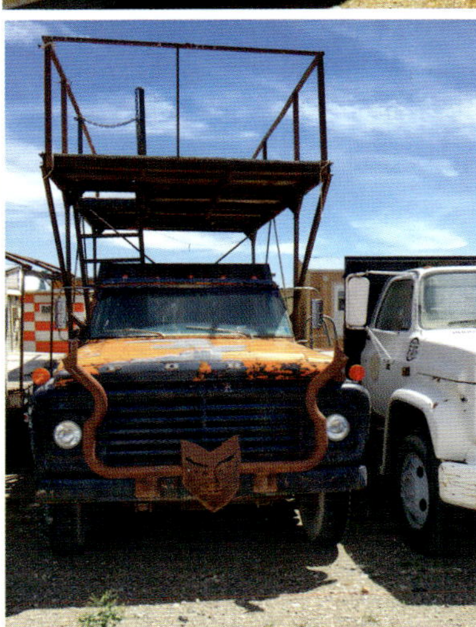
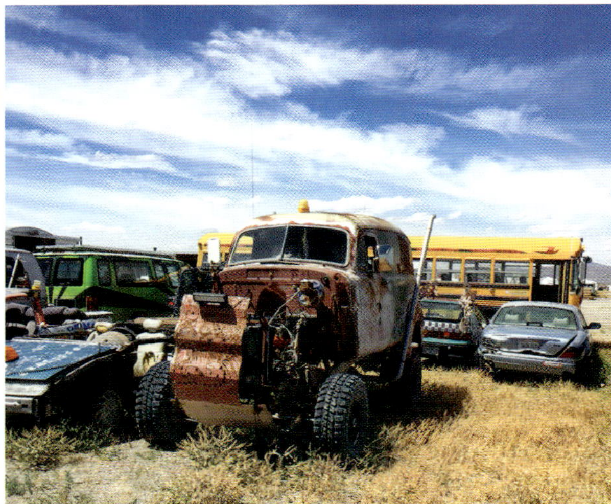
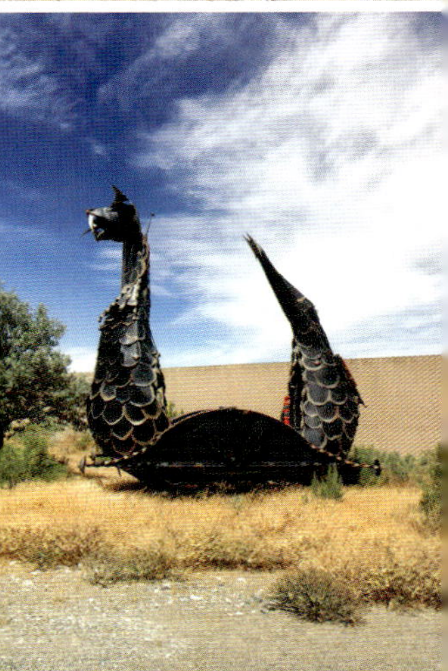

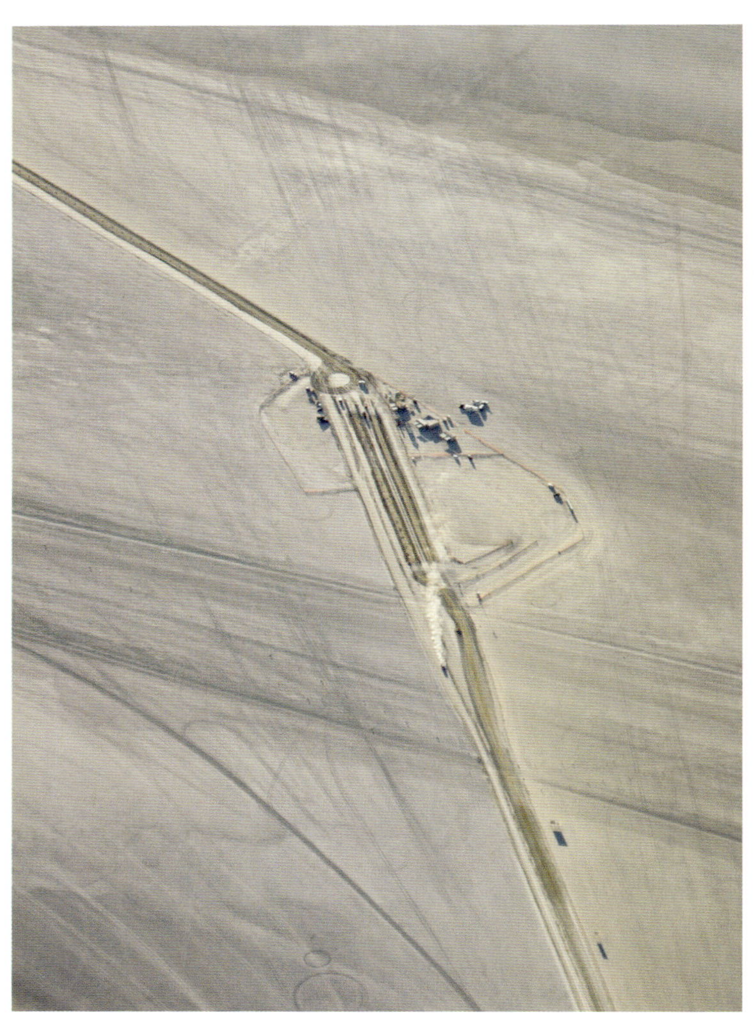

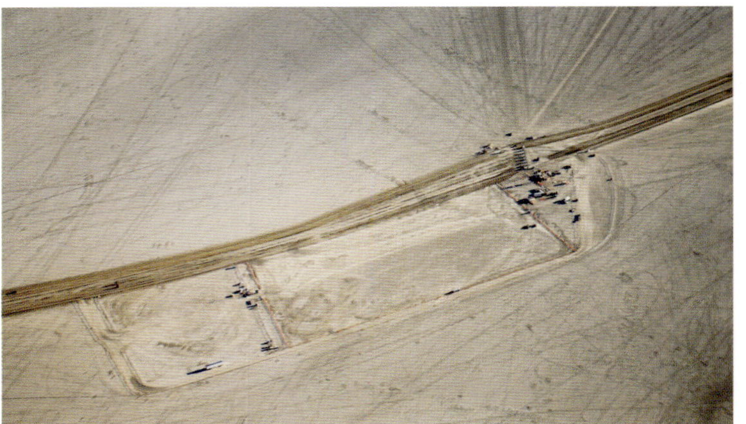

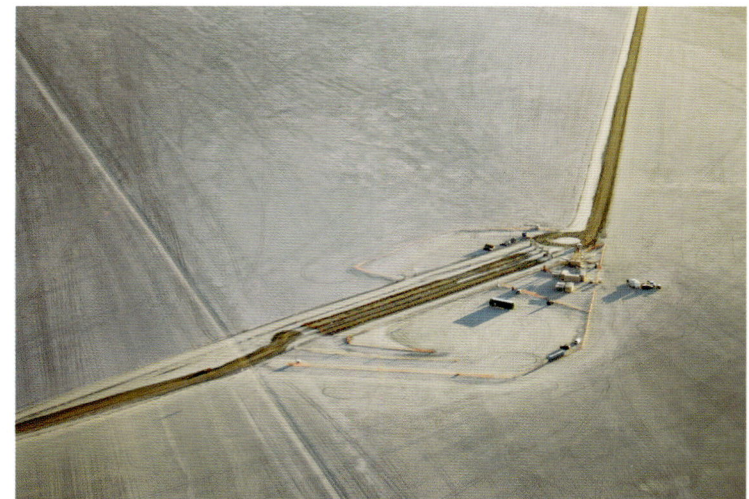

The Box Office, Gate and D Lot

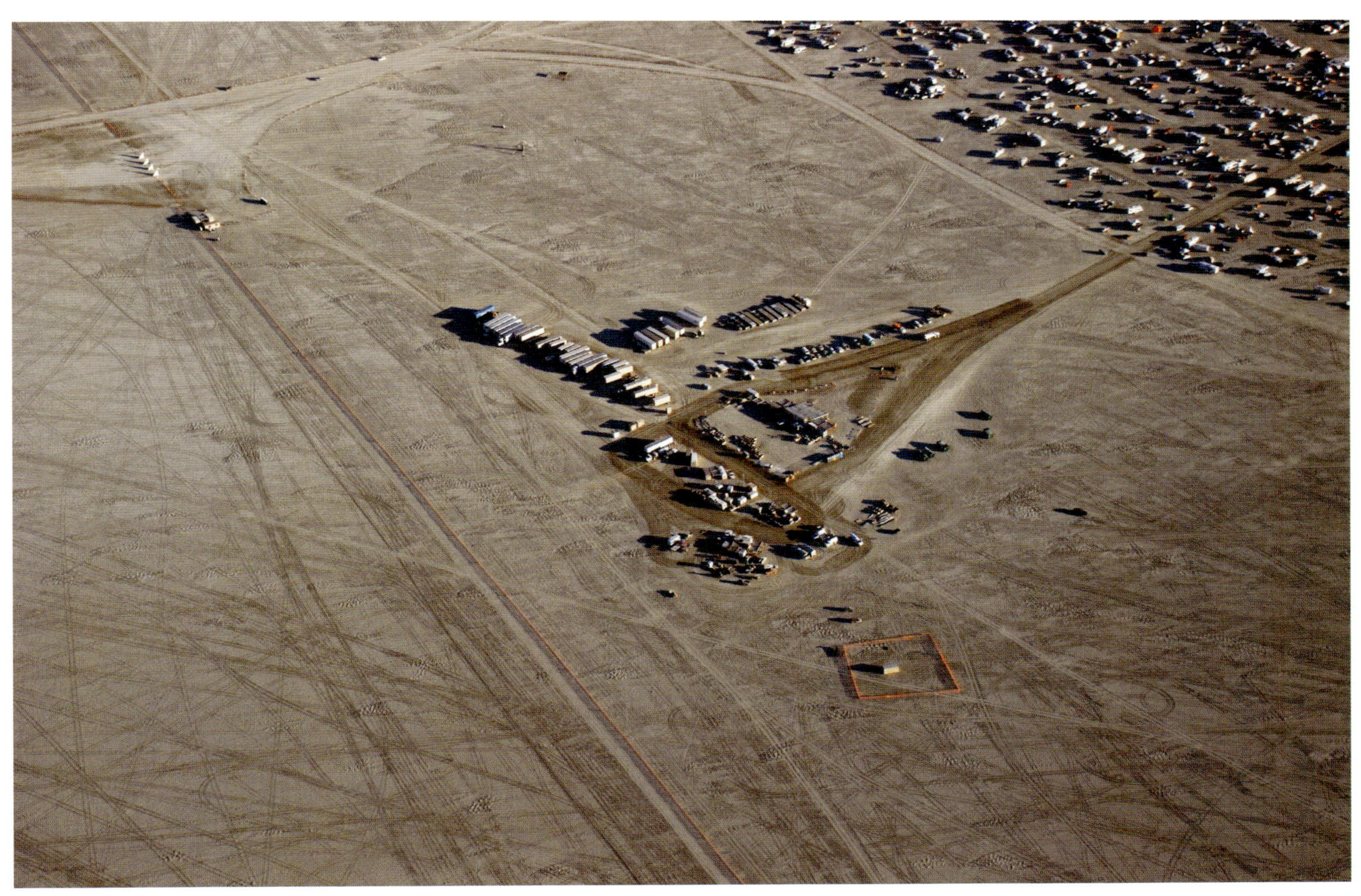

DPW Depot

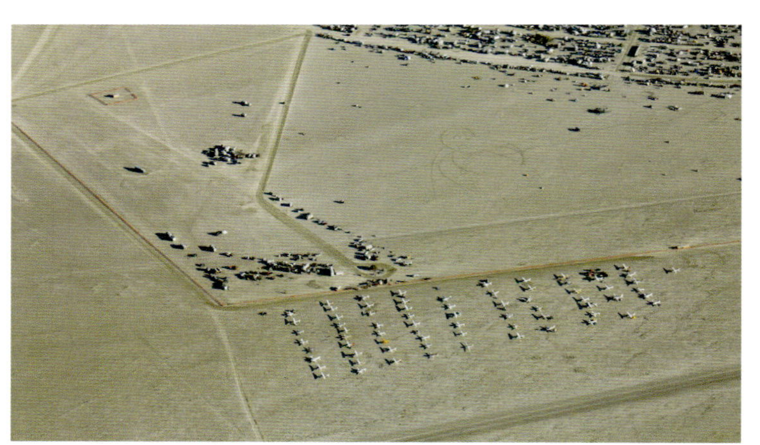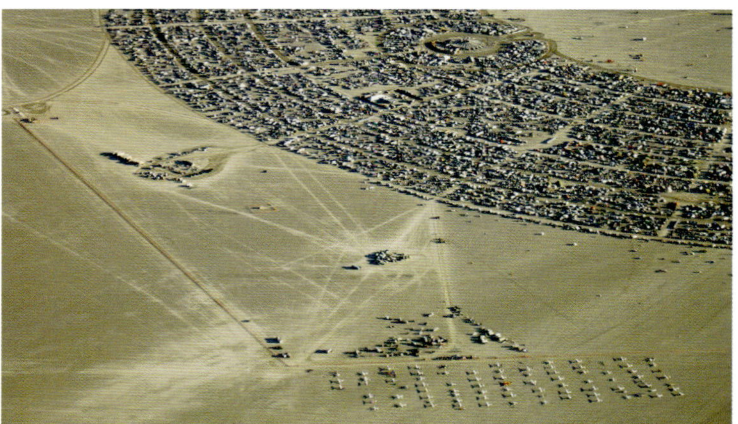

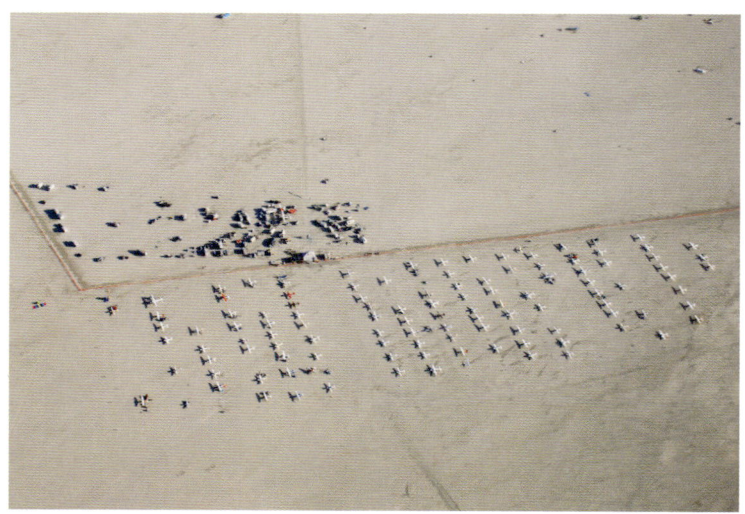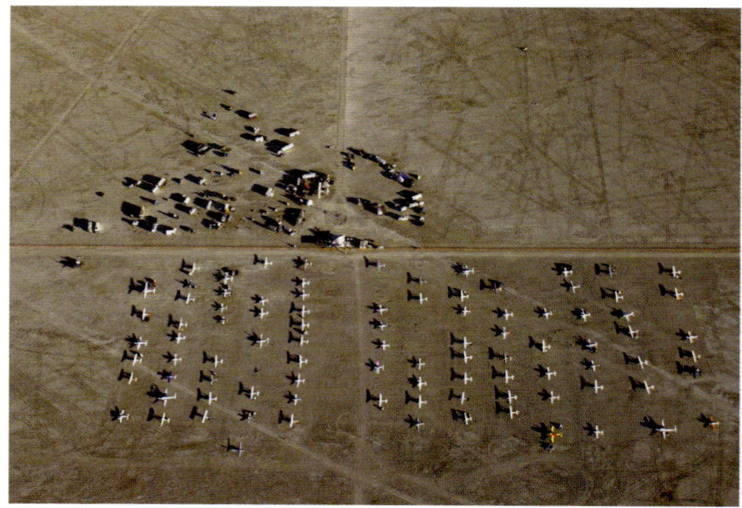

44

Above: top left to right: Black Rock City Municipal Airport (2005, 2006, 2007 and 2008)
Right: Black Rock City Municipal Airport. (2015)

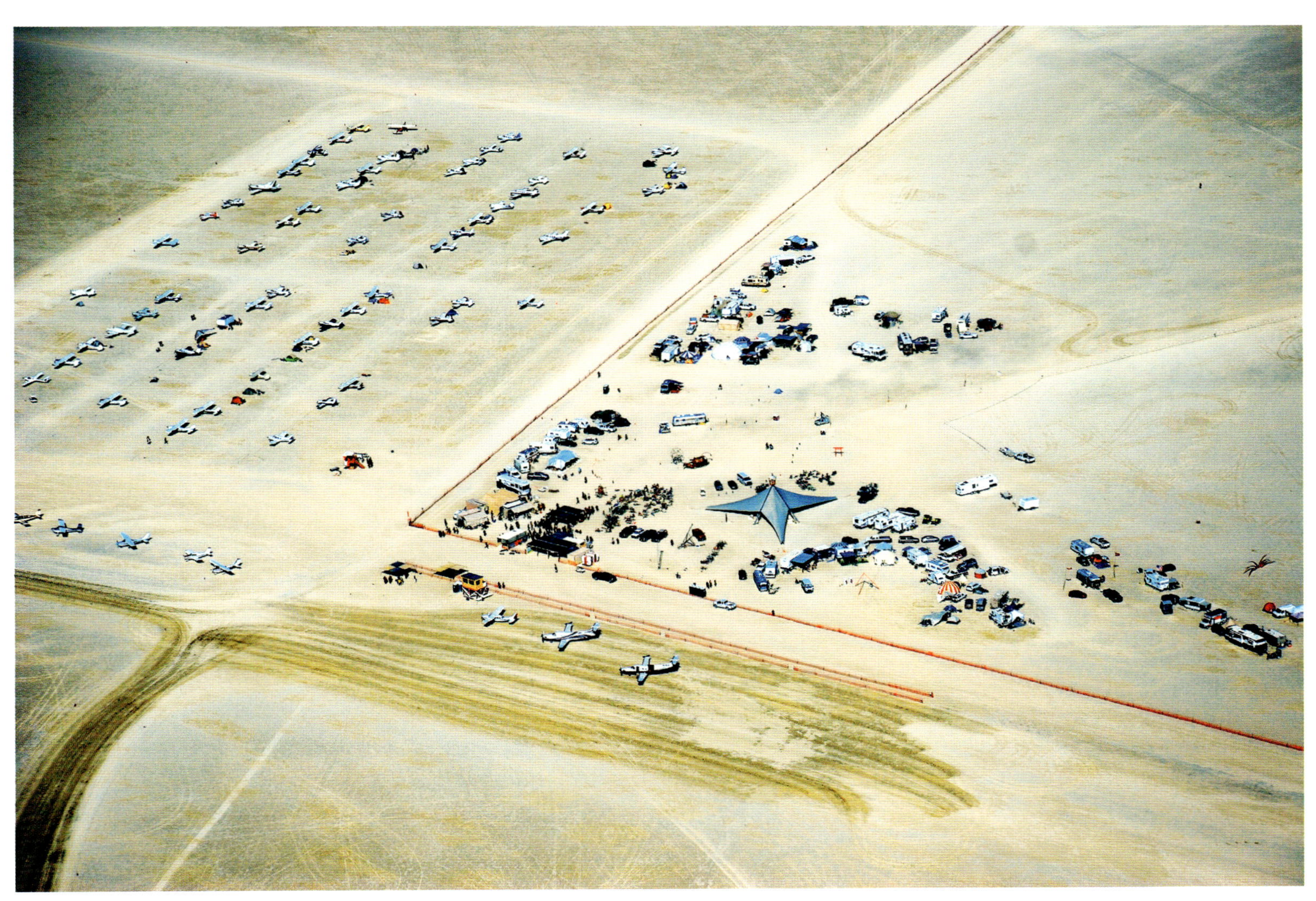

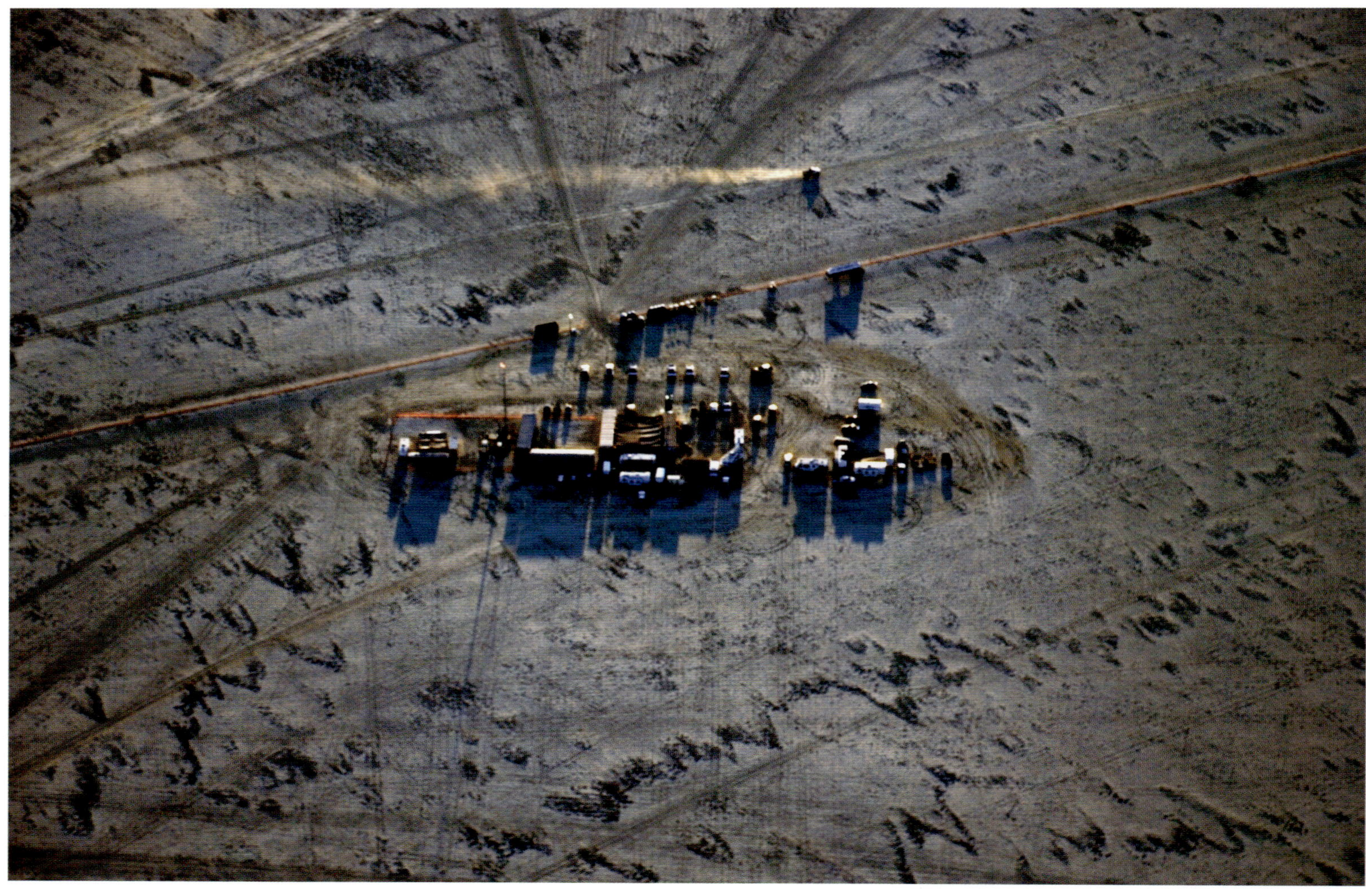

Above: DPW Depot (2009)
Right: Black Rock Station (2011)

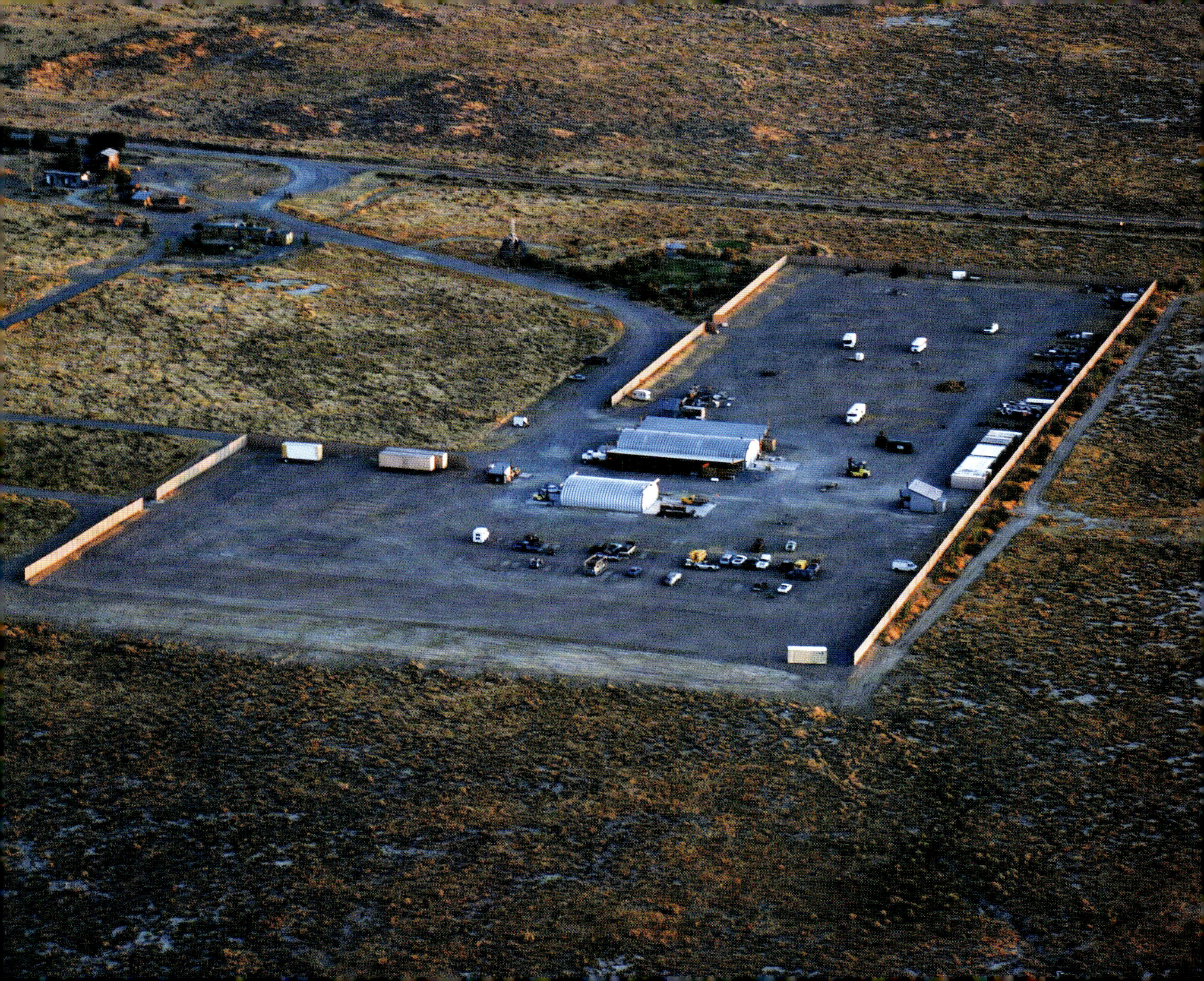

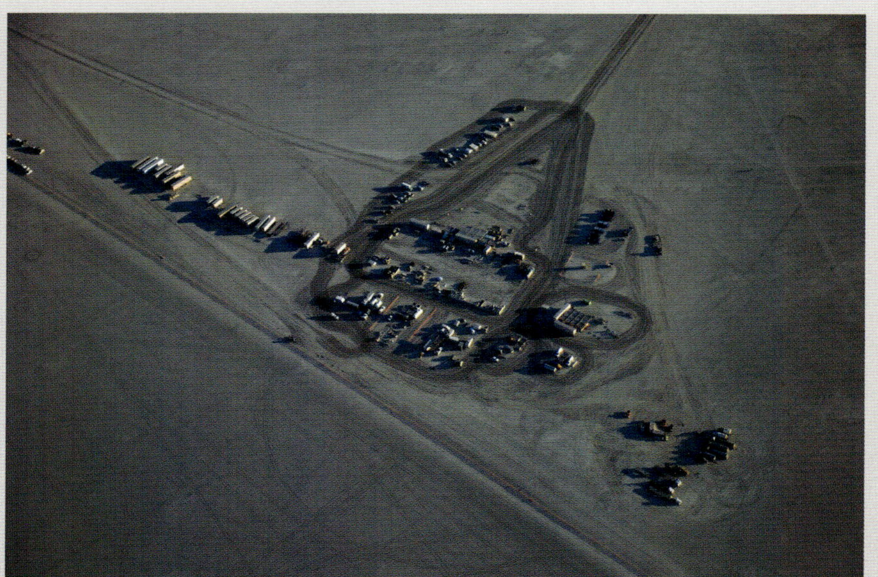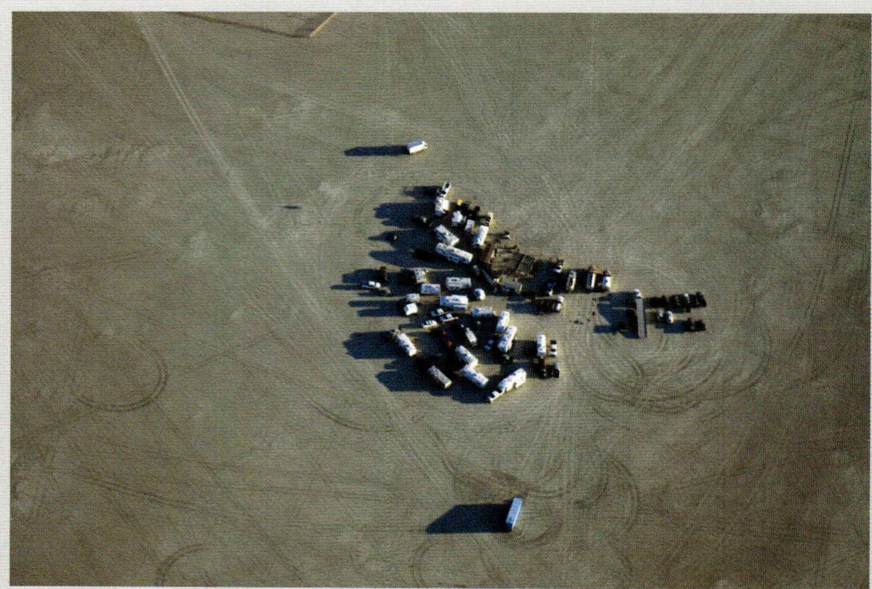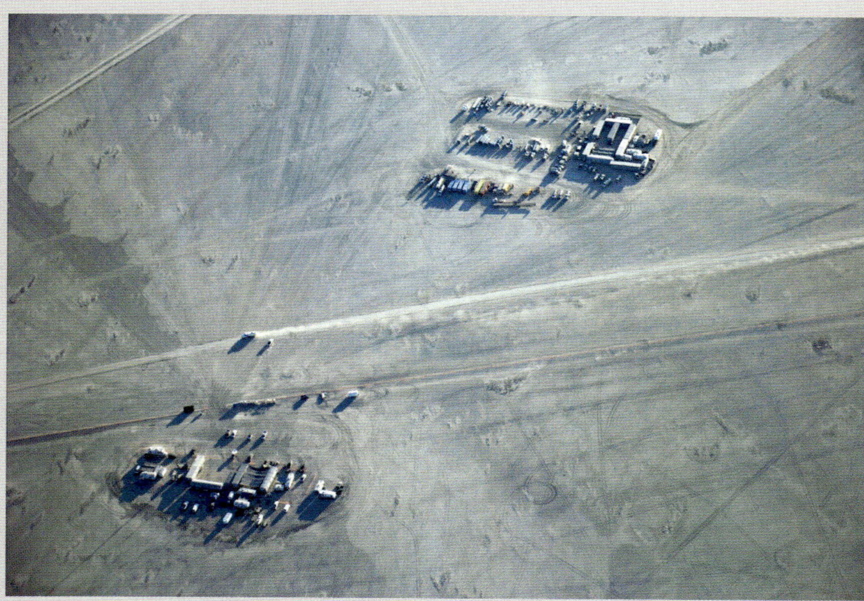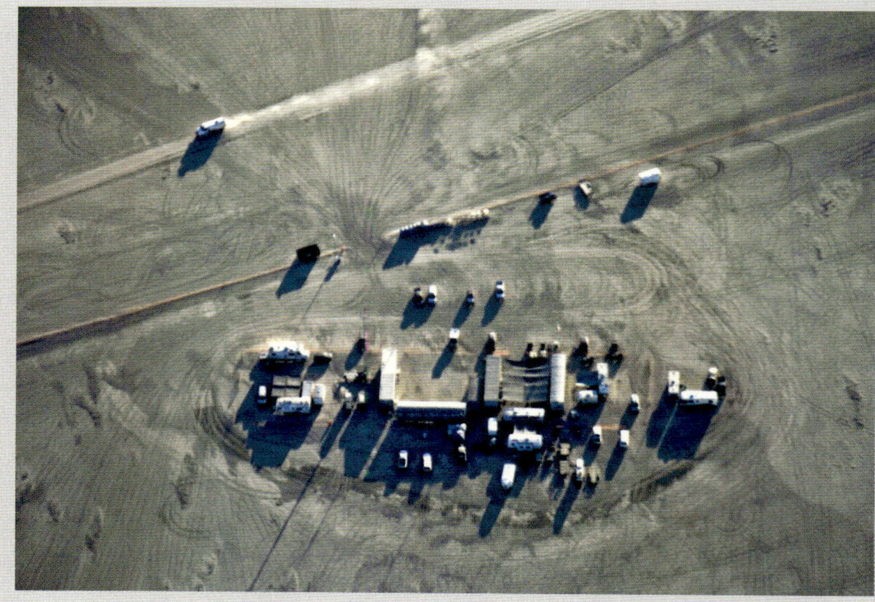

Above: *Left to right, top to bottom:* DPW Depot, Fire Suppression Area, Law Enforcement Compound and Site Services, Law Enforcement Compound (2011)
Right: Black Rock Station (2011)

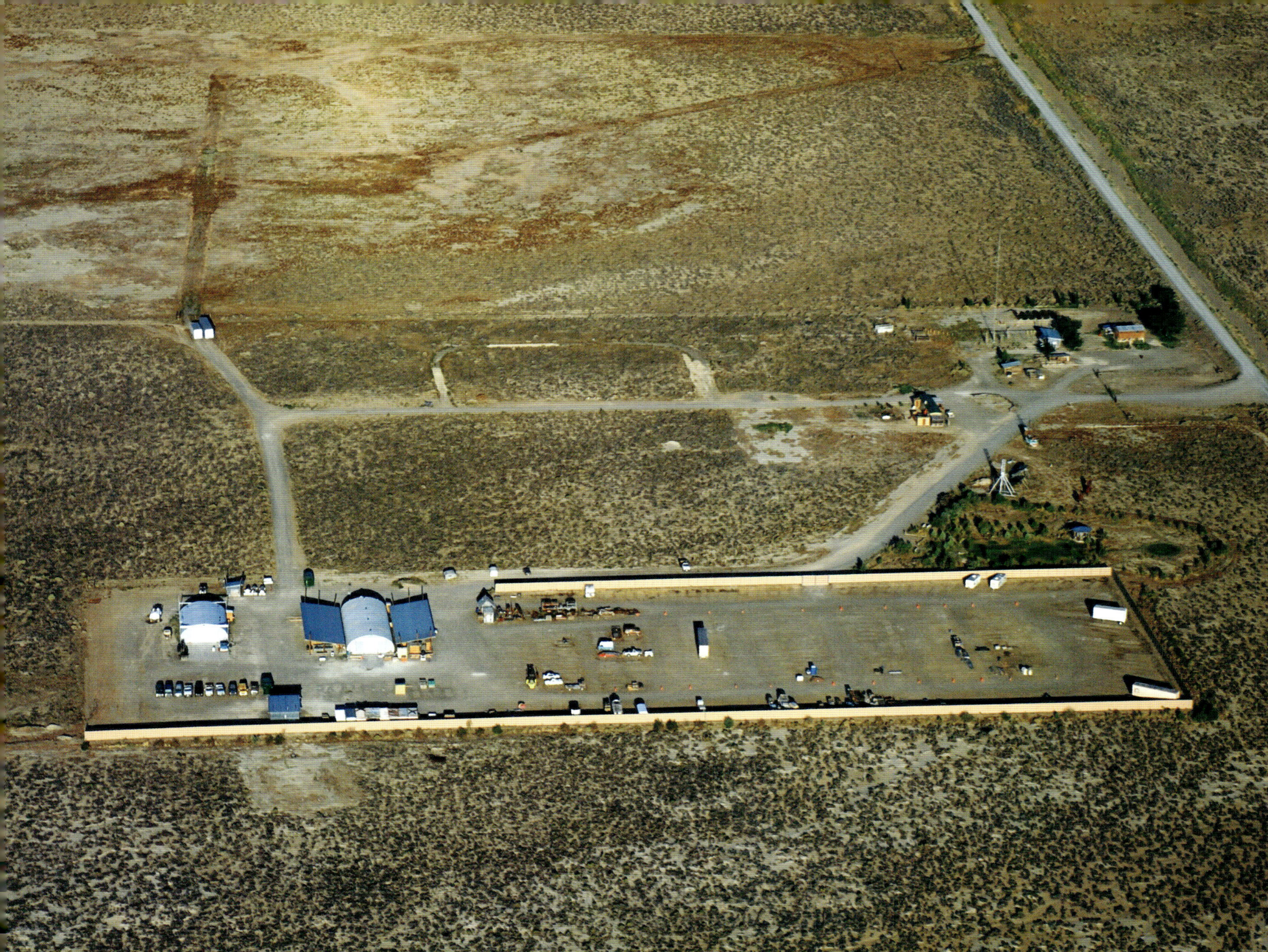

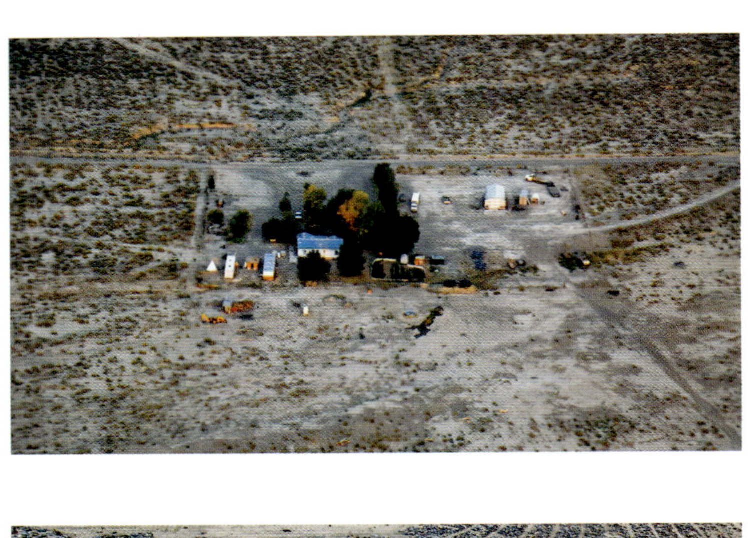
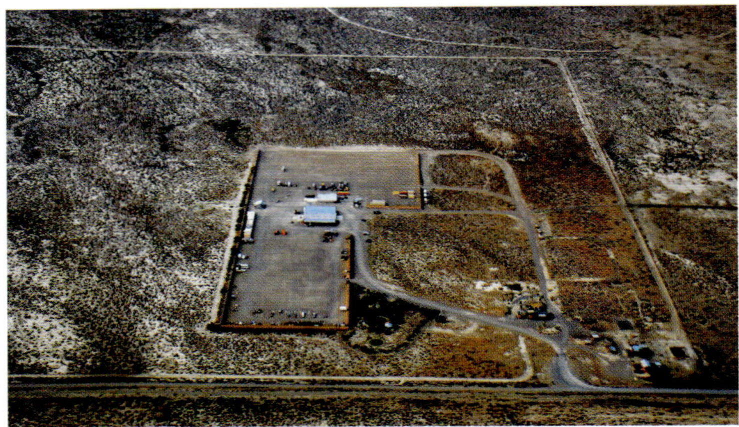
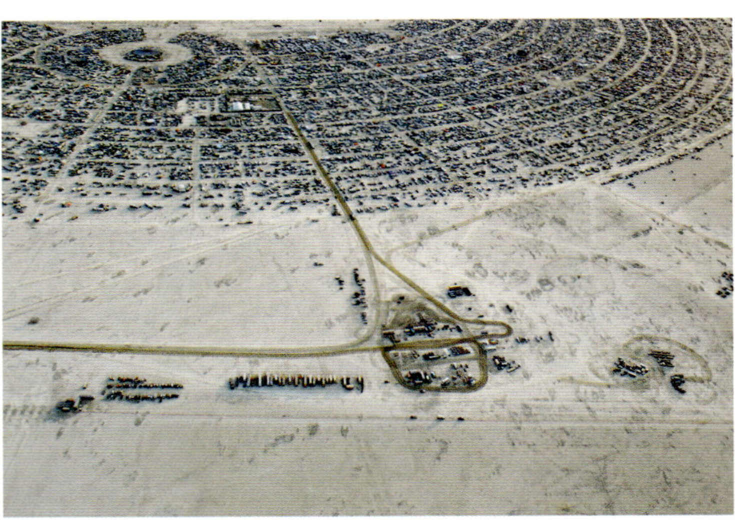
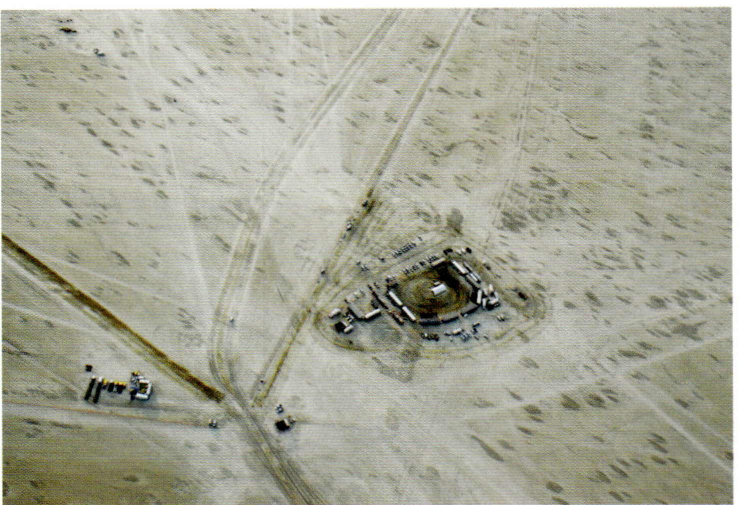

50

Above (L-R): *Jackson Ranch; Black Rock Station; DPW Depot; Law Enforcement Compound located inside the fence (2013)*
Right: *Black Rock Station (2009)*

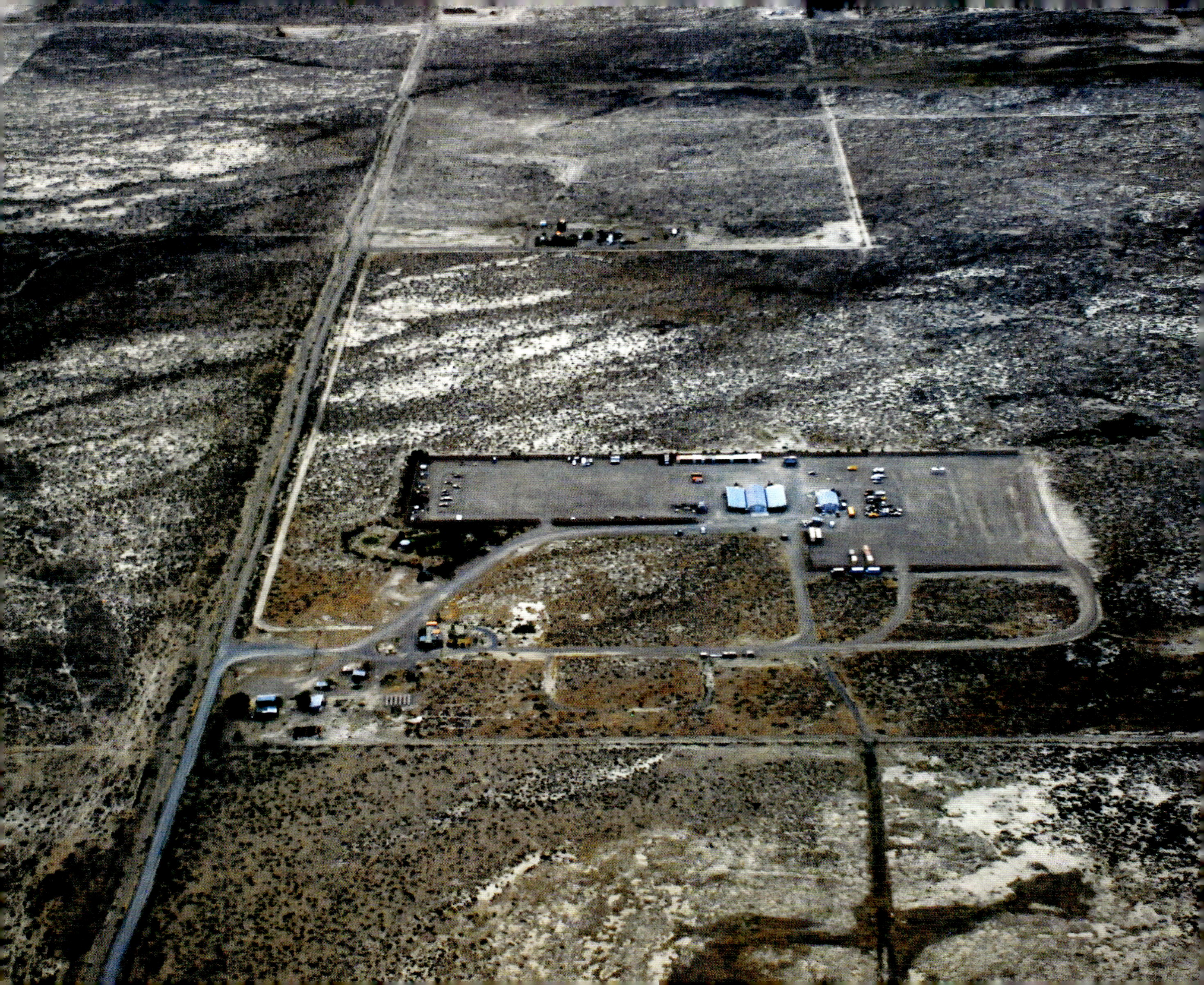

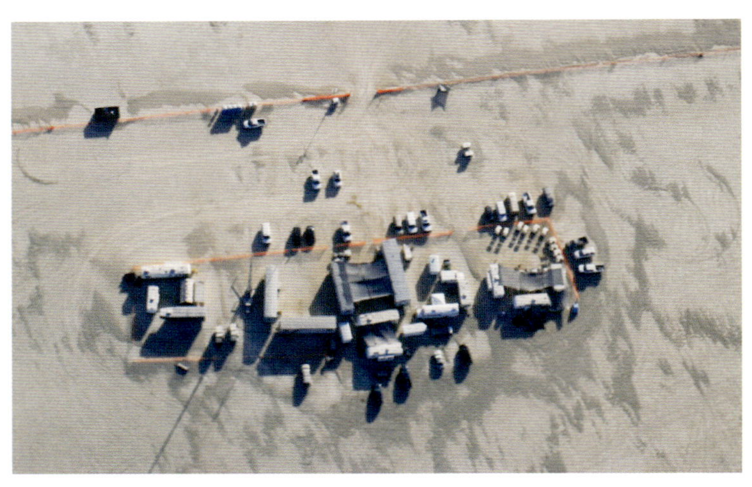

Law Enforcement Compound (2006)

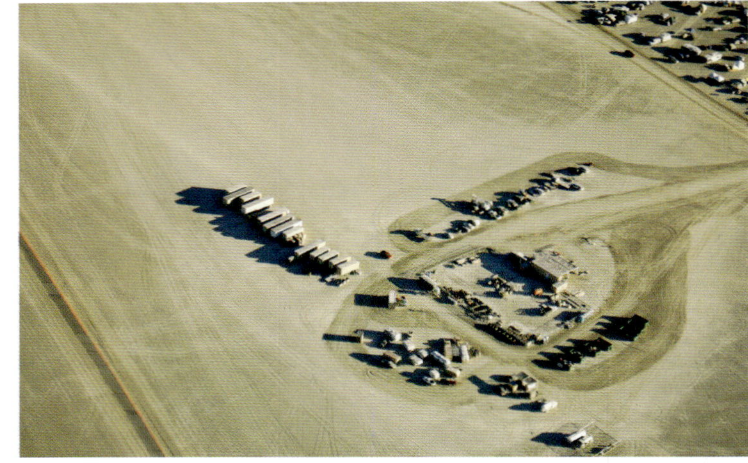

DPW Depot (2006)

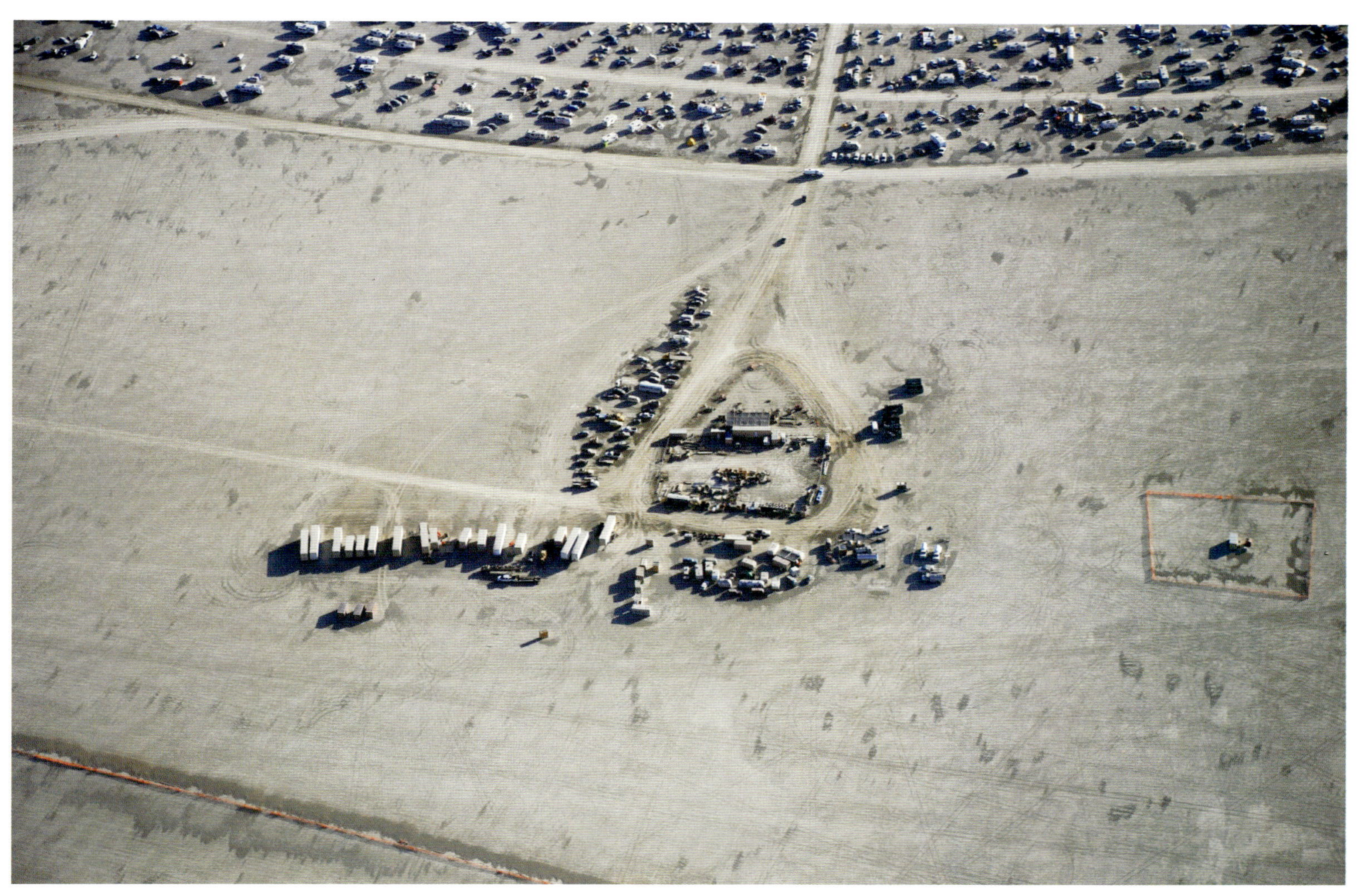

DPW Depot (2007)

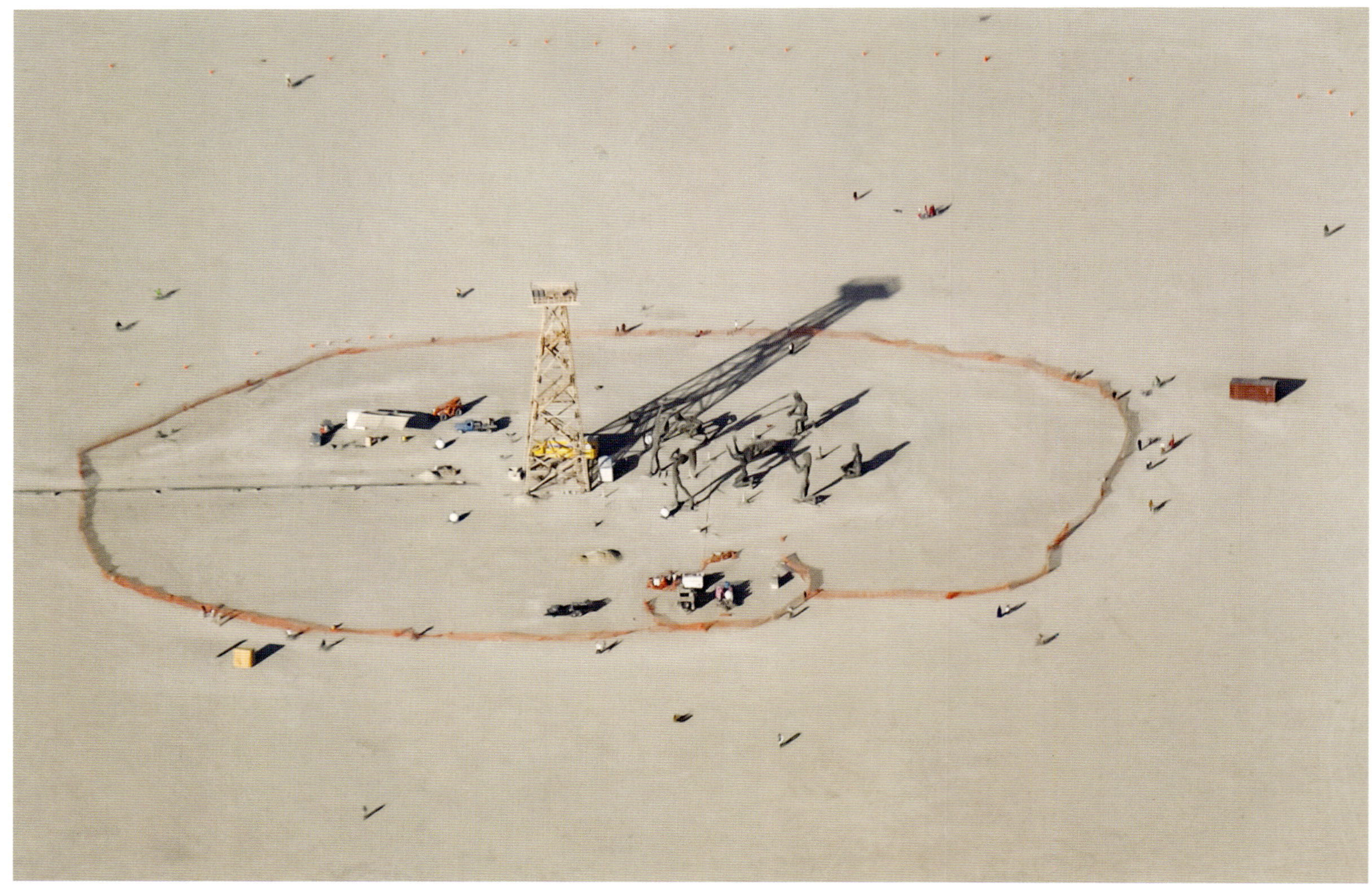

54

Above: *"Crude Awakening" by Dan Das Man and Karen Cusolito (2007)*

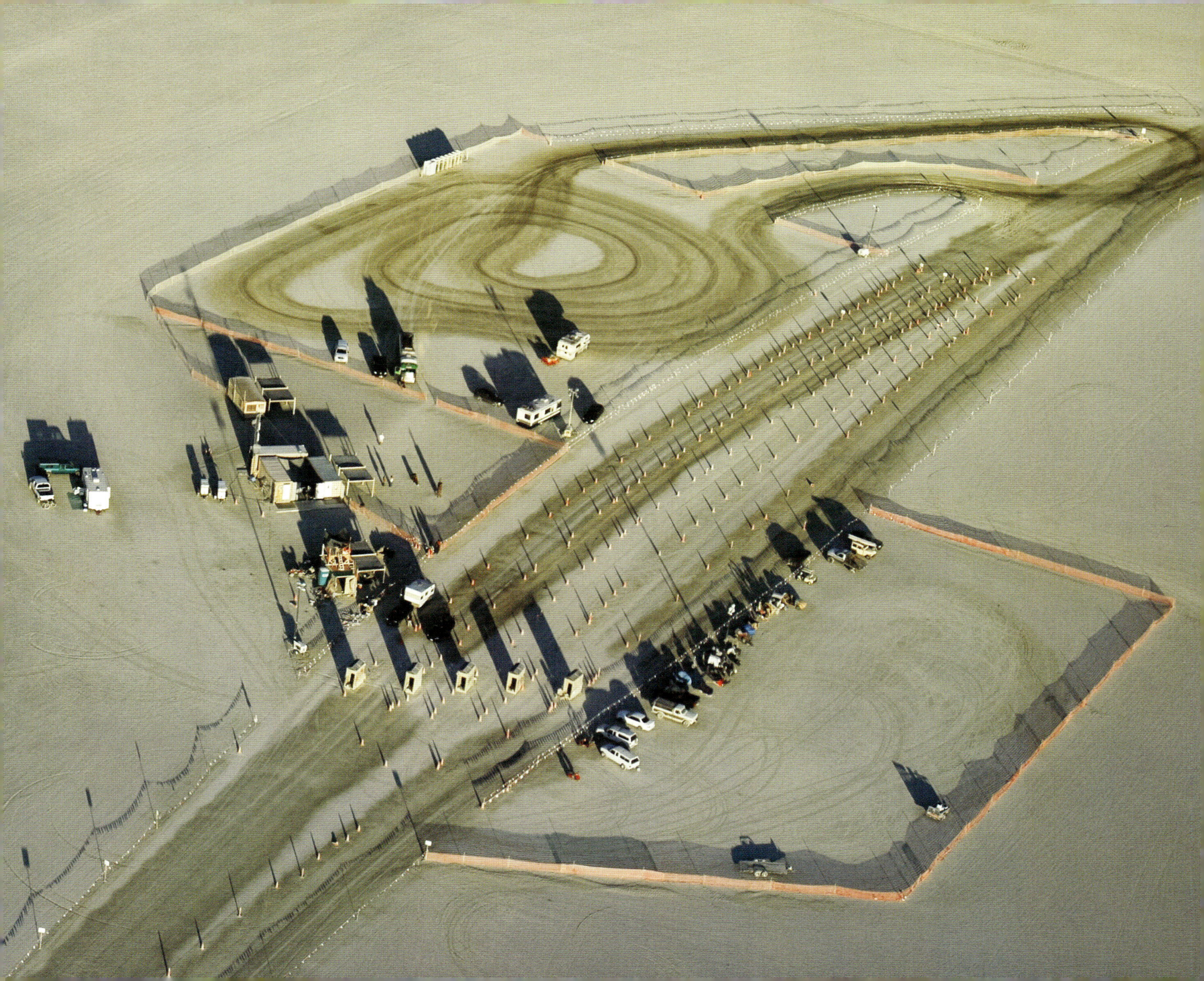

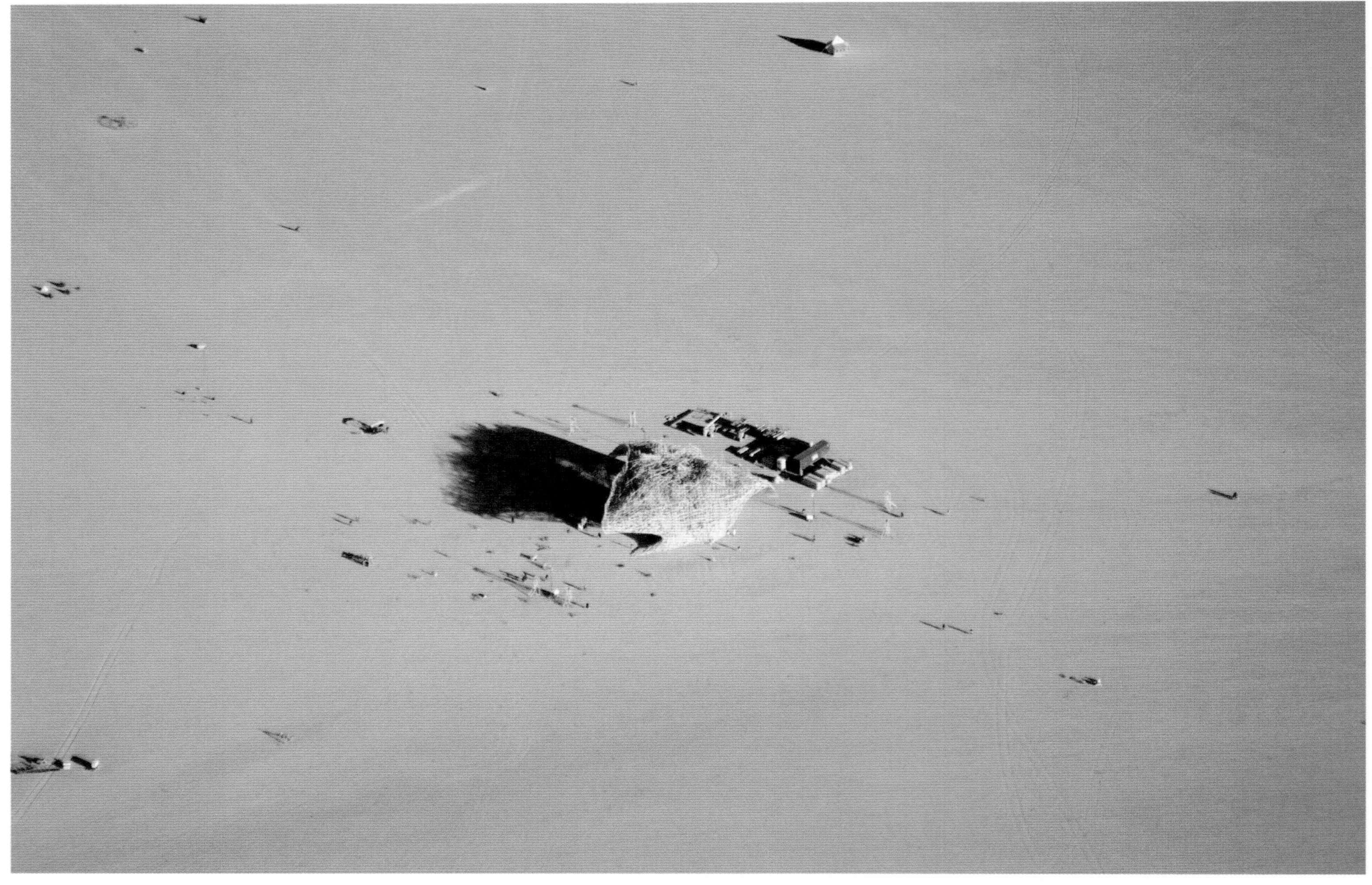

Above: *"Uchronia: Message from the Future" by Arne Quinze and Jan Kriekels (2006)*
Right: *Law Enforcement Compound (2015)*

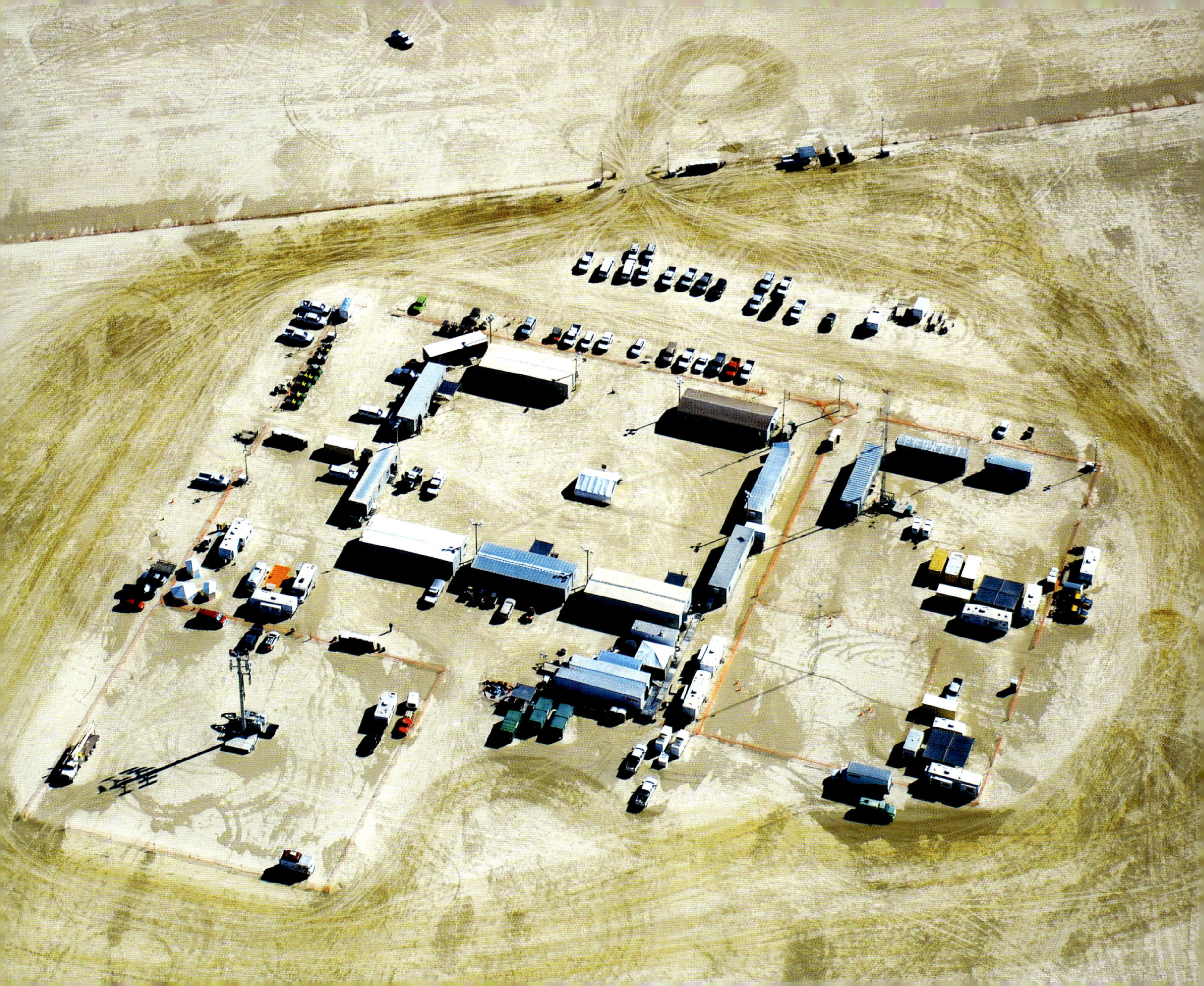

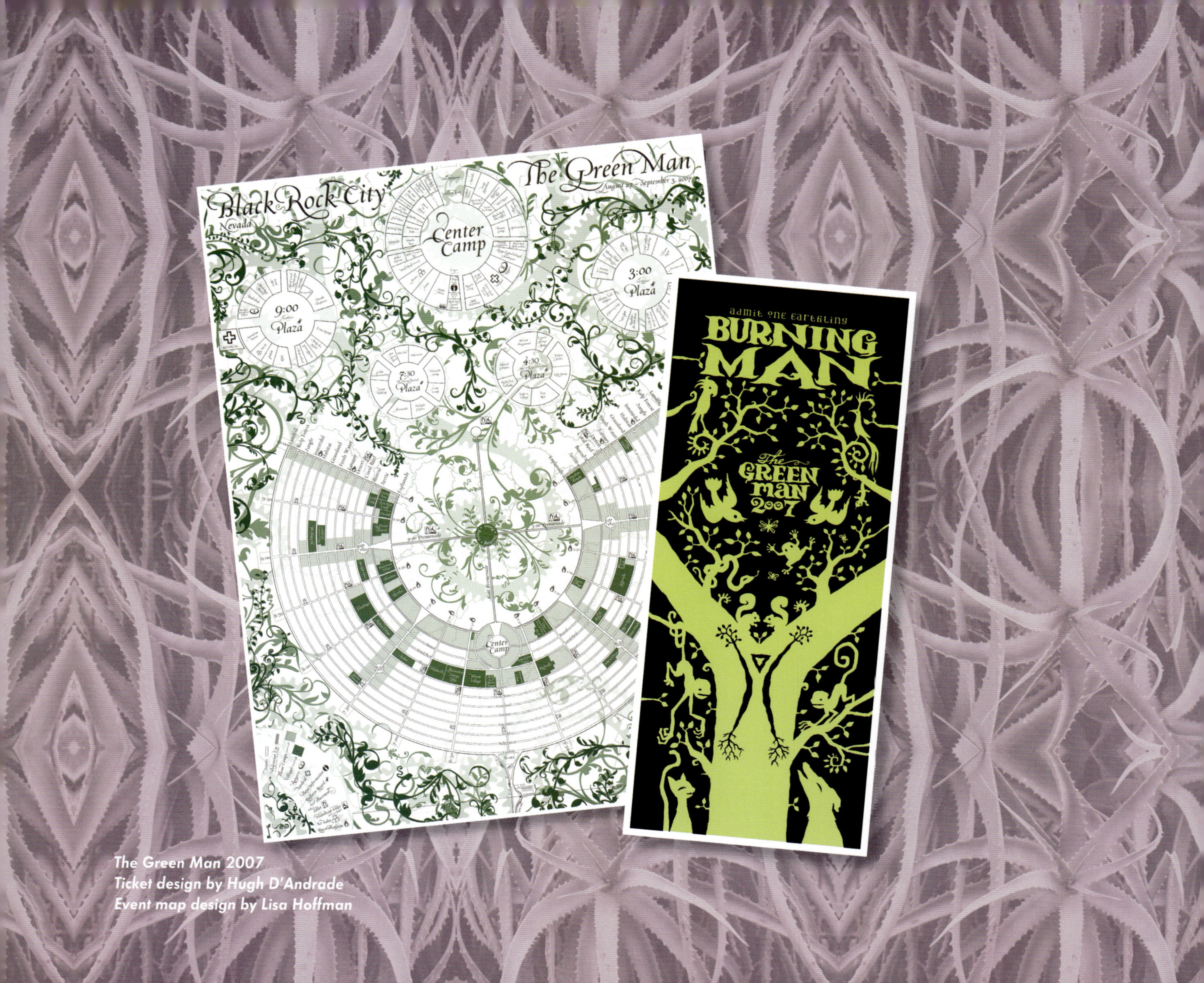

The Green Man 2007
Ticket design by Hugh D'Andrade
Event map design by Lisa Hoffman

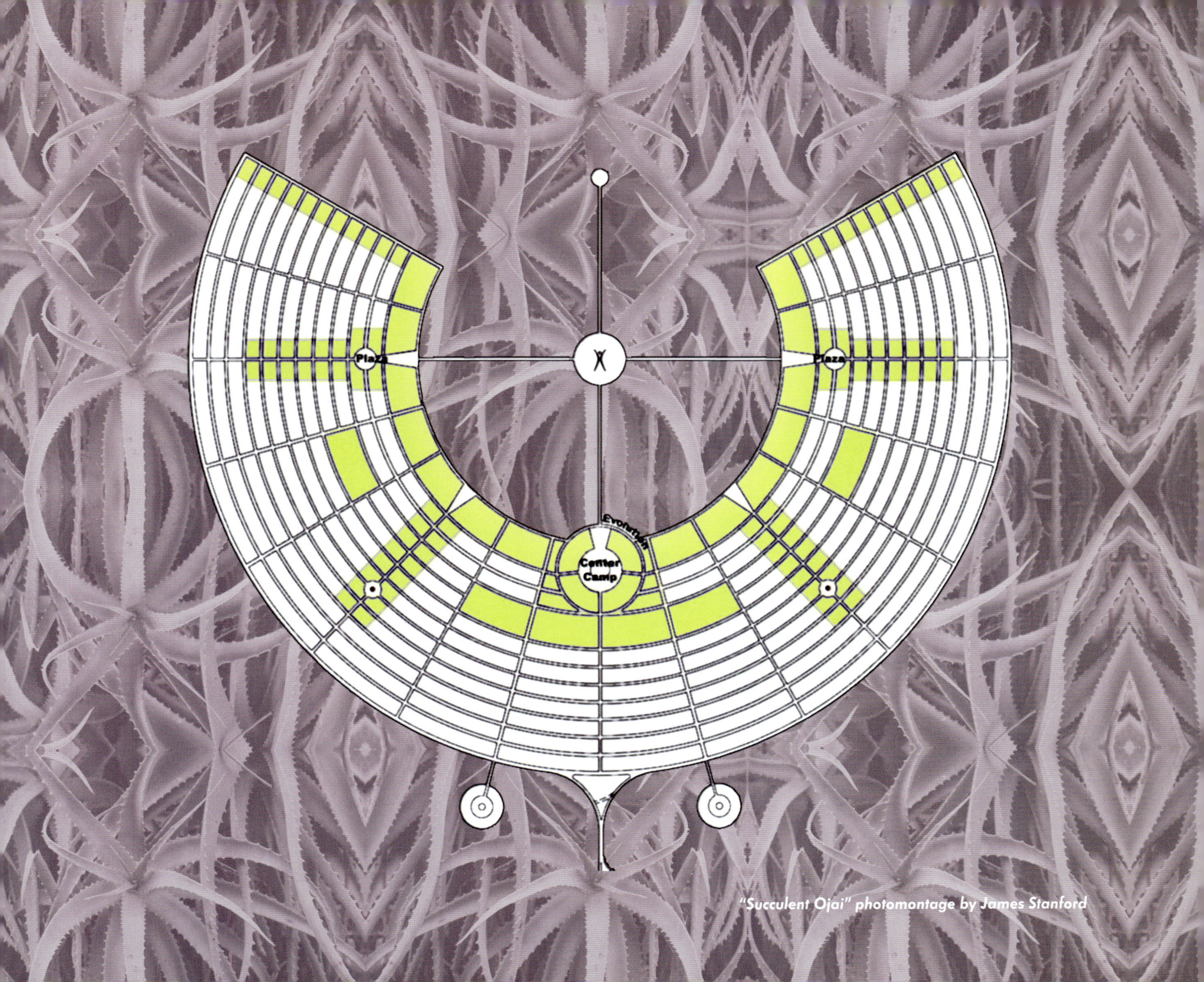

"Succulent Ojai" photomontage by James Stanford

Population 47,097

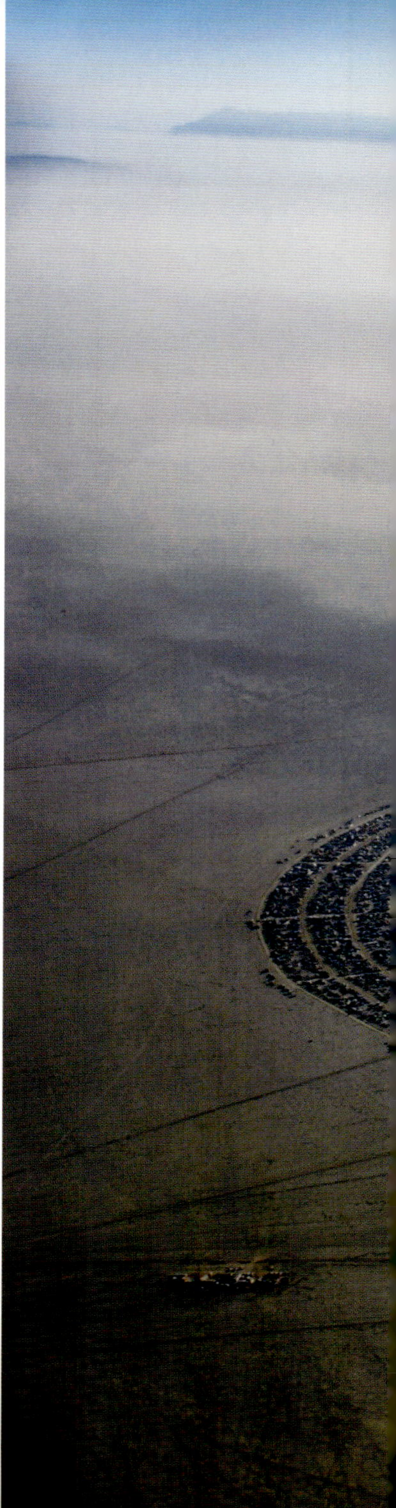

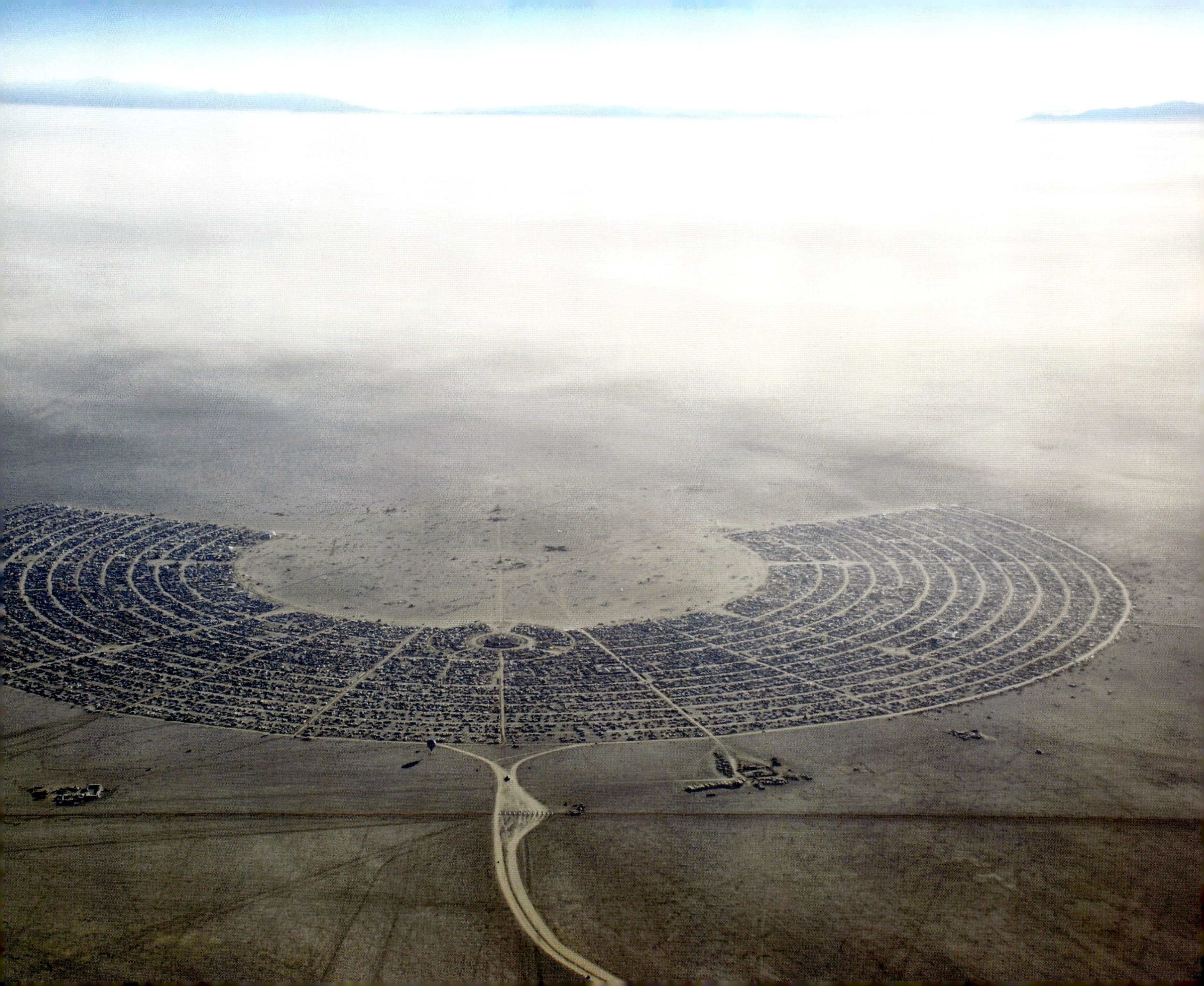

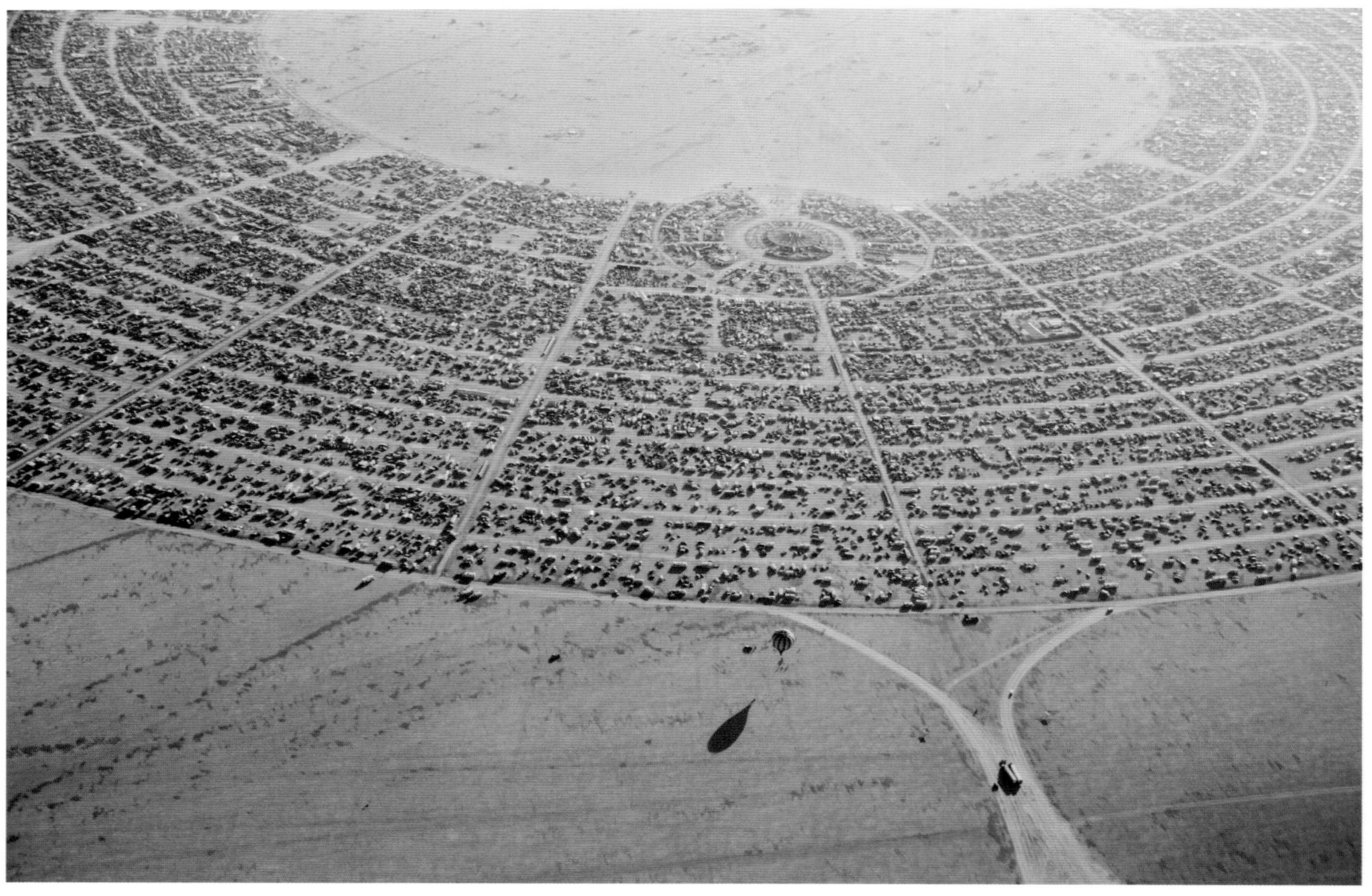

In 2007, the overall footprint of Black Rock City increased by approximately 20 percent more camping space as a result of adding more blocks to the city Over 750 camps registered as theme camps and 681 were placed as part of Black Rock City's urban planning efforts

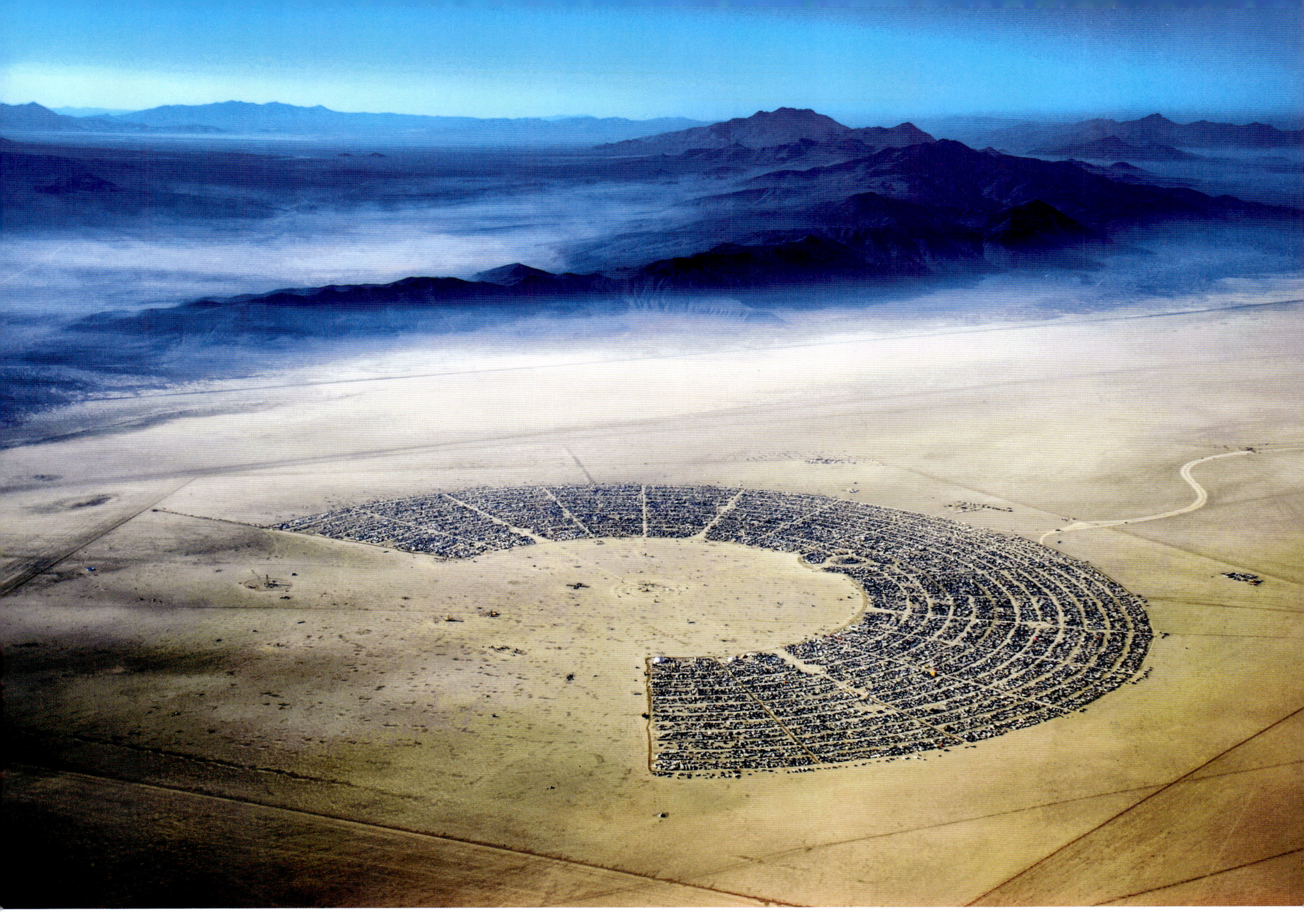

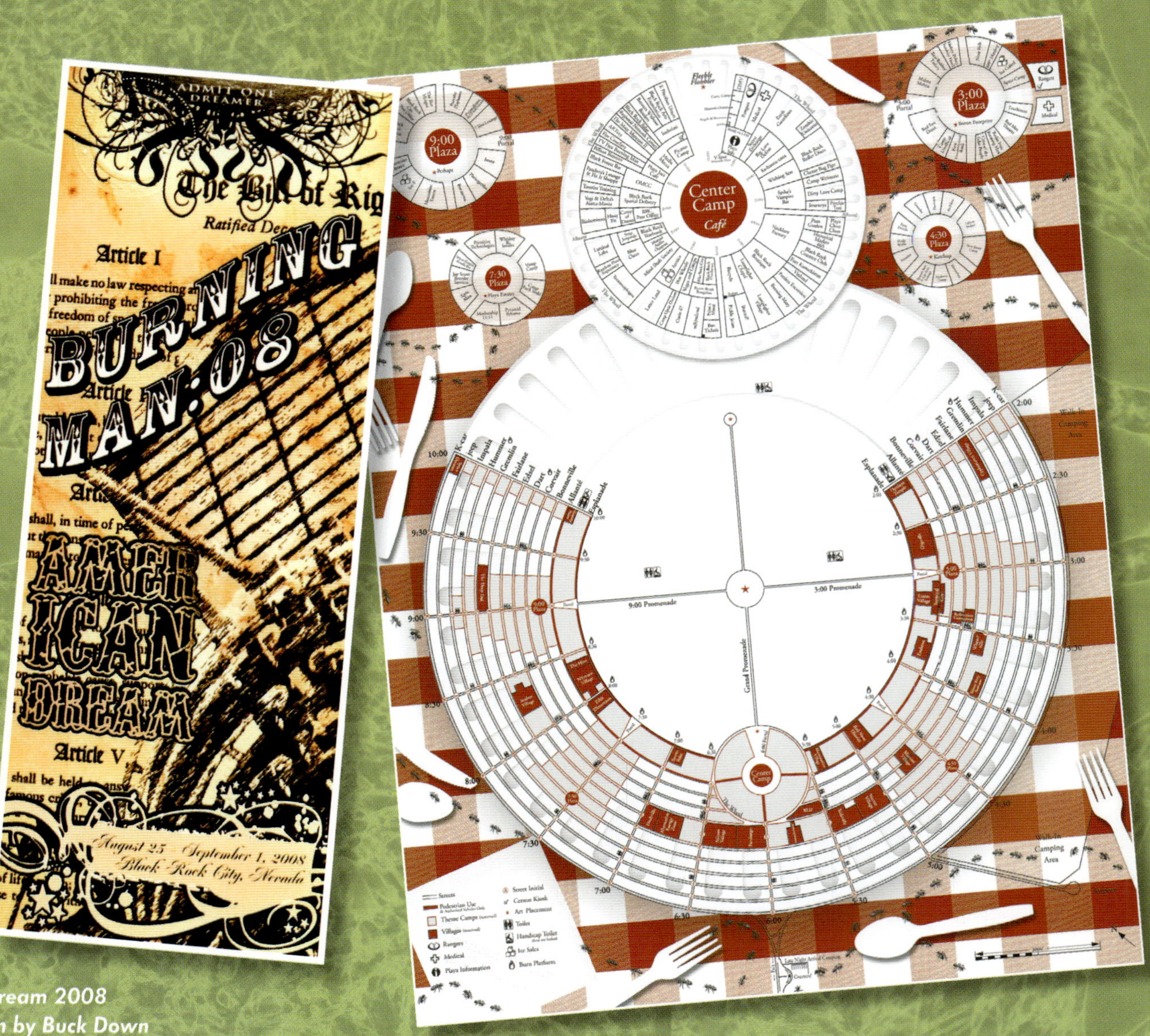

American Dream 2008
Ticket design by Buck Down
Event map design by Lisa Hoffman

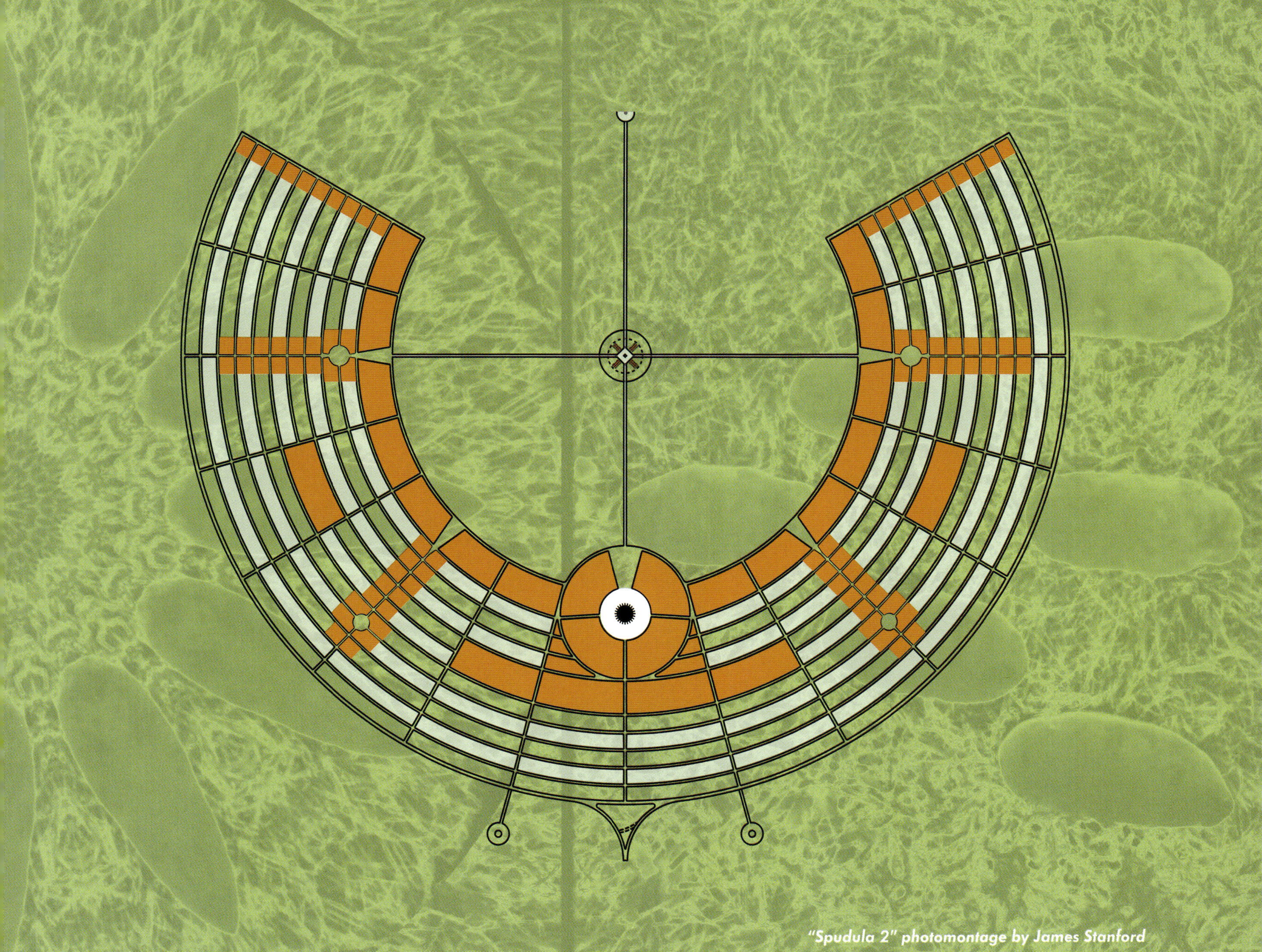

"Spudula 2" photomontage by James Stanford

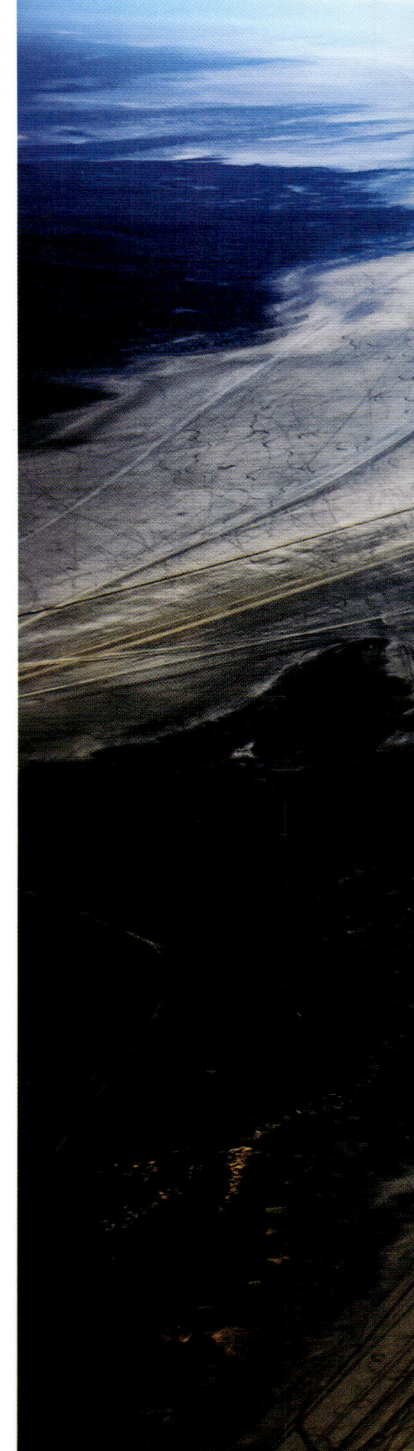

The location of Black Rock City moved another half mile northeast from last year's location as per the Bureau of Land Management's stipulations. The Burning Man Planning Department expanded the geographical layout of Black Rock City to accommodate the city's growth. Population 49,599

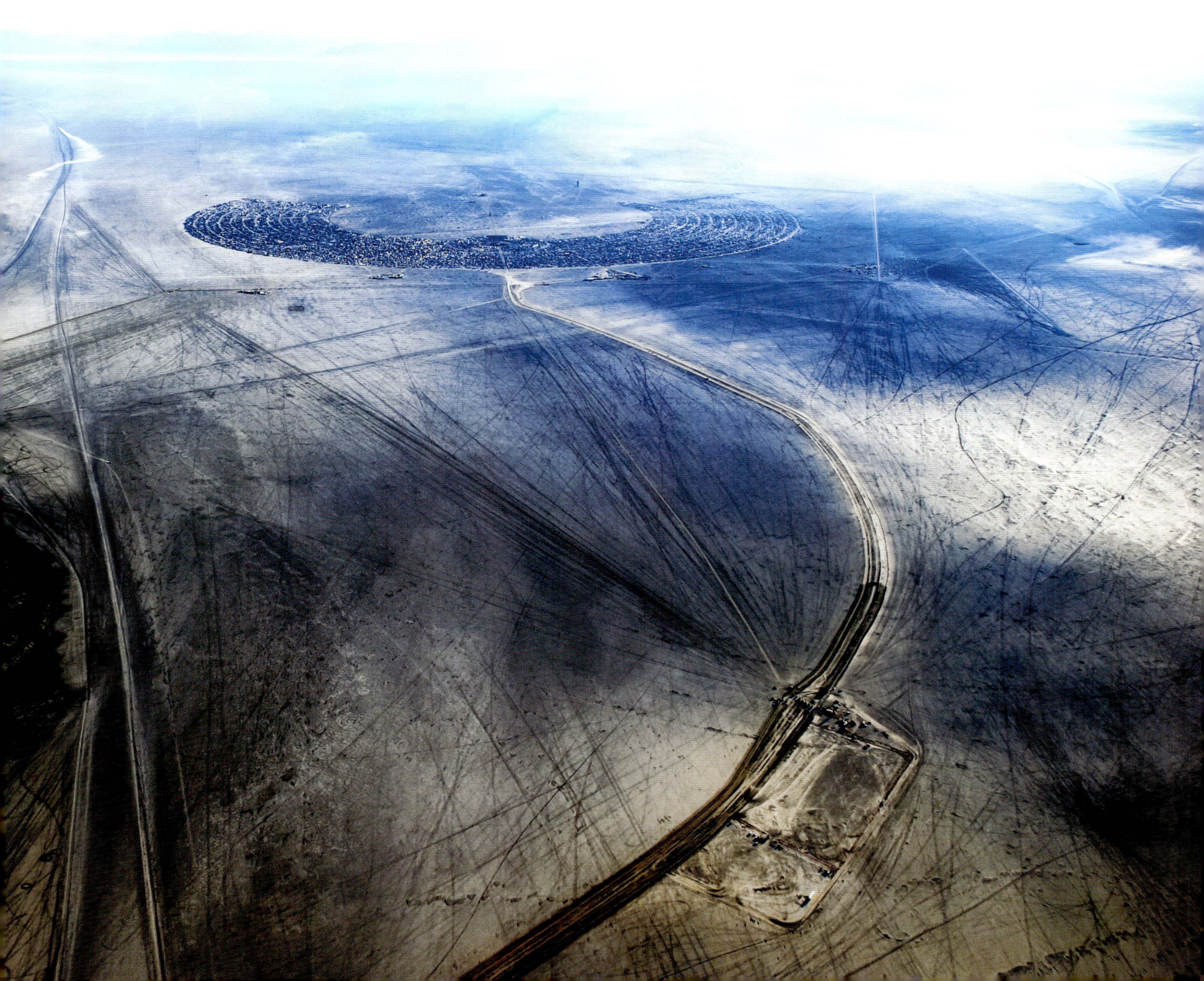

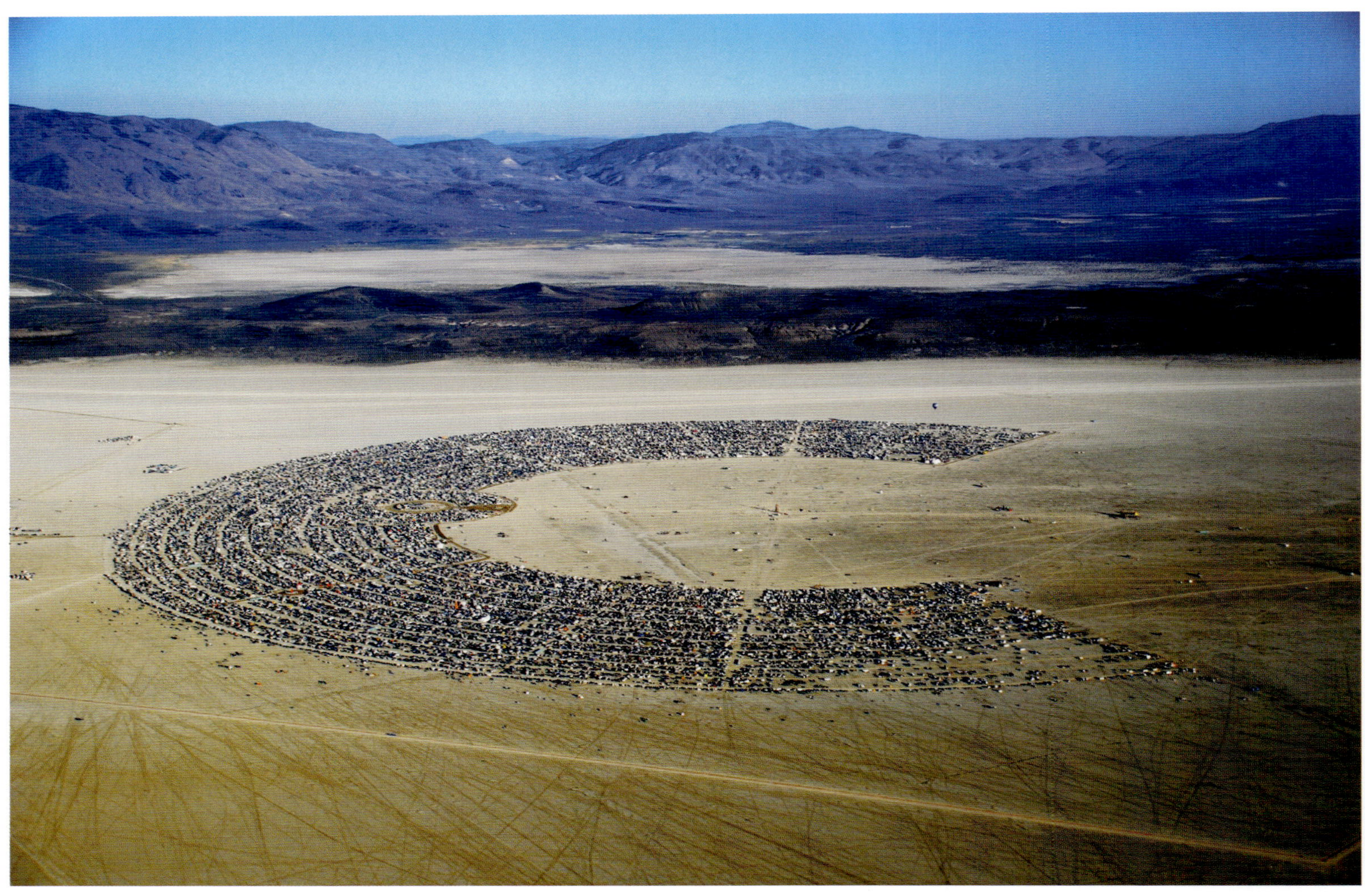

The distance from the Man to the Esplanade Road increased from 2,200 to 2,700 feet and the length of the Esplanade grew over 2,500 feet longer than 2007 Black Rock City's pentagonal perimeter fence grew as well

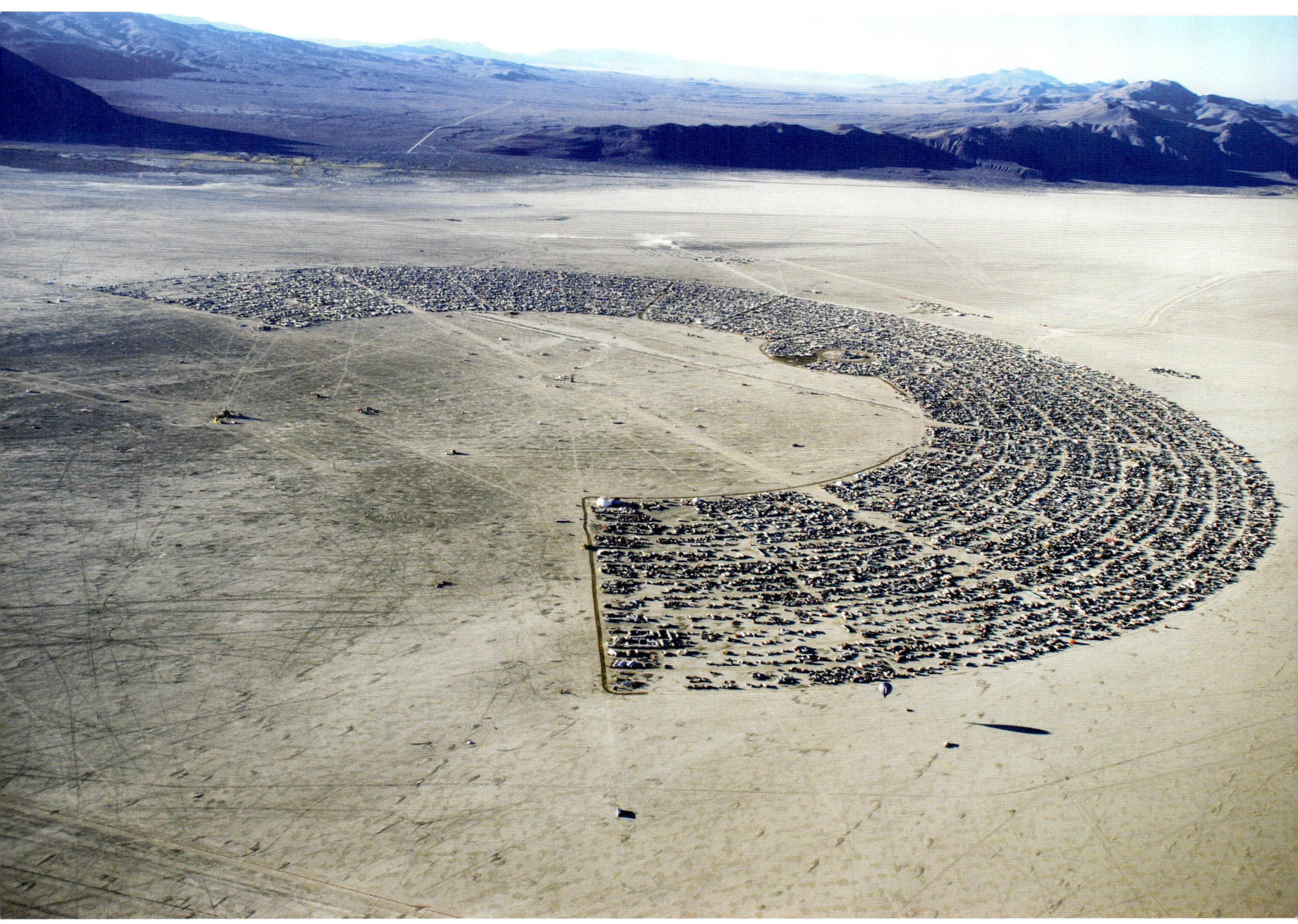

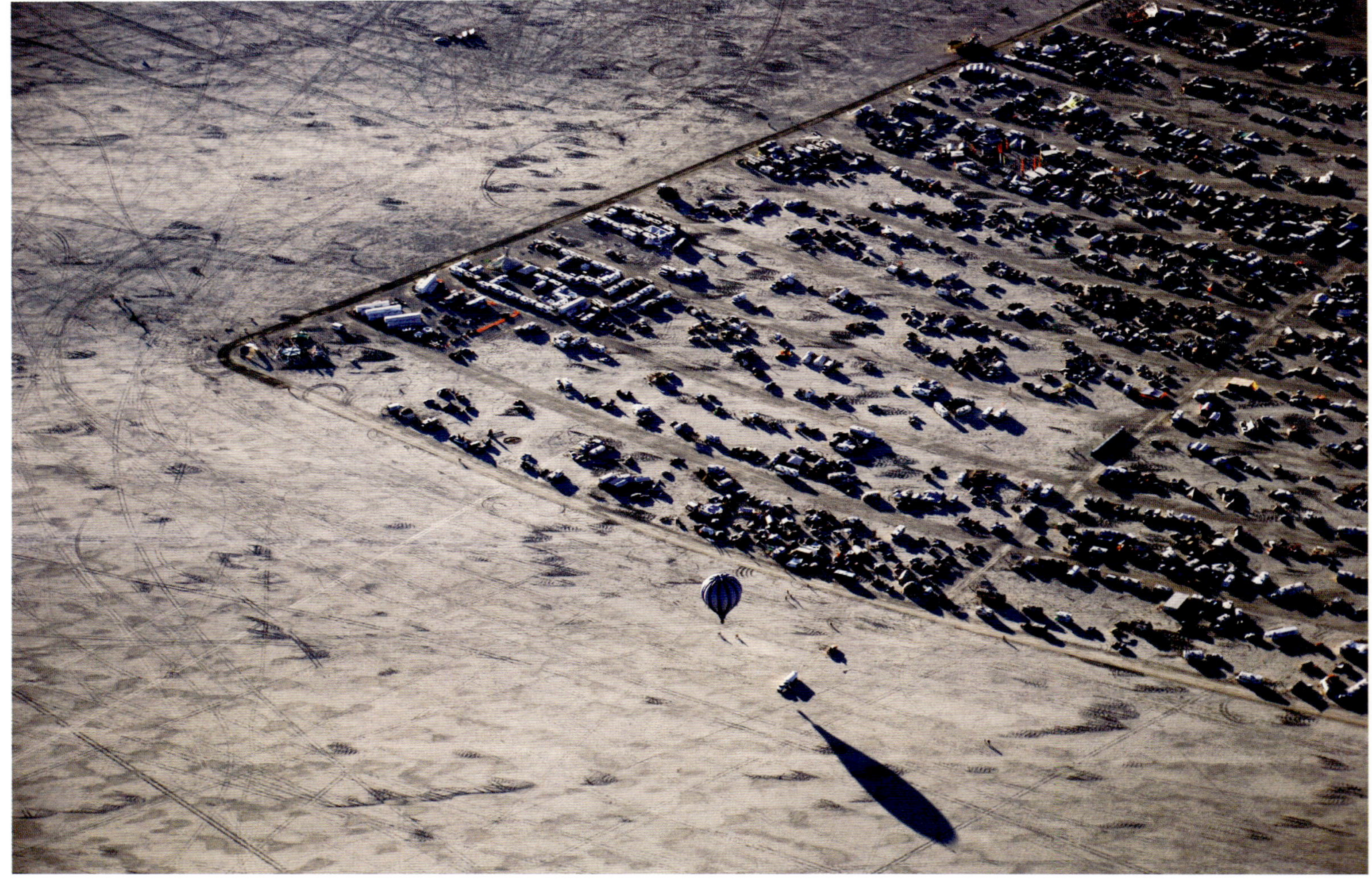

Above: Over 785 camps and villages requested placement, and 746 were registered and placed
Right: Black Rock City's Planning Department removed three inner blocks, Esplanade through C.
The inner playa (the space encompassed by the curve of the Esplanade) was expanded by 1,200 feet.
This made Center Camp circle larger

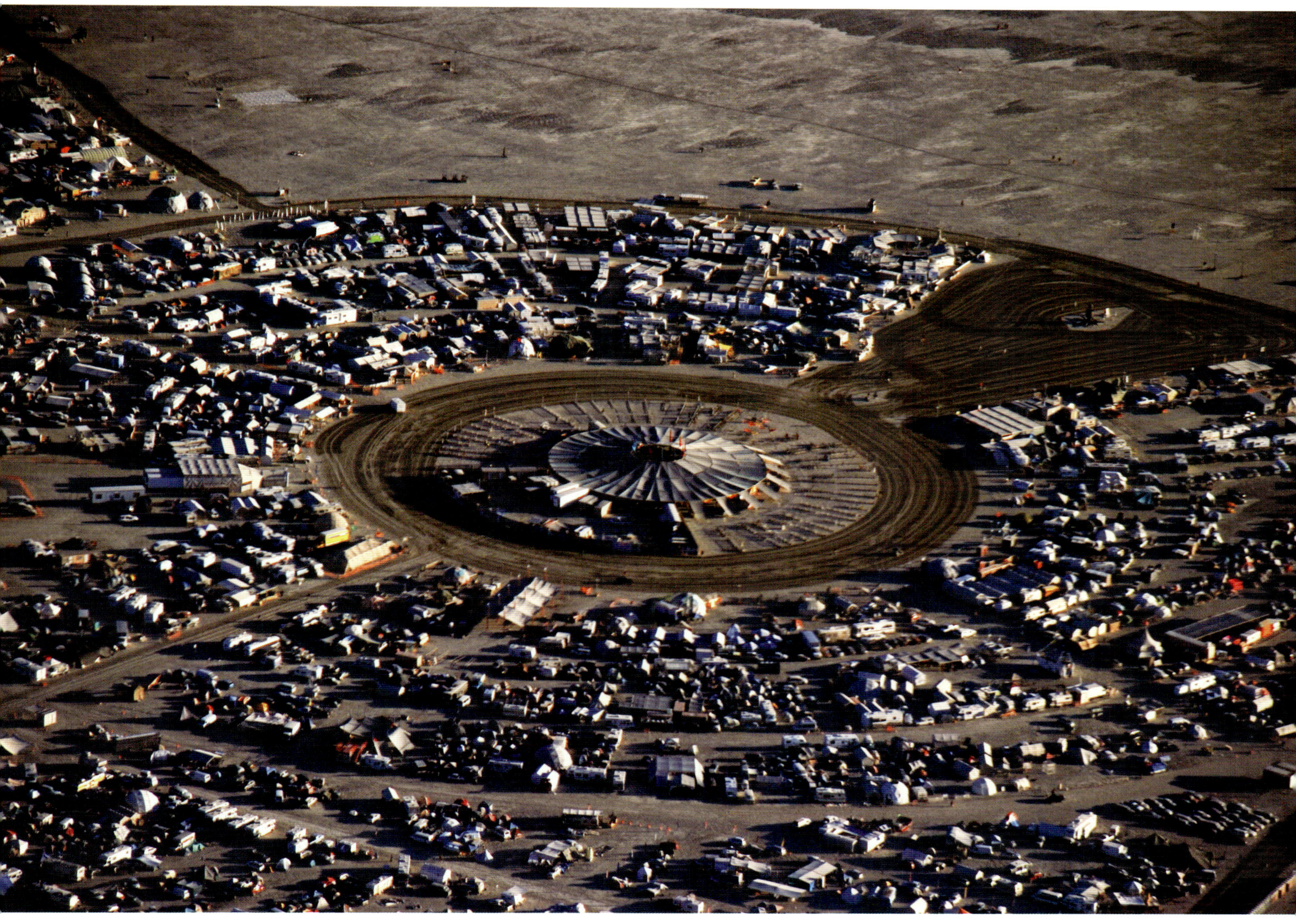

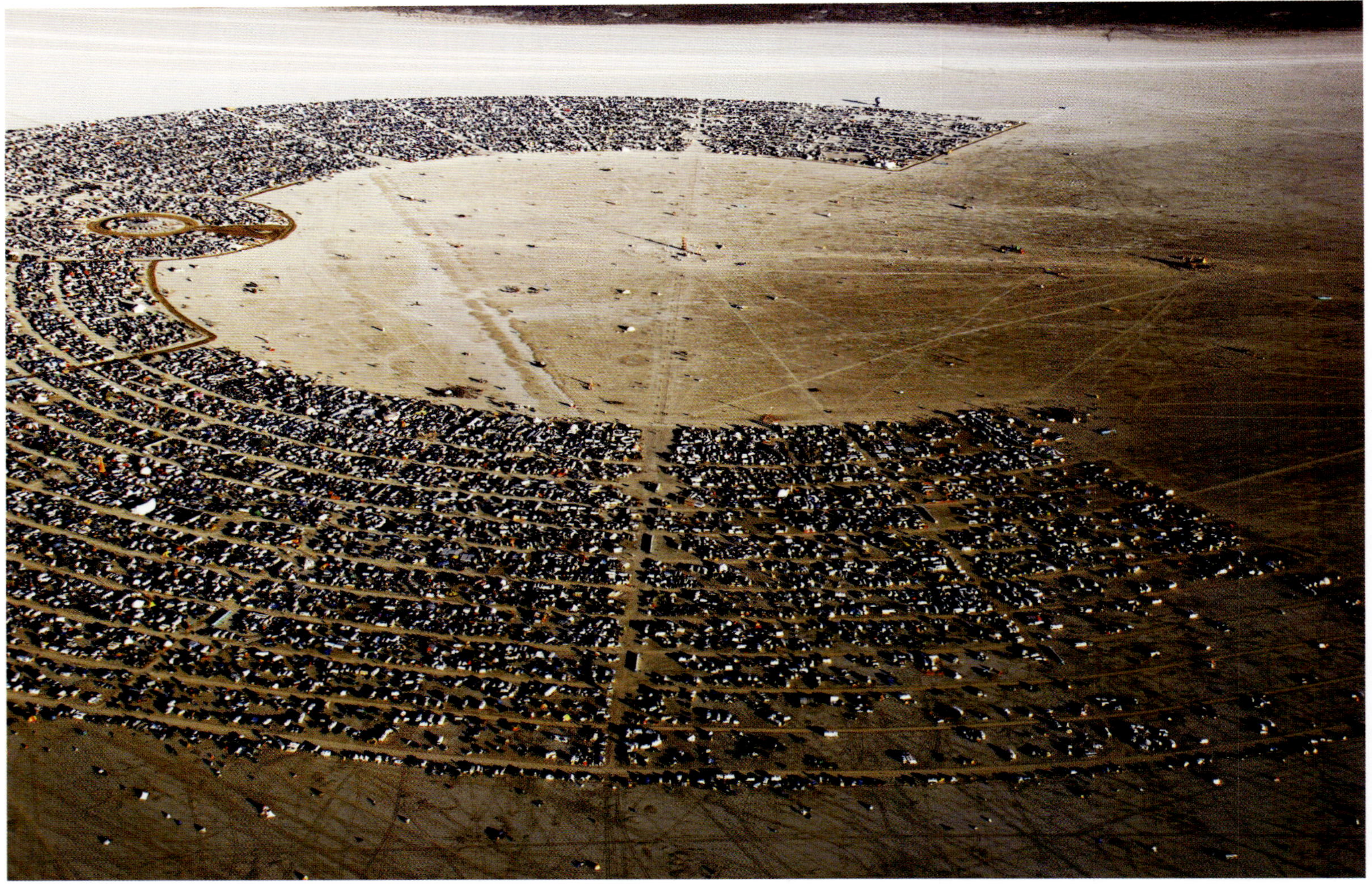

Above: *The playa was home to over 240 registered art projects, including 42 Burning Man funded pieces*
Over 600 vehicles were registered through the Department of Mutant Vehicles
Right: *Due to an unusually dry 2007-2008 winter season, the playa was riddled with heavy, wheel-stopping sand dunes and hard bumps*
The larger city made cross-playa travel difficult

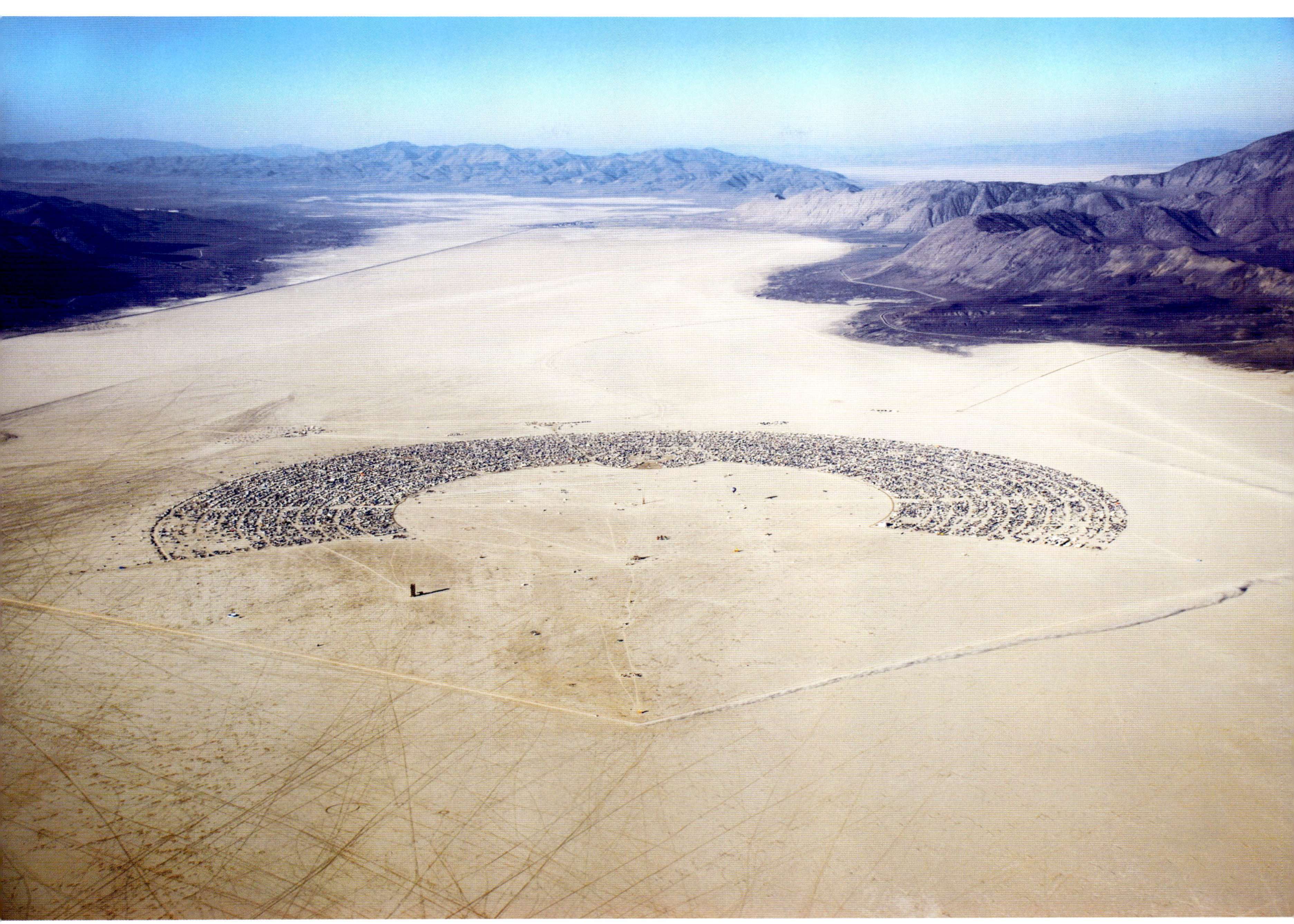

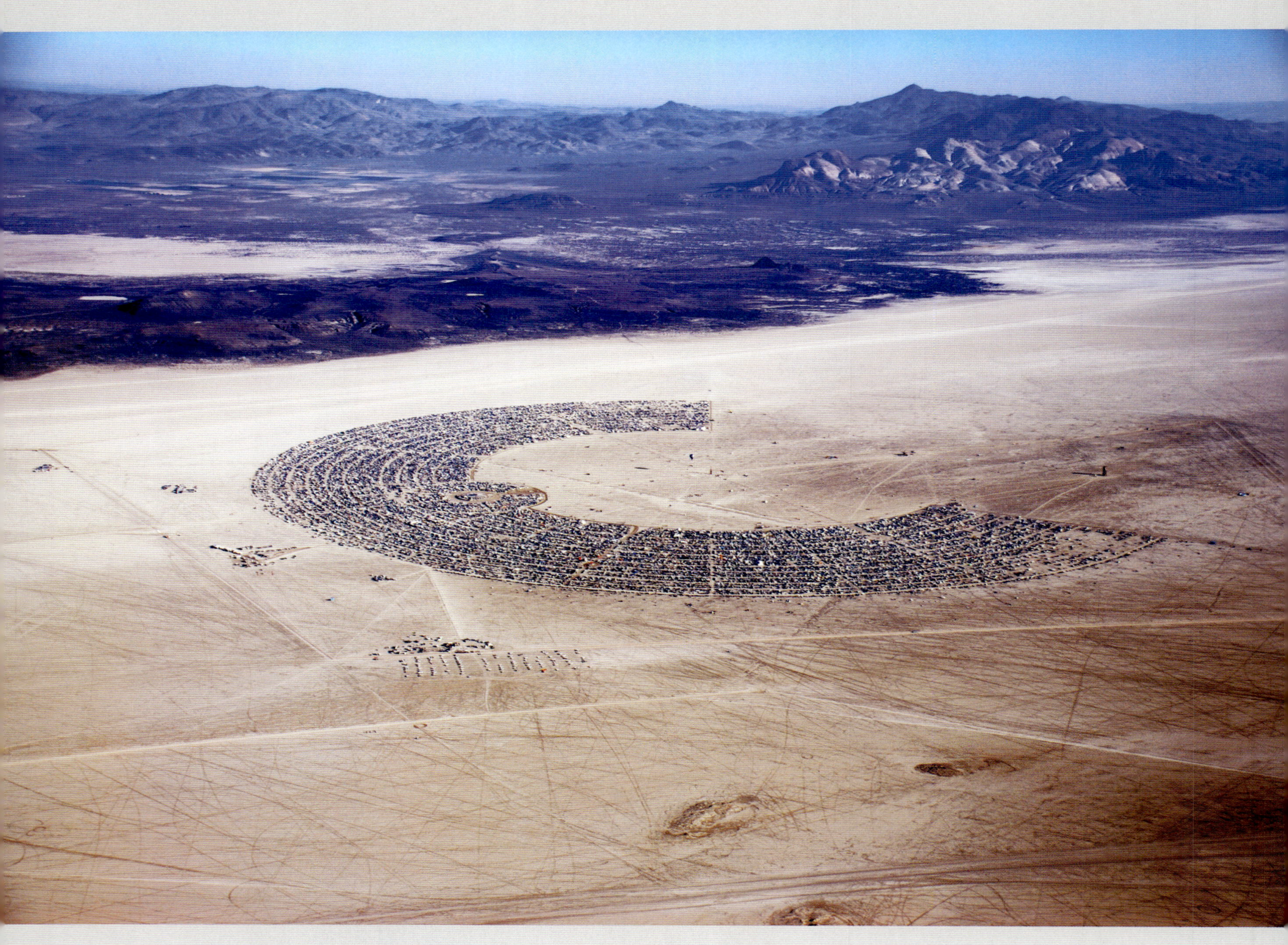

A Compass in the Wilderness

William L. Fox, Director of the Center for Art + Environment at the Nevada Museum of Art

The flattest state in the country is Florida, and a large chunk of its northwest corner—before the state's panhandle veers west—is the flattest place in the United States. The largest flat single geological feature in the U.S., however, is the slab of ophiolite that underlies the 20,000 square miles of California's Central Valley.[1] Some 435 miles long by 44 miles wide by 4-5 miles thick, it's a slab of oceanic rock that sits on the continental shelf from Bakersfield clear north to Redding. It might, in fact, be the largest single flat rock in the world. But the flat places on land that enrapture us are the great playas of the American West, and most especially those intermittently dry lake beds in Utah and Nevada respectively, the Bonneville Salt Flats and the Black Rock Desert.

Playa, which means beach in Spanish, is defined as a desert basin with no outlet that sometimes fills with water to form a shallow lake. Known to scientists as endorheic basins, and sometimes more casually as terminal or terminus lakes, there may be as many as 50,000 of them around the world. The Utah and Nevada playas are remnants of enormous Pleistocene lakes that existed during the last ice age. Lake Lahontan, which covered much of northern Nevada, was once 500 feet deep over what is now the Black Rock Desert. Standing on the desert floor, you can count the multiple wave-cut terraces rising above you like ancient bathtub rings marking various shorelines as the lake rose and fell over time. Under you are 9,000 feet of sediments that have eroded over the millennia since the mountains rose and the lake basin sank. In total, the geology you can view from standing in the middle of the playa ranges over 23 million years of uplift, dropping, folding, spindling, and mutilating. As John McPhee noted in his classic, Basin and Range, the geology of the Great Basin is among the most complicated and least understood on Earth.[2]

The Bonneville Salt Flats cover about 40 square miles, nowhere near as large a playa as Bolivia's Salar de Uyina (4,085 sq. miles) or Australia's Lake Eyre (3,668 sq. miles), but their clear white surface is located just off a major interstate freeway, thus offering drivers a convenient space upon which to inscribe the world's land speed record. The flats were used until the salts thinned and the cars became so heavy that the surface couldn't support them, whereupon the competitors were forced to find another great *tabula rasa*. In 1997, they settled on the Black Rock Desert in northern Nevada, about 100 miles northeast of Reno. The desert extends over approximately 1,000 square miles and within it lays North America's largest playa, which covers approximately 400 square miles. But it wasn't just tire tracks that

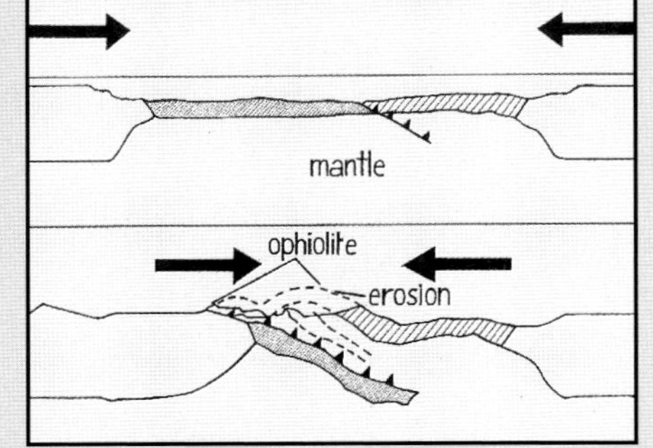

Above: *Ophiolite illustration (2018) by Zully Mejia*
Left: *Black Rock City (2008)*

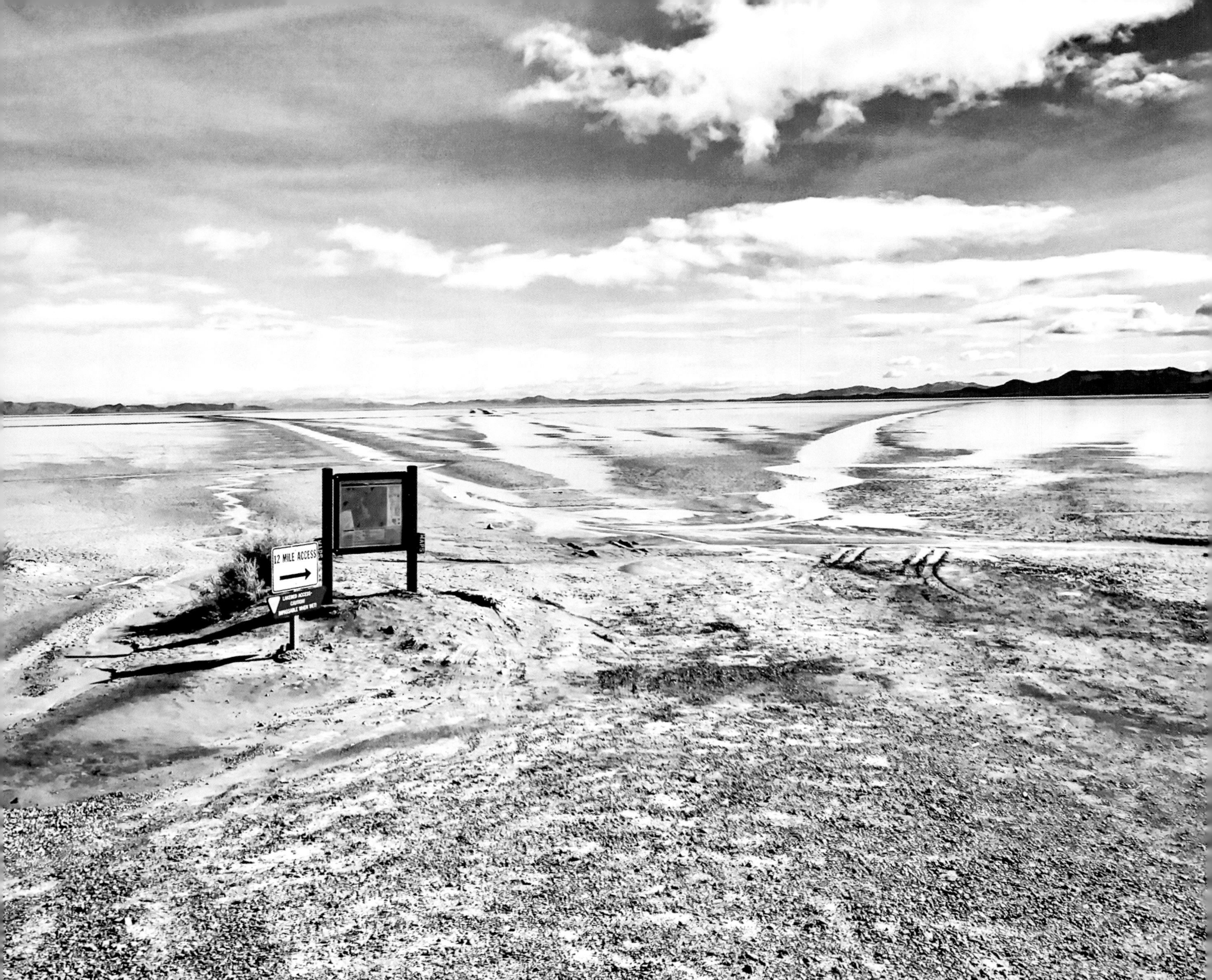
12 MILE ACCESS
LAKEBED ACCESS
CAUTION
IMPASSABLE WHEN WET
MAPS
MAPS

people were inscribing on the Black Rock; artists had already been working its surface for more than a decade, most notably during the nomadic annual gathering known as Burning Man.

The Black Rock Playa upon which Burning Man takes place is one of ninety basins sitting within the Great Basin, the last geophysical province to be defined in North America, and the only one into which water flows with no outlet to any ocean. Dry lake beds tend naturally to be flat and featureless, and that means that humans–primates that evolved to cope with the forests, broken woodlands, and savanna of Africa – are easily confounded by them. Humans tend unconsciously and unavoidably to scale themselves – scale the length of their own limbs – to the limbs of bushes and trees. That's a problem in the Black Rock, since when you are in the middle of it, you are where nothing ever grows. When the playa has been wet for a month or so, you might see fairy shrimp appearing out of their desiccated burials to breed, and on fall nights tiny pallid scorpions may arrive to dance across the surface. Moths, butterflies, dragonflies, coyotes, and deer all transit the polygonally fractured alkali flat—but no grasses, bushes, or trees grow in the middle of the playa.

Another neurophysiological basis people use for scaling is how things look bluer in the distance than they look up close – a shift in the atmospheric spectrum caused by the scattering of light by water molecules in the air. It rains less than eight inches a year on the Black Rock, and as I write this in mid-July, the humidity there is seven percent, considerably less than the 40-50 percent where most humans are comfortable. That means that less light is scattering over the desert, and things don't turn blue as fast as we expect them to. In addition, the air is clear and there are very few green plants on the distant mountainsides. Altogether, that means there's far less blue shift than we expect, and as a result, we vastly underestimate desert distances. When we overcome that cognitive dissonance and realize how large the place where we are standing is, it's very disorienting.

Then there's the problem of walking in a straight line in an isotropic environment, or a place where things look the same in all directions. Try walking a fixed line on the Black Rock, even while viewing a distant landmark such as a mountain peak. You'll find yourself veering ever so slightly to one side, most likely to the right, even if you're left-handed. A recent theory published in the journal, *Experimental Brain Research*,[3] is that "the brain's vestibular (balance-maintaining) and proprioceptive (body awareness) systems combine to enable regular spatial updating,

Above: Brine shrimp illustration (2018) by Zully Mejia
Left: 12-mile access, lake bed access: impassable when wet, to Black Rock Desert, photo (2017) by Laura Henkel

and it may be the vestibular system in the inner ear that malfunctions in the absence of visual clues."

The point is that big playas are difficult to navigate across physically, mentally, and emotionally. They are distressing spaces in which to find yourself precisely, because you're generally lost or at sea, as it were (the world's largest isotropic spaces being oceans, of course). That's a problem if you're not mentally prepared, not carrying enough water, or don't have access to shade in the summer and warm clothes and sleeping gear at night (again, that lack of humidity means it's both hotter and colder than you might expect). It's not just your visual input that's strained, but all of your senses. There's less variety of touch, smell, taste, and hearing as well as vision. That diminishment is actually useful if you're seeking to un-anchor your normal sense of reality, to approach an unexpected state of mind. It's not just tire tracks we aspire to run out across the playa, but new approaches to higher—or at least other—states of consciousness.

When you limit your sensory input, your mind begins to turn inward, and you begin to perceive the universe as an unending space. You get a sense of being both tiny and right-sized compared to your size in everyday life. A variety of related phenomena based on the limitations of sensory input have been measured using a functional magnetic resonance imaging unit (fMRI) on a variety of religious and meditating practitioners, and it's not a coincidence that the world's major monotheisms arose in deserts. One of the more interesting study findings is that when you are in a place where there are few, if any, familiar sensory clues, not only are you confused as to where you are, but the normal feedback mechanism—the constant input that confirms where you are and keeps you in place—is lacking.

Note that the above sentence contains the word "place" for the first time in this essay. Mostly I've been using the word "space," because that is what you experience before you begin to make it into place, or land into landscape, or terrain into territory. Terrains in which our distributed cognitive neurophysiology[4] fails us in this process of conversion are spaces where we deploy cultural means to compensate. And that includes using geometry at many different levels, the cartographic grid being the most familiar. Burning Man is a ritualistic gathering where people come to disorient themselves in a quest for new experiences, but geometry offers a handrail as they enter the Black Rock and the event.

Geometry

The oldest known visual awareness is that of single-celled organisms rising and falling in the ocean in response to sunlight. All creatures able to perceive light orient themselves to diurnal cycles, whether to seek sunlight or to hide from it, so it is no surprise that a very early human expression of geometry was governed by the apparent motions of the sun, moon, and stars. The earliest surviving examples of what we call artworks are petroglyphs carved into rocks, pictographs painted on rocks, and rocks arranged on the ground as geoglyphs. All three are found around the world and were often aligned to solar events, usually to first record and then predict a solstice or equinox. The oldest rock art presently known in North America is found alongside the shores of Winnemucca Dry Lake, Nevada, which you may pass when driving to the Black Rock Desert. Atop one of the lowest of those wave-cut terraces is a group of limestone boulders ten to fifteen feet tall, that are covered in carved geometrical figures and symbols clearly relating to nature. The markings may be as old as 14,800 years and date back to what is believed to be the first arrival of humans in the region.

The exact meaning of the abstract geometries is unknown, but when I visited the site in 1997 with the renowned Nevada rock art researcher, Alvin McLane (1934-2006), he pointed out several petroglyphs that he had recorded as possible solar interaction designs. Rocks have been used around the world to orient people to celestial events that marked the arrival of the seasons. This would be, even in pre-agriculture time, requisite survival knowledge about when and where water, edible plants, and game would arrive and leave. This was never more important than to desert cultures, where resources were less generous than in other climates. The evidence is abundant, from the geo-glyphs of the Atacama Desert to the Nazca Lines in Peru, or the greatest ensemble of rock art in the world, found on the arid shores of the Burrup Peninsula in Western Australia. Sites with solar interactions are generally accepted by anthropologists to have varying degrees of sacredness, because the sun would have helped humans predict events essential to survival. All of this bears on why the circle of Rod Garrett's design for Burning Man's Black Rock City is open at its eastern end—to admit the rising sun. And why 75,000 people give rise to a collective roar when the sun lowers every night behind the Granite Mountains to the west.

Black Rock City is designed as a wheel that is marked off in hours radiating out from the placement of the wooden figure burned at the height of the Burning Man event. It's an acknowledgment that time is a cultural invention, dependent upon that natural geometry of the circle drawn by the sun each day. And it makes getting around the city more feasible for people who may be under the influence, as well as providing public safety personnel a way to find you when you're in trouble. To live in the city is to inhabit a clock on the ground that is governed by the sky – which is another way of saying a compass. It wasn't always so.[5]

When I first attended Burning Man in 1992, the encampment consisted of tents randomly strewn across the desert floor with the then-40-foot-tall wooden man sort of in the center of everyone. Around 600 people were in attendance that

100 YDS TO BURNING MAN
ATTACHMENT C : SITE PLAN BLACK ROCK
RECEIVED
JUL 0 1 1992
DISTRICT OFFICE
WINNEMUCCA, NEVADA
PORTABLE TOILETS
PORTABLE TOILETS
30'
AXIS LANES & PARIMETER MARKED BY STAKES POLES & CAUTION TAPE
N
RING DIAMETER 270
750FT
COLOR CODED BY QUADRANT
CENTRAL PAVILLION
CAMPING AREA
CAMPING AREA 10.8 ACRES
NOTE NO POST HOLES WILL BE DUG POLES WILL BE GLUED & ATTACHED TO FLAT BASES
SCALE 3/8" = 30'
630FT

year, the third time the event had been held in the desert. Started as a party on Baker Beach in 1986, it required little sense of group design, although increasingly a fair bit of planning and construction. Burning Man arose from a milieu that had produced the Suicide Club and the Cacophony Society in San Francisco. These were neo-Dadaist gatherings, "Happenings" of a sort, where disorientation was a desirable and fundamental condition of the events. People were led, sometimes blindfolded, into unexpected places, such as sewers and the tops of bridges where meals, performances, and installations were variously staged. The idea was to knock you out of your sense of the ordinary and the bourgeois and in so doing, open a door to creativity. So urban planning didn't come naturally to the group when they arrived on the Black Rock. On the contrary, a certain amount of chaos was privileged.

Rod Garrett (1936-2011), who was originally from the San Fernando Valley, aspired at first to become an architect, then a landscape architect, but ended up moving to Oakland and studying Environmental Science at UC Berkeley. He was diverted from academia when he helped a friend next door with a backyard construction job, started making sculpture, and began hanging out with people such as the poet Gary Snyder and the comic Lenny Bruce. One of the guys working with him building decks and pergolas was Will Roger, a photographer who had moved from Rochester to Marin County. Both of them attended Burning Man for the first time in 1995. I attended Burning Man for the first time in 1994. Rod came in either 1995 or 1996.

As Garrett explained, "The original form of the camp was a circle. This was not particularly planned, but formed instinctively from the traditional campfire circle and the urge to 'circle the wagons' against the nearly boundless space. By 1992 the Bureau of Land Management had required the group to submit a site plan, and Burning Man founder Larry Harvey (1948-2018) drew one that featured a set of cardinal axes converging on a central pavilion for the Man. The north-south axis was shown to be 650 feet, the east-west a slightly longer, 750 feet. Everything was to be marked out with stakes. Garrett noted, "Compass headings added to the circle served our need to orient ourselves in that stark emptiness." Nonetheless, I still got lost that year

The first public lands permit for Black Rock City was received in 1992 from the Bureau of Land Management Winnemucca District Office based upon this site plan by Larry Harvey

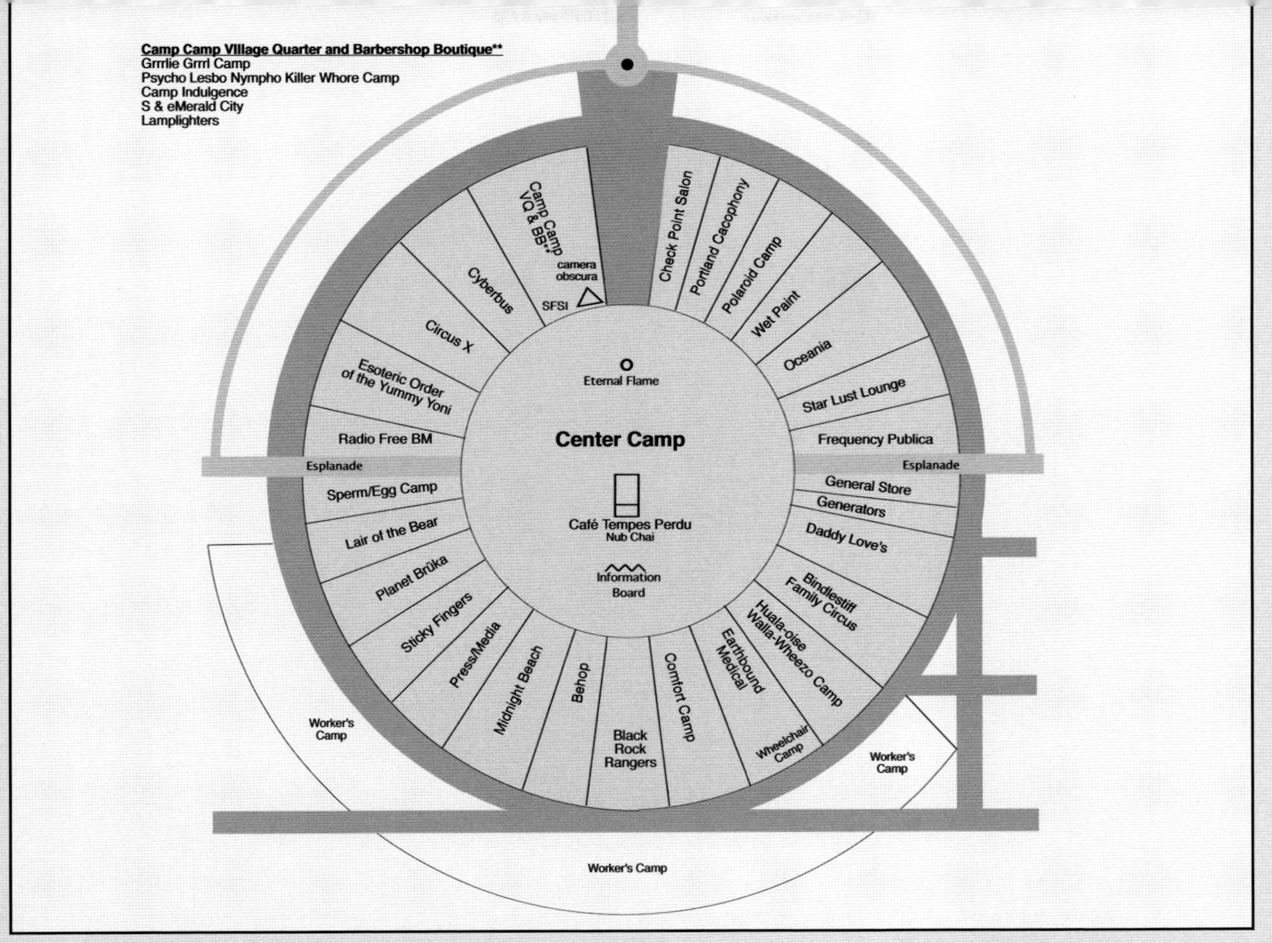

attempting to find my tent in the wee hours of the morning, a not uncommon experience in those days." The map was not the territory and, like I said, random camping. That was and remains the essential tension when camping on the Black Rock playa or attending Burning Man, situations into which one ventures in order to experience deliberate disorientation, yet a space in which one can use a handrail.

In 1996, with 8,000 people in attendance, the camp featured a center stage and a couple of ring roads that were more promenades than actual streets. One of these roads was lined with "theme camps." The event that year was themed appropriately enough as it turned out "Hellco," and Garrett described it as being in full "uncontrolled sprawl." The crowd pushed itself to the edge of chaos. There were several injuries and a fatality, and the Bureau of Land Management decided to deny Burning Man a permit for the next year. Larry Harvey asked Will Roger, who had previously been a volunteer, to assume control of desert operations.

A rendering by Rod Garrett (1997) and camp placement by Harley K. Dubois.

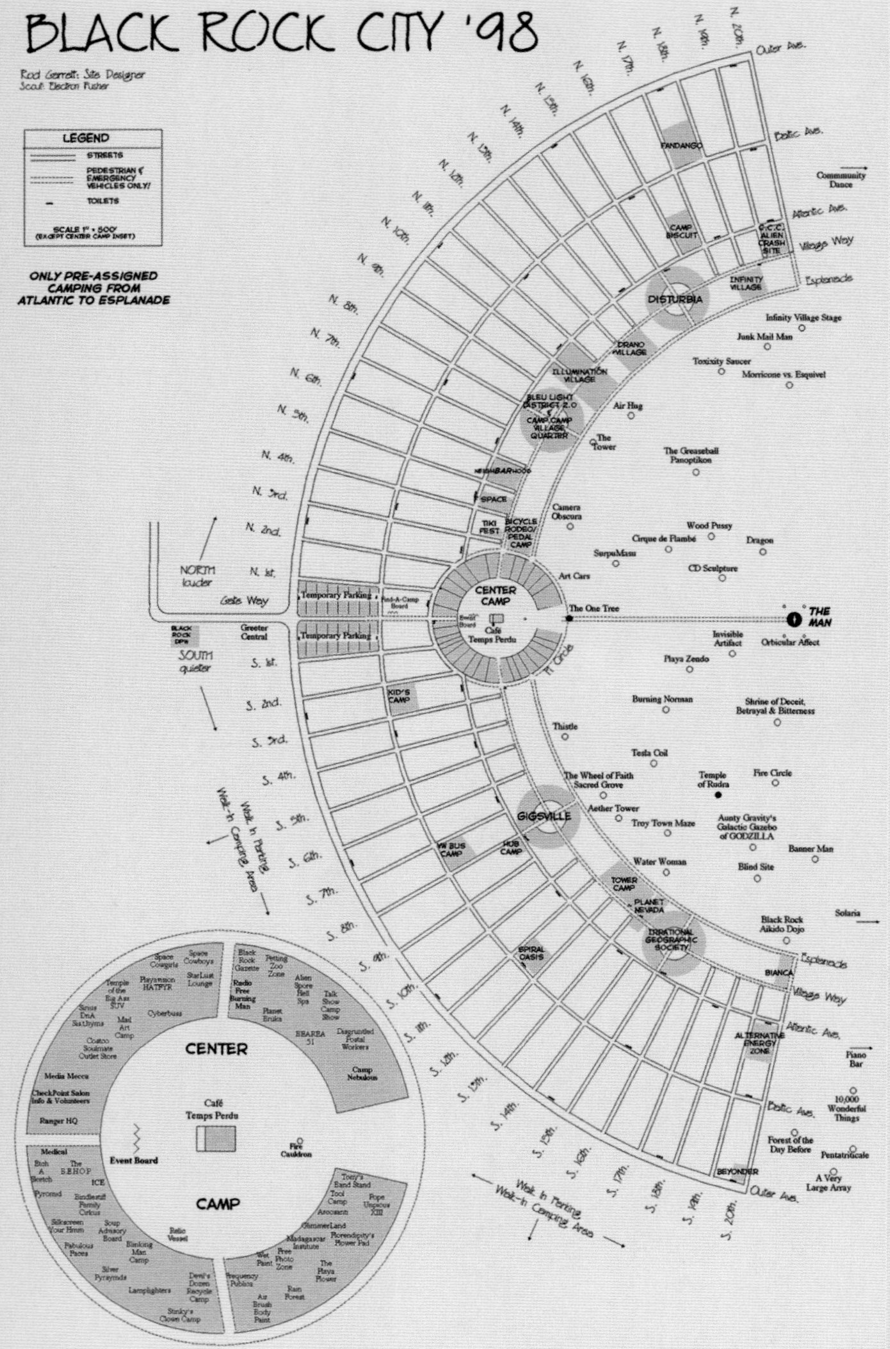

In 1997, everyone retreated to the smaller Hualapai playa to the north, and Roger issued a fervent request to Garrett for help with a more formal street plan. Although Garrett proposed an early version of the now-familiar semi-circular arc, it wasn't yet practical for the organization. For one thing, the Hualapai site was located partially on the shoreline of the smaller playa in order to avoid federal land, so there was no clear span across which to draw an arc. And, for another, no one in the organization knew how to survey a curve. After a few attempts, Garrett was able to devise a segmented series of rectangles that Roger was able to survey and build. That was the beginning of a deep collaboration between designer and builder that would last until Garrett passed away.

Upon Burning Man's return to the Black Rock the next year, Garrett designed several versions of the city. When he and Roger finally settled on one, they were able to survey his arc with blocks divided by radial streets projecting out to the west from Center Camp. That year Garrett also established zoning to accommodate and separate civic components such as the airport, walk-in camping, and large-scale music domains. In a 2015 interview with the online magazine, Dezeen, Harvey described in hindsight an almost counter-intuitive fact about the ongoing evolution of Black Rock City as being organized around boundaries.[6] "We discovered that you could delineate boundary lines

The basic structure of what the future of Black Rock City would look like. If you look at a clock face, this goes from four to eight o'clock. These are 15 degree radials. The signature clock design was not in use yet. City design by Rod Garrett

at any scale you pleased as long as people could see the line created by a succession of [surveyor's] flags. Therefore, you could craft space in an environment that was so disjointed. People craved orientation. It was a very basic, primal need. So we could create a boundary that served lots of functional purposes and especially create boundaries that people would camp along. Eventually that was the way we created everything: the streets, every aspect of the bounded environment."

In 1999, Harvey selected "Wheel of Time" as that year's theme, which led Garrett to rotating the blocks to line up with the curving streets and dividing them into 15 degree increments along the arcs. He realized that he had created a clock face, which led to the naming of the streets after hours and minutes. By eschewing a rectilinear grid in favor of a segmented radial arc, naming the streets after intervals of time, then alphabetizing the long latitudinal avenues that follow the curve, they were able to maintain simplicity and a focus on the Man as the pivot around which the city and its society revolved. Surrounding everything was the orange trash fence plotted as a pentagon, the shape that Garrett determined was the easiest to patrol in terms of line-of-sight. The city is now plotted by its Department of Public Works by driving a golden spike in the center of where the Man will stand and surveying the five-sided figure outward. Tony Perez (Coyote) became the surveyor and continues to create the Black Rock City layout to this day.

Every year, Black Rock City grows as its population expands. The limit to both how much traffic the highway leading to the desert can bear and how much walking people can endure to cross the city seems to be about 100,000 people. In 2017, Black Rock City had a population of 75,000, and the distance from the Man to the five outer fence pentagon points was 8,175 feet. Each of the five sides of the fence ran 9,610 feet, for a total length of 9.1 miles. The area enclosed was 3,650 acres or 5.7 square miles, and the Burning Man organization was extending the city as needed.

Thus, the event takes advantage of one of the larger and more disorienting isotropic desert spaces in the world, a natural void overlaid with a civic geometry based on celestial orientation, to celebrate what looks and feels like an ancient fire ritual. And, in fact, Harvey noted at the end of his Dezeen interview that the city design resembles a Neolithic temple complex seen from the air. "We weren't aware of that as we went along," he concluded. "We were an engineering society, but we weren't basing it on some elaborate intellectual construct." And that's exactly the point: the geometry was a navigational response to the natural world.

Thousands of years ago, a solitary mystic would wander into the desert wilderness to be transformed by sacred knowledge; now an entire city of people seeks to briefly inhabit a strict, unforgiving environment wherein enlightenment may be found—or at least have a sense of what that may have meant to earlier generations of humans. Gary Snyder has, for decades, served as a sage in such endeavors. He observes in The Practice of the Wild that "Wilderness has implied chaos, eros, the unknown, realms of taboo, the habitat of both the ecstatic and the demonic... it is a place of archetypal power, teaching, and challenge... People of wilderness cultures rarely seek out adventures. If they deliberately risk themselves, it is for spiritual rather than economic reasons."[7]

Ground Truth and the God's-Eye View

This convergence of desert, human cognition, design, and spirituality are apparent in Will Roger's aerial photographs of Black Rock City, which he has been taking annually since 2005. To understand how this concatenation occurred, it helps to understand Will's relationships to both photography, which came first, of course, and then to Burning Man.

As to photography, George Eastman began manufacturing photographic dry plates in 1880 –an alternative to the much more troublesome and expensive wet plates –in Rochester, New York. In 1888, he founded Kodak, which for most of the 20th century was the world's dominant photo film business. Based on the presence of Kodak, as well as Bausch & Lomb and other optical firms in the town, a Mechanics Institute was founded and by 1902 was offer-

ing classes in photography. That was the precursor to the Rochester Institute of Technology (RIT) School of Photographic Arts & Sciences, which would become worldrenowned in the 1930s and graduate hundreds of students annually by the time Roger arrived in 1966 to earn an Associates degree in analytical chemistry. After living in New York City and visiting its museums, he realized he wanted to be an artist, and he returned to RIT in 1970 to run their photography-chemistry laboratory for students while he earned a Bachelor of Fine Arts degree. He left again in 1973, then returned in 1975 to become the Assistant Director of the photography school and an Associate Professor. He stayed until 1989.

Will took on the Photo Workshop course once taught by the legendary photographer, Minor White, which is how he met the young photographer named Marilyn Bridges. In 1976, the 28-year-old Bridges had found herself in Peru on assignment for a travel magazine. After hearing about the famous Nazca Lines, she visited them but was frustrated by the inability to read much from the ground. So Bridges hired a single-engine plane to fly over them. This is now a de rigueur experience for tourists, but in those days was a more daunting experience, as the doors were taken off the aircraft, and only a single seat belt kept you in place. She was terrified of the flying but entranced by the mystery of the lines. She used color slide film to photograph the lines and showed her over-exposed images to Roger, who managed to produce decent prints from them while teaching her why black-and-white would be a better choice for aerial work. Bridges then flew back to Peru to take black-and-white images, and black-and-white became her medium.[8]

When Bridges entered RIT soon thereafter to work on her own BFA in Photography, Roger printed her negatives from Nazca. They were shown at the American Museum of Natural History in 1978. Bridges went on to earn her MFA in 1981, also at RIT, and received a Guggenheim the next year, which she used to charter an aircraft to fly over Yucatan and Chiapas so she could photograph temples from the air. In 1986, her first book, *Markings: Aerial Views of Sacred Landscapes*, was published from prints made by Will. Roger became her photography mentor. She joined a long tradition of photographers imaging sacred archaeological sites, starting with the 1906 photograph of Stonehenge by Lt. P. H. Sharpe. Georg Gerster's survey around the world includes his 1978 image of Pueblo Bonito, part of the Anasazi Chaco complex in northwestern New Mexico that was built from 900 to 1088 A.D.[9] That's also where Marilyn Bridges took her 1983 aerial view of the ruins of Penasco Blanco, its rooms arrayed in an arc that encloses a Great Kiva, a partially subterranean room used for the performance of religious rituals. Some of the remains in their photographs resemble the "Neolithic temple complex" that Harvey was describing.

Roger was married to Bridges from 1976 until 1988. They bought an airplane and both learned to be pilots, although most of the time Bridges hired a pilot so she could photograph while Will was working at the school. Bridges received multiple grants and awards for her work and has continued to image both sacred and secular sites from the air. In the meantime, Roger established his own aerial practice, one devoted to capturing the evolution of a single contemporary sacred site. Flying in a 1959 four-seater Cessna 182-B piloted by a fellow "Burner," he has taken both close-in and distant views of Black Rock City every year. At first giving prints as gifts to his fellow founders and board members of the Burning Man Project, now he is sharing them with a larger audience.[9]

As to Roger's relationship to Burning Man, after being named head of Desert Operations and founding the Department of Public Works in 1998, he went on to become one of the six "cultural founders" (the group constituting the legal entity Black Rock City LLC) and was the first chair of the Burning Man Project (the nonprofit that actually puts on the event) for seven years until 2018. For 20 years, he was responsible for or guided the construction, maintenance, demolition, and clean-up of the city, post-event. He oversaw the surveying, fencing, and road construction, then the BLM-mandated environmental sweep afterwards. If Garrett,

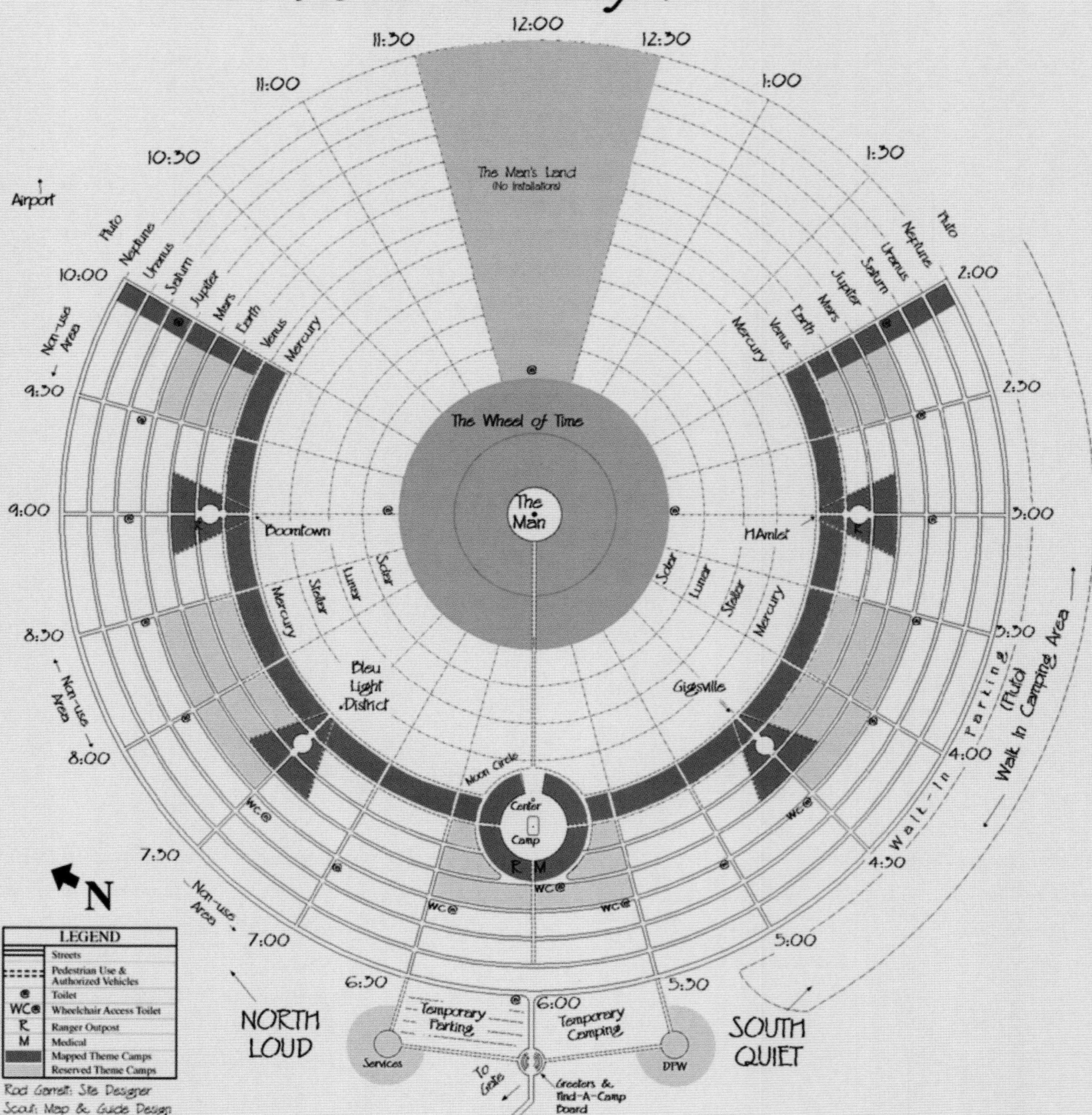

Black Rock City 1999
12:00
11:30
12:30
11:00
1:00
10:30
1:30
Airport
Pluto
Neptune
Uranus
Saturn
Jupiter
Mars
Earth
Venus
Mercury
Pluto
Neptune
Uranus
Saturn
Jupiter
Mars
Earth
Venus
Mercury
The Men's Land
(No Installations)
10:00
9:30
2:00
Non-use Area
2:30
The Wheel of Time
9:00
The Man
3:00
Boomtown
Hamlet
Solar
Lunar
Stelar
Mercury
Solar
Lunar
Stelar
Mercury
8:30
3:30
Non-use Area
Bleu
Light
District
Gigsville
Walk-In Parking (Pluto)
Walk-In Camping Area
8:00
4:00
Moon Circle
WC
WC
Center
Camp
7:30
R M
WC
4:30
N
Non-use Area
WC
WC
WC
7:00
5:00
LEGEND
Streets
Pedestrian Use &
Authorized Vehicles
Toilet
WC Wheelchair Access Toilet
R Ranger Outpost
M Medical
Mapped Theme Camps
Reserved Theme Camps
6:30
5:30
6:00
Temporary
Parking
Temporary
Camping
NORTH
LOUD
SOUTH
QUIET
Services
To
Gate
Greeters &
Find-A-Camp
Board
DPW
Rod Garrett: Site Designer
Scout: Map & Guide Design

his best friend, was the designer of the city as compass and clock, Roger was the person who built the instrument. In addition to serving as construction wrangler and master logician, he was also the liaison to local businesses in Gerlach, the nearest town, and the Nevada representative to federal, state, and local officials in the field. There's more on the year 2000 job description I'm quoting, but that's enough to explain how, when viewing the city from the air, he understands everything he sees in terms of structure and function.

Aerial images offer us the ability to discern structures and patterns not apparent from views on the ground. This is precisely why archaeologists have been using them since the second decade of the 20th century in the Middle East and elsewhere to locate sites.[11] But aerial views of settlements started long before that with the earliest yet known example: a small mural inside a house excavated at Çatalhöyük, a neolithic settlement in Anatolia that flourished 9,000 years ago. Although painted from the imagination of its creator, the aerial depiction of the settlement was an accurate mapping of its layout and relationship to the landscape. Likewise, the beautiful and stunningly accurate aerial painting of the Italian town of Imola by Leonardo da Vinci in 1502, which was a radical innovation, was painted from his mind's eye, albeit based on measurements he made on foot.

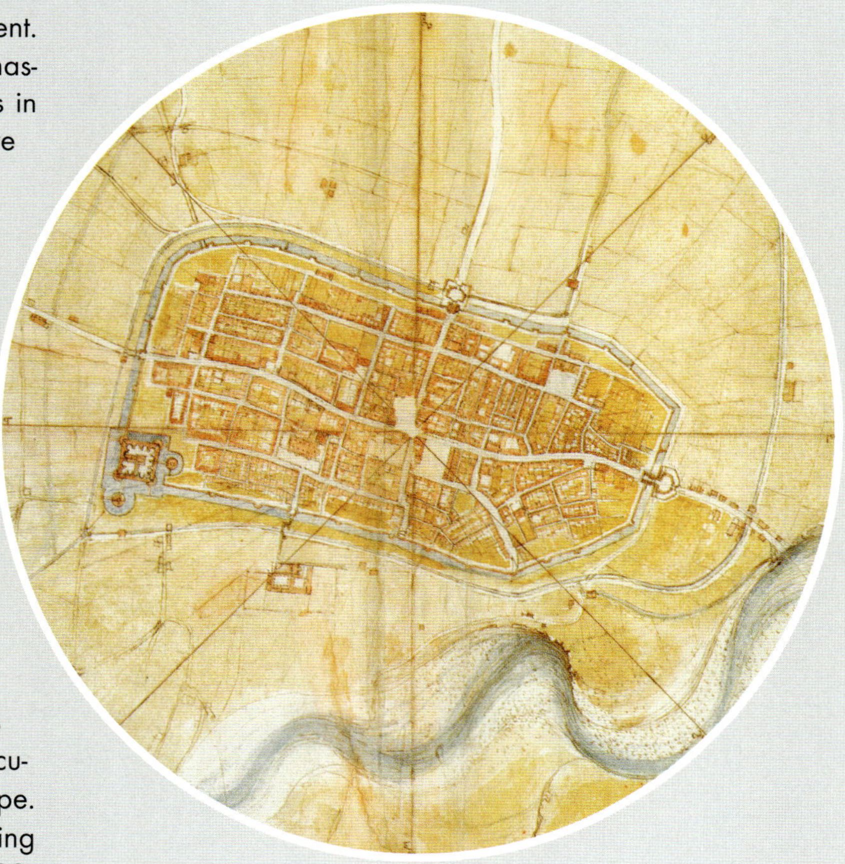

City Plan of Imola (1502); Illustration by Leonardo da Vinci

Left: The 1999 city design by Rod Garrett

"Bird's-eye" views of towns became increasing popular throughout Europe during the following centuries. The paintings and prints provided citizens a sense of where they lived, as their towns became cities too large to perceive all at once from the ground—but they also served as advertisement for the stature of the cities themselves. These handsome aerial views were both chart and art and even today provide reliable information about the orientation and evolution of cities in Europe and around the world. Most of Bridges' views of sacred sites were made from this perspective, an oblique image taken from not too far off the ground, usually under 1,000 feet or so, and thus well in the "nap of the land," as contemporary aerial photographers call it.[11]

As cities grew larger, airplanes more capable, and photographic optics more precise, artists began making views from well above that distance, sometimes oblique views but also directly vertical ones from 2,000 up to 10,000 feet and higher. And these latter are often referred to as "God's-eye views." Images made with civilian cameras in airplanes at those elevations increasingly lose the resolution of individual figures and then vehicles, but in turn bring us the context of the city. Shorelines and mountain ranges bordering the cities are in the view, providing environmental context, and local atmospheric conditions become apparent. And, inevitably, the eye begins to perceive (and sometimes construct) patterns not perceivable from the ground.

Will's early images from 2005 set out much of what will preoccupy him while over the camp: an overall oblique view of the city taken from a fairly high altitude with a horizon apparent in the distance; a tighter and slightly steeper view of Center Camp at the apex of the arc; and a much steeper, lower image of a detail, such as an art project, a theme camp, or the airport. In looking over the set of three images chosen by Roger from each of the 12 years from 2005 through 2017, it's remarkable how different the images within each category can be. Depending on the angle of the light, the vagaries of winging a composition while flying at a 125 mph and bouncing in the wind, and the variability of airborne dust from tens of thousands of people shuffling their feet—all that and more go into determining which images work best from year to year. This means the views are never oriented in exactly the same direction or taken from exactly the same vantage point. Nonetheless, you can see the growth of the population, how the arms of the city begin to close slightly over time in response to that growth, and, in fact, how the city has been walked progressively northeast toward the center of the playa as it requires more breathing space.

What's ultimately revealed is how the pentagon and the arc constitute a framework that works at any scale, and upon which nature and culture display mutations. Will, an artist trained as a scientist, has worked both to construct a place and then to picture it – a bounded place within an unbounded space. The city's inhabitants, who seek the disorientation of the unfamiliar, must juggle a profound and familiar act of balance between the wild and the civilized.

If the playa as pure space is a wilderness, then (per Snyder) one of its aspects is eros. This would imply, if not require, that the civic plan, the mapping of the playa, has an aspect of logos. The former, in Jungian terms, leads toward the relational, as the latter leans into the objective. The transcendence of space meets the rigors of place,

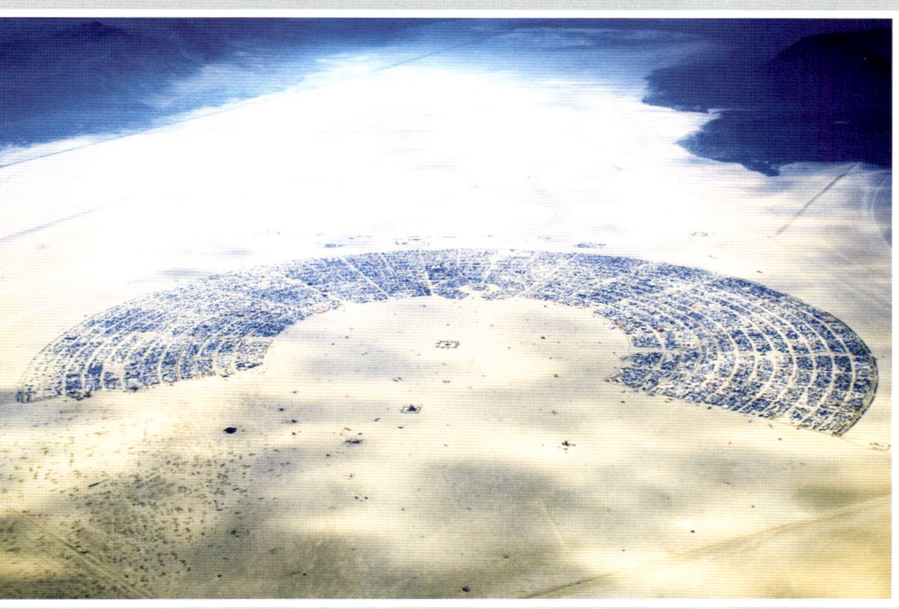

which makes Black Rock City a coherent jumble or entanglement. Chaos is there, but it's complicated and constitutive of its opposite, order. Such is the case with all dualities.

Roger, though, in picturing the living community of Black Rock City adds a vertical dimension to the great horizontality of the playa, and the photography is an act of devotion to a figure collectively inscribed in a sacred space. Looking down at the photographs which look down at Black Rock City is to realize that Will, even as he has a serial scheme of repeating certain kinds of images annually, is also at play with the tension of eros and logos, making images that include both, as he has the pilot soar high and low. And it is play that exemplifies the spirit of Burning Man, that embraces both the wilderness and the compass of the city. Roger is at play with the collective practice of Burning Man and making it three-dimensional in a very specific manner. This elevates his work, in a literal and metaphorical sense, above the boundaries: Play is exactly where the tension between eros and logos is resolved.

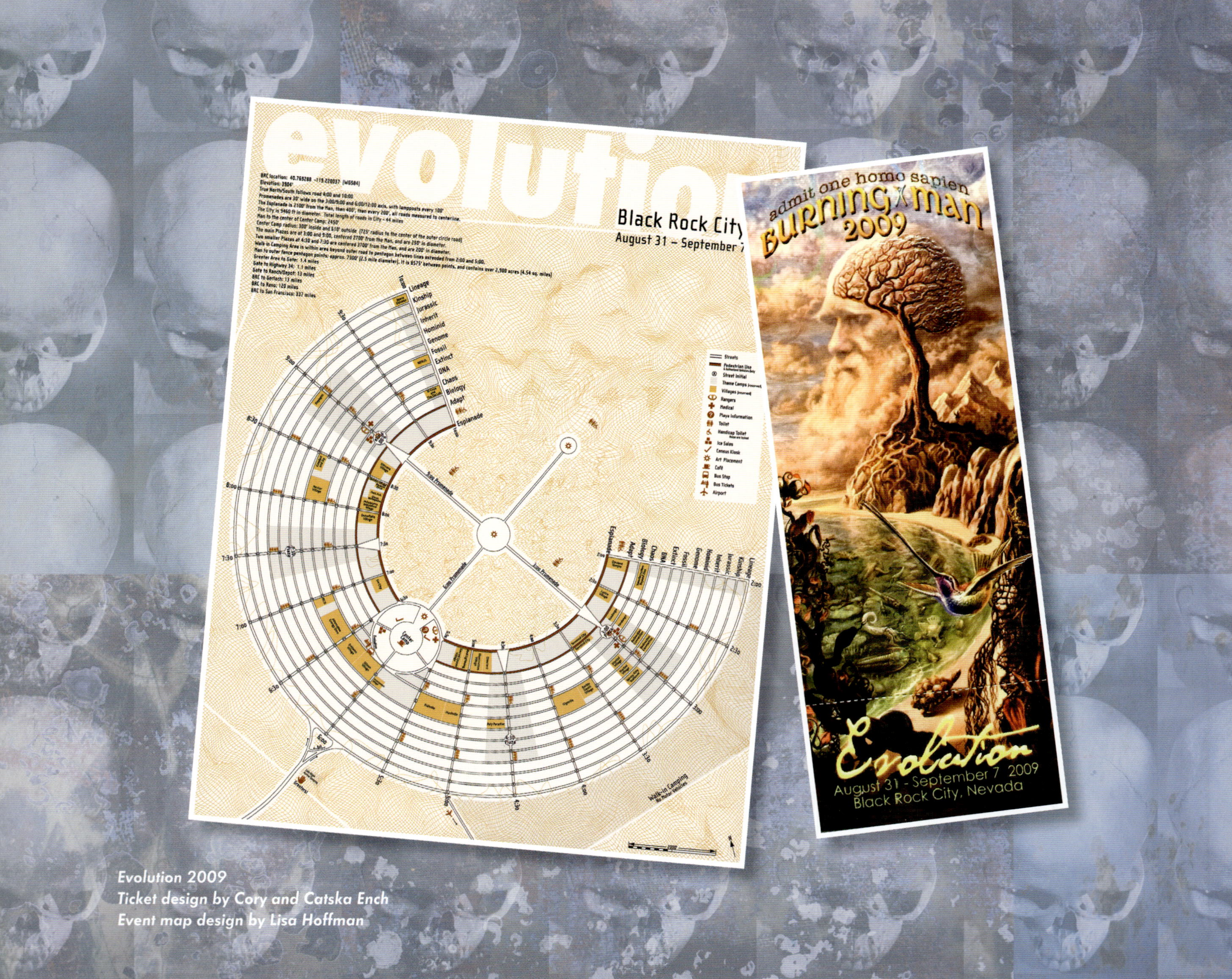

Evolution 2009
Ticket design by Cory and Catska Ench
Event map design by Lisa Hoffman

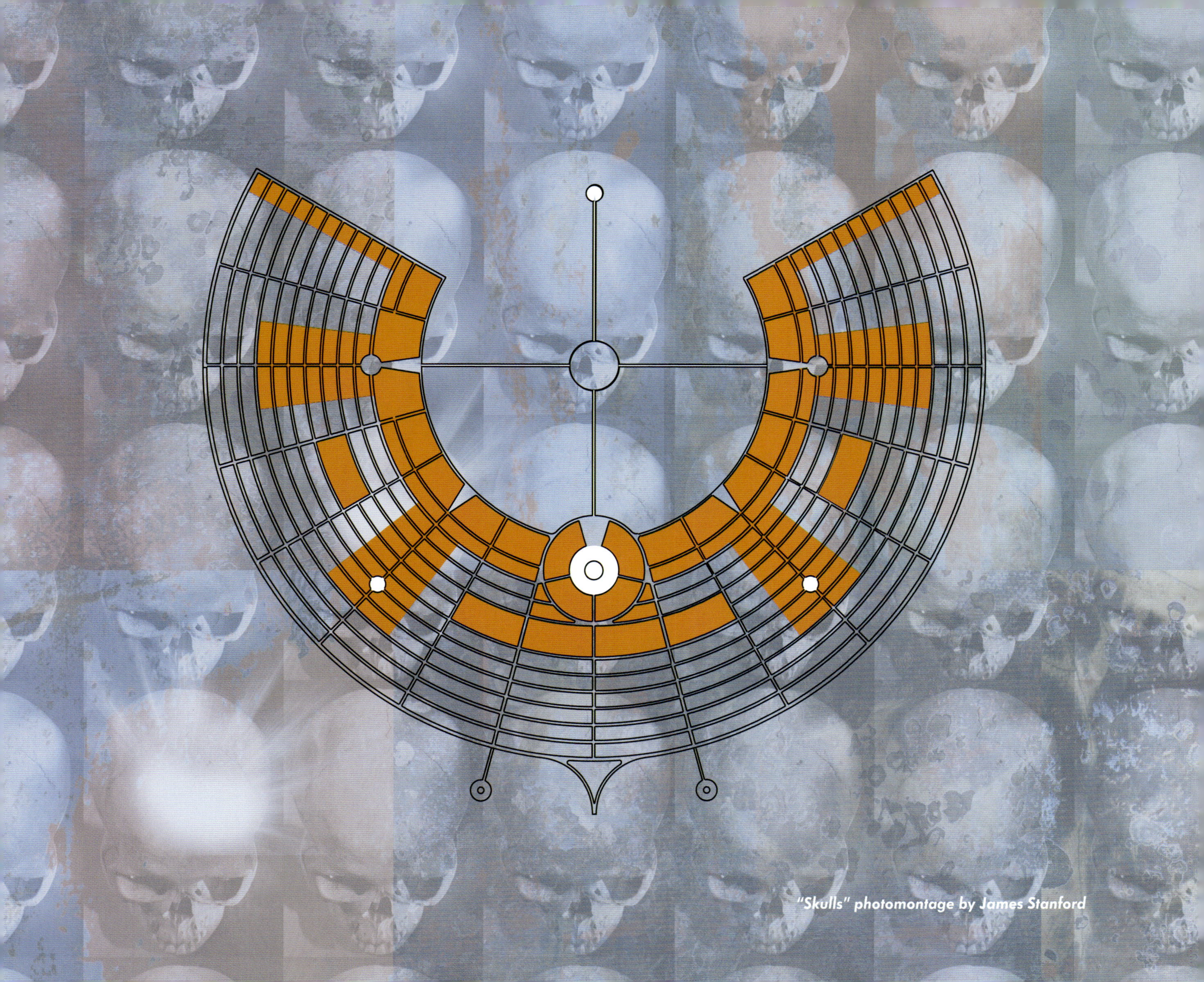

"Skulls" photomontage by James Stanford

The location of Black Rock City was moved a half-mile southwest from 2008's location as per the Bureau of Land Management's stipulations. Population 43,558

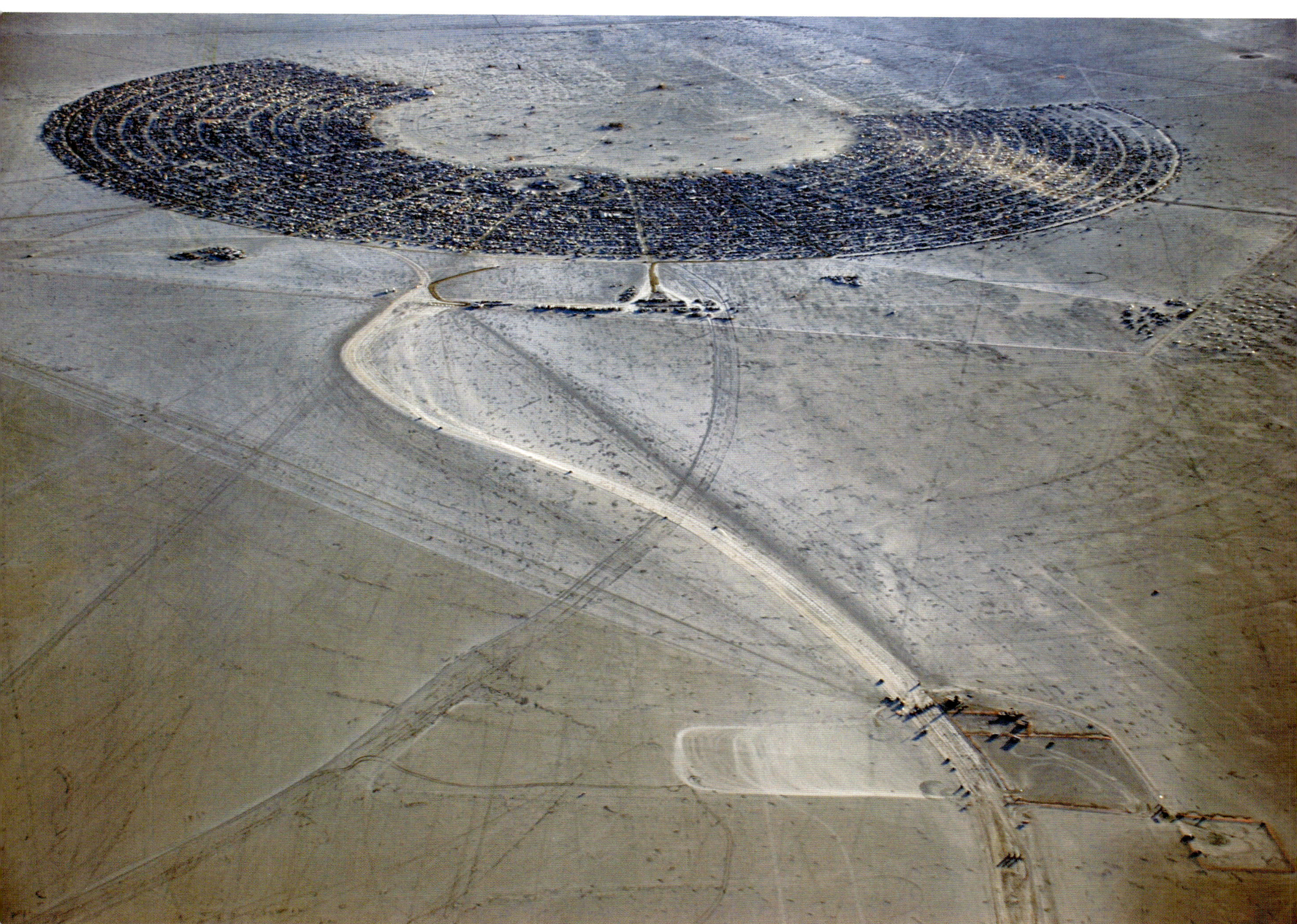

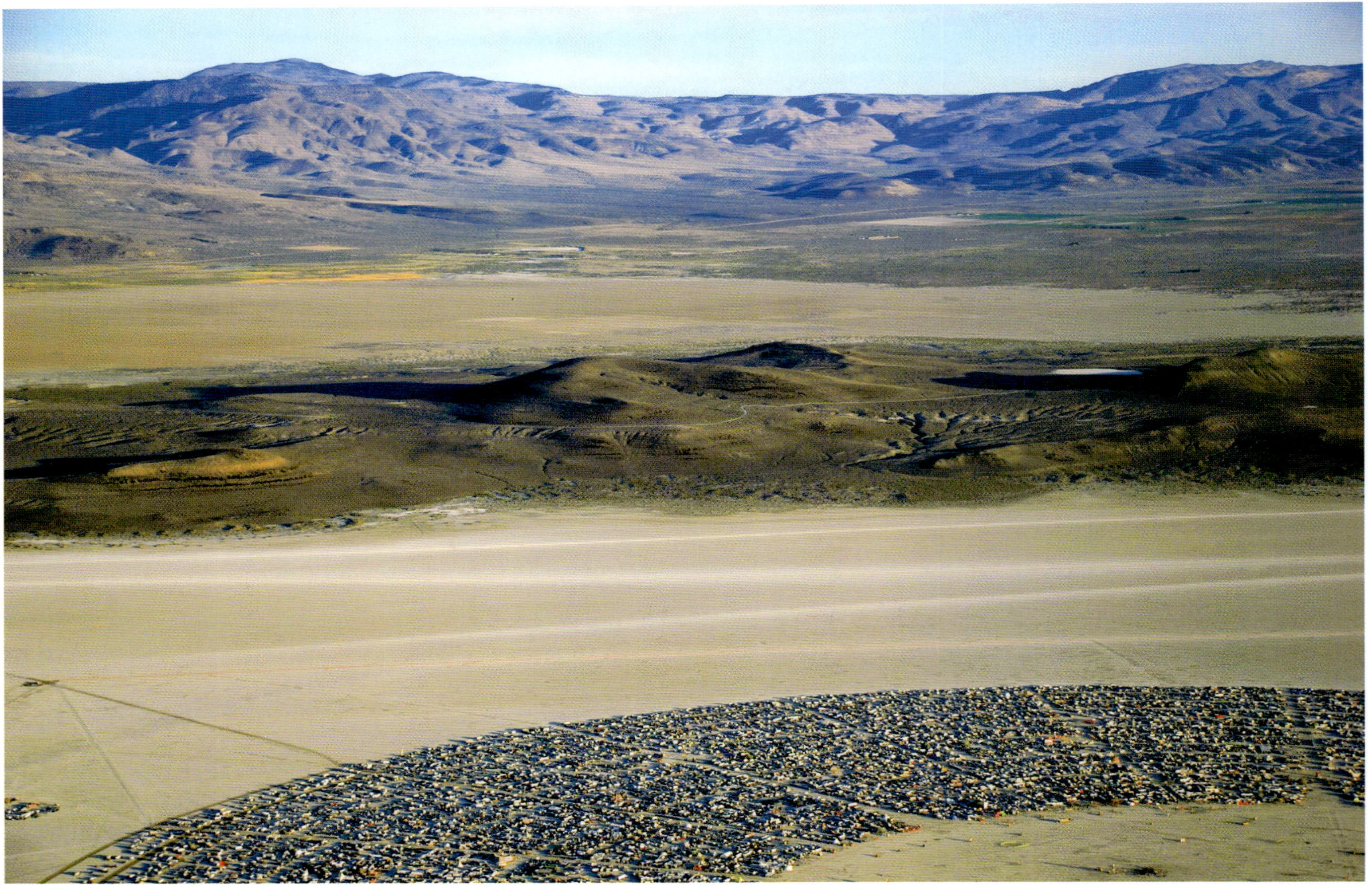

Above: *The playa extends for approximately 100 miles northeast from the towns of Gerlach and Empire, between the Jackson Mountains to the east and the Calico Hills to the west*
Right: *The flatness of the Black Rock Desert's lake bed surface is ideal for experimental land vehicles. In 1983, Richard Noble drove the jet-powered Thrust2 car to a new record of 634.015 mph. In 1997, Andy Green drove the world's first supersonic car to a record 763.035 mph*

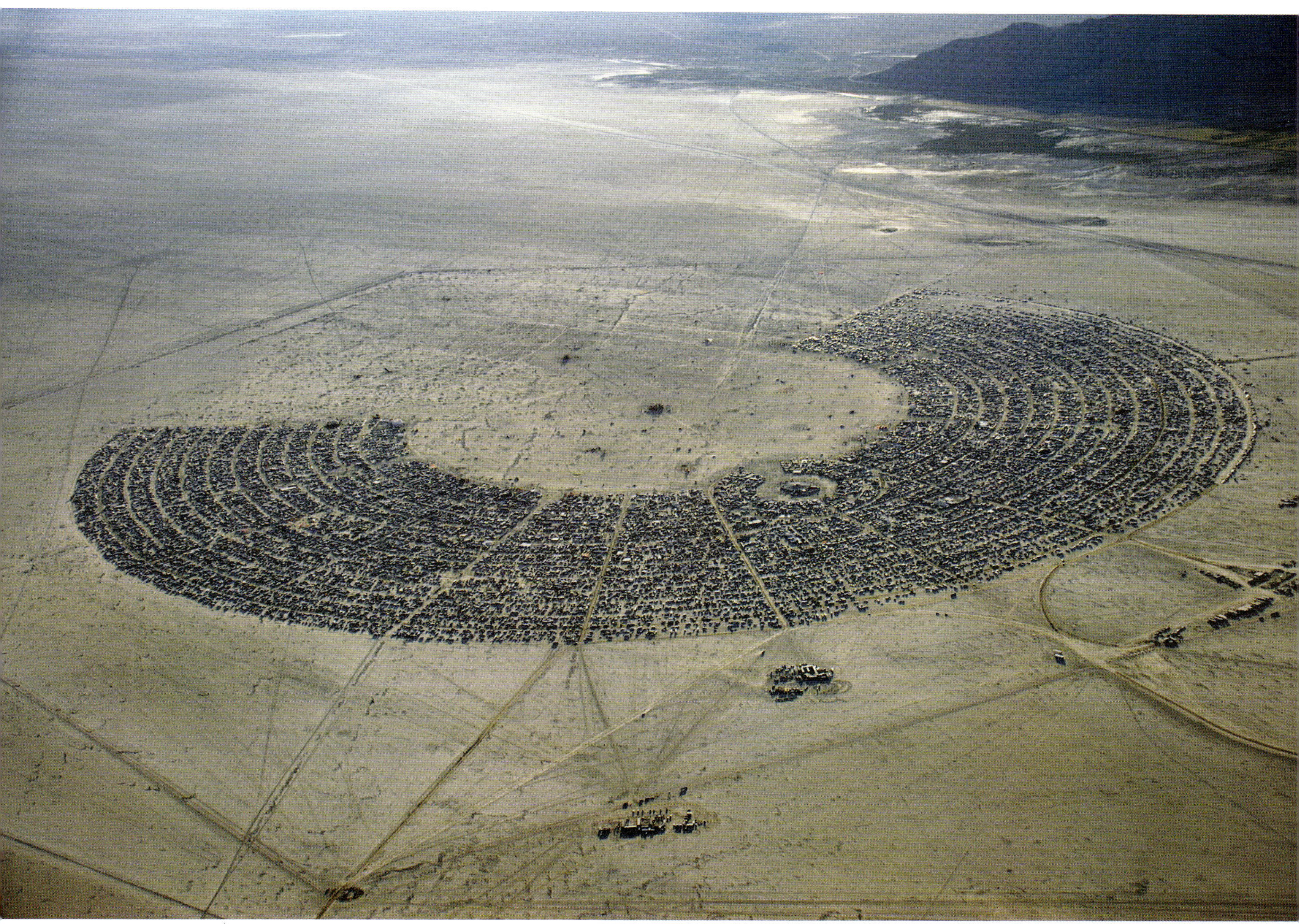

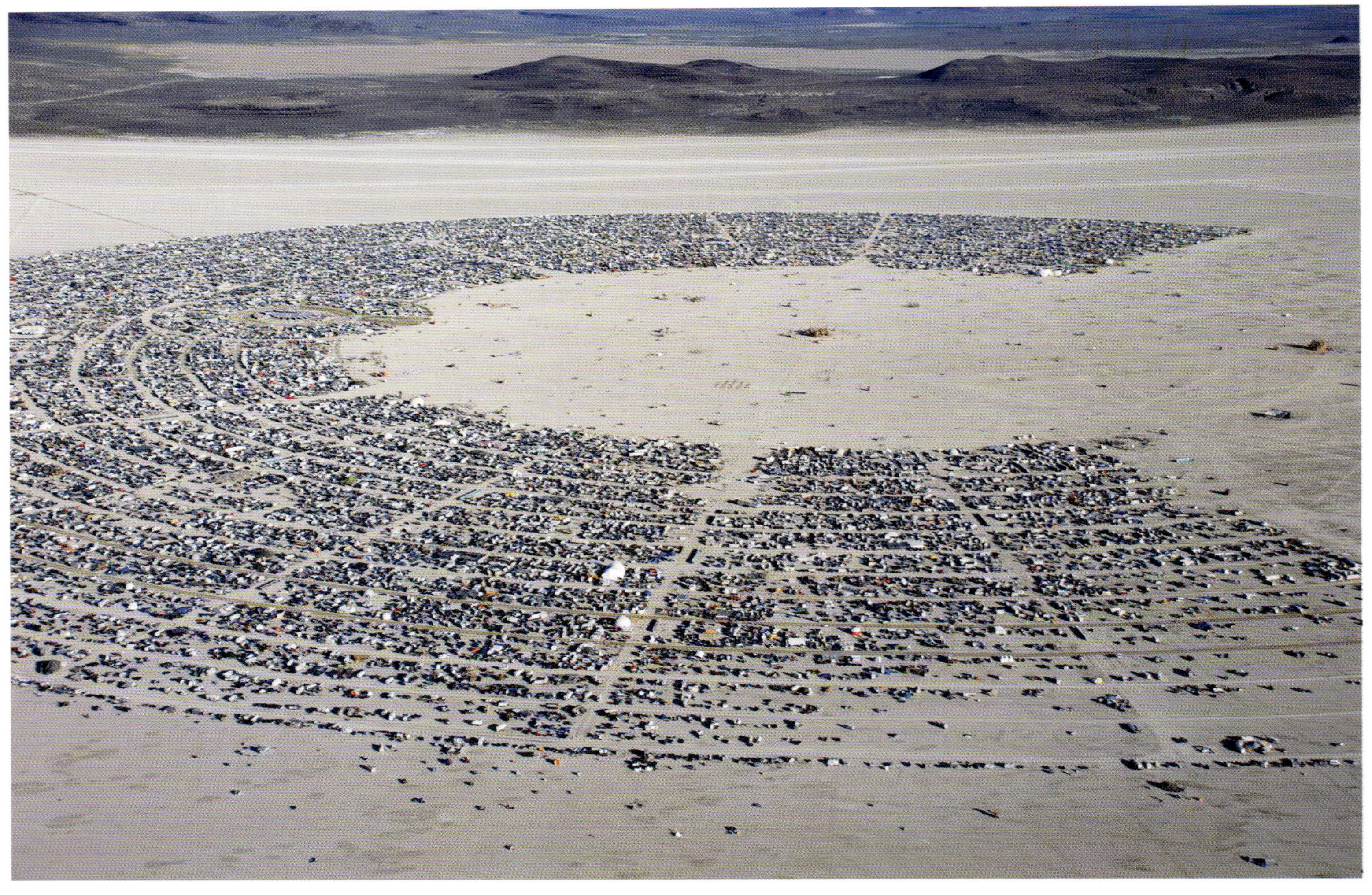

Above: *There were 749 camps that requested placement and 618 were placed as part of Black Rock City's urban planning efforts*
Right: *The speed limit in Black Rock City is 5 mph and 10 mph on Gate Road*

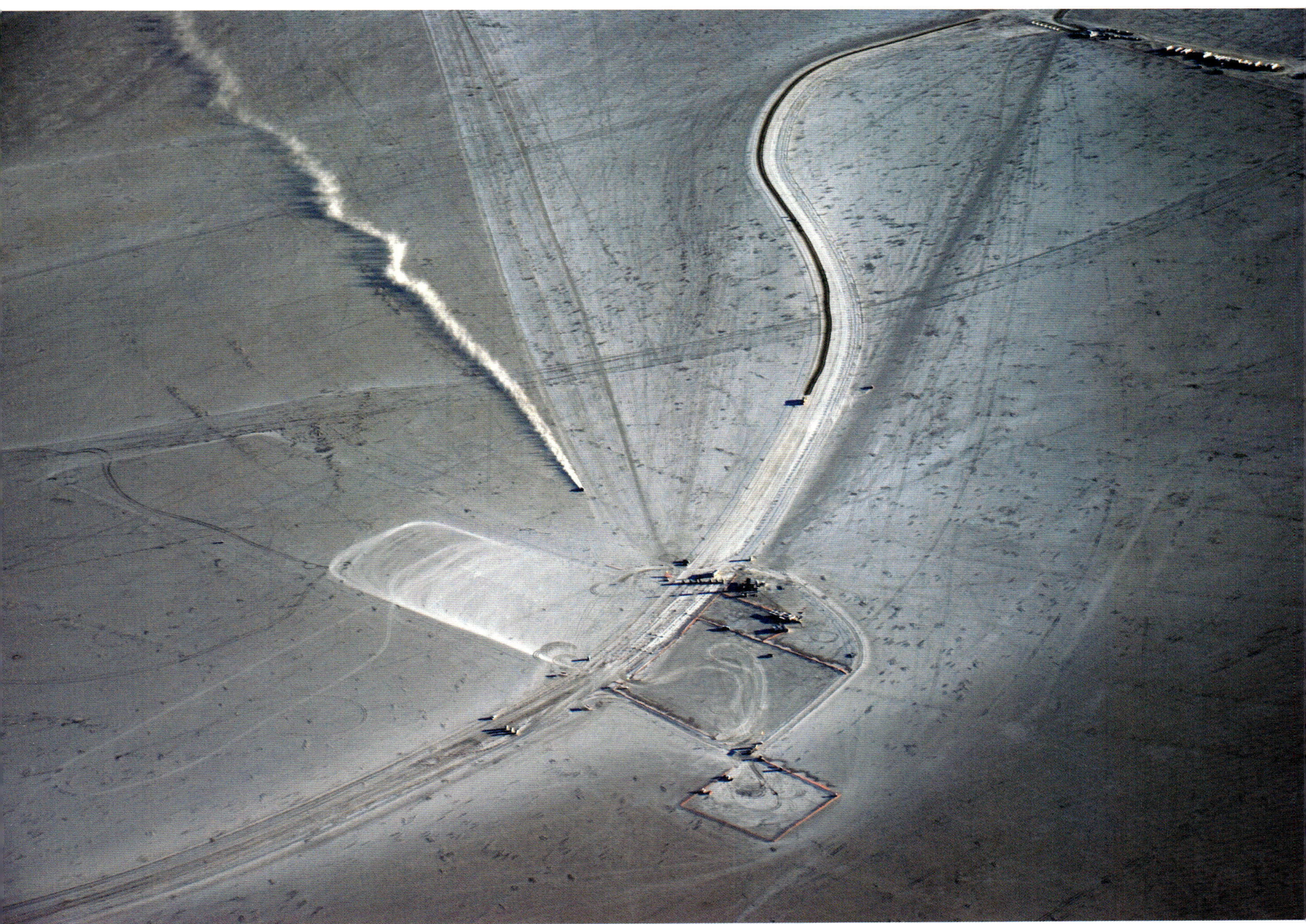

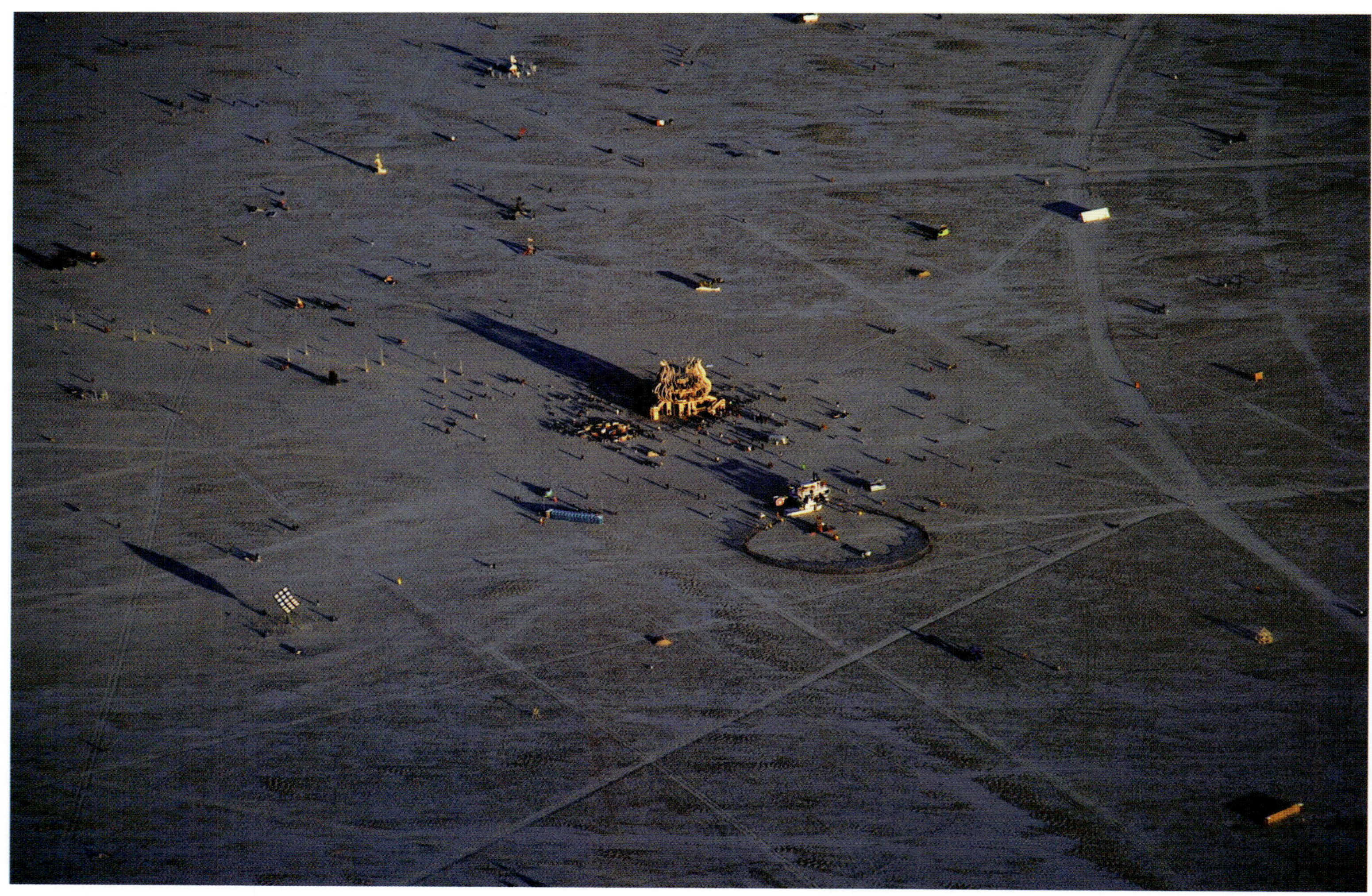

98

Above: *"Fire of Fires" Temple by David Umlas, Marrilee Ratcliffe and Community Art Makers (2009)*
Right: *The size and layout of Black Rock City was returned to roughly the same as the 2007 event*

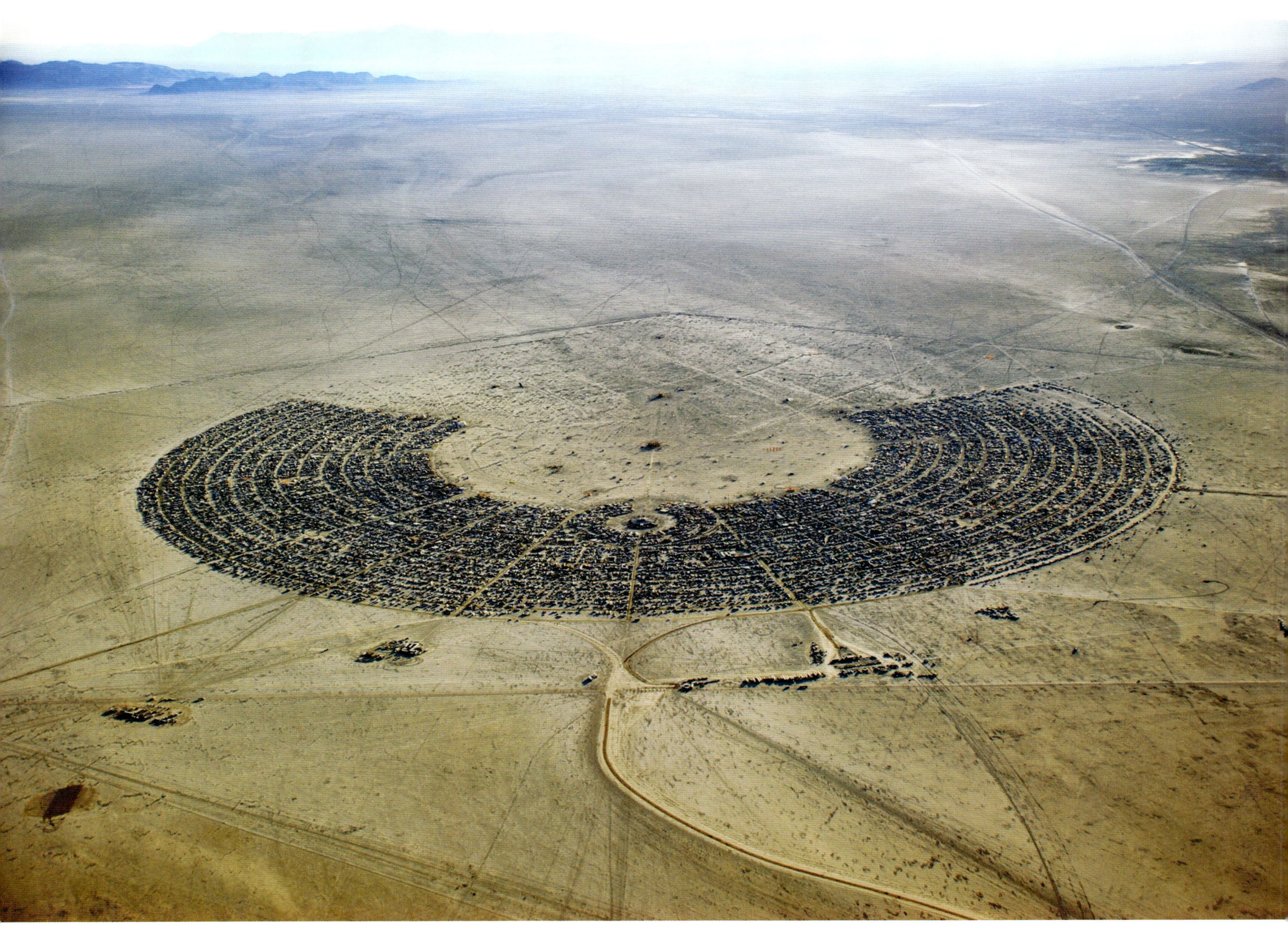

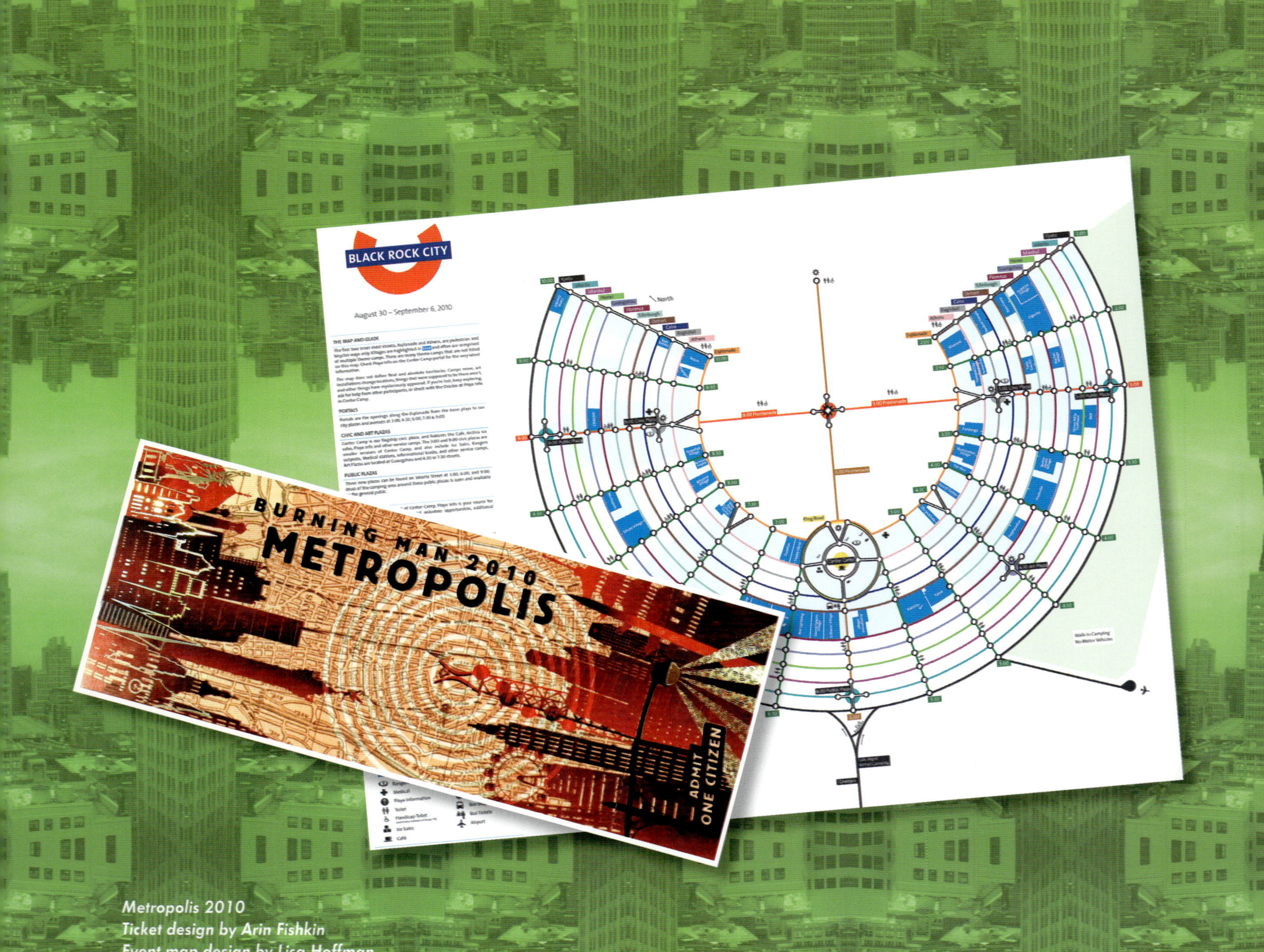

Metropolis 2010
Ticket design by Arin Fishkin
Event map design by Lisa Hoffman

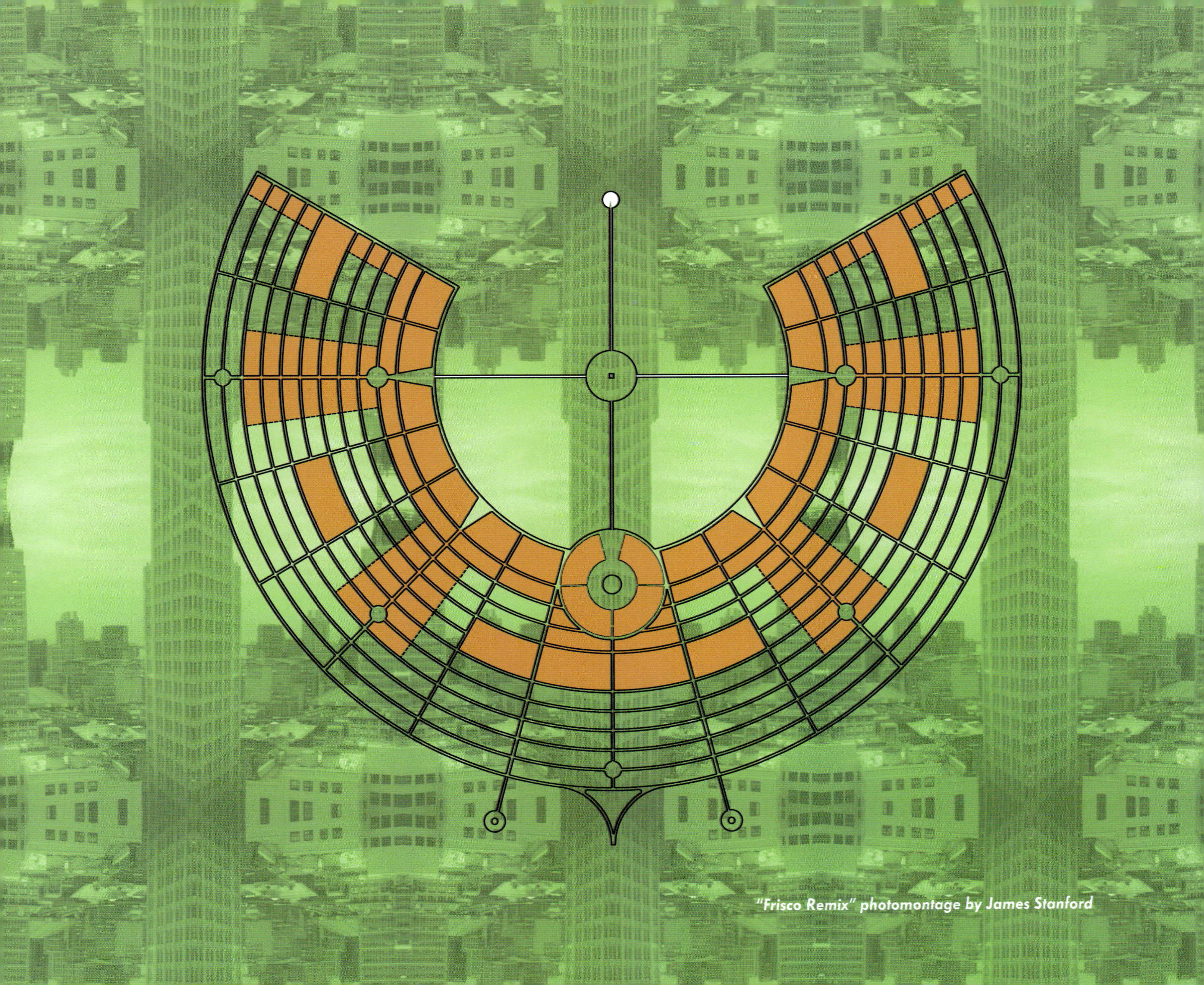

"Frisco Remix" photomontage by James Stanford

High winds, frequent dust storms and rainstorms make for a challenging year. Population 51,525

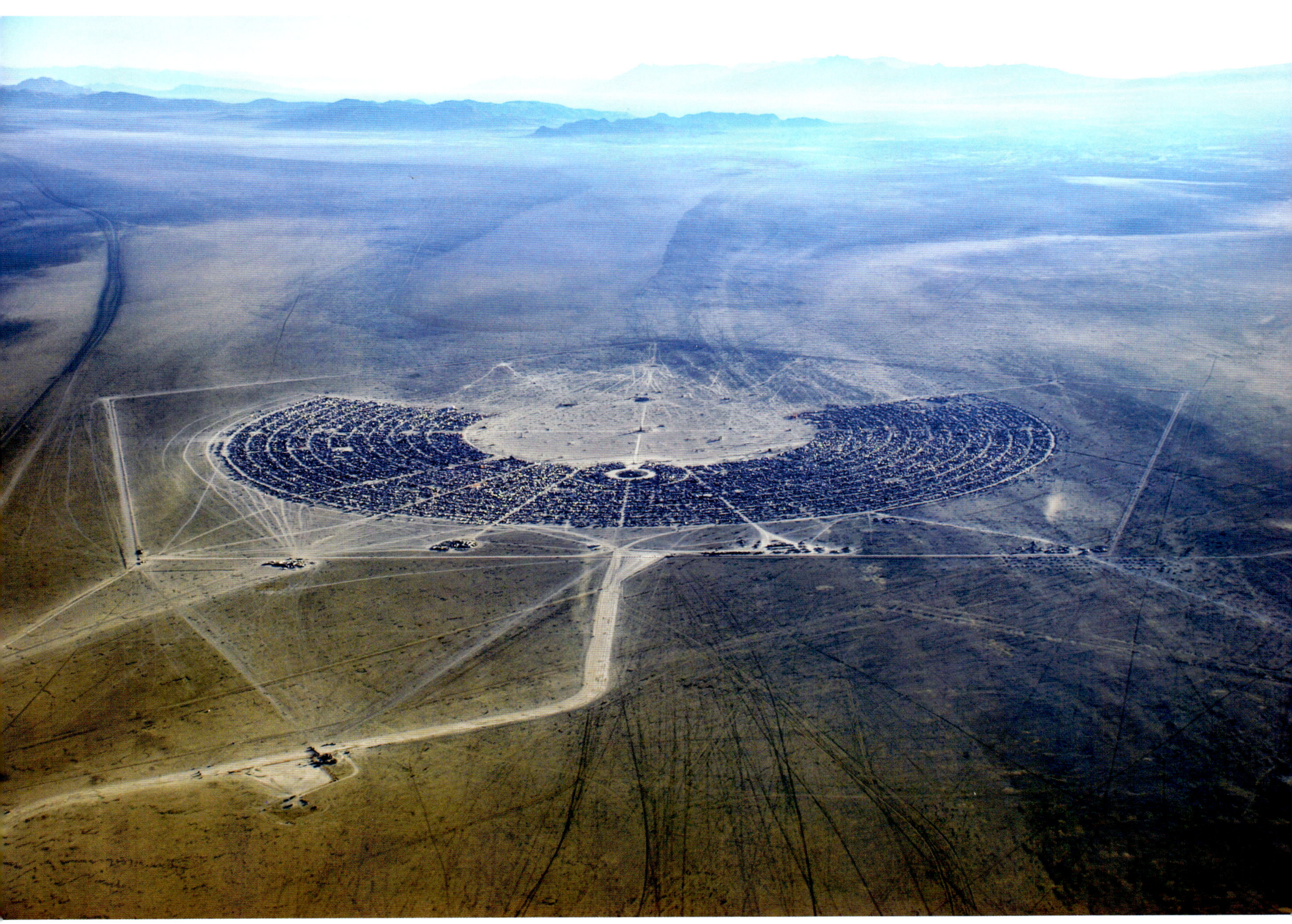

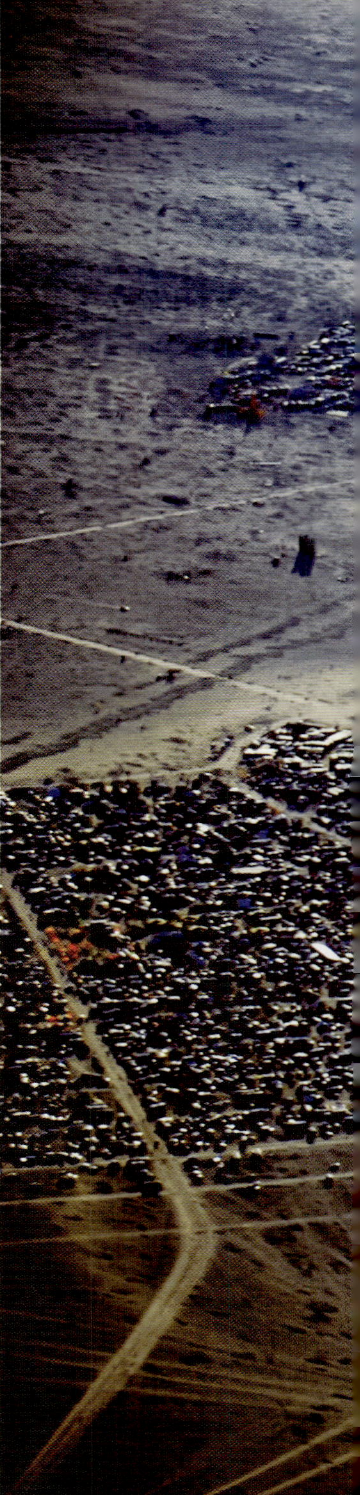

About 700 registered camps were pre-placed; of these, 626 were theme camps, 39 were villages and 35 were other camps
There were 275 registered art projects on playa, including 36 honoraria projects that were funded by the Burning Man art grants program

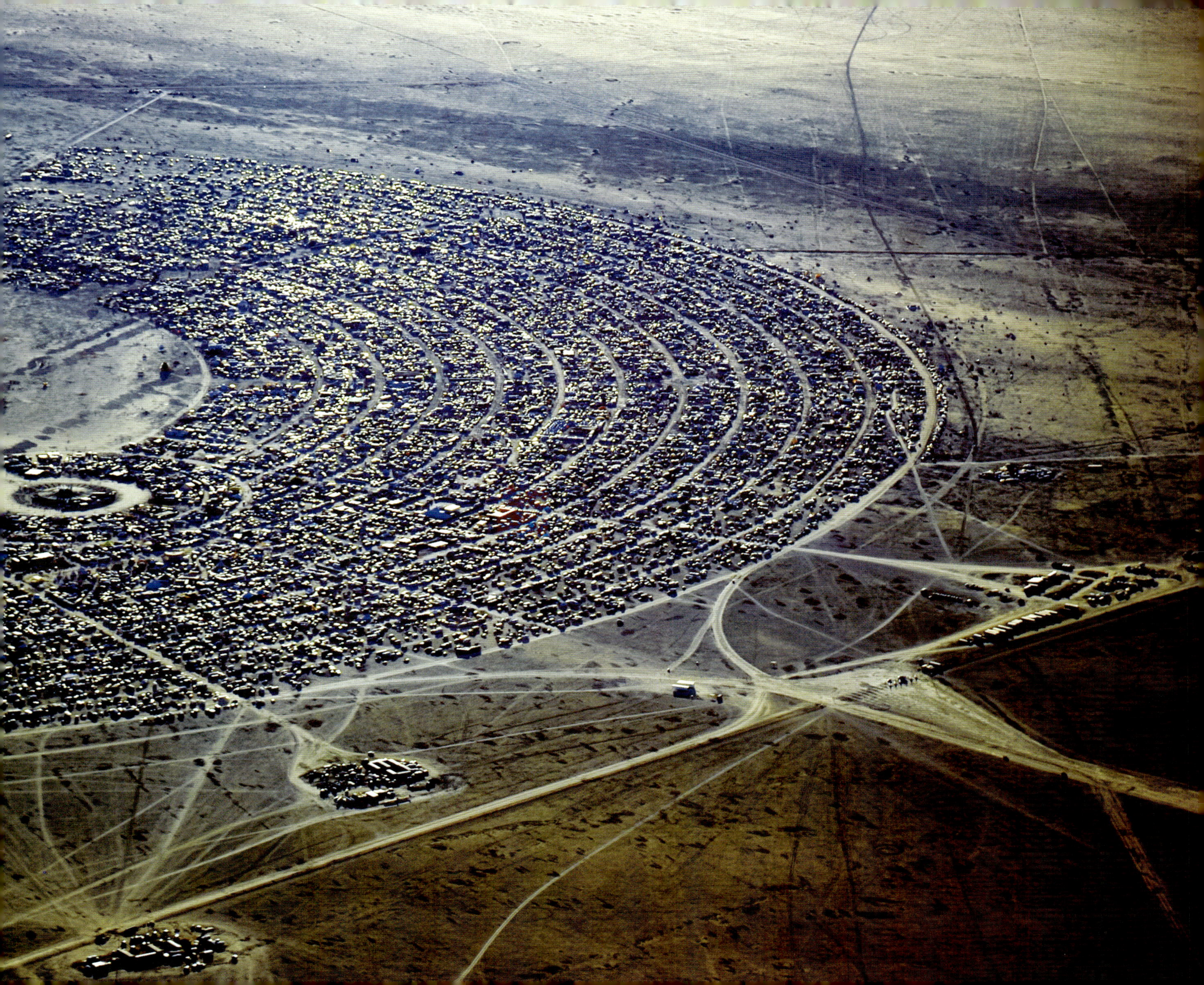

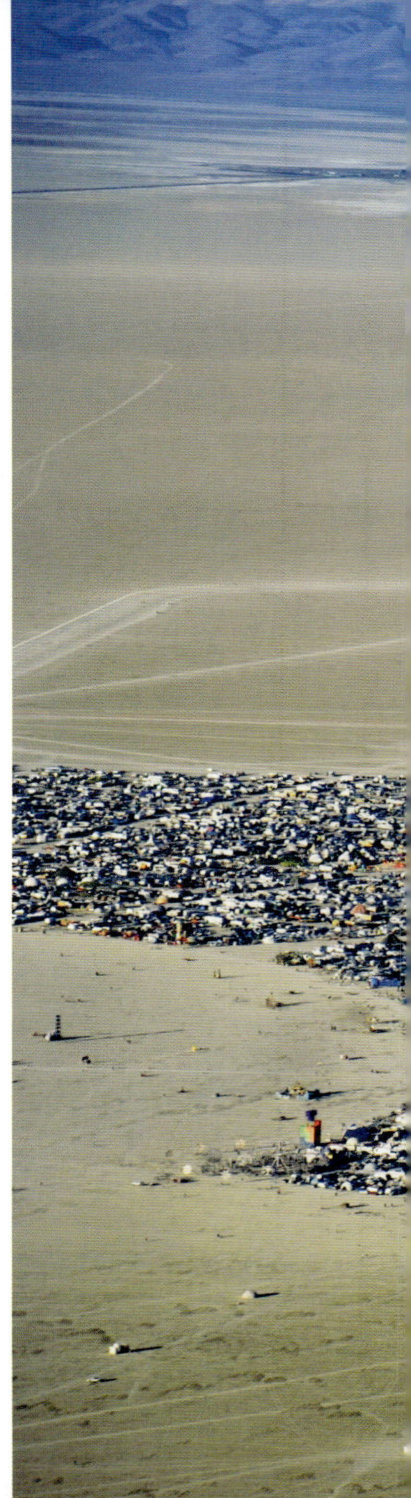

To accommodate the anticipated increase in population, two concentric streets (L and M) were added to the back of the city mid-event

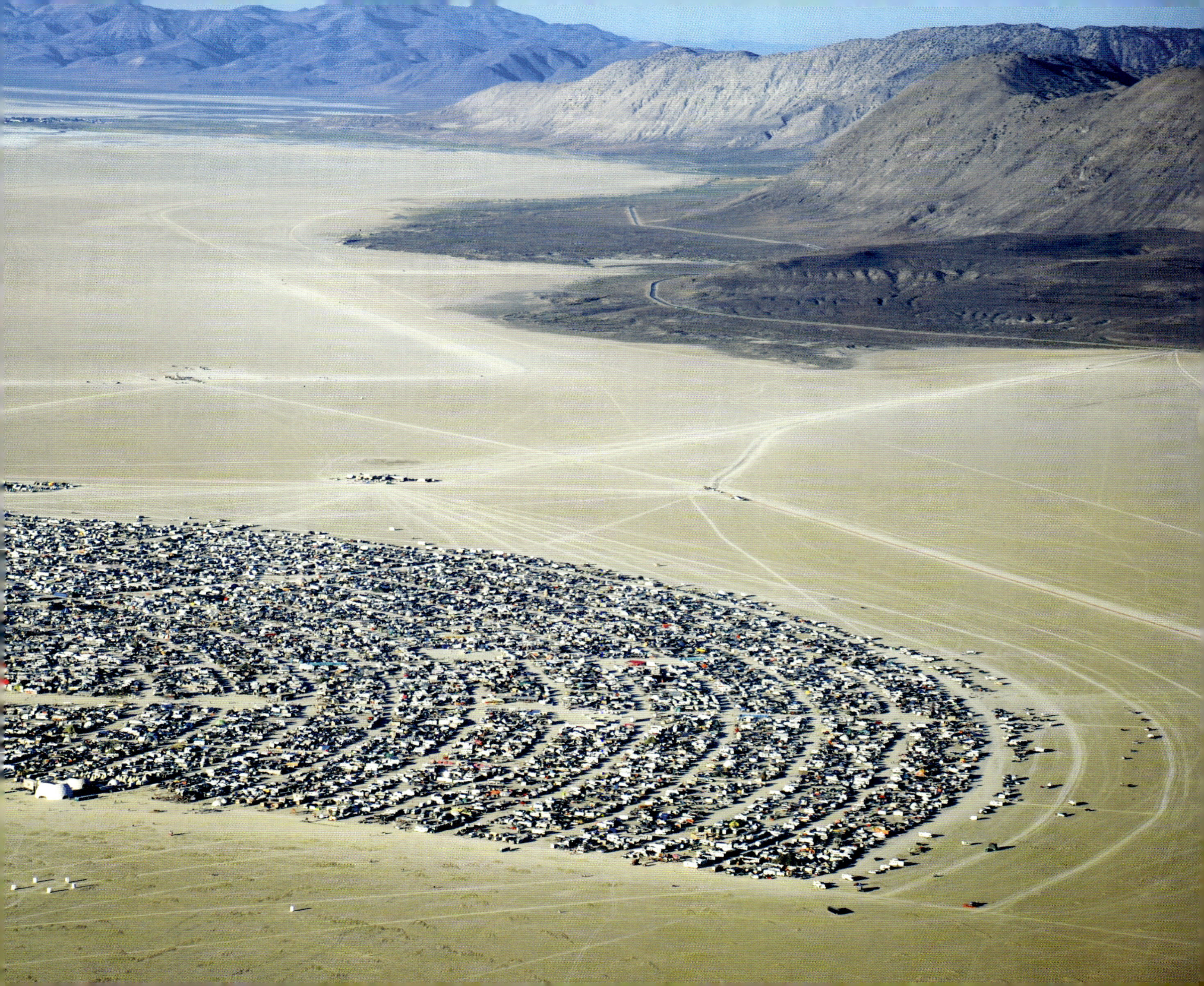

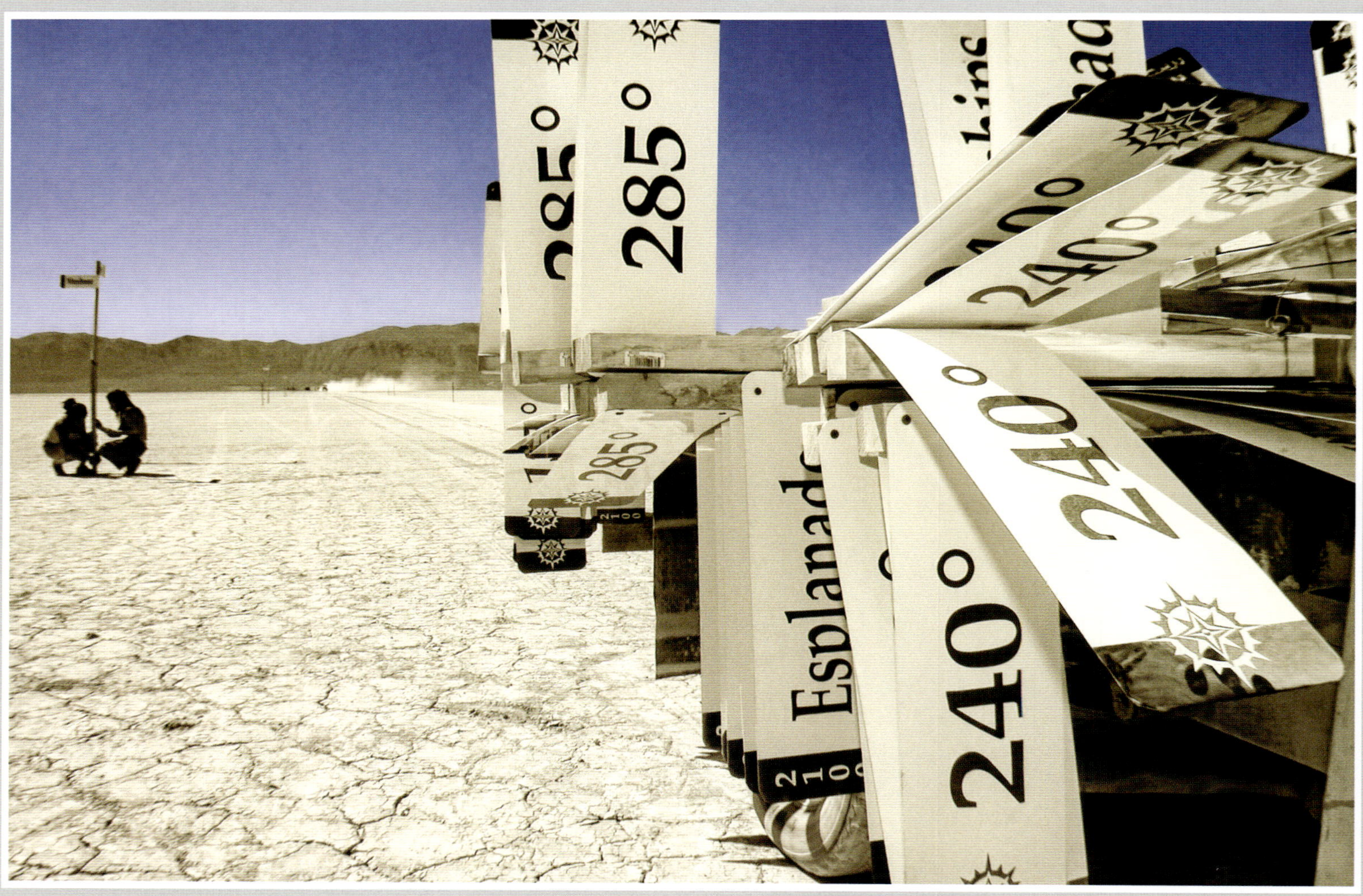

Street sign installation, photo (2002) by Craig Morse

Cuckoo Clock

Tony "Coyote" Perez-Banuet, Superintendent, Black Rock City

Standing atop the hay bale platform that was soon to be the site of the Man, I looked out to the city we just built. It was Black Rock City, 1998. Camps were starting to pepper a grand boulevard called The Esplanade that was the leading edge of the new city grid. Black Rock City had begun its urban sprawl. The new grid formed a circular amphitheater, pivoting around a center point and resembling a grand pinwheel that swept over a mile wide and several blocks deep. It was a giant blue heron stretching its neck to the Man and circling its wings around us, as if ready to take the entire township into open flight, a beautiful fortress of security opening out to the playa in a trumpet of freedom.

When does a nomadic group of hardy campers become a city? When do they decide to take up residence and start pushing in stakes? What defines a city in the first place? Is it the framework of streets and pathways or is it – as Mr. Stuart Mangrum suggests – when the plumbing arrives?

"Plumbing, coffee, and a newspaper are what define civilization," was his learned conclusion. Harley K. Dubois might say it's when the people bond into a cooperative community. She would know, as she was the founder that swirled this township into a living being like the pinwheel of imagination it has become.

So, when did Burning Man first start to define itself as a city? It was Stuart Mangrum and his good friend, Chris Radcliff who made the sign that called Burning Man "Black Rock City" back in 1995. Then it was no more than a loose circle, opening to the deep playa in an expanding "V" shape that acted like the bell of a horn and seemed to stretch to infinity. It was still a strong gathering space, a communal circle around a center camp, with the Man standing out in the "V" horn. The Man was not the center of the circle until 1998, when the city plan was a giant blue heron. In fact, the city plan wasn't a clock until 1999 when the theme of that year's event was "Wheel of Time," and it has remained a clock up to the present day, except for 2002, when the event theme was "Floating World," and the city was a compass. The participants voted it out organically by replacing the compass signs with clock signs, though. The clock idea was such a damn good one that it simply prevailed.

So, why did this gathering in the desert form its first city grid of numbered blocks and streets in the first place? It was when Burning Man, the runaway teenager of San Francisco, grew up and had to come of age. It was when Burning Man formed itself into a company. It was when Burning Man had to take a hard look at the word, "liability," and become responsible for the safety of its citizens.

I was a fly on the wall of despair on the morning after the fires of Burning Man 1996. The city had lost control and flew too close to the sun, melting its wings in an adolescent display of hubris. The organizers of the event carried the weight of the transgressions of a foolish rabble that streaked the night, and Larry Harvey sat at its center. He spoke the words that changed Burning Man forever. He spoke the words that turned the key on the tumbler of society. He spoke the words that fueled the forge of a city.

"The city's gotten too big for us to do nothing," he said. "Either we don't do this again, or we drastically change our approach. We'd have to turn this into a real city that protects its citizens. We've created a dangerous environment that has become injurious. We must find a way to confine it, so we can become responsible for one another."

The city needed to become a design that works to cap the explosions and turn them into an engine that drives a community.

We build the world's largest clock face. (It has never formally been entered into the *Guinness Book of World Records*, but I welcome any challengers.) It's the city grid of Black Rock City. It's where the citizens of our city reside for the season it is there. It is the home of Burning Man.

It takes a week of building in the August triple-digit heat of the open playa of the Black Rock Desert (a dry pluvial lake bed in northwest Nevada that covers about 1,000 square miles). It takes a seasoned desert-ready crew of about 25, camping under the stars. It takes low tech analog systems that won't fail in a corrosive, anti-electronic world. It takes keen eyes that can hold focus in the glassy warp of a sorcerer's world of mirage and illusion. And it takes doing most of the work in the vivid break of dawn and last lights of dusk.

Is it truly the world's largest clock face? It matters little to me. It's our world's largest clock face, with the diameter of the city grid exceeding two miles. For us, it's the art that we bring to the event. It's the largest art piece of all — the city itself.

There were some among us who didn't quite embrace the notion that this city was a work of art. Even in our open-minded world of permission, we have our fair share of critics. But, the artisans who build this city know better. Every year, toward the end of summer, the city places its thumb print on the whiteboard playa that can be seen from the heavens.

It's always the sound of a chopping board and the smell of sizzling bacon that wake me in the pre-dawn during the survey of Black Rock City. It's our camp cook who's up before the rest of us, even though he was passing the whiskey into the night with the champions of the survey team. His name is Citizen, and he holds the cooking hearth of the camp, which in turn holds the heart of the team. I can hear him just on the other side of the walls of our octagon-shaped survey station that also acts as the open sky shelter where we sleep. We are the survey crew that lays out the city grid of Black Rock City, and our work begins just as the morning glow behind the eastern mountains sheds enough light to outline a crewmember in the field through the Leica lens of my theodolite.

"In range at 8:30 and 'J'," says the crew member over the two-way radio.

"Three inches left," I return over the radio, while peering through the crosshairs of the scope. The crew member moves the marking stick three inches left.

"Mark! 8:30 and 'J'," I say when the stick is in the crosshair.

"Marking, 8:30 and 'J'."

I had a visiting observer once ask me, "Did you just adjust the marker by three inches even though it's about a mile away?"

"Well, yes," I answer. "This is the foundation of the city. If we don't pinpoint this part, it gets pretty wiggly down the line. Next thing you know, we've taken a 30-foot bite out of someone's camp."

This is only experience talking. For most every system we have in place, an ample mistake put it there.

People routinely tell me how lucky I am to be the one who gets to build our now-famous clock city. They also routinely ask me where I went to school to learn how to survey. I tell them what I've been telling them for years: "I'm a sax player."

Truth is, I got the job of surveying Black Rock City by doing the job. It wasn't luck. It was hard work and willingness to fail. We were all city kids outside of our comfort zones when we first started scratching out roads on the cracked clay of nowhere. In fact, in our first attempt at organized blocks, in 1997 on the Hualapai Flat, we resorted to straight lines, due

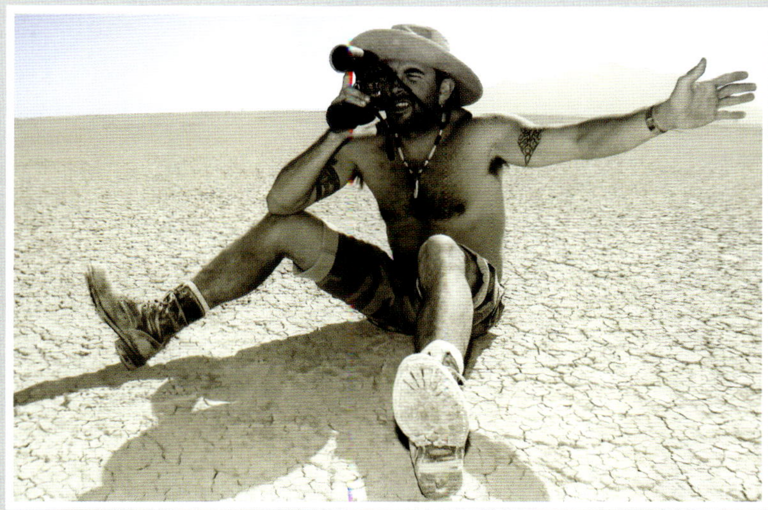

Tony "Coyote" hand signaling survey. Photo (2002) by Craig Morse

to the Sheriff's confusion, safety concerns, and our blatant admission of not knowing how to draw circles in the desert.

But we came back in '98 with some know-how and a beautiful plan designed by Rod Garrett, and the grand sweep of the giant blue heron was etched into our history.

It would be a city planner's dream to get a clean slate to re-build on every year, and this one comes with a full log of clumsy attempts at what did and didn't work in previous seasons, as we fumbled around with this new disappearing city. Black Rock City is like a giant Etch-A-Sketch that's forever erased and improved upon—a disposable prototype that can be made better every season. Blocks were expanded as the population grew. "V" shaped entrances to strategic radial streets lancing the arc acted as vacuums, pulling the energy of the front of the city into the outer blocks. Destination plazas and theme camps were intentionally placed to the back of the city to draw the spirit of the community inward. And every year, Rod Garrett would hand me down a revised clock plan that ticked even better than the last year's.

"You're asking me to build a bigger city in less time," I would say.

"You can do it," he would reply. "You're the Coyote!"

Whenever he called me the Coyote, I knew that he had upped the game once again.

Over the years, we've been able to work our methods into a pretty slick system. To the casual watcher, we're a well-oiled machine. What they don't know is that our systems were born of failures. They're kiln baked products of struggle, as we continued to re-invent the potter's wheel, and there were a lot of broken pots. We tried to measure the width of blocks with ropes that would stretch, causing major whumps in the circles. We tried to drag 200-foot chains behind trucks, and the chains would twist, tangle, and sometimes snap back at us in a dangerous whiplash. There was delay after delay and countless do-overs. For a number of seasons, we would assemble a line of about 30 crew members and trudge along in a massive pinwheel, pulling these 200-foot chains in what became "The Great Chain Drag." It was extremely labor intensive, but accurate enough to dial in a solid era of beautiful clocks. Rod and Will were always very pleased with the aerial shots. The first transit scope I used was a turn-of-the-century railroad transit, (now sitting under glass as it travels with a museum exhibit). It had clouded lenses, and it would hitch and jam in the perpetual dust, skewing the measurements again and again. I'm amazed the cities got built at all. We had yet to get any reliable radio communication, so all the measuring was done with flag semaphore and hand signals. One season about halfway through the survey build, a co-worker of mine had been checking the work with one of the only GPS units that were out there. He came to me with the bad news that the outside greeter station on the edge of the city was about 800 feet from where it was supposed to be! Back then, we would orient the city with a compass, and I had checked it countless times when putting in the cardinal points of the grid. The fact remained that the entire city was twisted off its mark by a full three degrees, putting everything out of whack by hundreds of feet in many cases. It was a simple oversight that would not be repeated. I learned never again to wear a metal watch when hand-holding a compass. The Man burned anyway.

Now we use laser range finders (an outdoorsman's tool) to achieve our distances, and I have an instrument called a theodolite in the Octagon station that replaced the various transits and scopes I had enlisted. It is able to pinpoint the coordinates to a razor's accuracy. The only time we use the GPS systems is to replace the compass in orienting the city. We find the Man — we find south — another Black Rock City is born.

It was the steady quest for safety that first forged our city blocks in 1997. The final design was a result of pressures from the local sheriff in conflict with Rod Garrett, who was trying to keep a sculptor's approach to the sterile world of safety. It was the start of an endless dance of politics between Black Rock City and law enforcement. In 1999, we suffered a county line border dispute with the Pershing County sheriff. It was also the first year of the Gold Spike ceremony, which was performed three times that year as the city kept getting shoved back and forth over the border like an unwanted plate of Brussels sprouts. The Pershing County sheriff despised Burning Man and used the power of his office to ban the event from his county.

"There will be no public nudity in my county!" was his battle cry.

But when Will Roger and I visited the proposed site just over the line into Washoe County, we found ourselves standing in a mud bog.

"We can't have the event here," said Will. "Let's move the Gold Spike north a mile. I'll deal with any fallout with the Sheriff." Will Roger was a bold man.

Will wanted to make the building of BRC ceremonial, so he fashioned the Gold Spike ceremony after the transcontinental railroad Gold Spike. We invited a *Reno Gazette* news reporter, the county commissioner, several of the local town folks, and anyone who cared to join. There was a lot of hand shaking, photo ops, some champagne, and congratulations all around. After this, Will gave me the honor of setting the spike –an honor that I enjoy to this day. The Pershing County sheriff did not attend. It was the first year that the city was a clock, and I was in charge of the survey crew for a second season. We were just five people. By the third day of work, we had figured out how to build this thing and had most of the blocks outlined and in place. We were enjoying the artisan's buzz of the build.

That afternoon, our one-and-only radio crackled to life with a message from Will.

"Coyote, stop building the city and bring your crew into Gerlach for a meeting."

The Bureau of Land Management, (the federal law enforcement agency that policed this land) had stepped in on behalf of the angry sheriff and informed us that we were in violation of our usage permit and needed to move the event back into Washoe county where it was originally planned. Will was furious. We were furious. We were natural-born rebels and didn't see no borders in the desert. But the sheriff sure did. He knew exactly where his county line was. We had to go back out there and pull up all the flags and move the Gold Spike into the mud bog. The second Gold Spike ceremony was just the five of us standing around it in a dejected circle. We set the spike and got to work. BUT – the silver lining was that we got to re-do our work right away and fix all the mistakes we had made. A solid system was forming, and it was the foundation of the methods that we still use today.

So, what about the third time we set the Gold Spike? In the

days that followed, Will wrote a letter to the BLM explaining our plight and the potential for the 10,000 expected people to be stranded in a mud bog. Three days later, the BLM weighed the situation against the possibility of having to rescue 10,000 people with the National Guard, and they went over the head of our angry sheriff. We were allowed to go back to our original spot. So, the third time the Gold Spike got set was by me, and me alone, banging it into the playa in a wash of curses. The third time building that damn clock, we had it dialed!

Building the city anew every year has honed our systems into a fine machine. I can speak for my crew in saying that it is truly our favorite week of the year. It's a special honor to carve out the beautiful image of a two-mile-wide clock, a wondrous work of art that seats 75,000. The crew becomes a human pinwheel as it clicks out block after block. And then in the evenings, we camp in the open magic of the Black Rock Desert, as the stars fill us with the stories of our times. We sit in the lap of prestige — truly the first Black Rock City citizens of the season.

As a young man, my dream was to receive a Grammy. That dream was set on a shelf on the day that I stood atop a hay bale platform and looked out upon the sweeping beauty of the giant blue heron city that we had just built and called home. Every year, I await Will Roger's aerial photographs to see the fruits of our labor. I no longer wish for a Grammy. Instead, I receive my annual award of being the honored one who gets to build the largest art-city-cuckoo-clock in the world. Black Rock City.

The Gold Spike ceremony was created in honor of the transcontinental railroad Golden Spike of 1869

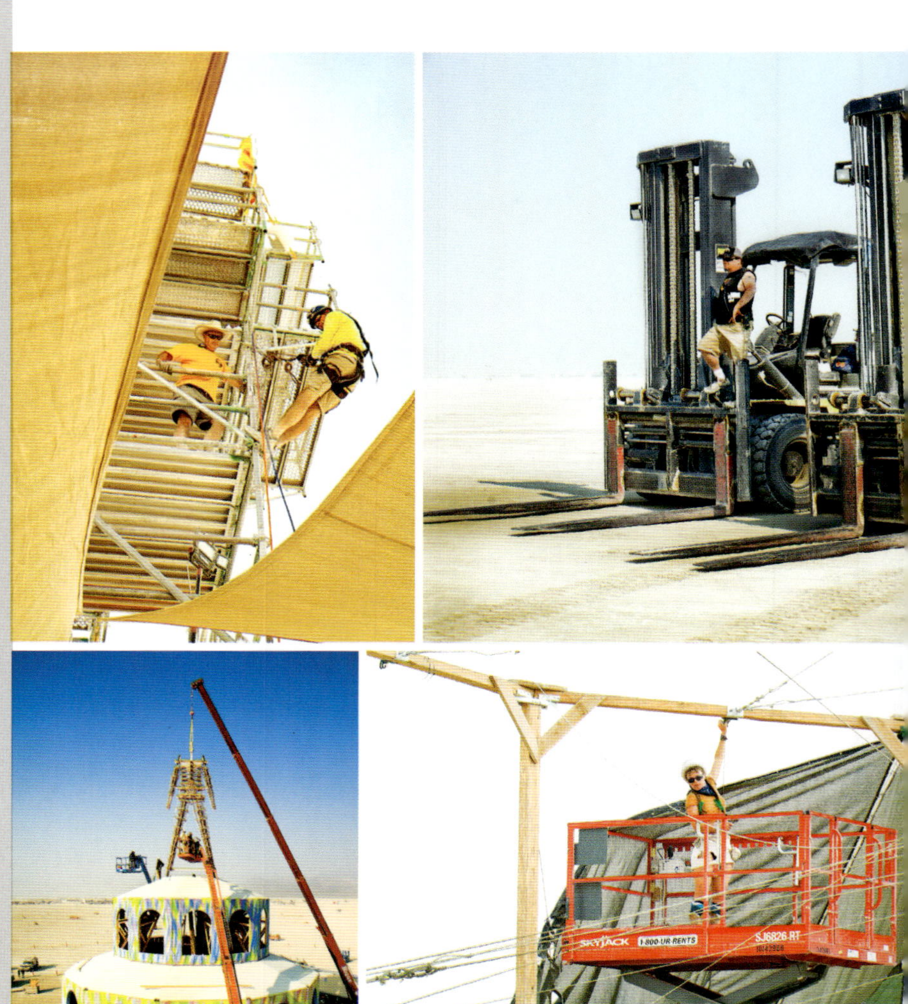

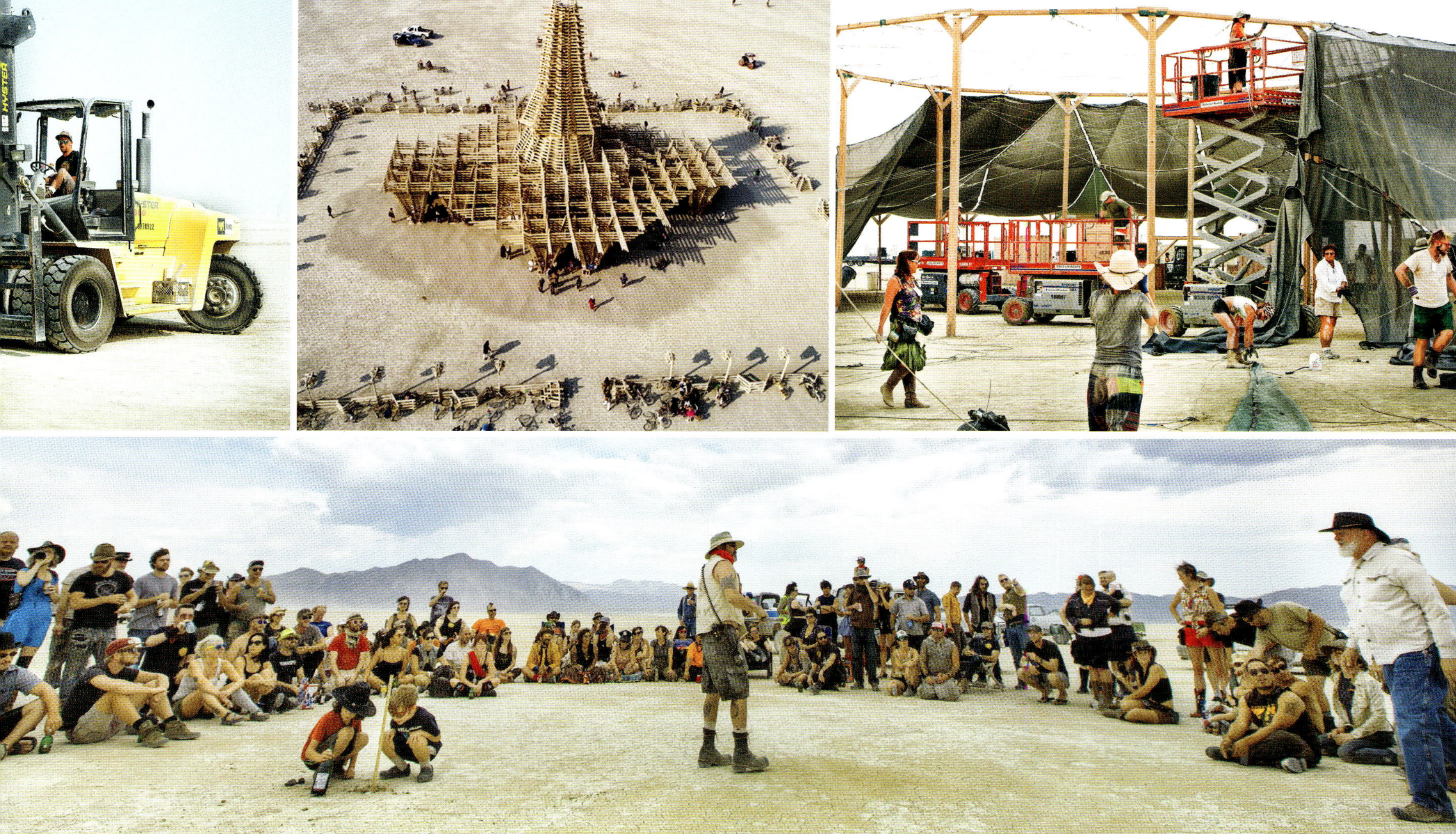

Top, L-R: *Emergency Services Department Fire Training, photo (2017) by Lisa Ferguson; Heavy Equipment and Transportation (HEAT), photo (2012) by Garry Geer; "The Temple" by Steven Brummond, Marisha Farnsworth and Mark Sinclair, drone photo (2017) by Will Roger; Cafe Crew workers building Center Camp Cafe, photo (2004) by Garry Geer*
Bottom, L-R: *Raising The Man atop the Pavilion, photo (2012) by Garry Geer; Cafe Crew workers building Center Camp Cafe, photo (2004) by Garry Geer; Tony "Coyote" and his twin sons Atticus and Colby at Gold Spike ceremony, photo (2012) by John Curley*

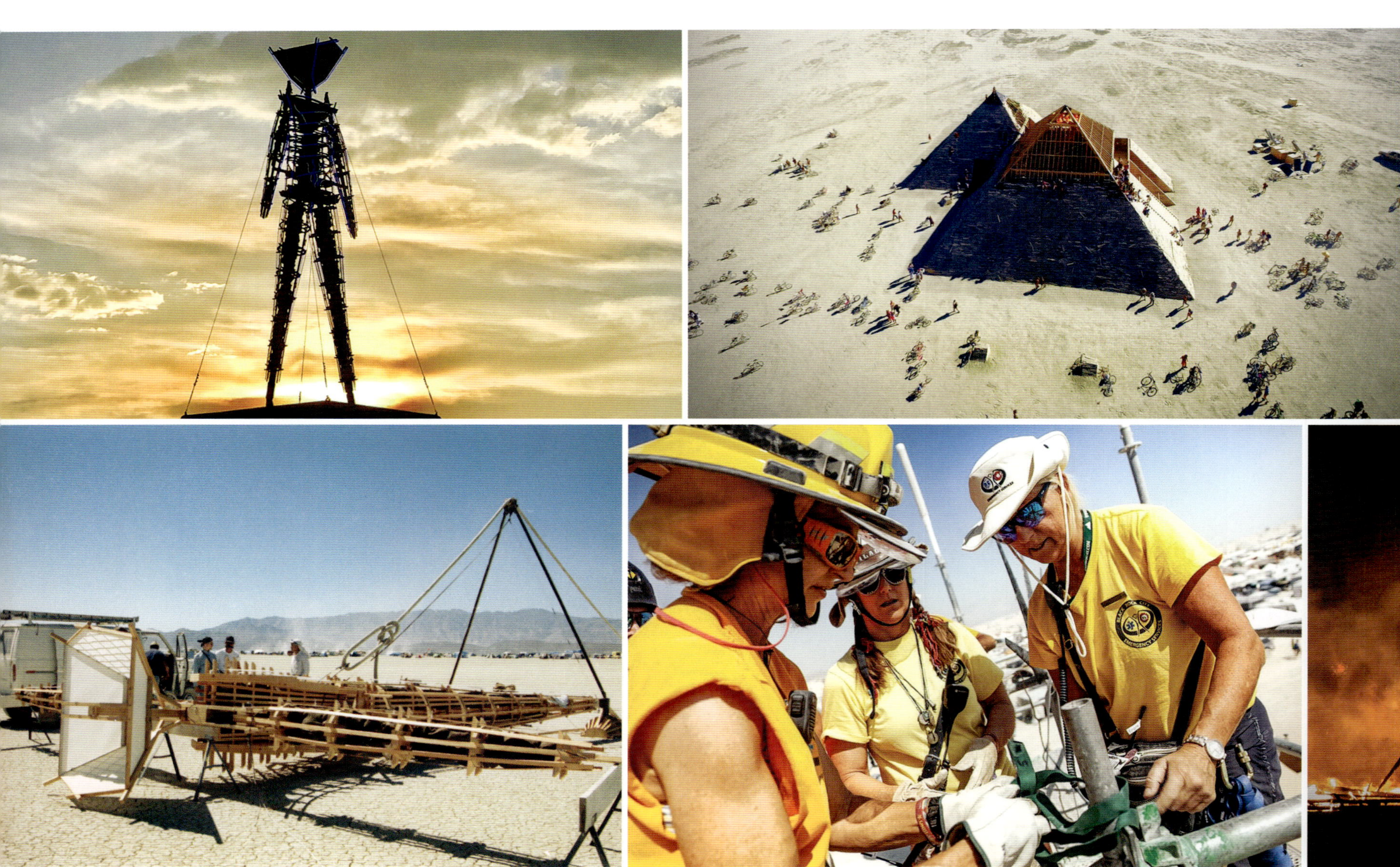

Top, L-R: *The Man, photo (2018) by Will Roger; "Catacomb of Veils" by Dan Sullivan and Catacomb Crew, drone photo (2016) by Will Roger; Crimson Rose and Will Roger camping on Black Rock Desert, drone photo (2018) by Will Roger; "Cowboy Carl" Brucker, a legend of the Trash Fence, and Will Roger, photo (2012) by Garry Geer*
Bottom, L-R: *Raising the Man, photo (1995) by J. Absinthia Vermut and Nevada Museum of Art, Center for Art + Environment Archive Collections; Emergency Services Department Fire Training, photo (2017) by Lisa Ferguson; "Temple Galaxia" burn, photo (2018) by Eleanor Pregor; Will Roger at First Camp, photo (2012) by Garry Geer; Greeter Pods, photo (2011) by Dan Adams*

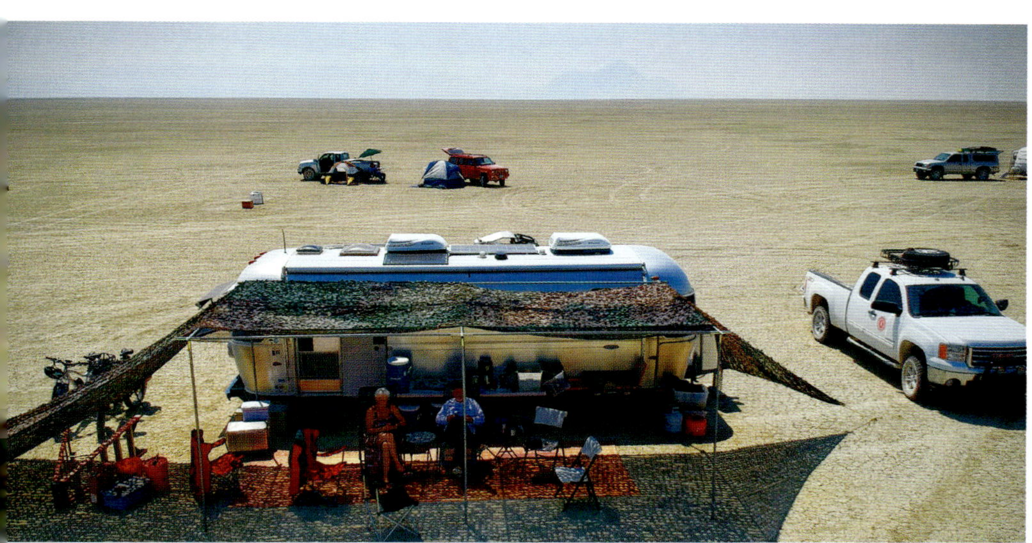
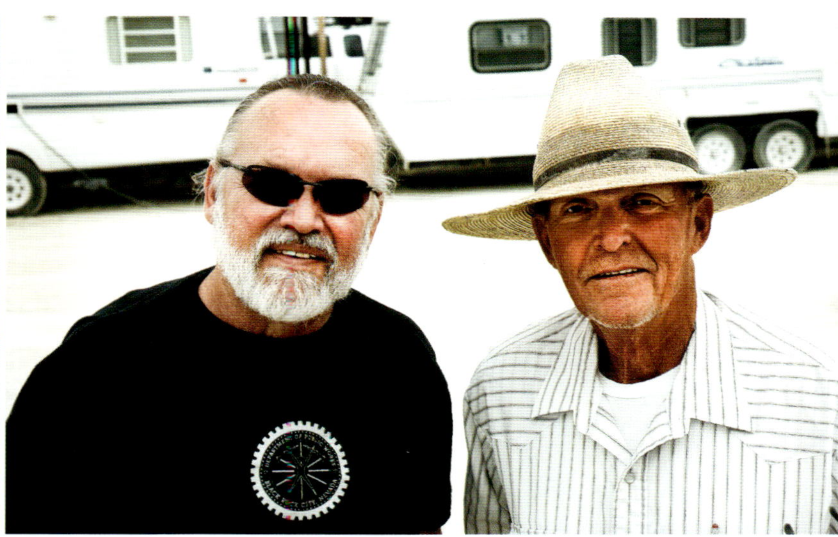
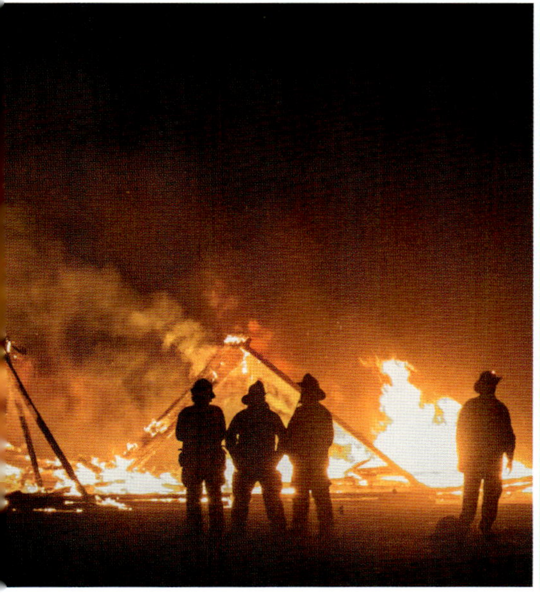
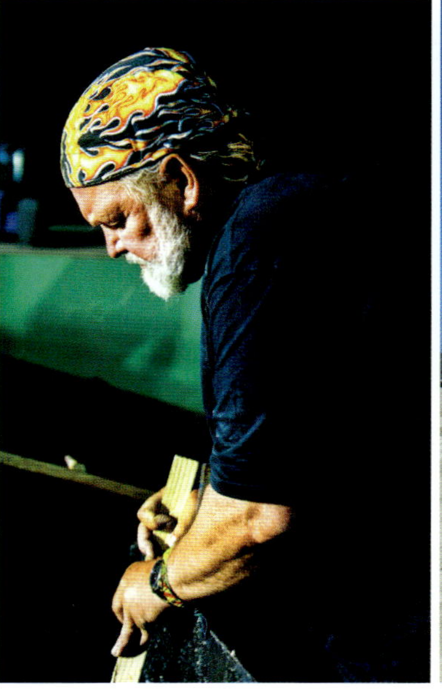
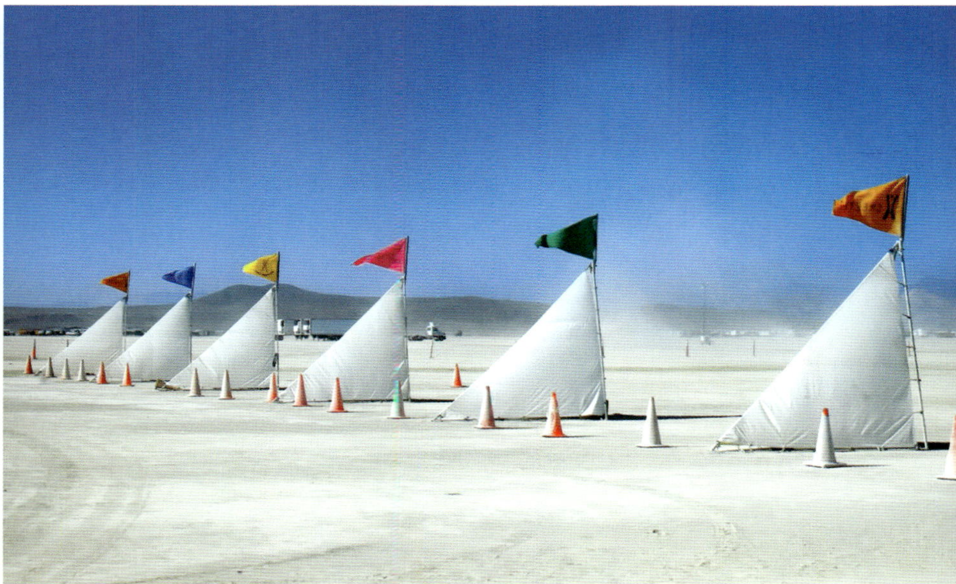

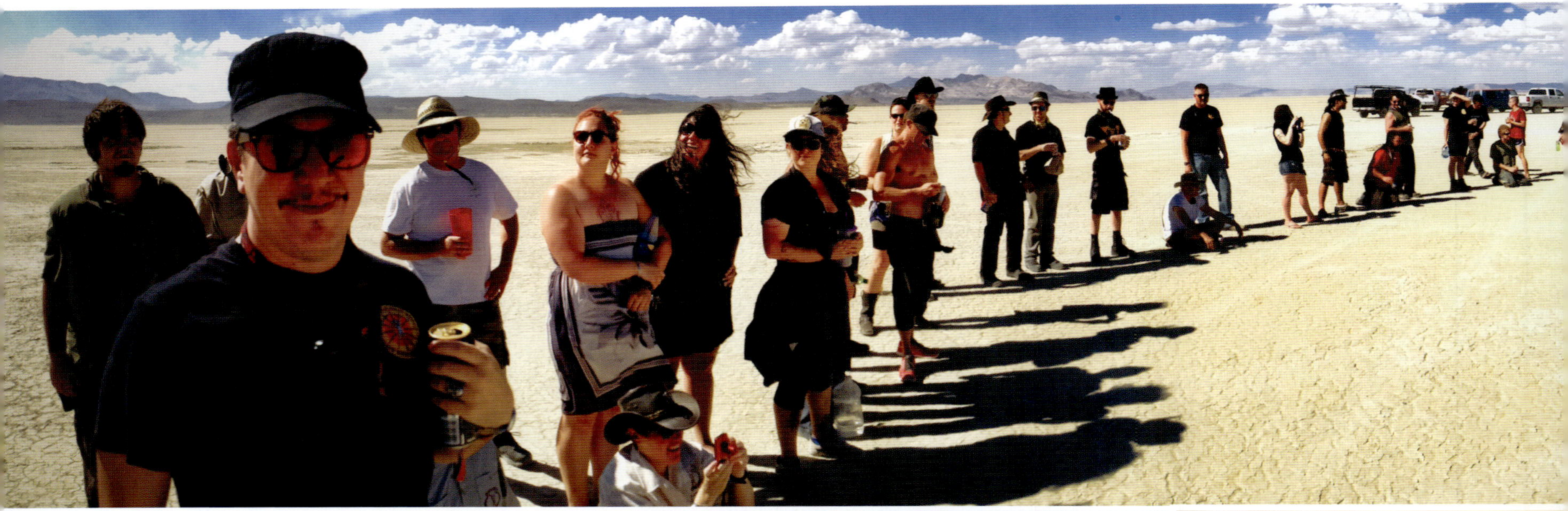

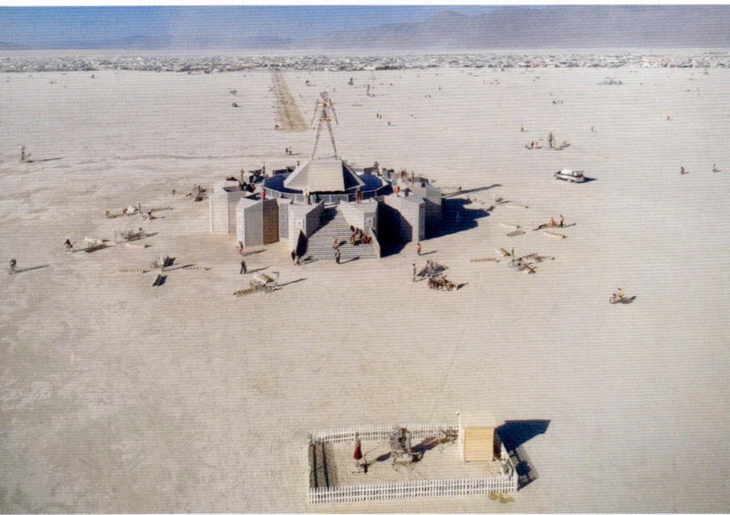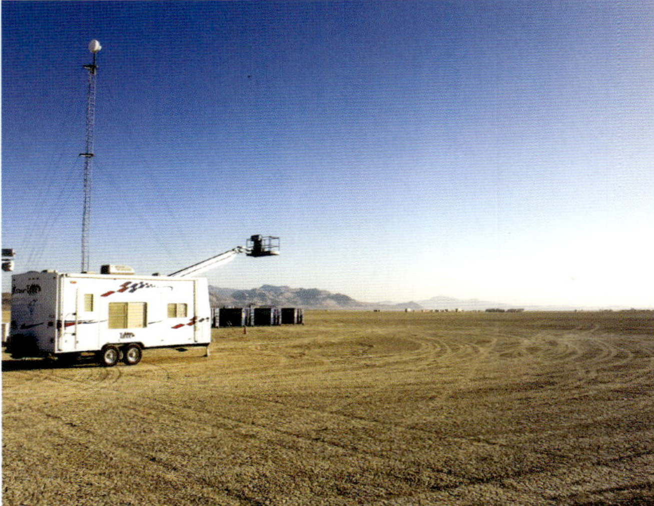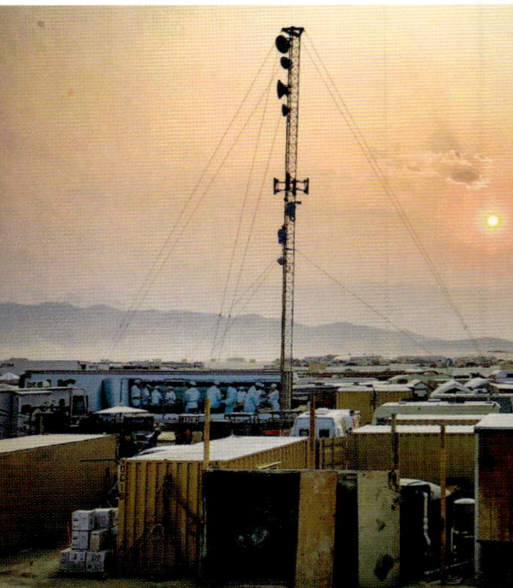

Top: *Gold Spike ceremony, drone photo (2013) by Will Roger*
Bottom: *The Man atop the Pavilion, photo (2018) by Will Roger; Temporary radio tower, photo (2011) by Brent Chapman; Temporary radio tower, photo (2018) by Will Roger; HEAT equipment, photo (2012) by Garry Geer; Camping on the Black Rock Desert, drone photo (2018) by Will Roger*

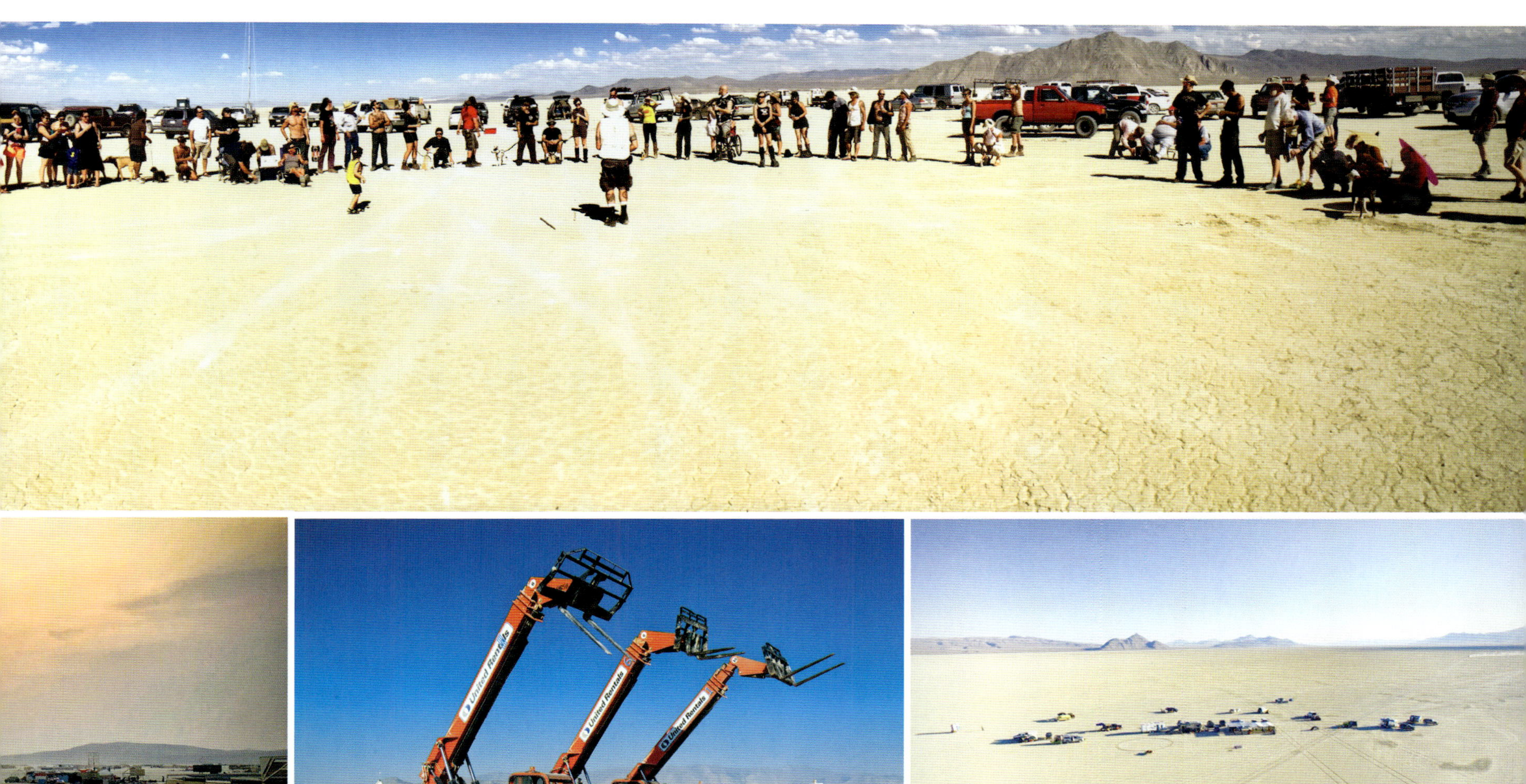

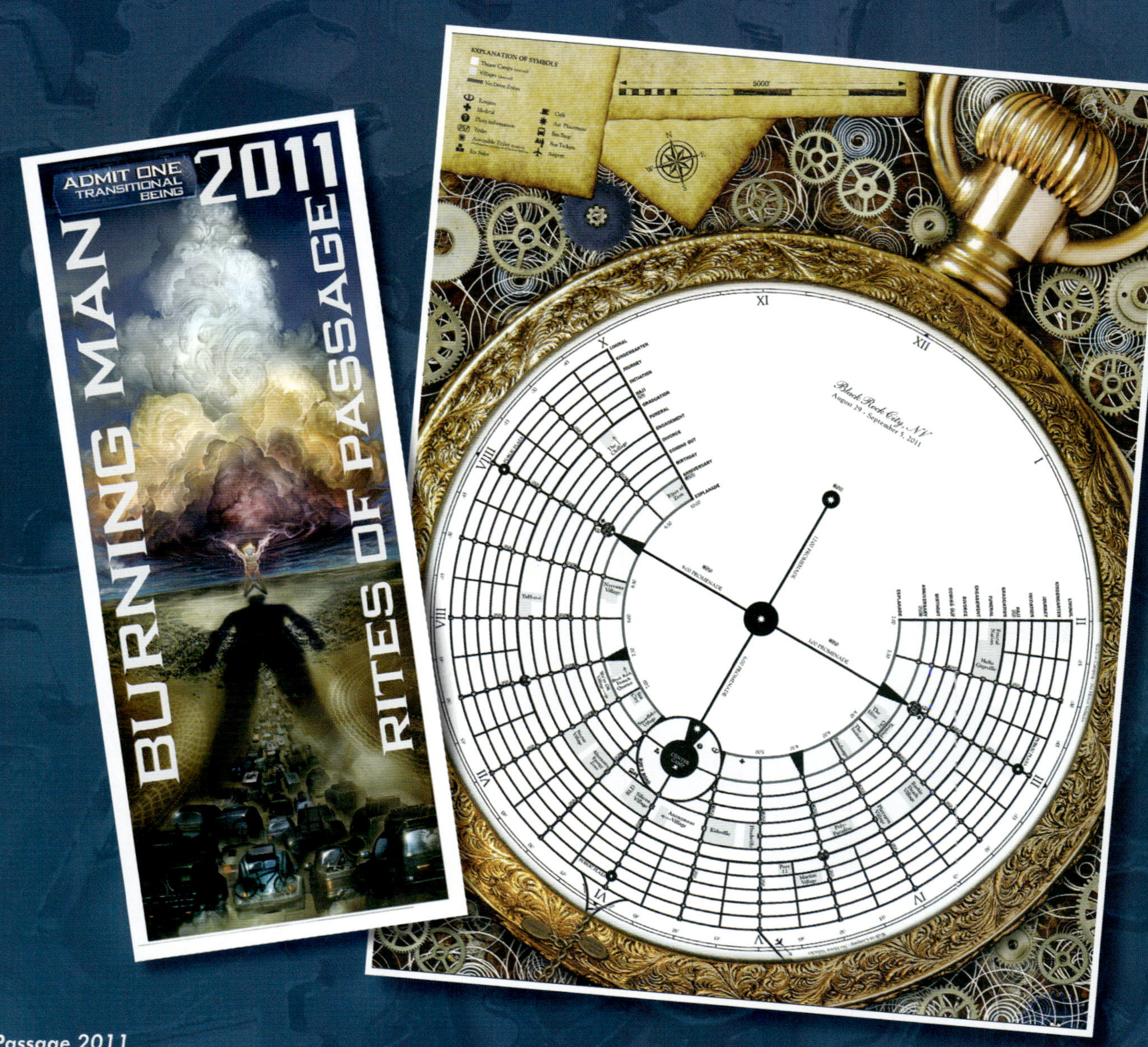

Rites of Passage 2011
Ticket design by Android Jones
City map design by Lisa Hoffman

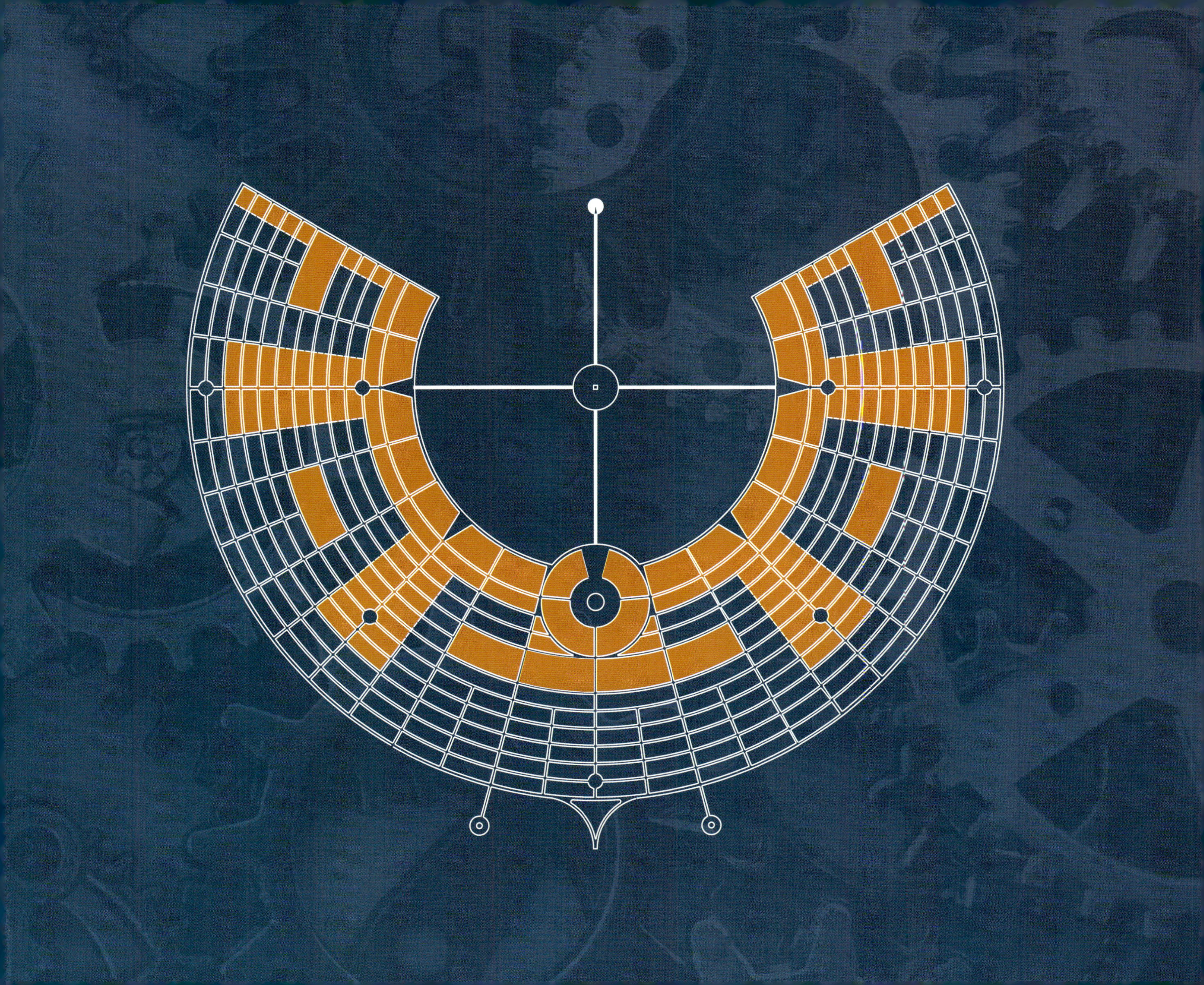

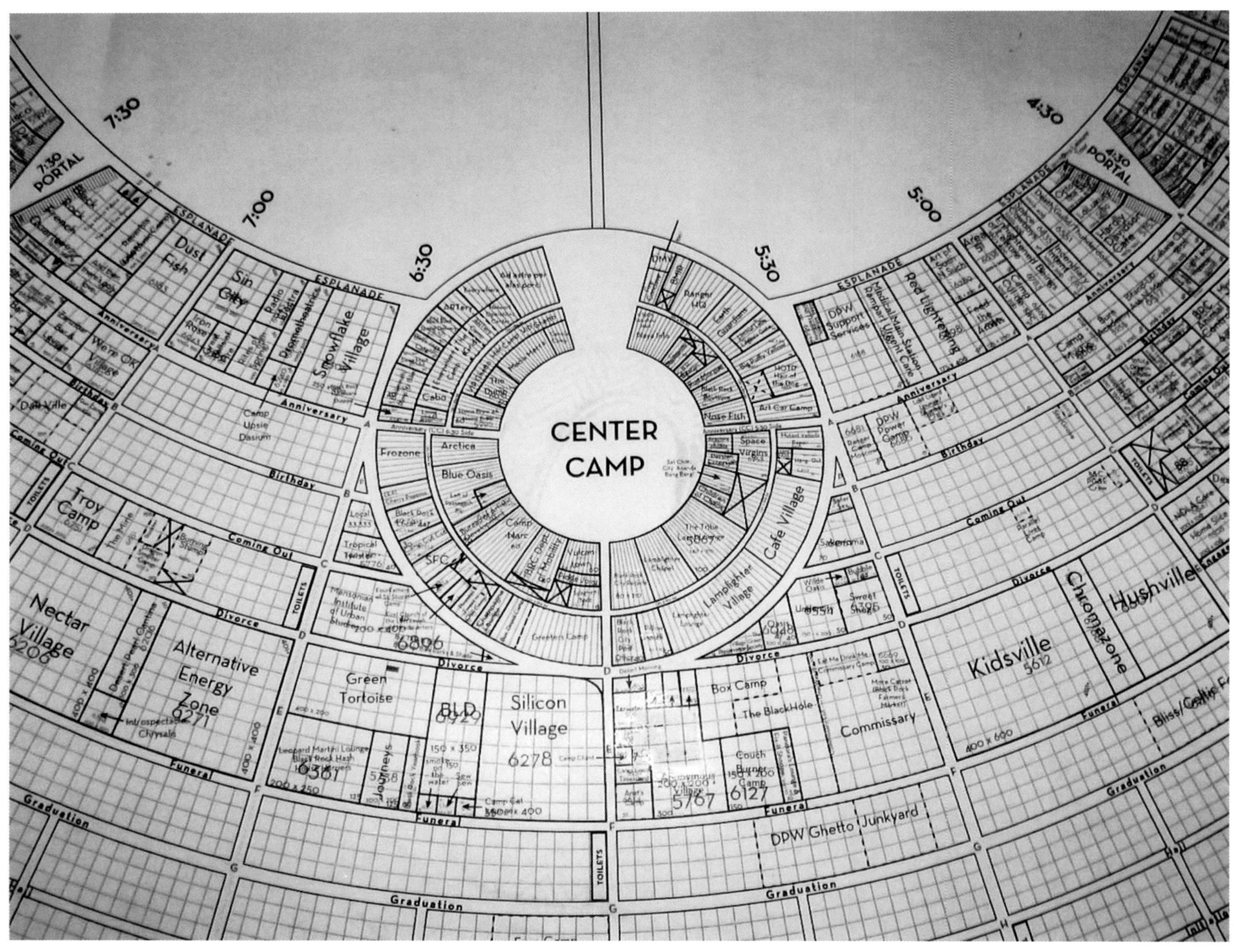

7:30
7:00
6:30
CENTER CAMP
5:30
5:00
4:30
7:30 PORTAL
4:30 PORTAL
ESPLANADE
ESPLANADE
Anniversary
Birthday
Coming Out
Divorce
Funeral
Graduation
Dust Fish
Sin City
Snowflake Village
Troy Camp
Nectar Village
Alternative Energy Zone
Green Tortoise
Silicon Village
Box Camp
The Black Hole
Commissary
Kidsville
Hushville
Chromazone
DPW Ghetto Junkyard
Blue Oasis
Arctica
Frozone
Cafe Village
Red Lightning
DPW Support Services
TOILETS

Above: Camp placements (2011)
Right: Population 53,963

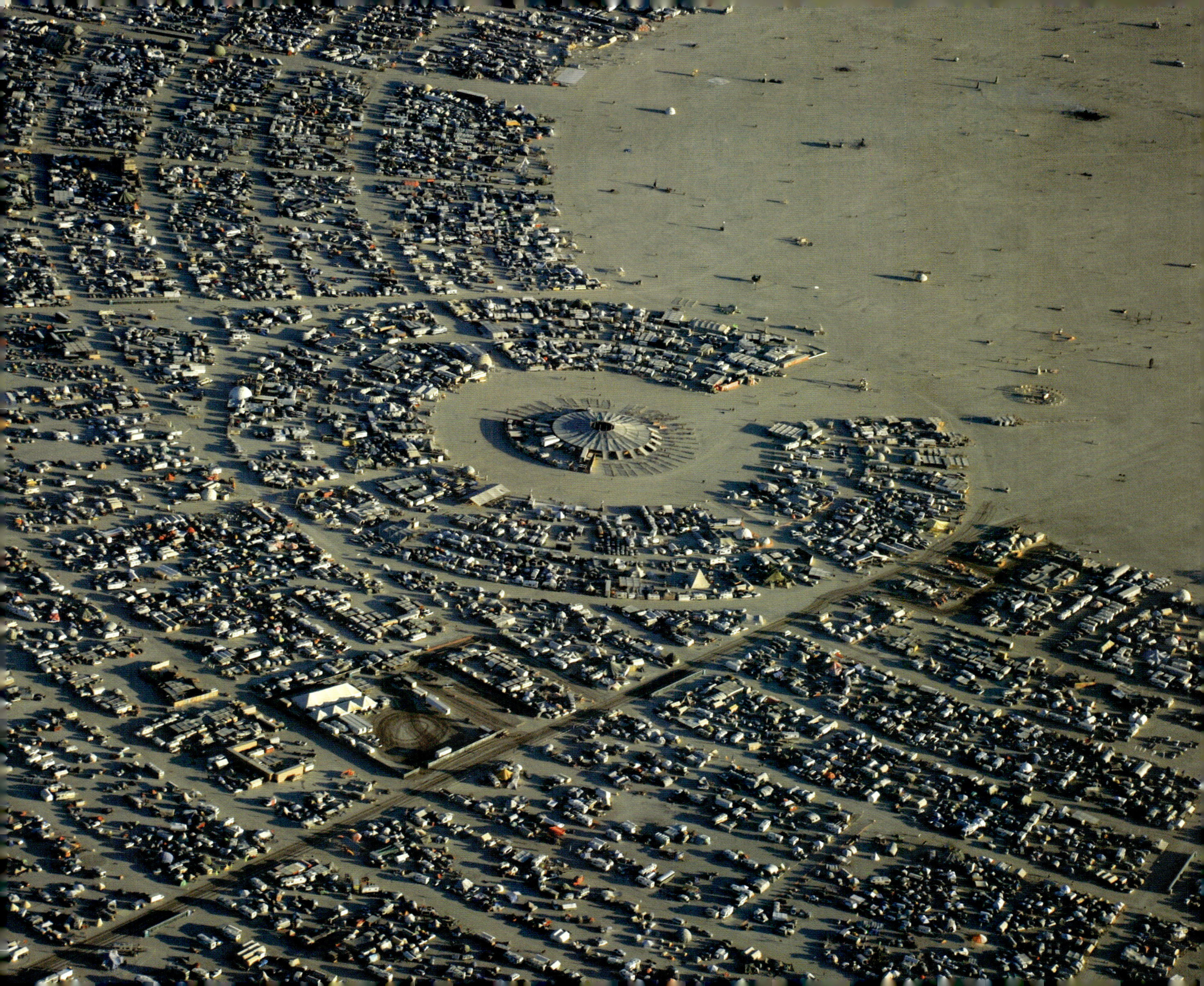

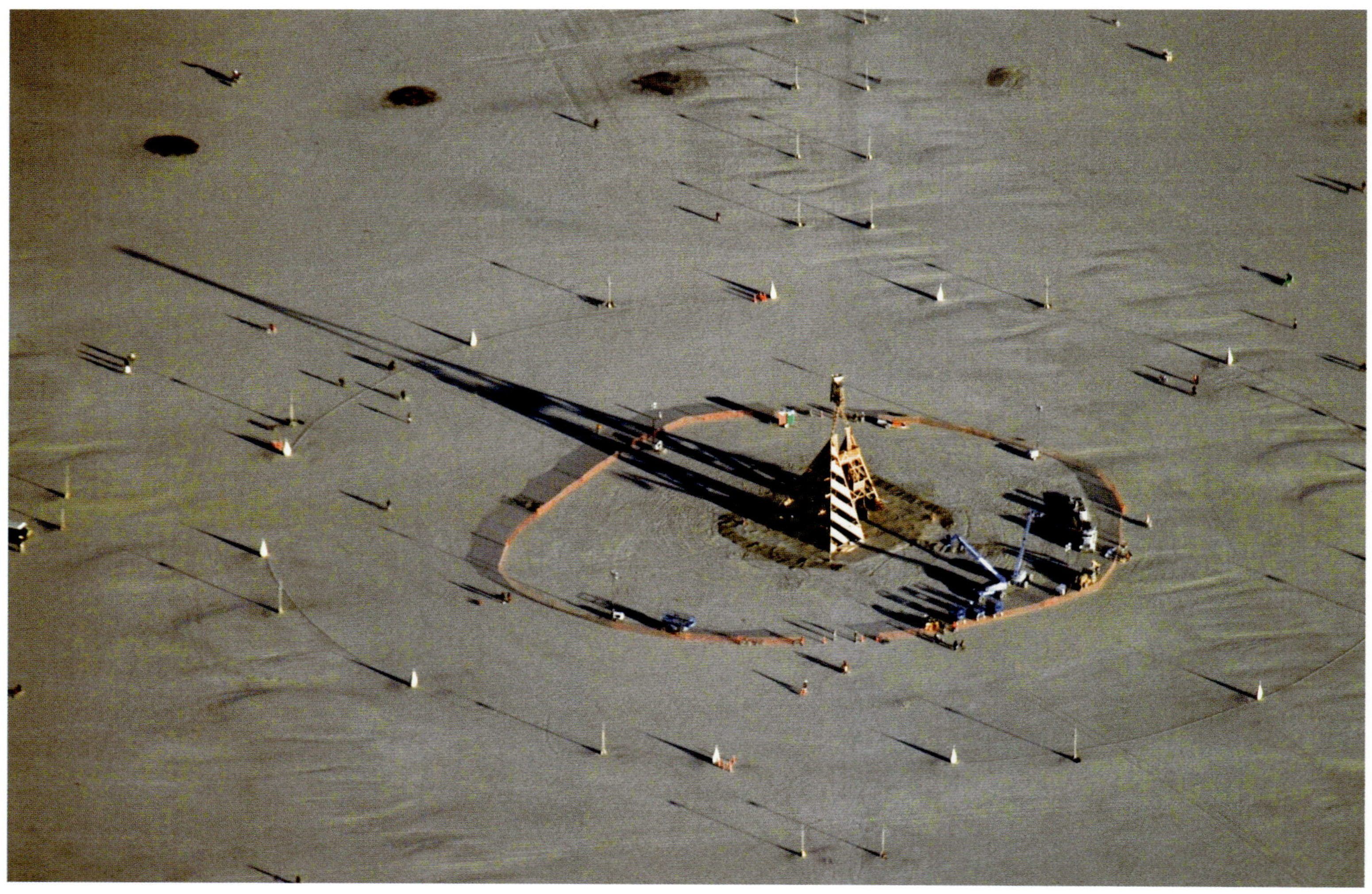

124

Above: *Preparing the Man and Pavilion for the burn*
Right: *This year's pentagonal perimeter fence expanded to 9.2 miles*

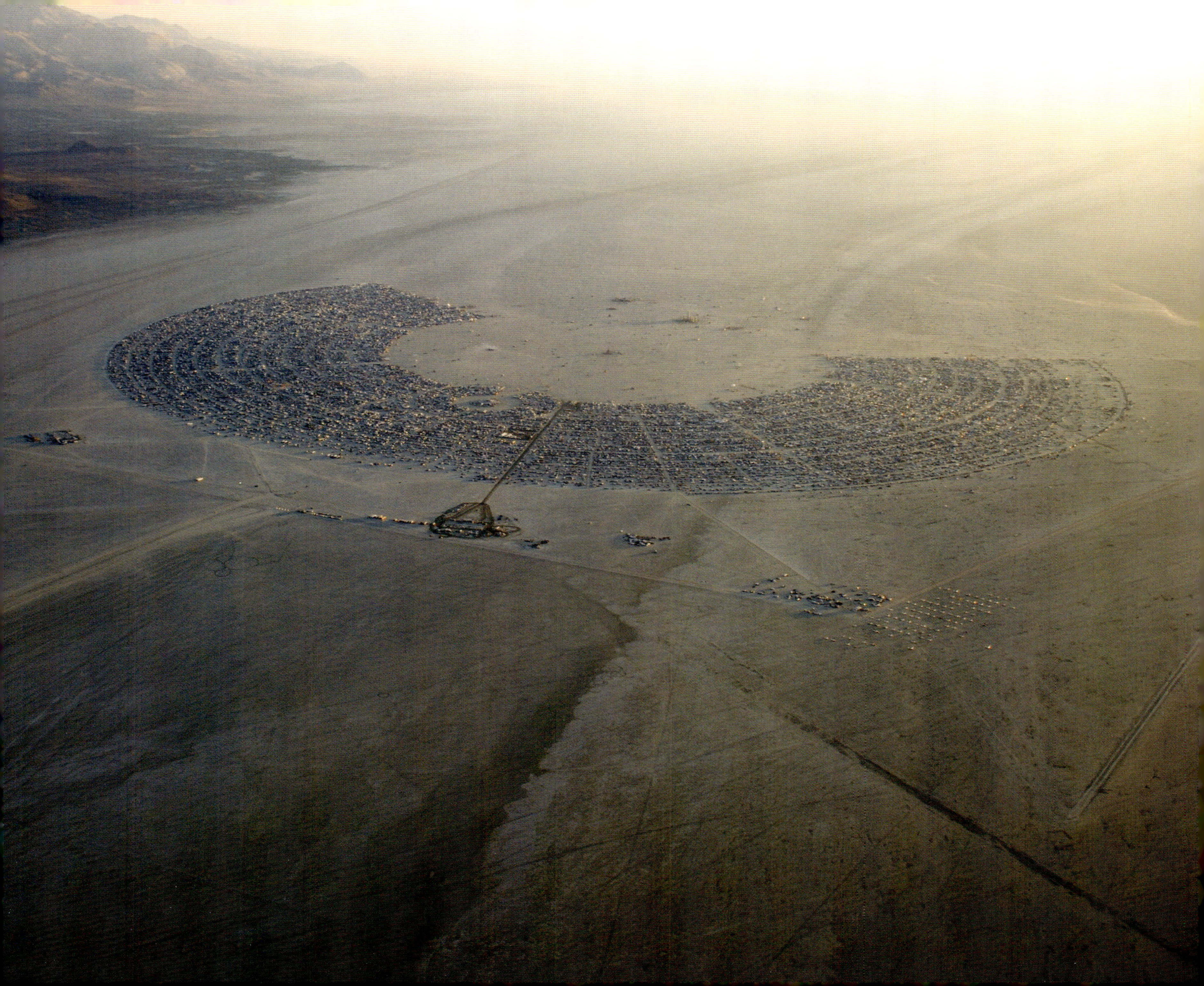

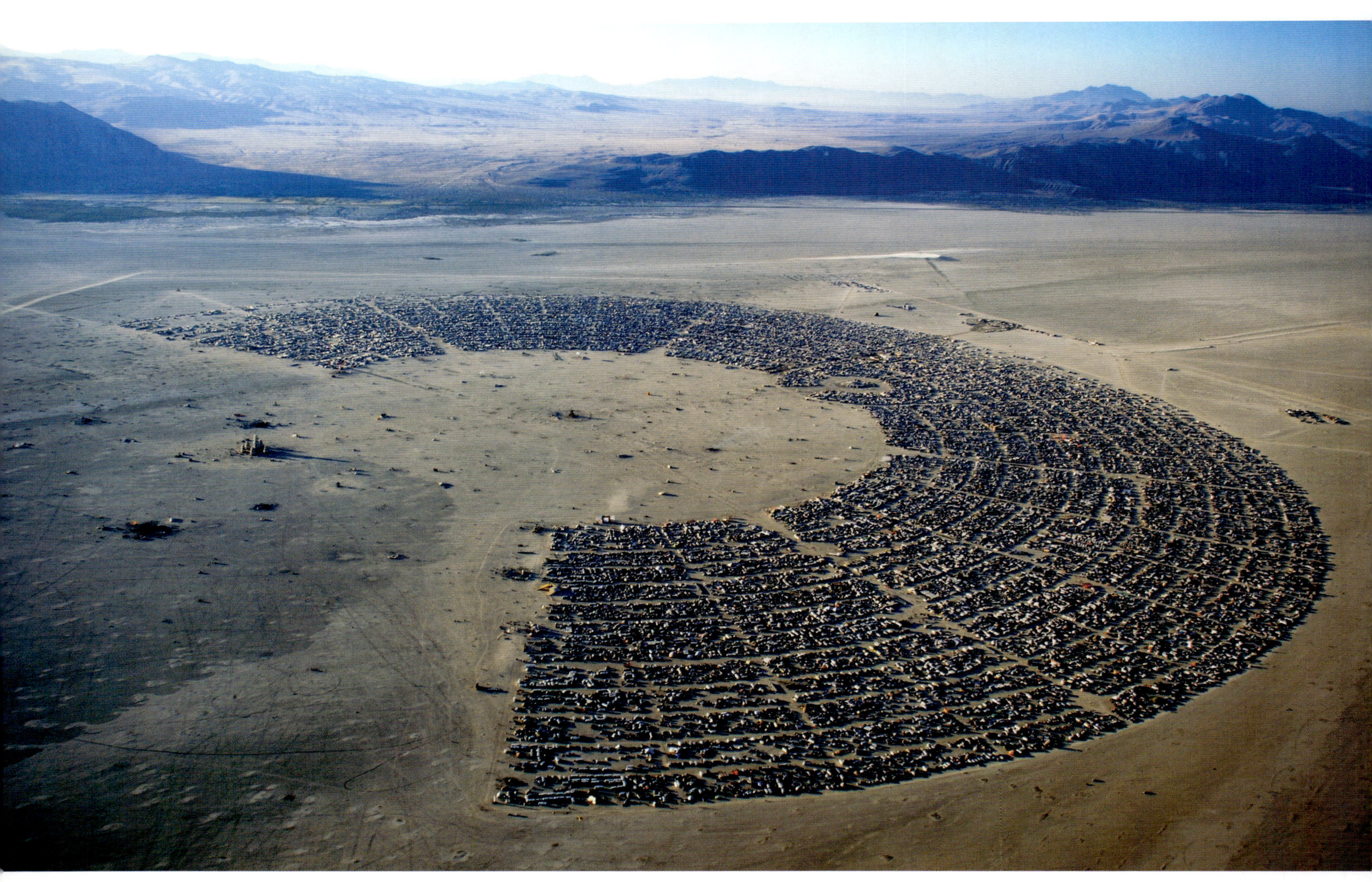

Above: *Over 920 theme camps placed*
Right: *"The Temple of Transition" by International Arts Megacrew and helmed by Chris Hankins and Ian Beaverstock. "Abraxas" dragon mutant vehicle (lower left)*

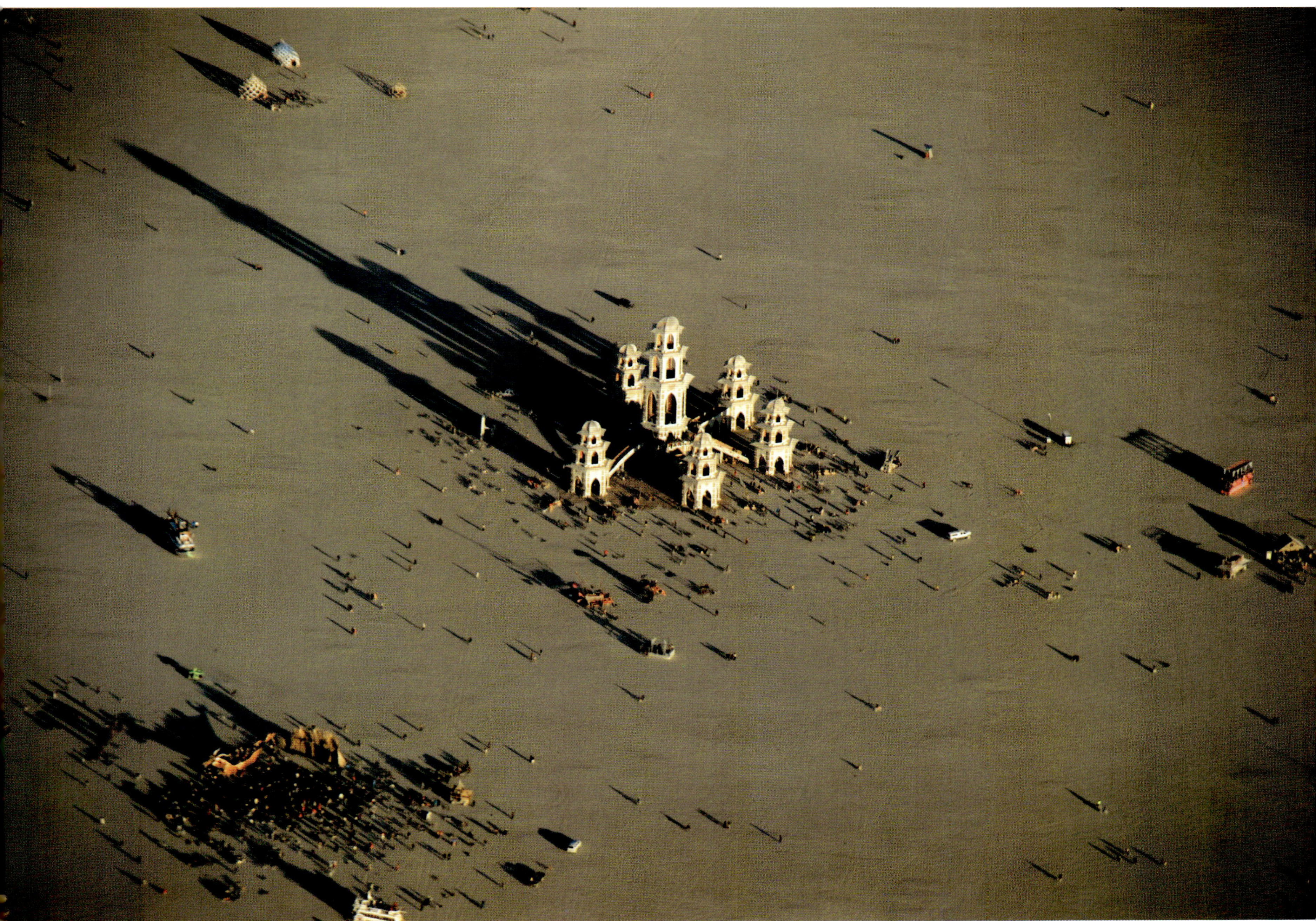

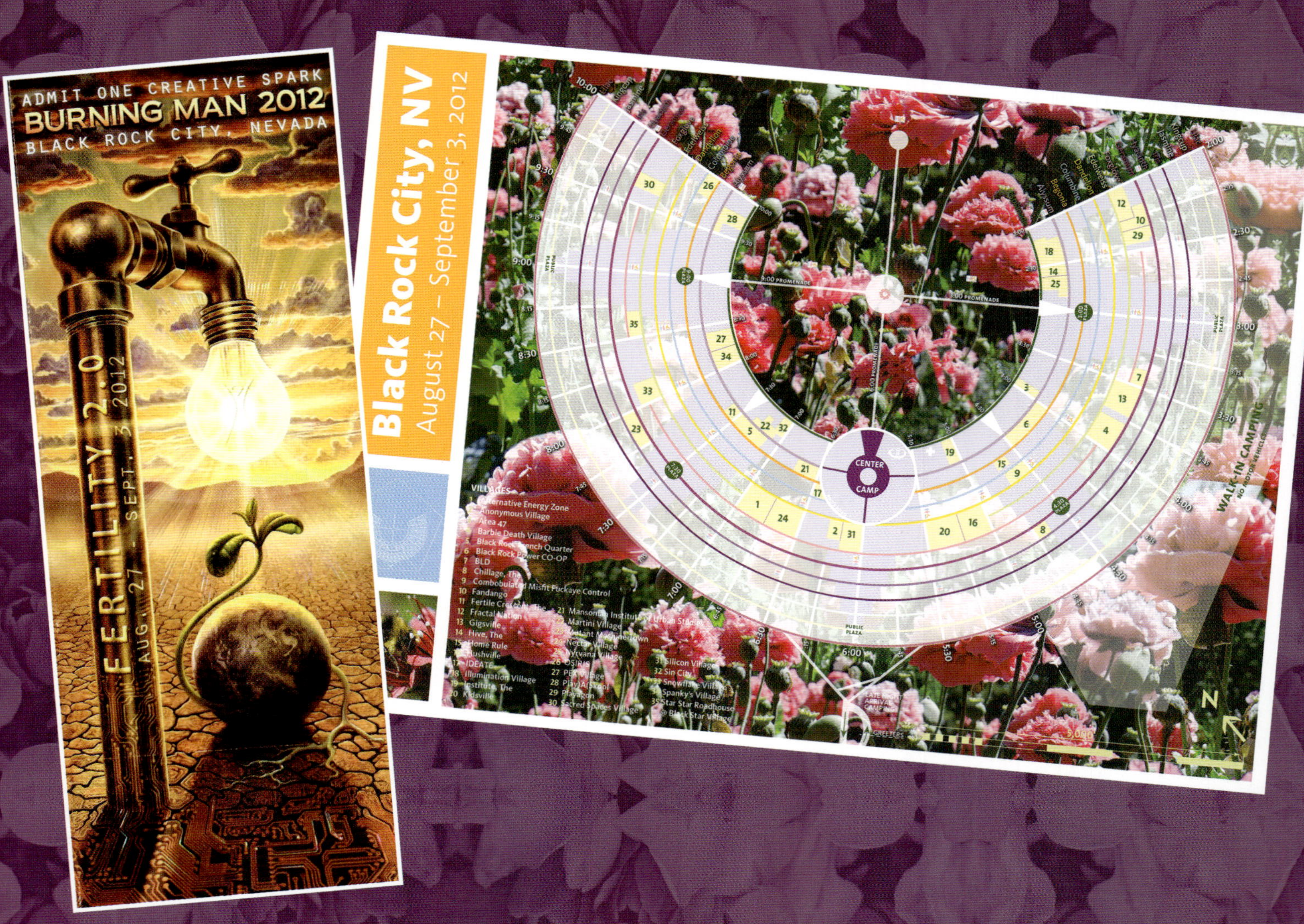

Fertility 2.0 2012
Ticket design by Cory and Catska Ench
City map design by Lisa Hoffman

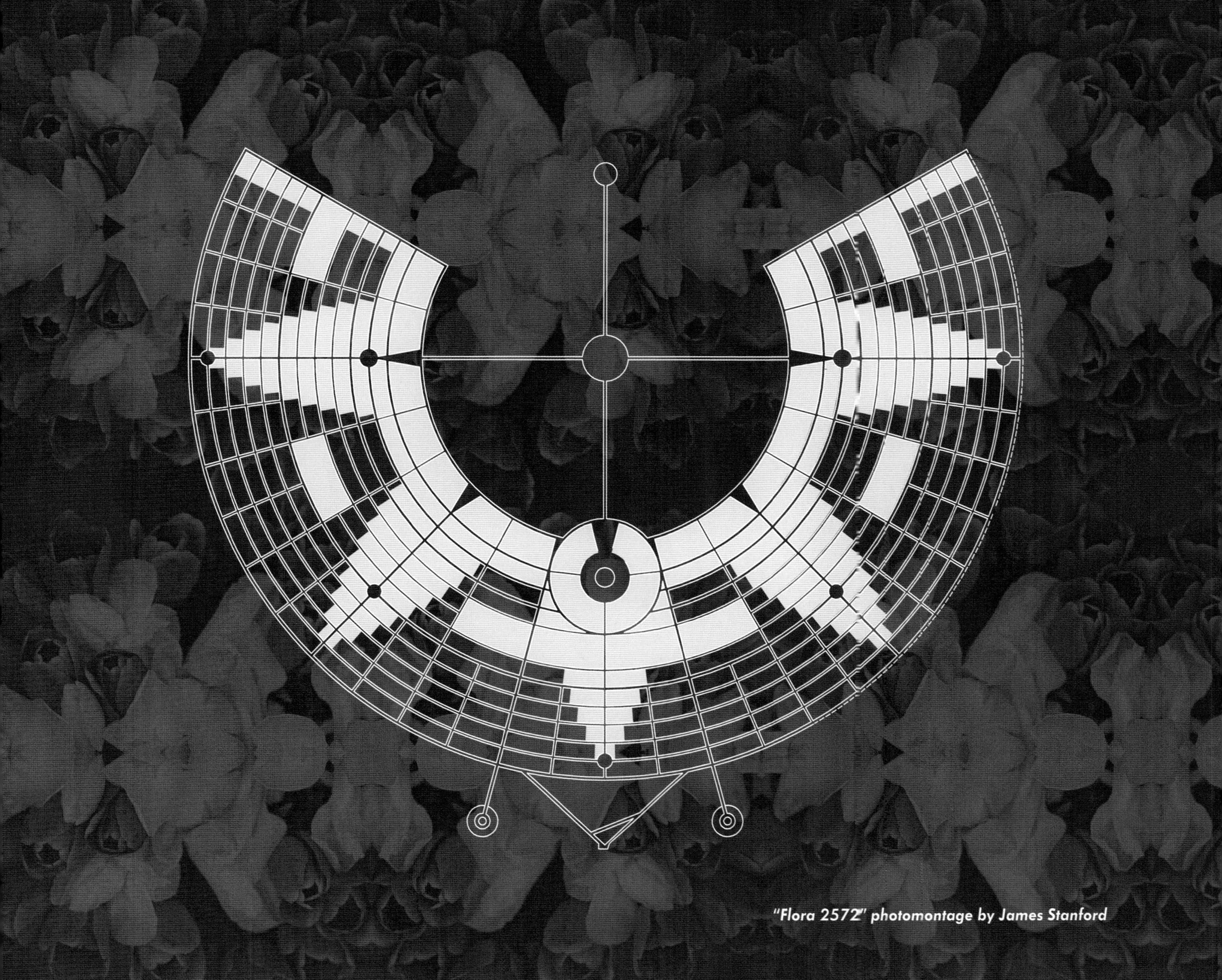

"Flora 2572" photomontage by James Stanford

Right: Black Rock City at 10,000 feet in the morning light. The lack of winter rain produced intense dust storms
Population 56,149

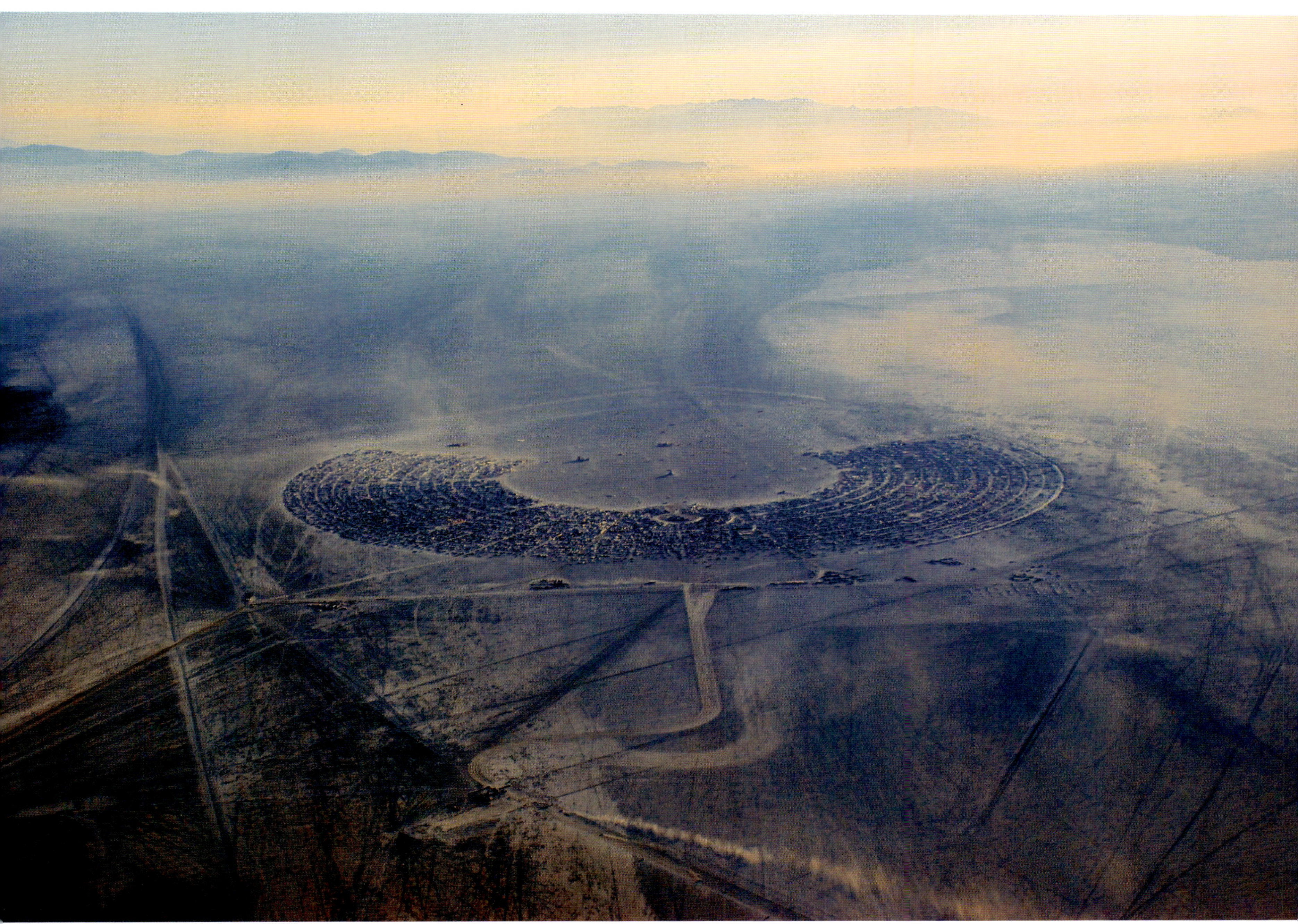

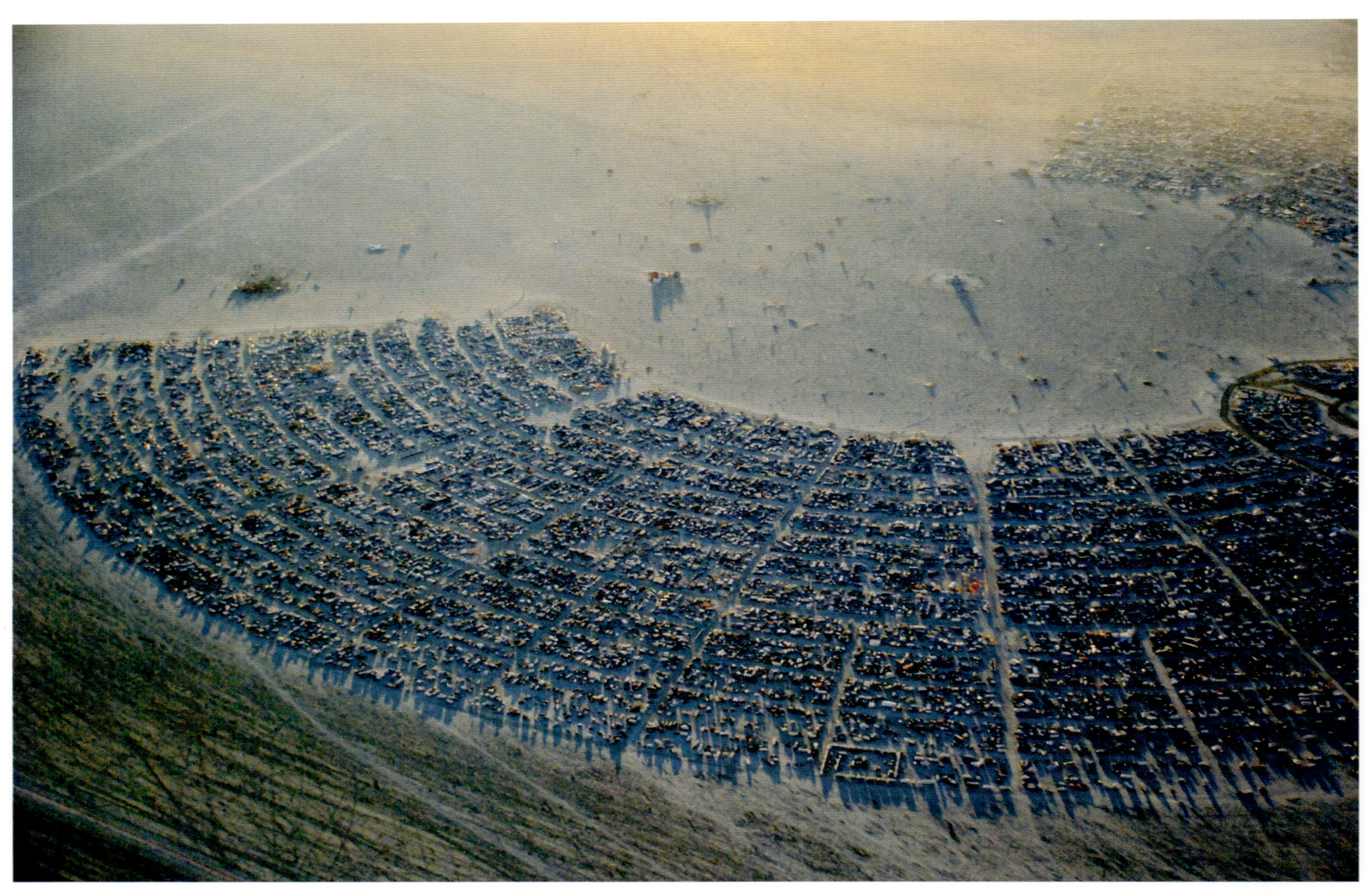

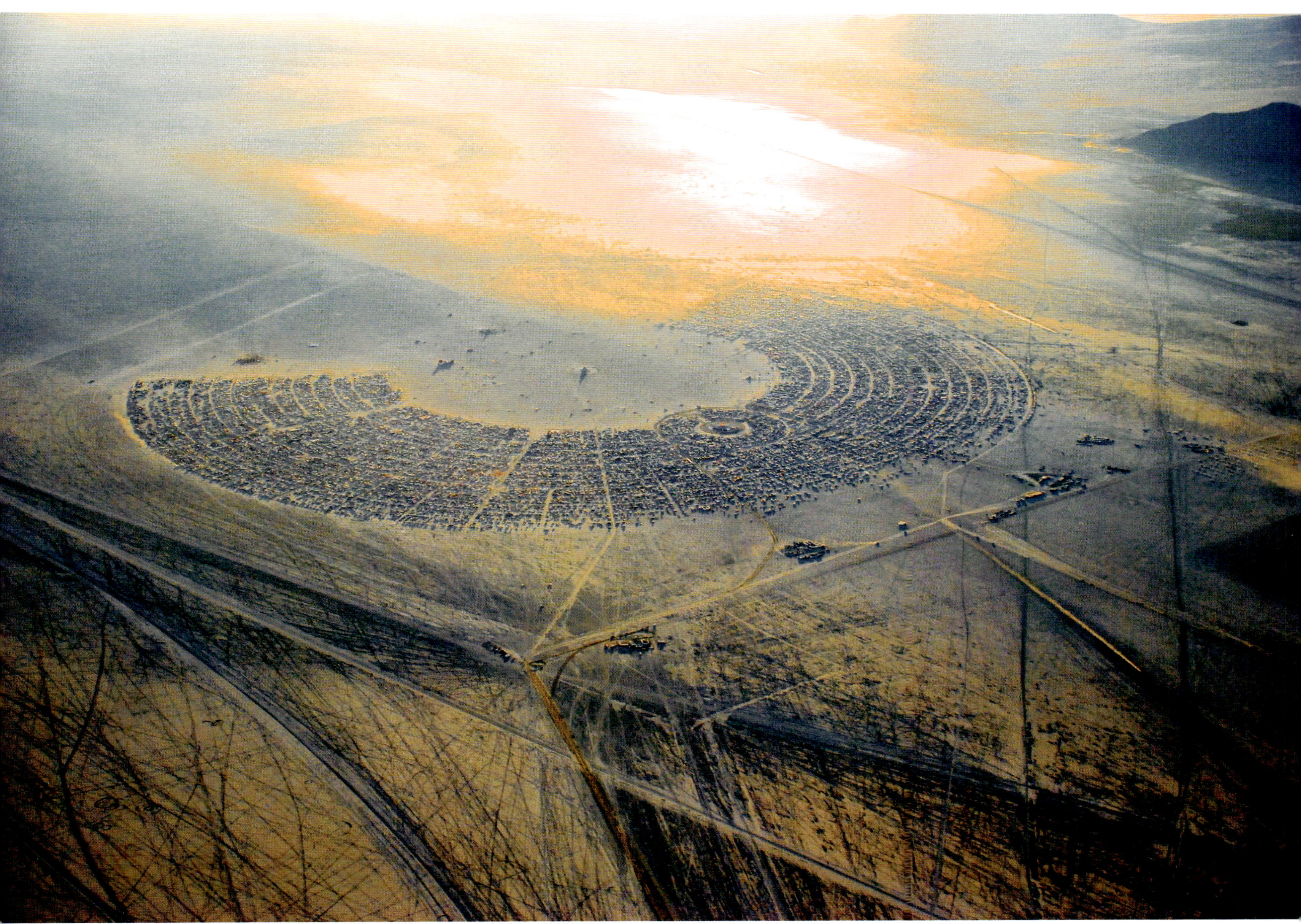

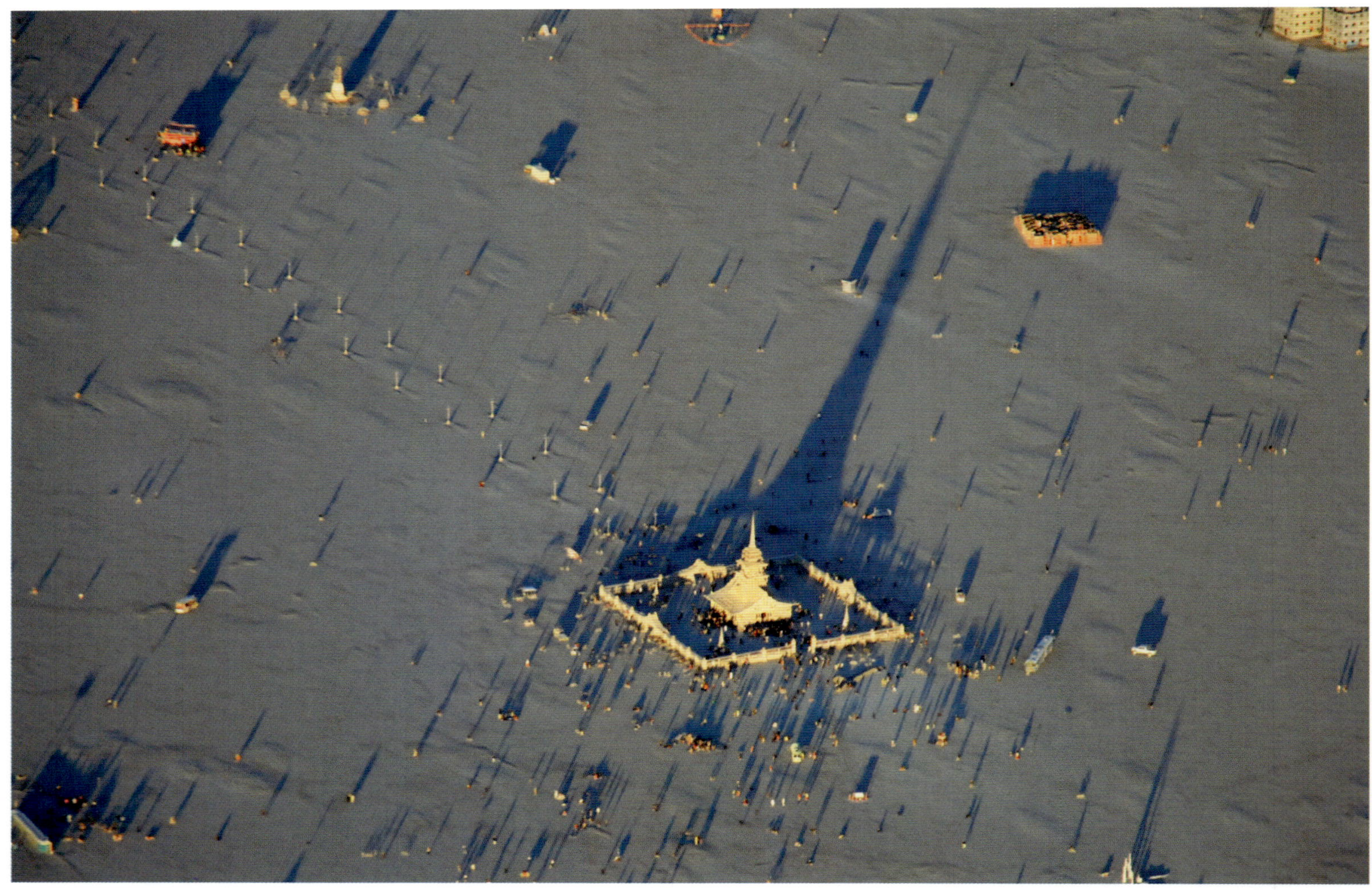

134

Above: "Temple of Juno" by David Best
Right: The Man stood above the honeycomb-designed Pavilion. It was the last structure conceived by Rod Garrett
The Pavilion held up to a thousand participants at a time

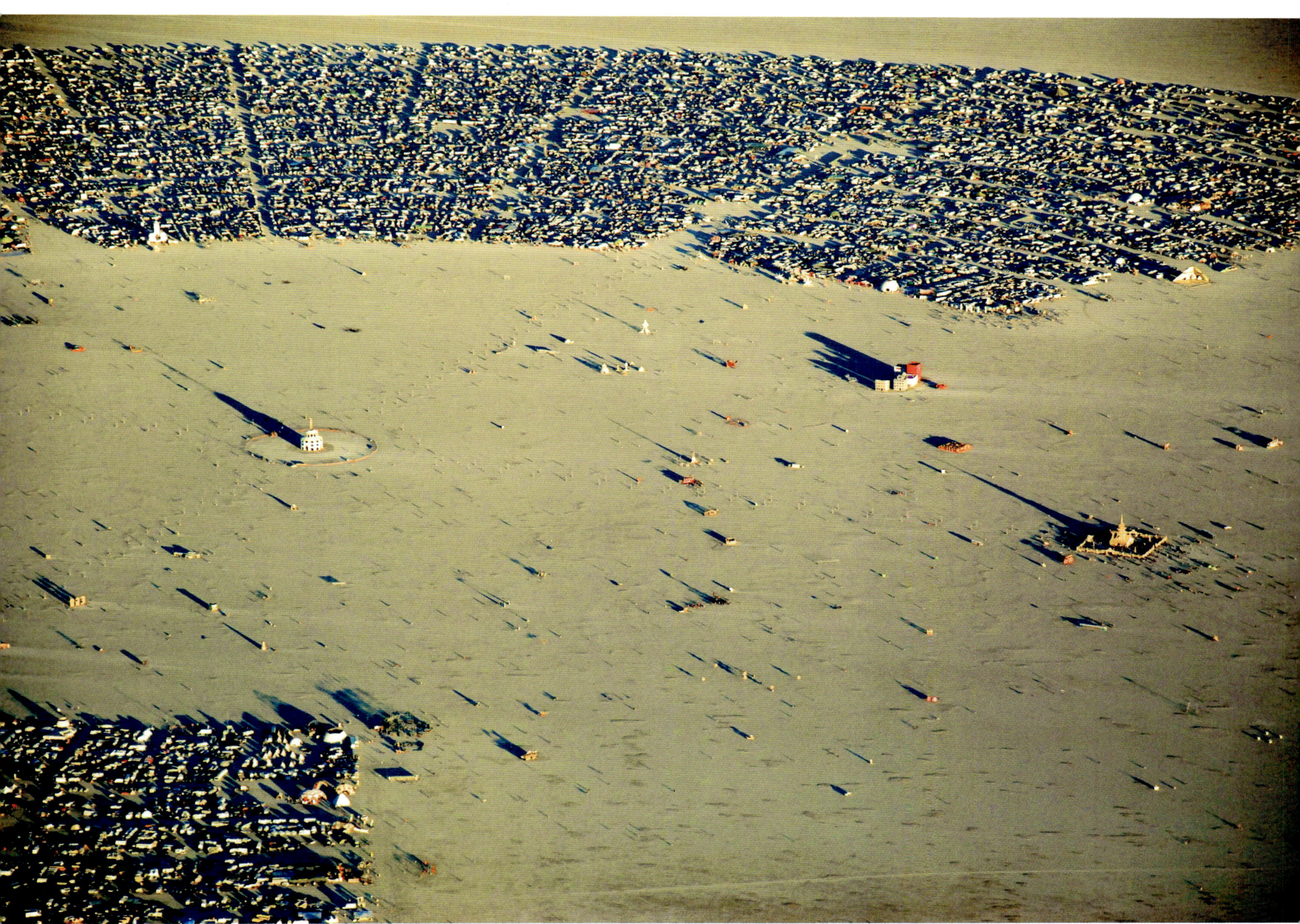

A known landmark, Old Razorback is to the east of Black Rock City

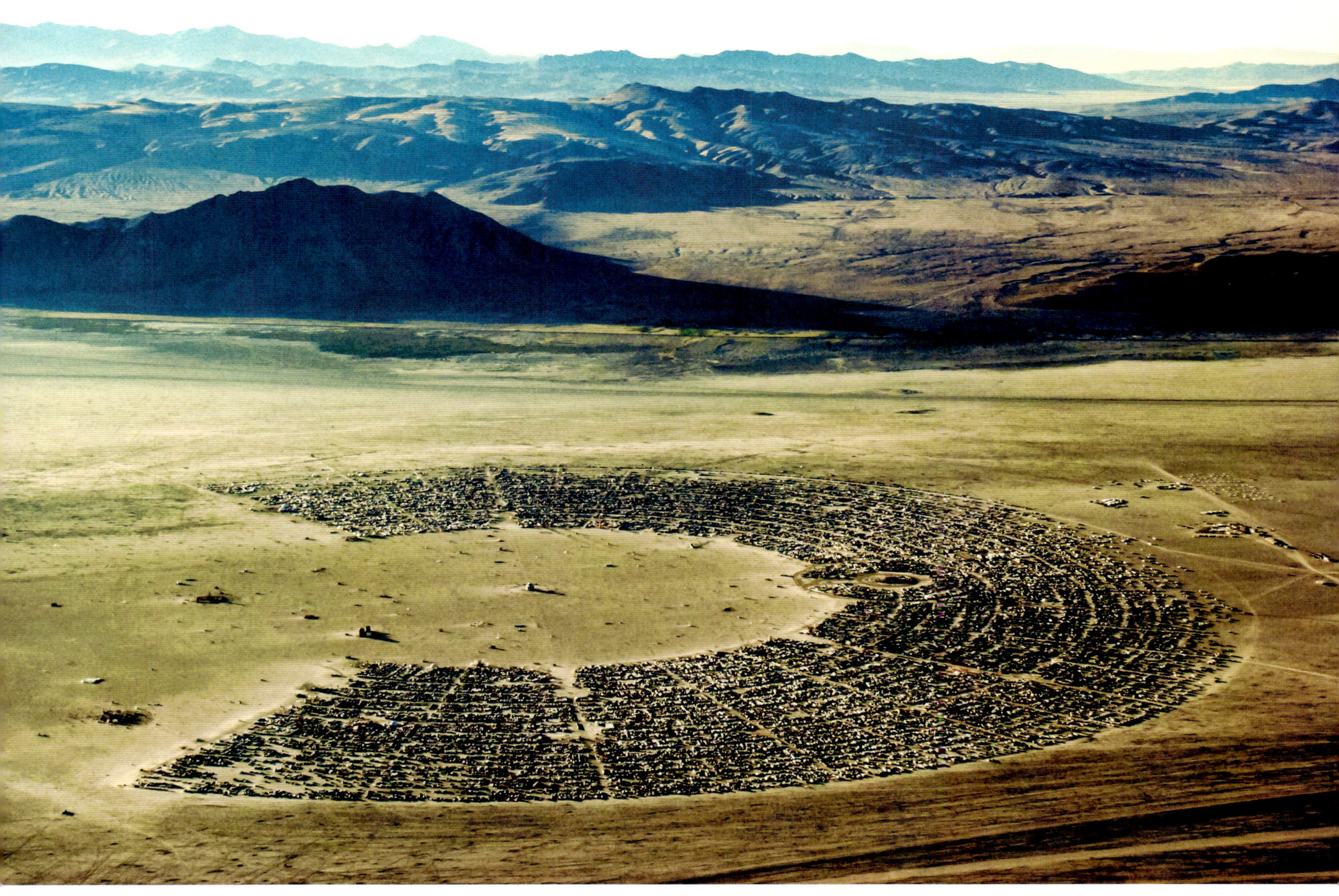

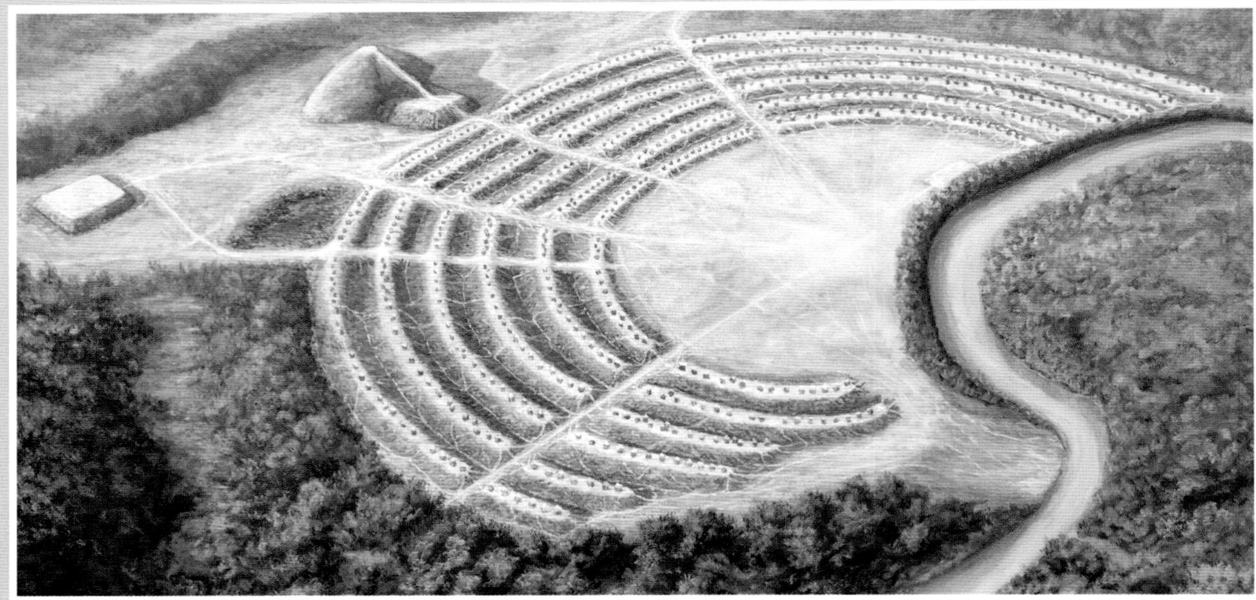

Poverty Point 1200 BCE

138

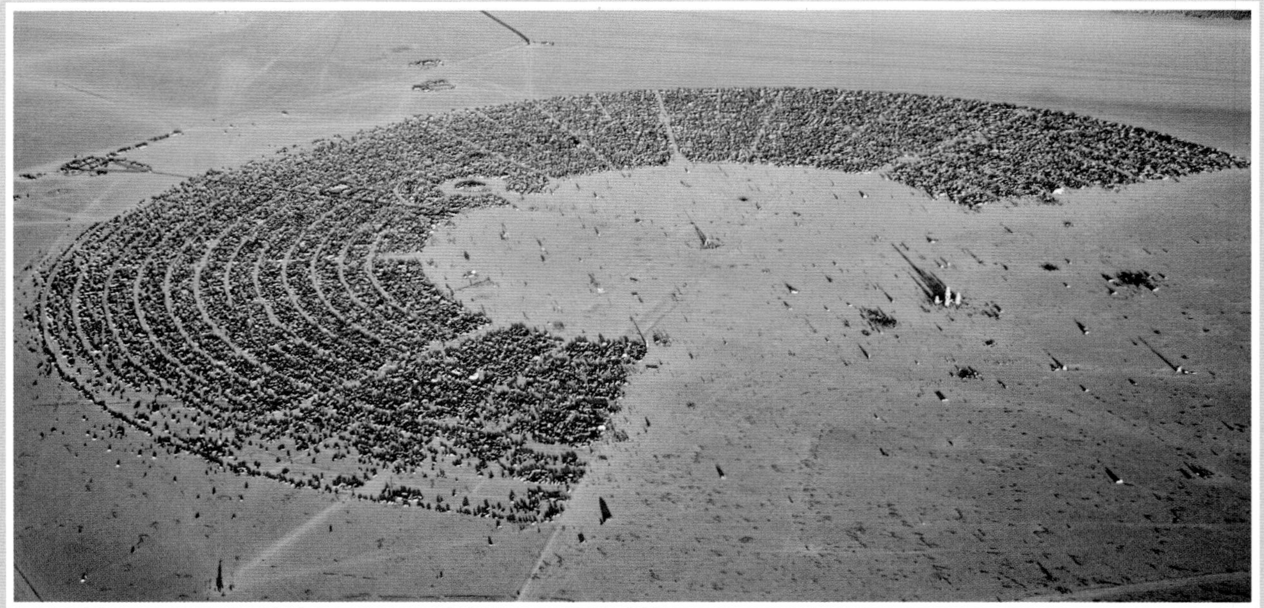

Black Rock City 2011 AD

Ephemeral City, Eternal Memory

Alexei Vranich

— I —

From the first aerial view, it was obvious to an archaeologist like me that the designers of Burning Man were inspired by Poverty Point, a 3,000-year-old archaeological site in northwest Louisiana. Considered one of the earliest sites in North America, Poverty Point hosts substantial constructions of earth, stone, and wood. In a class on ritual, religion, and festival that I taught at UCLA and Berkeley, I would place the above images of Burning Man and Poverty point side by side and talk about the similarities in design and concept when it came to sacred design and architecture.

Candidly put, on the ground, Poverty Point is not much to look at. Pictures of eroded mounds and broken pots and arrowheads do little to interest students distracted by today's modern technologies and a deep anxiety over the financial potential of their carefully chosen, ultra-competitive majors. However, bringing Burning Man into the syllabus transformed a class from a small discussion group in a classroom to a popular lecture in a packed hall. The effect of comparing a pre-Columbian site with what the students thought was a colorful event in the desert rendered the past more relevant, and thought-provoking discussions revolved around the desires and experiences that make us human. This also had the effect of transforming and legitimizing Burning Man from some type of anomaly—a drug infused rave, according to its critics—to a continuum of the evolution of society. I emphasized the deeply historical, if not deeply psychological, symbolic value of the design, as I introduced the work of several important theorists and some basic concepts of sacred design. As a result, I was able to teach a diverse group of mostly non-liberal-arts students basic concepts in sacred architecture and religious theory, and it made great sense to them.

Projecting both images on the screen, I would start by pointing out how an important structure sat towards the center of the semicircular areas of both. At Poverty Point, archaeologists found the remains of a substantial wooden structure that had been built several times over and had served as the location for important and elaborate rituals. It was a representation, perhaps, of an *axis mundi*—the center of the world—where all the powers of the heavens and the underworld met and were mediated on earth. Aligned along the center with the *axis mundi* was a large earthen mound, dirt and stone brought in from distant locations. As a point of comparison, at Black Rock City loomed The Man, set to burn as the festive climax of the week, along the central axis between Center Camp—probably the most diverse location when it comes to people and activities—and The Temple, the viscerally intimate point of visitation for all attendees, consumed by fire in a final act of collective and personal introspection.

The radial pattern is the most distinctive and intriguing aspect of both designs. The roads at both sites converge on and accentuate the center. Unlike the European city where

139

Top left: Illustration (2014) by Herb Roe
Bottom left: Photo (2011) by Will Roger

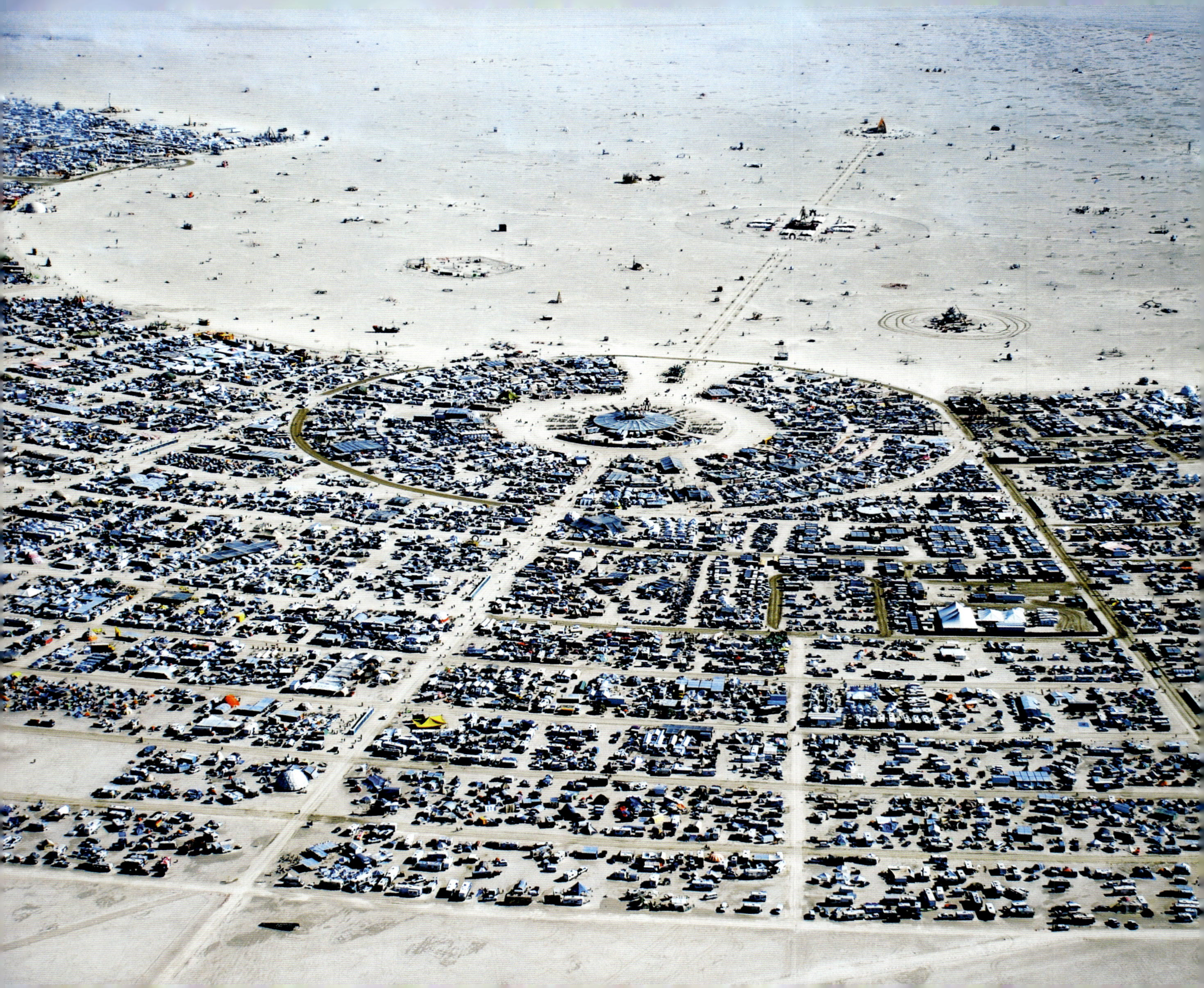

a plaza is the center of the town and the grid radiates from that point, the radial pattern calls to the surrounding landscape, as if it were designed from the outside in. These roads serve to move people back and forth, to be sure; however, in the pre-Colombian case, the roads also called to the distant landscape – aligning to sacred mountains and cosmological bodies and acting as a conduit designed draw their energies magnetically towards the center of their universe.

It is interesting to note that, in both cases, the site is more impressive from the air, almost as if there were a second audience for the ritual performance. When I pointed out this insinuation to my students, I also introduced another relevant term to them: *Imago Mundi*—Heaven on Earth—which in prehistoric times meant that the design was created by the gods and handed down to the lowly denizens of Earth. Another year of fair weather and good harvests would be guaranteed if these divinely inspired rules of perfect design were adhered to, and the movements of people were choreographed in a manner that would mimic the motions of the cosmos. At Black Rock City, the curves of the radial are so slight that from the ground the "Burners" don't even notice the radial form, even from one of the higher pieces of art or miradors. Notwithstanding, by utilizing art and photography, one can appreciate and grasp the importance of the pattern of this temporary city that both controls and directs the flow to and from the playa and the central feature.

Both sites are located on Earth but, conceptually, they live in another dimension. This point, underscored in the Sacred and the Profane, I would repeat in one context or another in every class. Theorists such as Mircea Eliade and Joseph Campbell (of The Hero's Journey and Star Wars fame) have made sure that this binary is a common one in literature, movies, and even in everyday conversations.

At sacred sites worldwide, the process of moving from the profane to the sacred begins well before arrival at the actual site. The travel to the site—the pilgrimage—initiates the transformation of moving from the mundane world to a magical place. The first view of the site is often accompanied by ritual and acts of cleansing the body and soul; many more rituals follow before passing a well-marked boundary into the actual site.

"We arrived at this vast plane," narrated Burning Man co-founder Michael Mikel in the film, Spark, *"I took a stick and I drew a line on the ground, and I said, on the other side of this line, everything will be different. And everything has been different."* On one side is what Burners call *"home,"* the area outside the default world, but the boundary and the concept are the same as Sacred and Profane: you are entering a place where everyday rules do not apply.

— II —

The immediate similarities of Poverty Point and Black Rock City are indeed astounding; nevertheless, these design elements can be found in pre-Columbian sites from the Mississippi Valley down the continents to the deserts of Chile. For the more theologically inclined, this similarity in form may relate to a common human spirituality; in a similar vein, a psychoanalytical approach would find this pattern to be a Jungian archetype—a product of the manner in which our brains are hardwired. One anthropologist in the late 1960s referred to this as the Psychic Unity of the early American population, the product of the similar shamanistic religious tradition brought by the small group of people that crossed the Bering Strait and rapidly populated the continent over the next few thousand years.

Consequently, it came as a surprise to me many years later, as I visited the founders and veterans at First Camp, that I received blank looks when I mentioned Poverty Point. As we can see from the introductory chapter here by Will Roger, the design for Black Rock City began in a near-casual manner, drawn on a napkin, and its form developed over several years in response to various pressures from stakeholders. The fact that the founders independently created the same design as their pre-Columbian equivalents, separated by thousands of years and an even wider chasm in culture and religious beliefs, makes the similarities more striking. Through a strange convergent evolution, ancient Native Americans and modern event builders arrived at the same solution as to how to manage people and convey meaning. To an archeologist, this phenomenon begs for further investigation.

The reason for the similarity in form is based on the imperative to quickly create a unified community with a core identity. There is, of course, a world of difference between the participants in an ancient religious ceremony and modern Burning Man attendees. Few of the latter would arrive driven by the motivation and fear of a Supreme watching over them and willing to grant them posthumous rewards – or believing that that their actions could somehow affect the weather and other fortunes for the upcoming year. In sum, both places brought together a diverse group of people for a brief break in their everyday lives, allowing them to experience something fantastic and feel a sense of purpose and unity with their fellow attendees and pilgrims. Most importantly perhaps, it could leave them feeling transformed by their encounter with something greater than themselves. It was the French philosopher Durkheim who called these brief and awe-inspiring moments those of "collective effervescence," which can be created in both a religious setting–such as during hymns in a cathedral–or in the last moments of a nail-biting sporting contest.

The design of Black Rock City focuses everyone on the communal playa, specifically on the Man and the Temple. All vision and motion are directed to this central focus. These structures are then activated, that is, made meaningful by people interacting in both private and communally playful manners.

The other common variable is location: more likely than not, it will be some god-awful place, far from anything of value or interest. In fact, the conditions often tend to be downright hostile. Consider the locations of some of the holiest places on Earth: Jerusalem, Mecca, Lhasa, or – to make it more relevant to our modern lives – the entertainment city of Las Vegas or Coachella in the the Palm Springs desert. Each requires a journey in order to arrive at the location; and once there, the harsh conditions are exacerbated by the crush of people. People have disparate types of experiences at Black Rock City, but this year we did share the common experience of the arrival, the long exodus back home, and the moment a dust storm snapped us out of our personal journeys and forced us to take refuge and secure the camp with both friends and strangers. The hardship of the trip and the stay most certainly bonds people within a common experience.

– III –

Other sites similar to Poverty Point rose and fell across the New World. Compared to the size and longevity of cities in the Middle East, these pre-Colombian sites were small and short-lived. In my region of specialization, the Andean Highlands, we term these places, "explosive" affairs, defined by

a large, singular area lasting a few generations, perhaps surrounded by a few small outposts that are miniature religious versions of it. These bordering indigenous populations would go about their subsistence-based lives more-or-less as they had before. The biggest effect was the iconic art produced in these centers, usually in the form of lightweight icons that would be carried across the landscape to end their days as personal property in the graves of their owners or as cherished heirlooms of their descendants. Clearly, the people felt strongly about the site, to the point that they wanted to take a physical manifestation of it to the afterlife. Archaeologists could then define a slice of time by the presence of the art and its style and wonder what mechanism brought this object so far from its origin.

In a similar fashion, when Burners leave after their short stay in this temporary city, they leave with symbols of the Man or representations of the design of Black Rock City in the form of icons and even on their bodies in the form of temporary or permanent tattoos. In this manner, Burning Man is distinct from the other events and entertainment centers that have developed in the last few decades. People have a memorable time in Vegas, go to Coachella for the music, and may even return a second time. But I haven't met anyone who even partly self-identified with those locations. Black Rock City is temporary, and intentionally so, but the effect is to create memory and propagate it through narrative. The smell of the

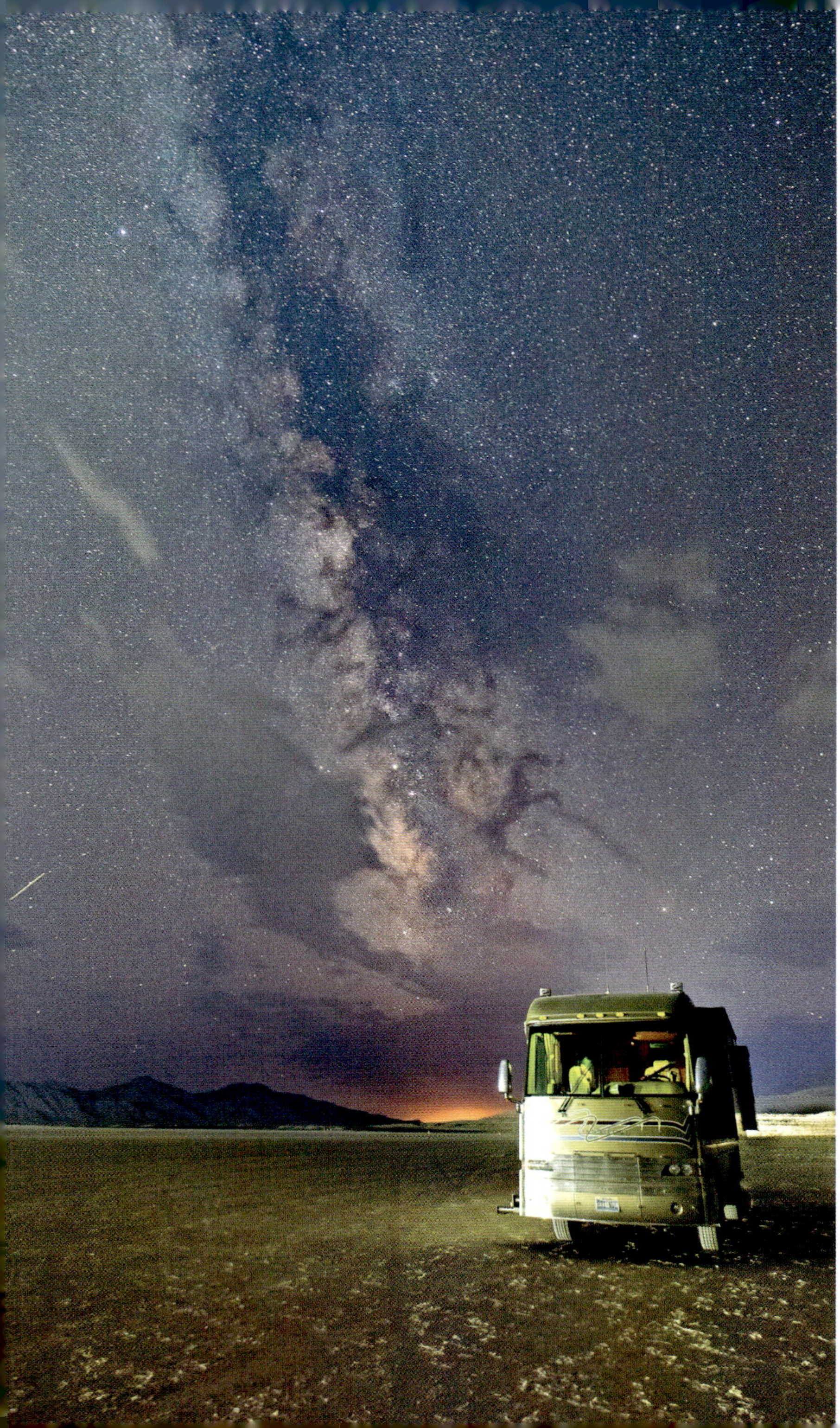

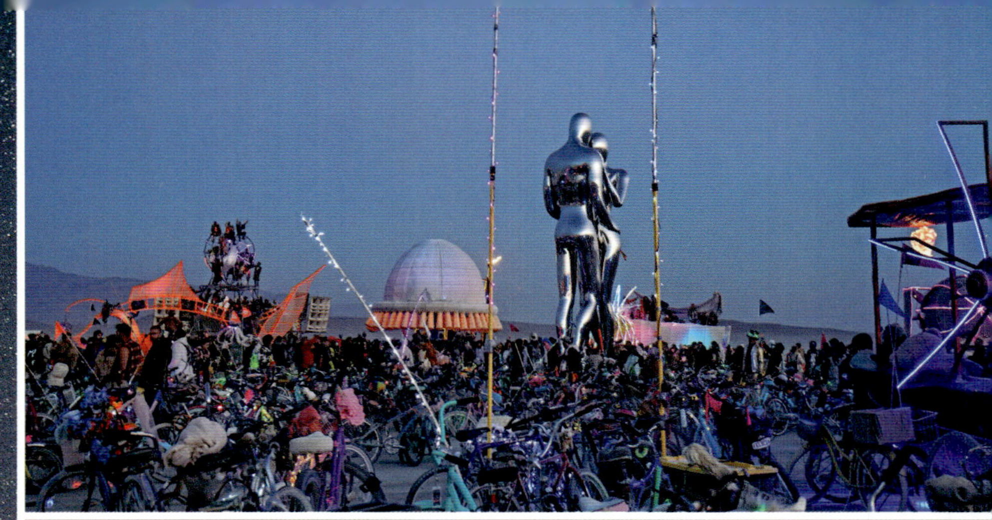
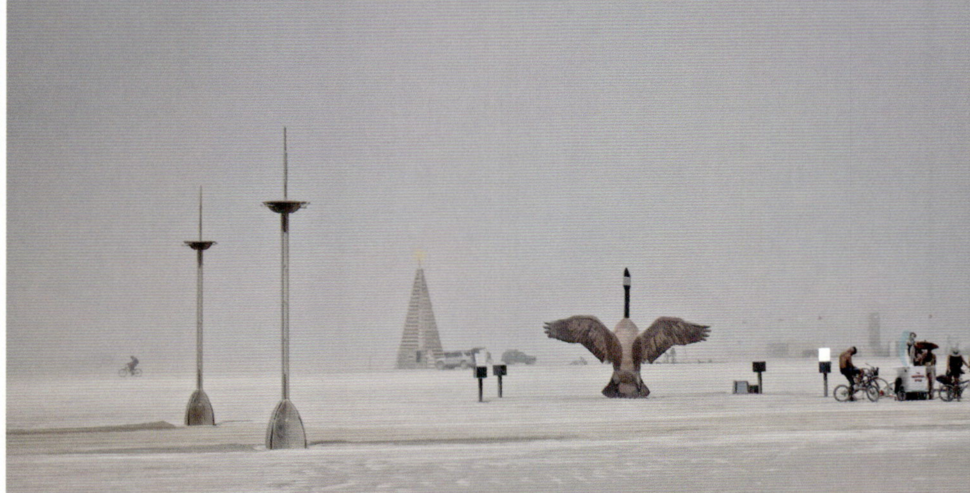
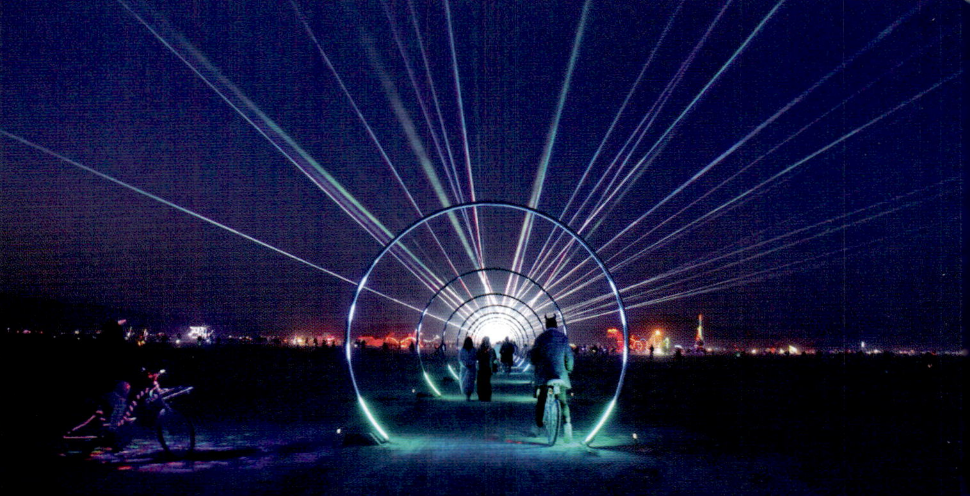

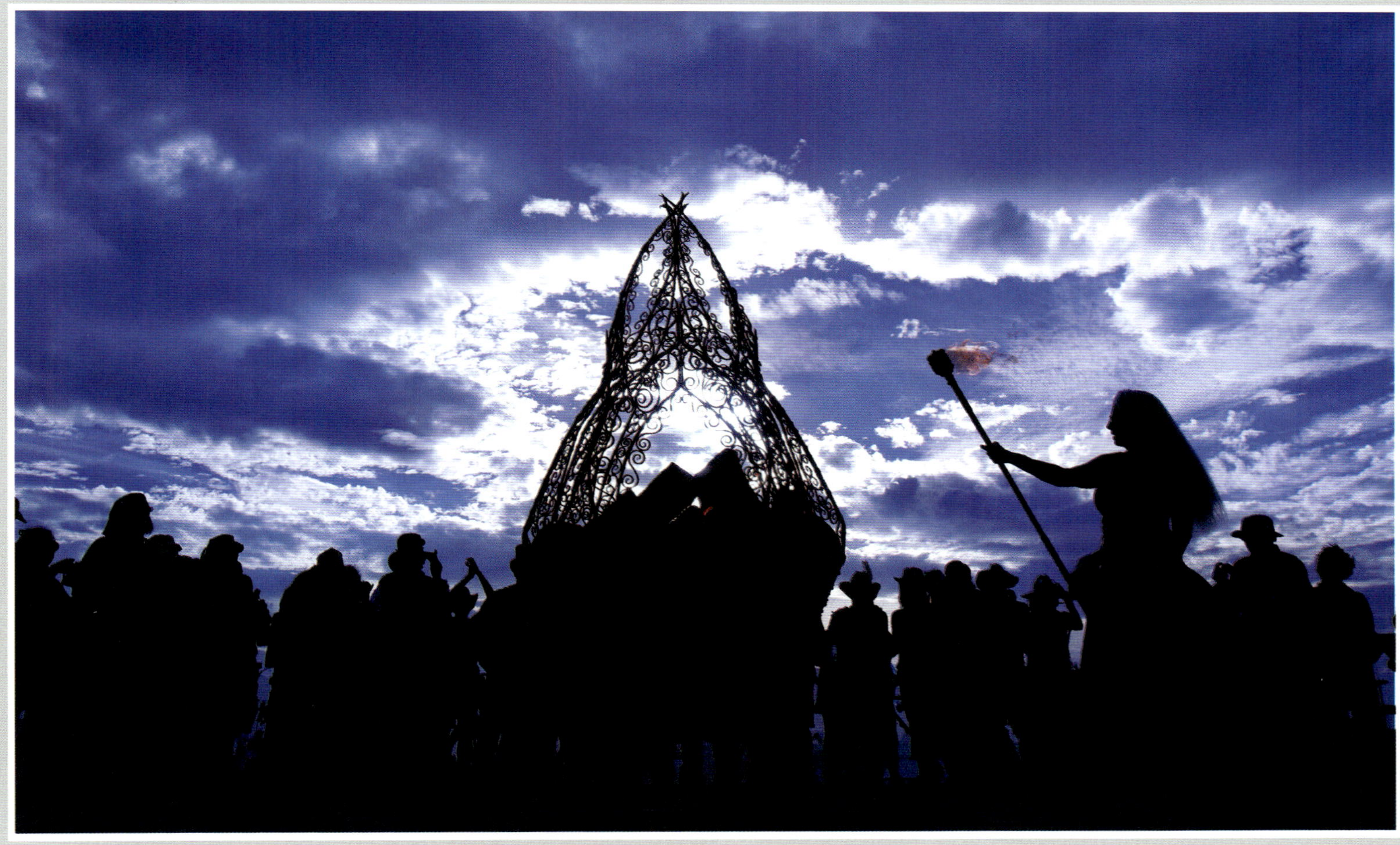

dust in one's clothing and equipment will immediately evoke a memory, as would the malodorus smell of a port-a-potty. Even without these olfactory reminders, Burners are notorious for turning any conversation topic back to Burning Man. I would even consider it a step beyond memory and say that the purpose of the experience, then, is to transform identity—or at least one facet of a person's identity. Black Rock City is an ephemeral city made permanent through individual and collective memory. The unending narratives serve to entice the next generation to make the arduous and taxing pilgrimage.

Above: Crimson Rose extracting a flame from El Diabla, a special cauldron at Center Camp. Photo (2016) by Mark Mennie
Far Left: Milky Way and Bus, smoke from distant California wildfires helped to create a cloud-like formation
Left Top to bottom: "In Every Lifetime I Will Find You" by Michael Benistry and "Robot Heart" sound car by Jason Swamy (2018); "Penny the Goose" by Mr & Mrs Ferguson stands tall in a dust storm (2015); Standing in the middle of "Sonic Runway" by Rob Jensen and Warren Trezevant, starburst light provided by "Mayan Warrior" mutant vehicle (2018). All photographs by Vanessa Franking

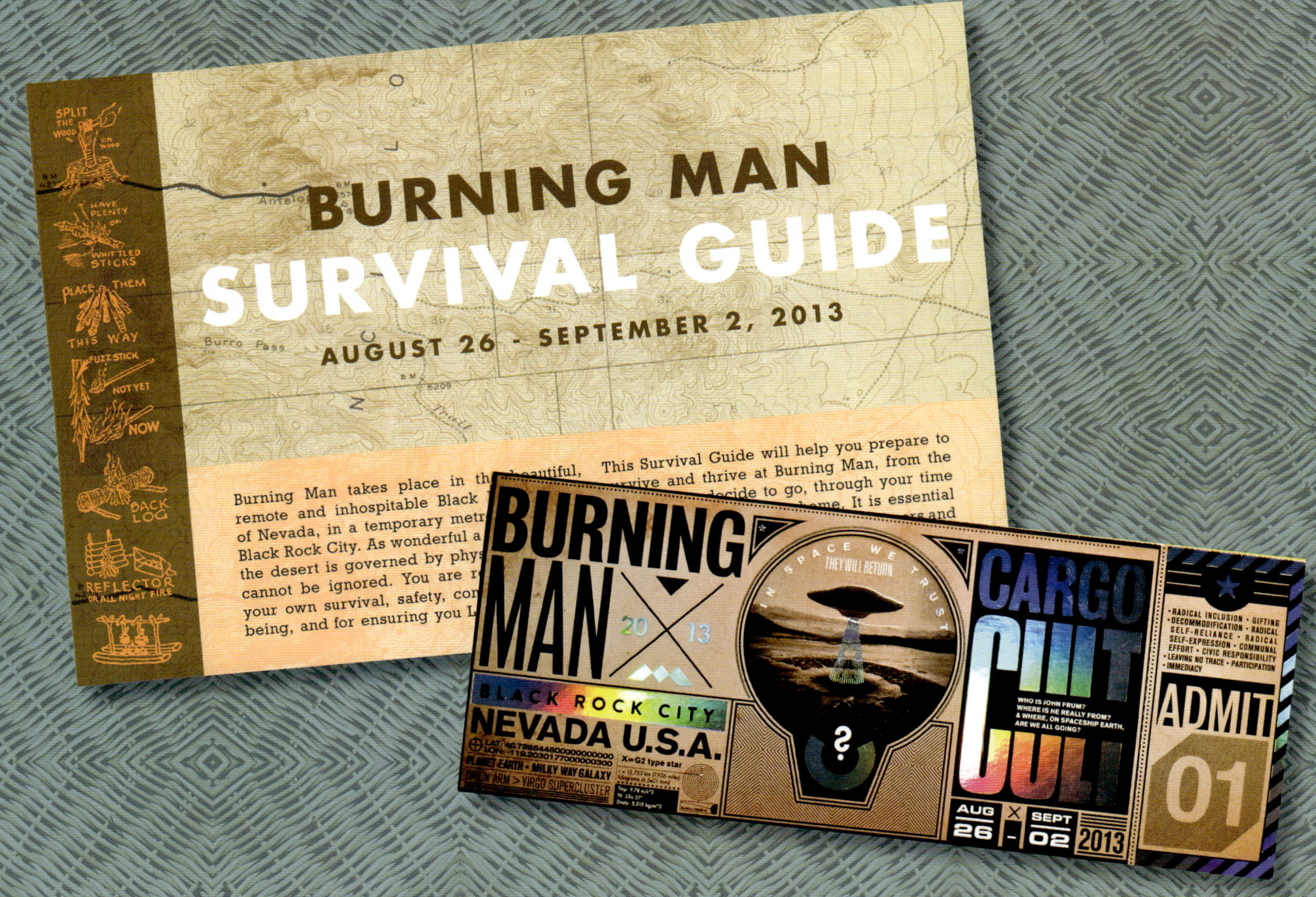

SPLIT THE WOOD
ON END
HAVE PLENTY
WHITTLED STICKS
PLACE THEM
THIS WAY
FUZZ STICK
NOT YET
NOW
BACK LOG
REFLECTOR
OR ALL NIGHT FIRE
BURNING MAN
SURVIVAL GUIDE
AUGUST 26 - SEPTEMBER 2, 2013
Burning Man takes place in the beautiful, remote and inhospitable Black of Nevada, in a temporary metr Black Rock City. As wonderful a the desert is governed by phys cannot be ignored. You are r your own survival, safety, con being, and for ensuring you L
This Survival Guide will help you prepare to rive and thrive at Burning Man, from the decide to go, through your time home. It is essential
BURNING MAN
20 13
BLACK ROCK CITY
NEVADA U.S.A.
PLANET EARTH • MILKY WAY GALAXY
ORION ARM > VIRGO SUPERCLUSTER
X=G2 type star
IN SPACE WE TRUST
THEY WILL RETURN
CARGO CULT
WHO IS JOHN FRUM?
WHERE IS HE REALLY FROM?
& WHERE, ON SPACESHIP EARTH,
ARE WE ALL GOING?
AUG 26 — SEPT 02 2013
RADICAL INCLUSION • GIFTING
DECOMMODIFICATION • RADICAL
SELF-RELIANCE • RADICAL
SELF-EXPRESSION • COMMUNAL
EFFORT • CIVIC RESPONSIBILITY
LEAVING NO TRACE • PARTICIPATION
IMMEDIACY
ADMIT
01

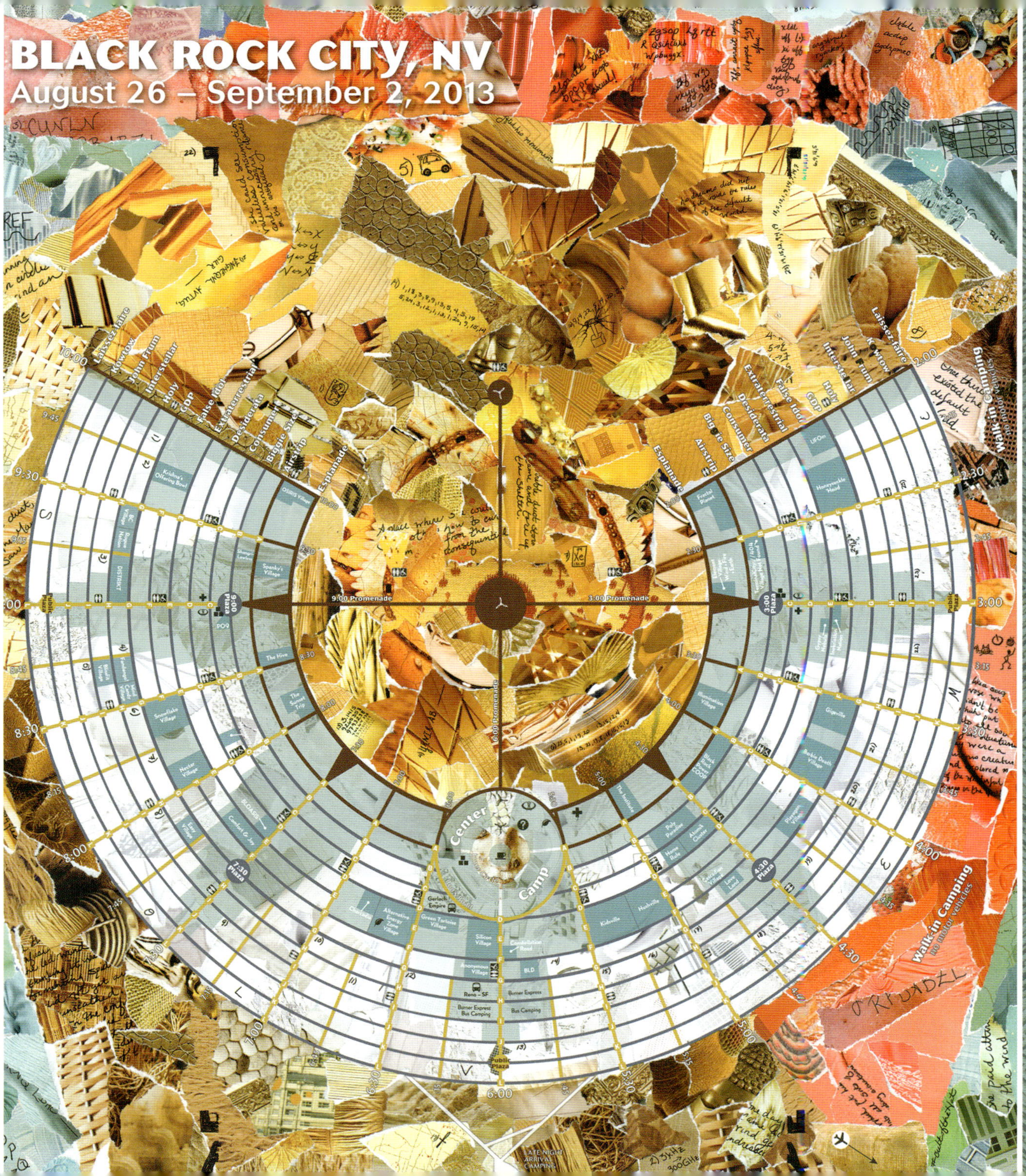

"Thatch 2" photomontage by James Stanford

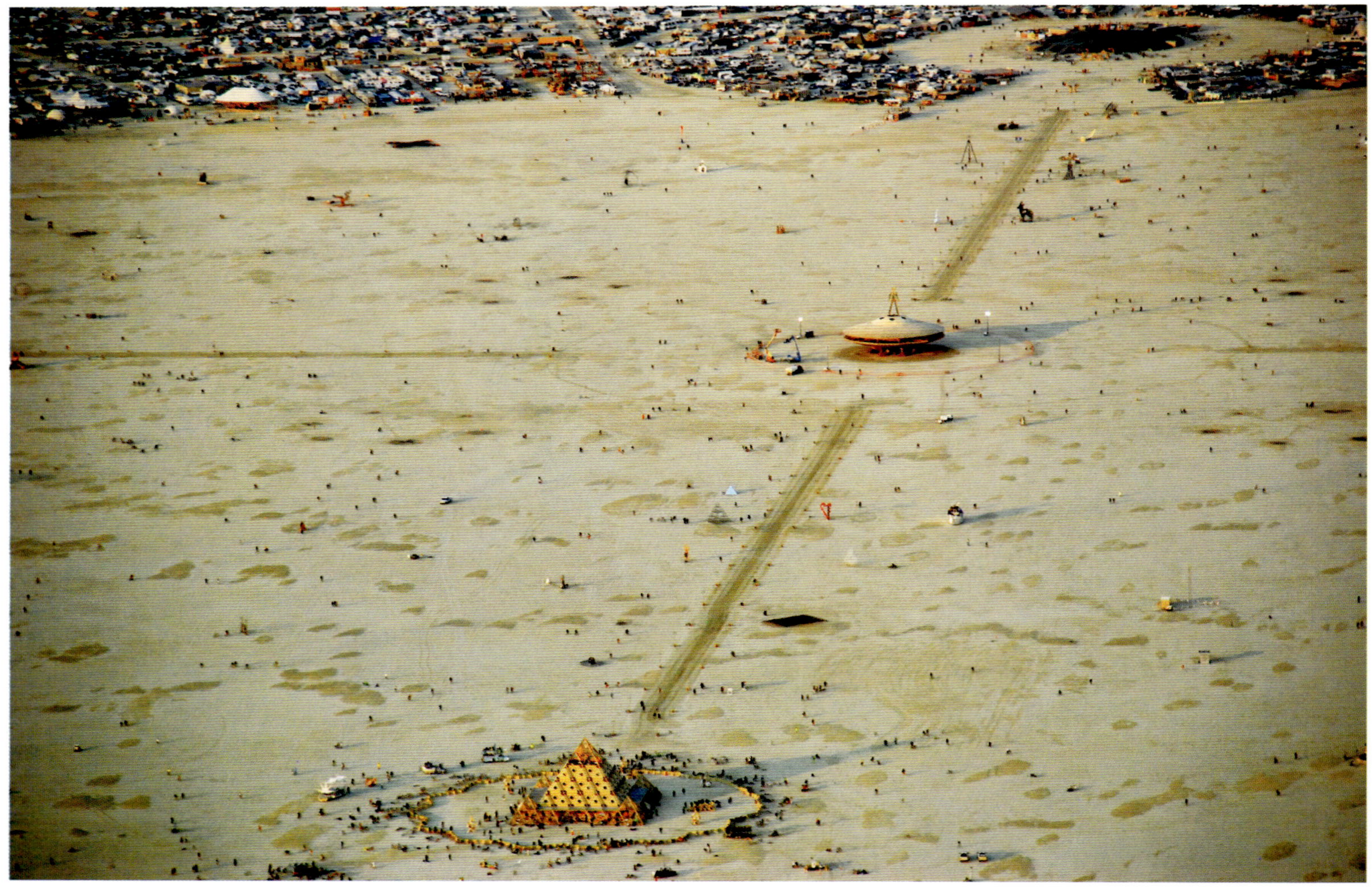

Above: *"Temple of Whollyness" by the Otic Oasis (Gregg Fleishman, Terry Gross and Melissa Barron) looking towards the Promenade to the Man and Center Camp*
Right: *This year 382 art projects, including 66 honoraria projects funded in part by art grants sourced from Burning Man ticket revenues. Population 69,613*

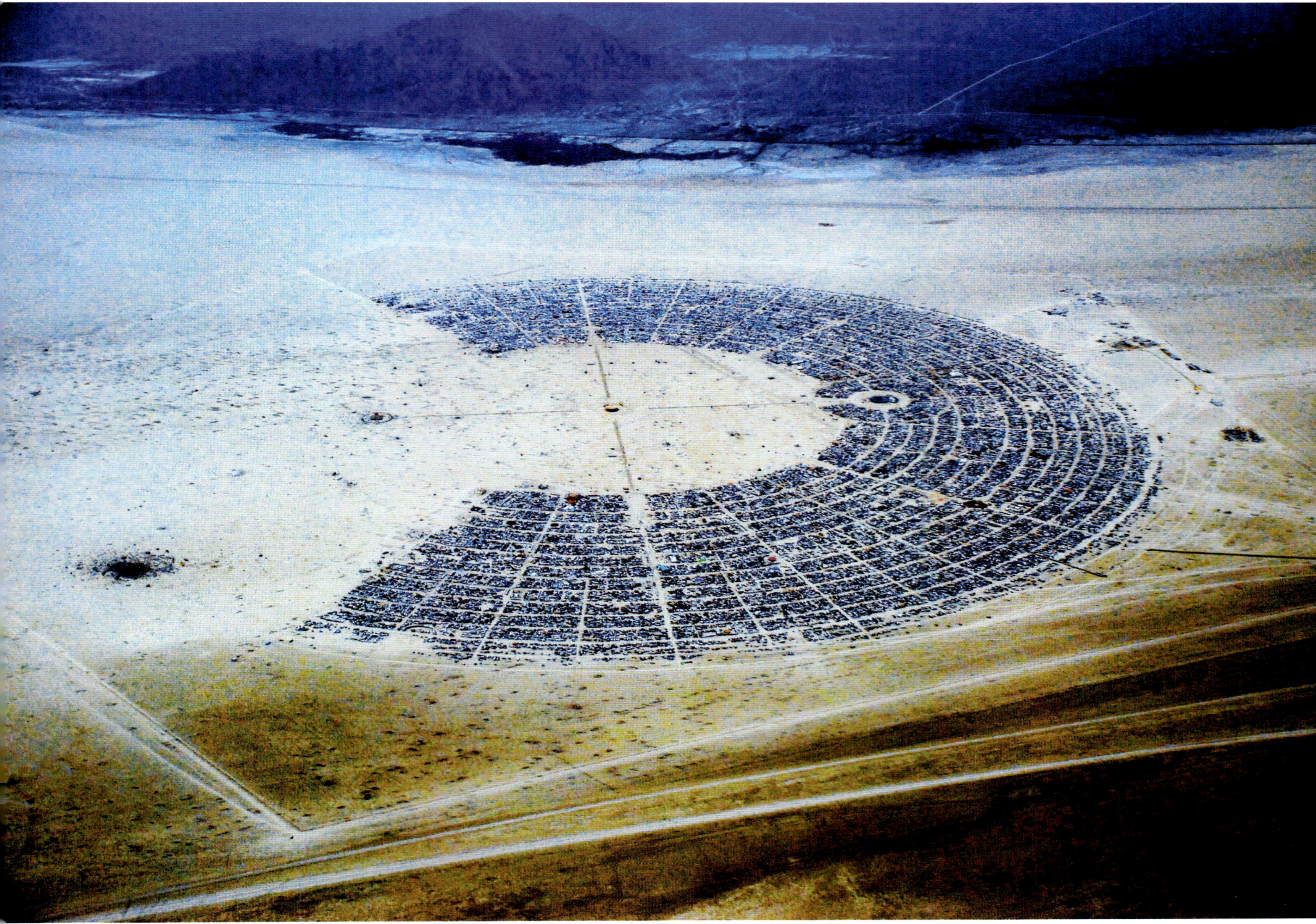

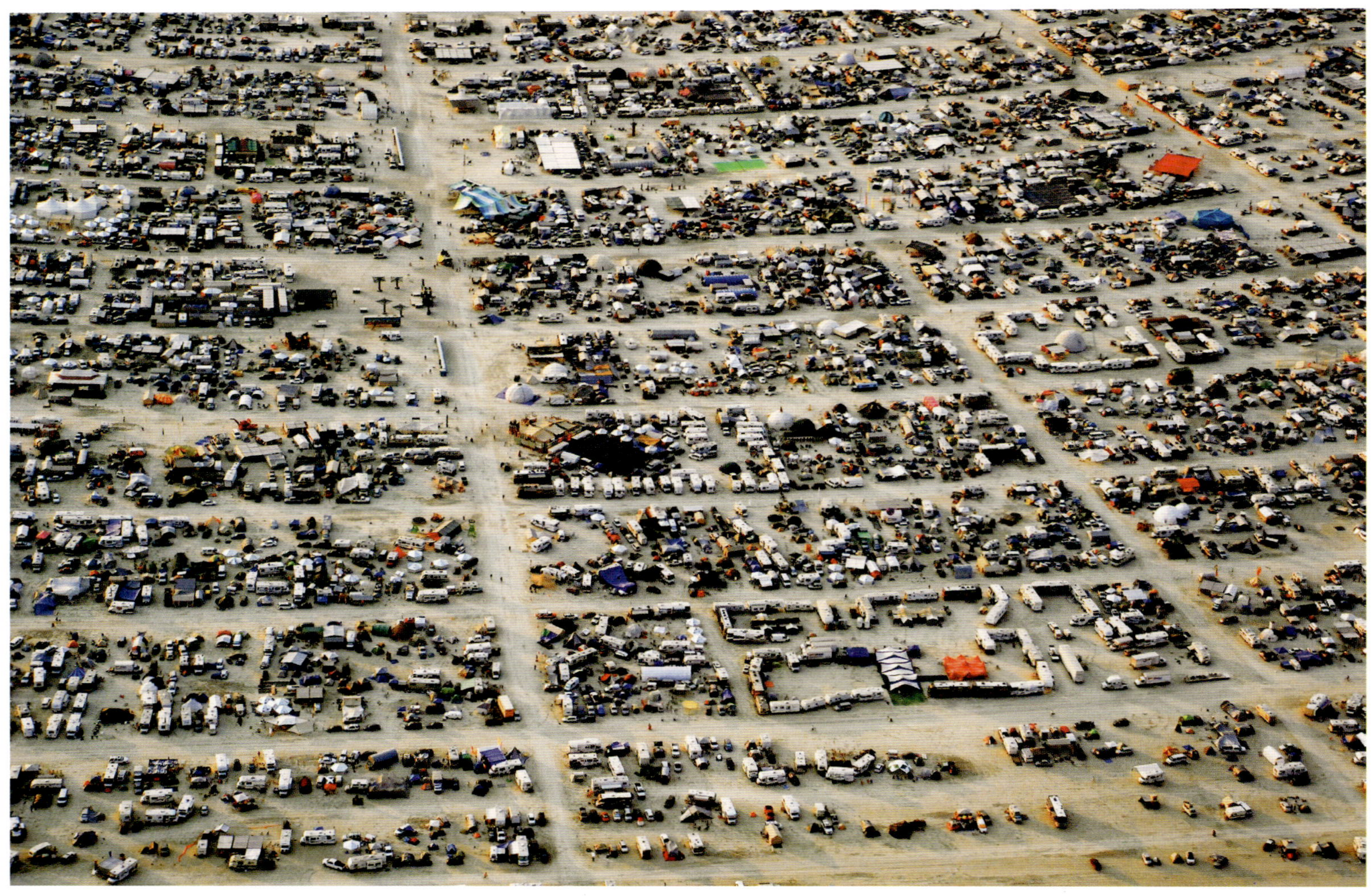

Above: *There were 844 theme camps and villages approved for pre-placement in Black Rock City*
Right: *A number of significant pre-event rainstorms occurred and smoke from the forest fire in the Sierras often blocked the sun during the day*

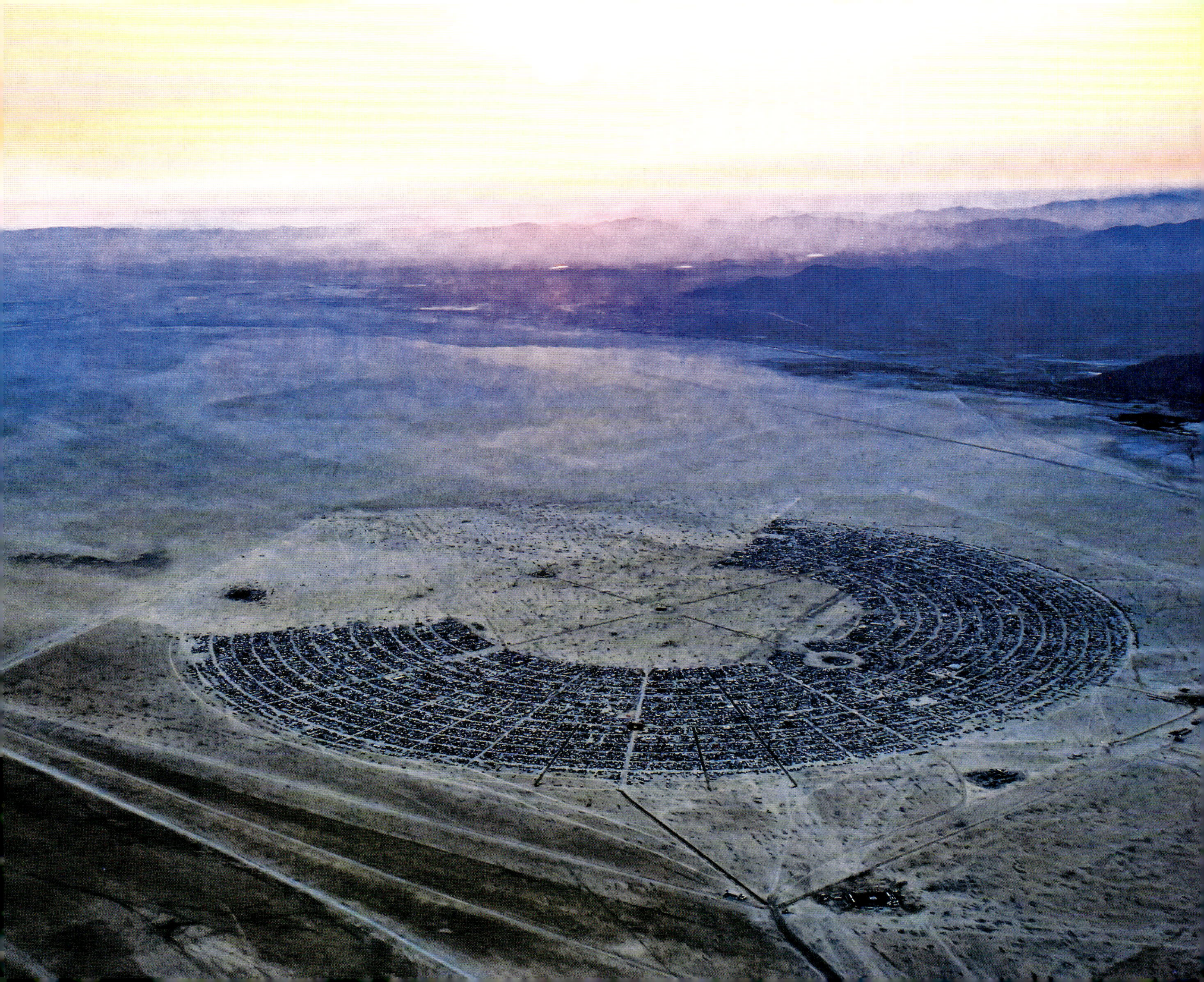

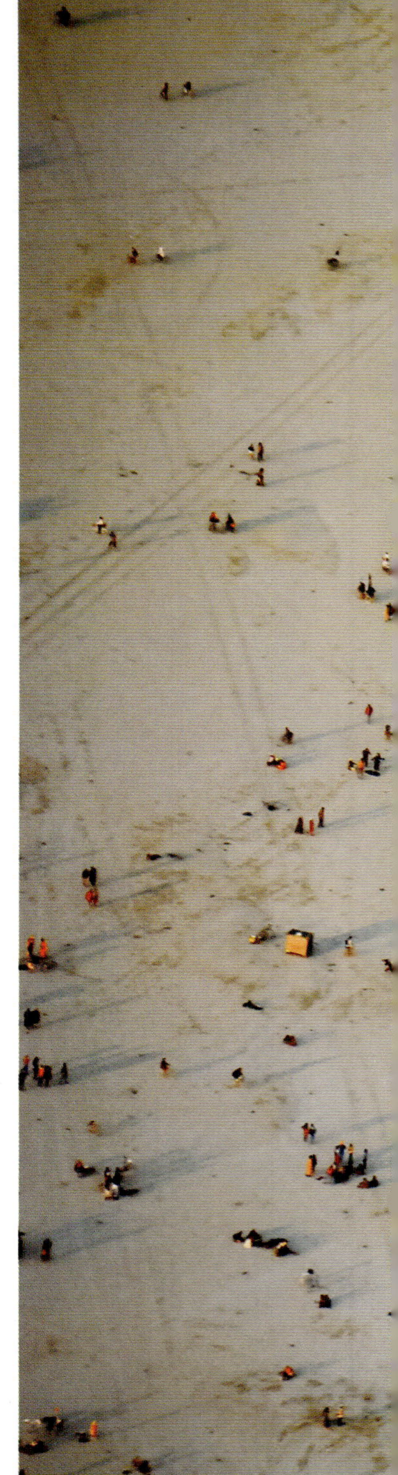

An early morning dance party on the playa. "Disco Duck" and other mutant vehicles

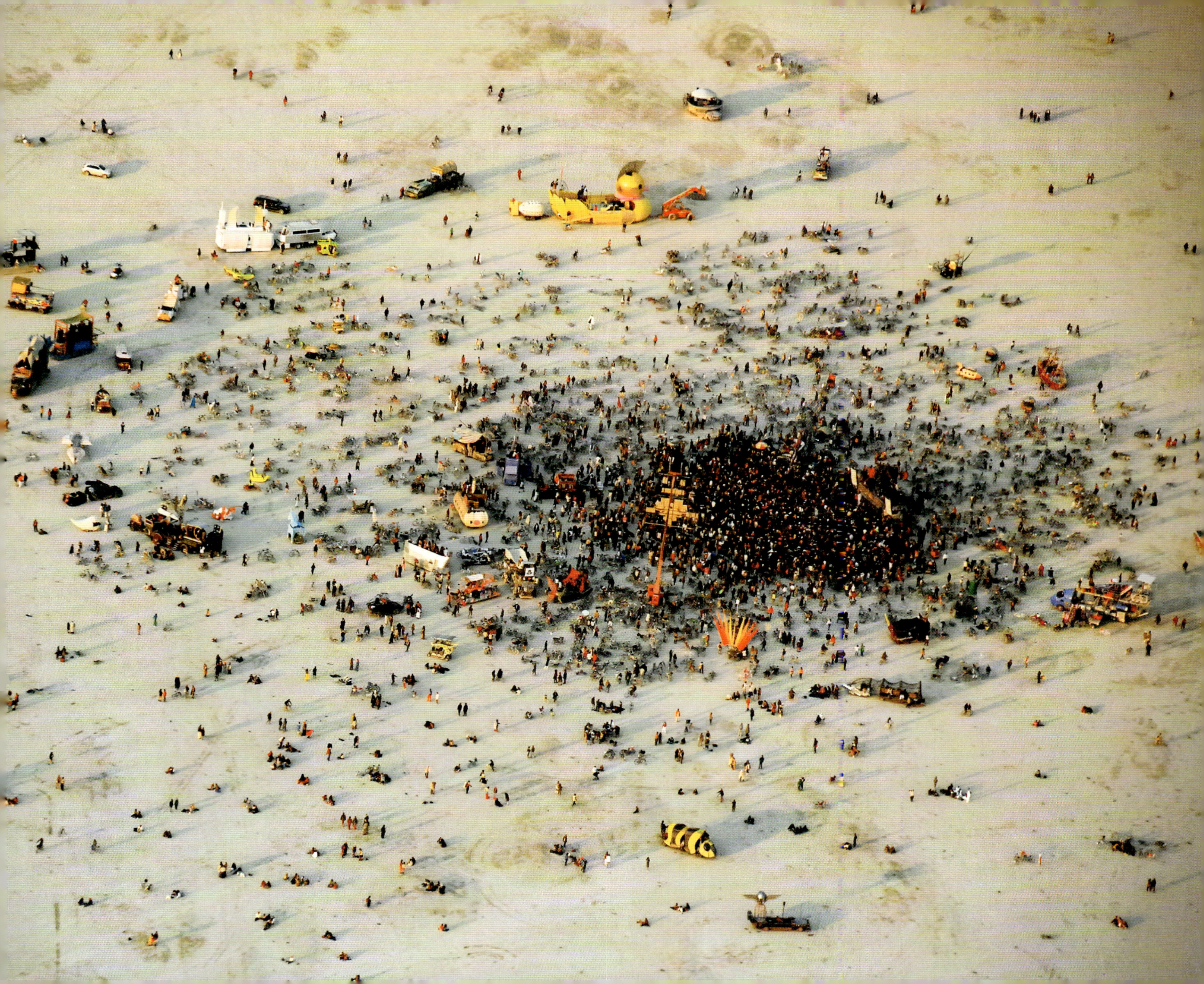

Morning sunrise on the playa

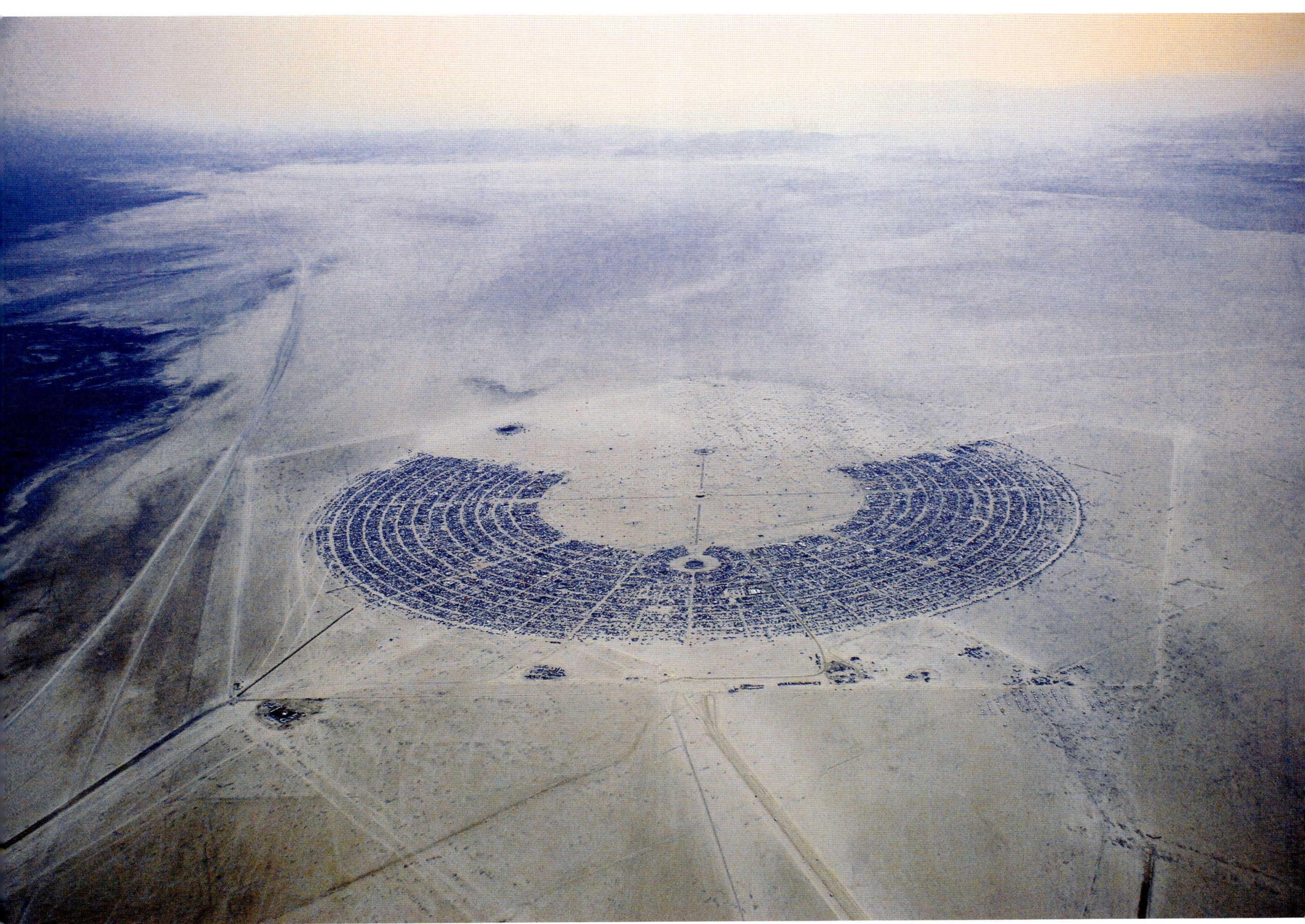

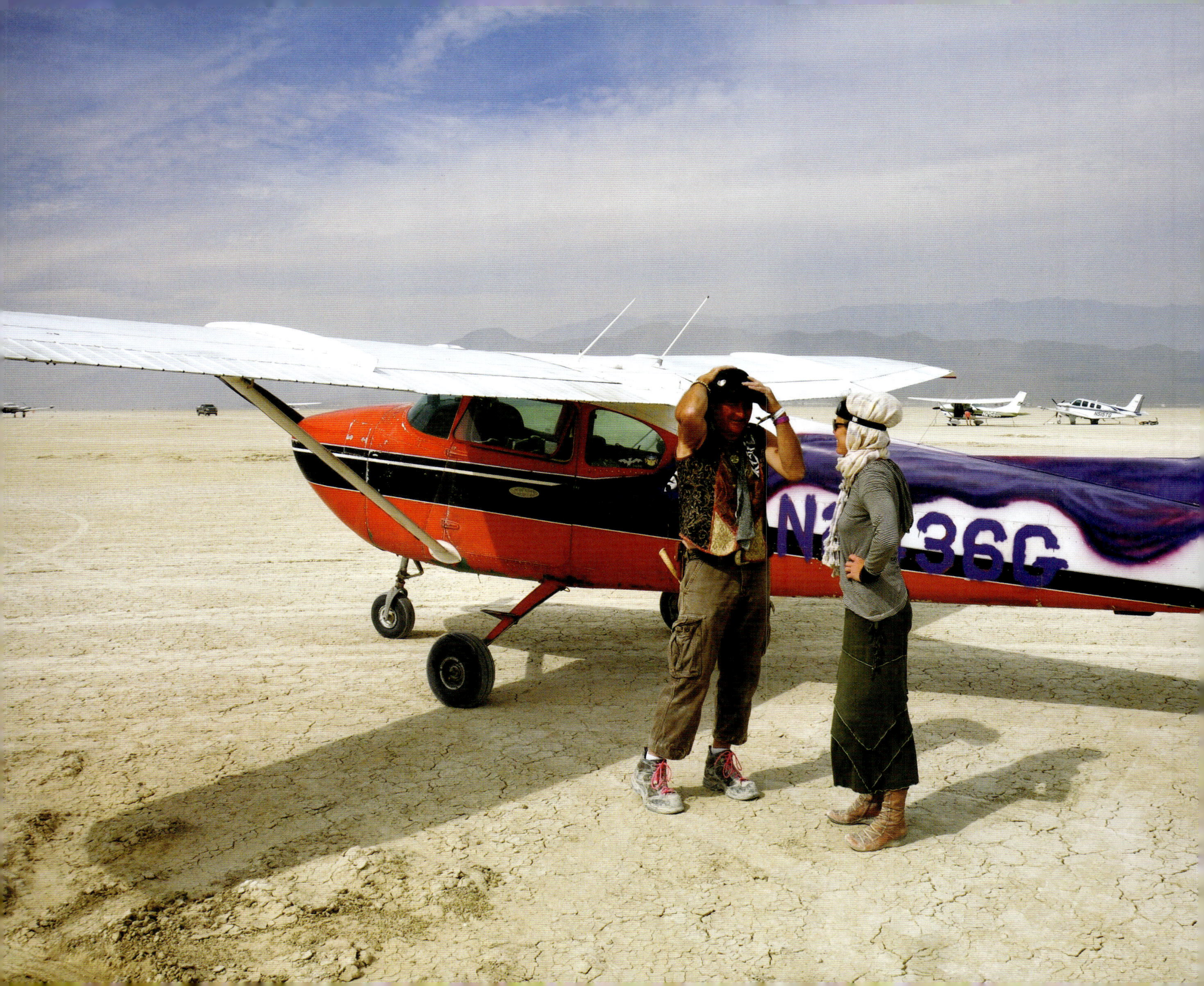

N1 36G

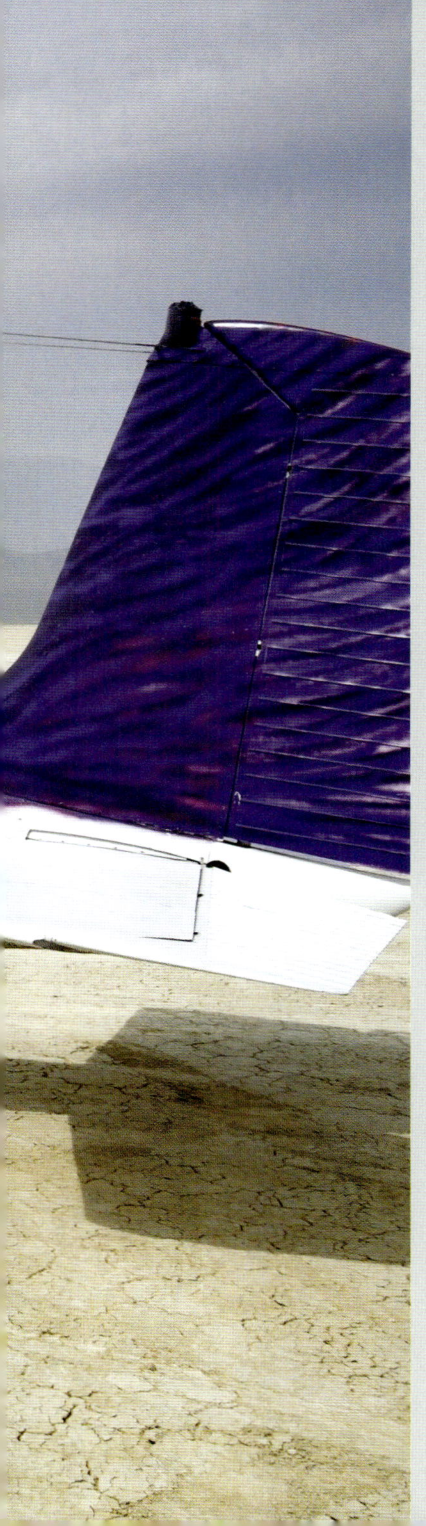

Afterword: Compass of the Ephemeral

Will Roger, Co-Founder, Burning Man

I began photographing Black Rock City in 2005 as a gift to our staff and partners. I'd select the "money shot," make 200, 13"x19" signed prints, and give them to staff as a holiday gift. Just this year it became clear that I had enough material for a book if I included some of the details that have never been seen.

All images were taken with a Nikon D-70, D-80, or D-90. The primary lens is a Nikon Nikkor 28-80 zoom. I photoshoped the images for contrast, brightness, and hue.

Each year presented a remarkably different challenge. Weather and atmospheric conditions are mercurial on the Black Rock Desert. Some years the dust, smoke from wild fires, or clouds made it difficult even to see Black Rock City from above. I trusted that my camera would see enough for me to work with.

I've done this series with two pilots. The first few years, my pilot was the late Berk Snow, a legend in the Burning Man flying community. Berk was a pleasure to fly with and a superb back-country pilot. A tie-down spot appears in his name at the Black Rock City International Airport each year as a memorial. After we lost Burk, my pilot became Dave Barrett, playa name Purple Haze. Dave is a great pilot with lots of experience flying in the high desert. We communicate in the cockpit with hand signals, mostly to drift the plane to get the wing or strut out of my view. We gain altitude to 10,000 feet, roughly a mile above Black Rock City, to get a good oblique perspective. I've always been in awe of how beautiful and organized Black Rock City appears from this perspective.

Dave "Purple Haze" Barrett and back seat passenger Suzy after the aerial photo flight next to his 1958 Cessna 182 (2016)

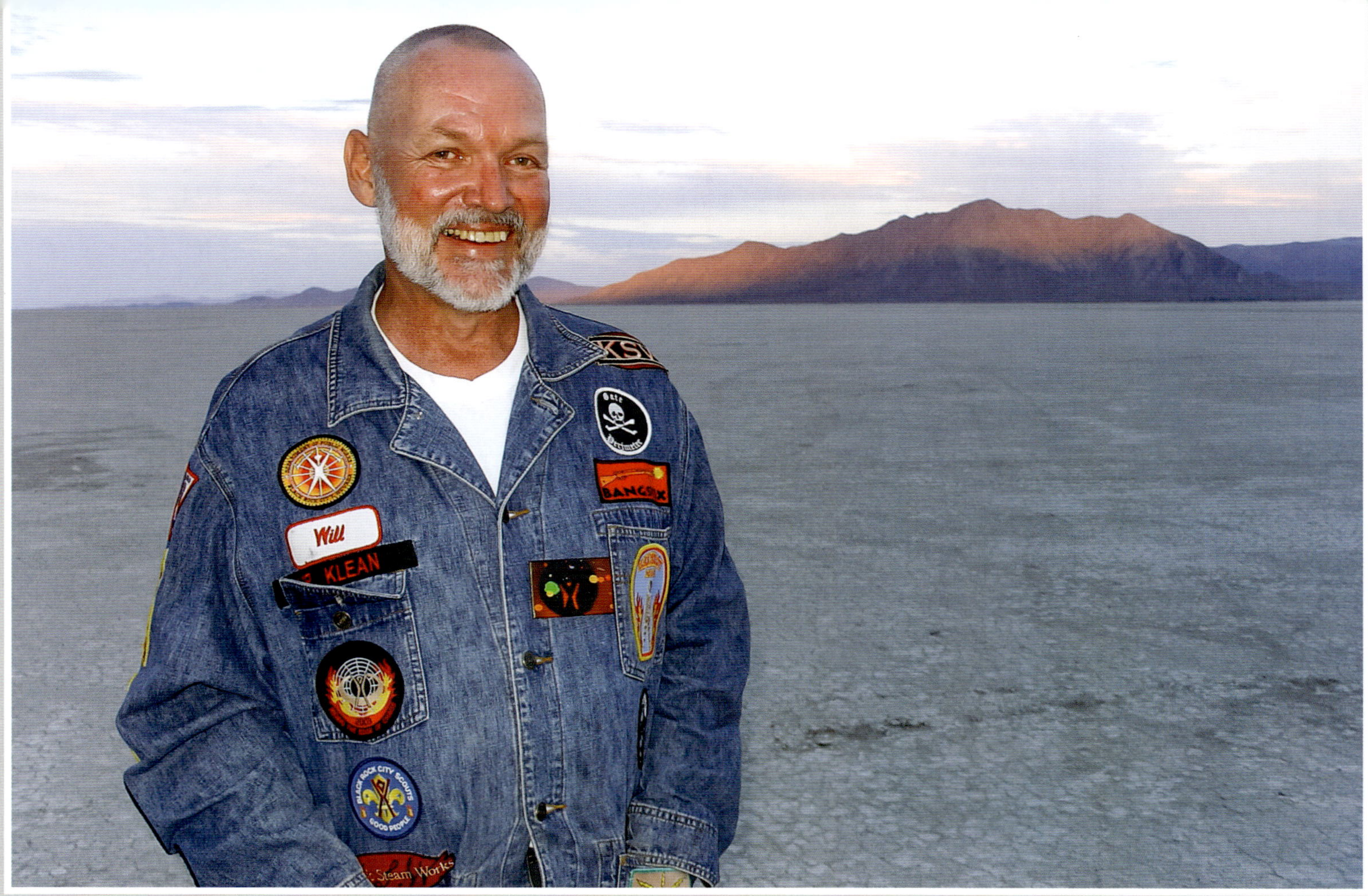

"The desert could not be claimed or owned — it was a piece of cloth carried by winds, never held down by stones, and given a hundred shifting names long before Canterbury existed, long before battles and treaties quilted Europe and the East. Its caravans, those strange rambling feasts and cultures, left nothing behind, not an ember. All of us, even those with European homes and children in the distance, wished to remove the clothing of our countries. It was a place of faith. We disappeared into landscape. Fire and sand. We left the harbours of oasis. The places water came to and touched ... Ain, Bir, Wadi, Foggara, Khottara, Shaduf. I didn't want my name against such beautiful names. Erase the family name! Erase nations! I was taught such things by the desert." – Michael Ondaatje, *The English Patient*

Desert Songs: The Art of Will Roger

Rosa JH Berland

In this series of astonishing aerial photographs of the desert and its various majestic natural wonders, from expanses of sand to mountaintops illuminated by the bluest of skies, Will captures a moment of wonder, the cities like calligraphic sketching, forming semi circles, and reminding one of all typography letters spread out like a Zen garden. Still other photos fluctuate between otherworldly moments of fog, sfumato and clarity, a dance of beauty across the landscape. The desert is a place that when you stand in the middle seems that it has no beginning or end. Still other views seem fogged by sunlight, a sort of veiling. These misty pictures have a quiet magnetism, pushing and pulling the viewer through the clouds allowing one to feel as if in flight. The aerial view is a unique perspective. We are able to see the great land's edges, furrows, and peaks. At once, the viewer is above this monumental place, the Nevada desert, but is also made aware of this place's formidable power, and awe-inspiring allure. Perhaps for a moment, we can be reminded of the rather foolhardy impulse of American settlers to conquer this vast and dry space, its power of erasure and remaking, deadly and magical. For his part, Will has long been committed to conservation efforts for the preservation of the Black Rock Desert.

Photo (2007) by Marnee Benson

Artist, Teacher, Innovator + Environmentalist

The desert of North America and beyond is a place of enduring mystery, power, and natural beauty. It is a ruse that this space of earth possesses a kind of blank canvas quality, and man is so often tricked into believing that the desert can be owned, harnessed, conquered, and taken. The winds will show such ambitiousness: the truth, through veils of heavy sand–blinding, erasing, wounding, starving, and burying. For its unrelenting power, beauty, and majestic spirit, many artists have come to love, respect, and even fear the desert. This dualistic way of interacting is very much at the core of American artist Will Roger's photographic practice.

Will is a conservationist, creator, and teacher. Having served as Chairman of Sierra Front, North Western Great Basin Resource Advisory Council, and President of the Friends of the Black Rock-High Rock, he is the sort of forward-looking artist and radical thinker you would want to know. His approach has an openness and fearlessness that we could all learn from. So, after encountering his work, it is no surprise that this man is also a cultural co-founder of Burning Man. In all of his work, Will requires of his audience openness to the power and mystery of the natural world, whether it be from a panoramic aerial perspective of the Black Rock Desert, the multi-faceted and intellectually engaging black-and-white photography, or his deeply sensual studies of flowers. There is a playful fluctuation between object, participant, viewer and voyeur.

Will began in analytical chemistry, working as a photo chemist at the Rochester Institute of Technology. Interested in finding new ways to understand the world, he would go on to earn his MFA in photography and serve as an Associate Professor of photography at RIT, working at the prestigious institute for over twenty years. There, he created and taught the course, "In Search of the Mystical Image." Today, Will is noted for his creative formal or technical approach, notably a distinctive style of stop-motion photography. Moreover, the artist's work is well respected for a fluency of movement, certain enigmatic lyricism, and a truly esoteric quality that fascinates.

As one develops intellectually and artistically, physical movement is often the impetus for real growth. So, seeking a new space and challenge, in the early 1990s, Will decided to move to California and focus on portraiture. He would eventually become involved in the wonderfully mind-blowing gathering of risk takers and creativity called Burning Man. The extraordinary freedom would act as catalyst for new and exciting work that seems to exist between two worlds: the surrealist photography of early twentieth century Europe and the Bacchanalian spirit of this world-renowned desert event. As well, the heroic and fantastic allure of the desert would come to be a key motif in the artist's work, including astonishing aerial photographs.

A Fullness of Form and Emptiness

Will's signature in-motion style gives the impression of a dancing world of loveliness, both in the erotic dancer studies or in the flower series. From Will's erotic portraits to his images of underwater ecologies or the grandiose beauty of the desert, one experiences a fullness of form and an emptiness, allowing both balance and intrigue. Will is a creative *tour de force* whose luxuriously beautiful photos intersect with a sense of the analytical; critics say this is a man who makes his subject dance through light, color, and stop-motion photography. Within this movement, there is a certain freedom to the work, a place where bold color, dramatic landscapes, or charged images of sexuality merge with quiet space.

A Man Fulfilled

Will Roger spends his time between the San Francisco Bay Area and the Black Rock Desert region with his partner and muse, Crimson Rose.

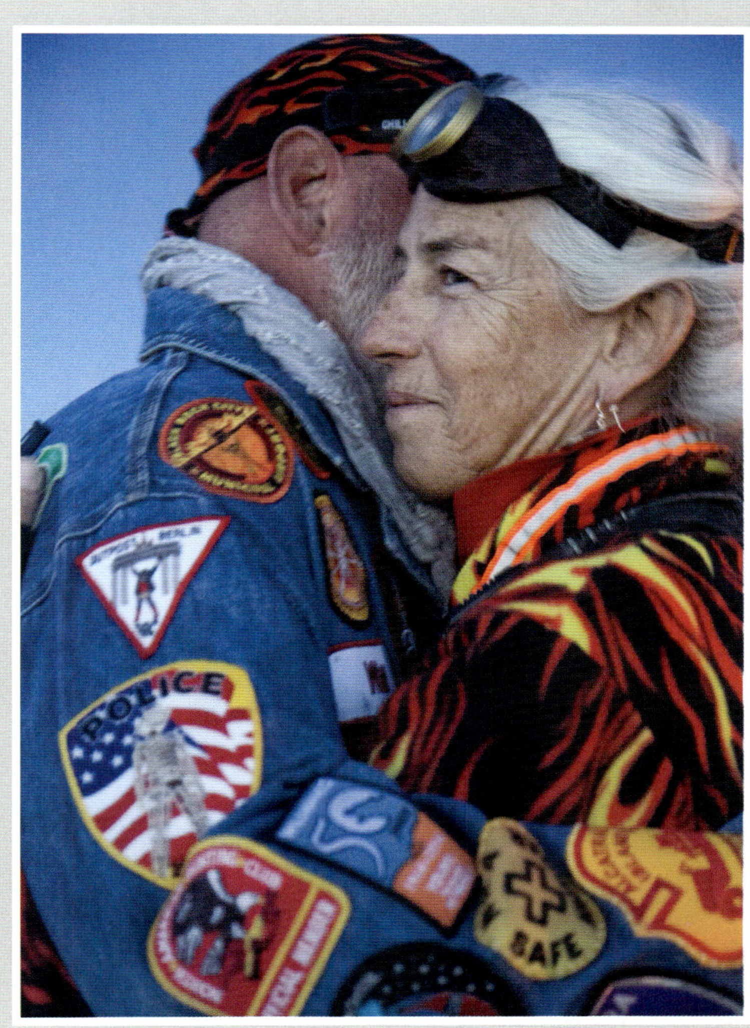

Will Roger and Crimson Rose embracing on burn night.
Photo (2017) by Eleanor Pregor

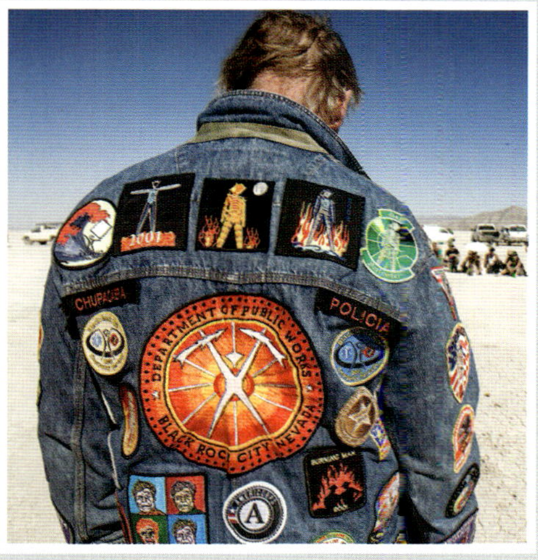

Will Roger's iconic DPW jacket, adorned with many patches, exhibits in museums.
Photo (2012) by John Curley

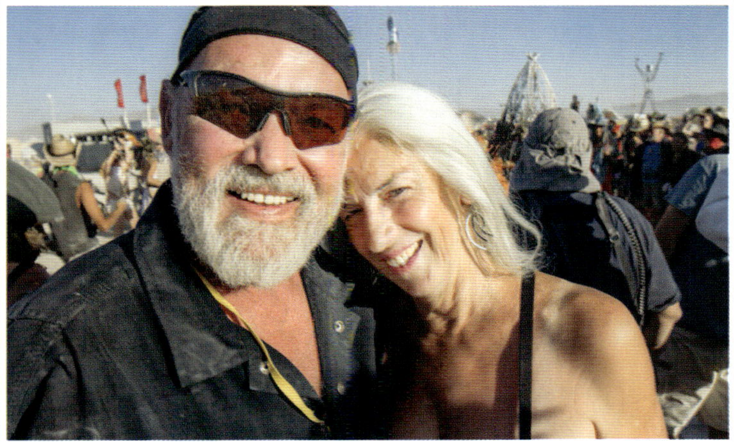

Will Roger and Crimson Rose. Photo (2017) by John Curley

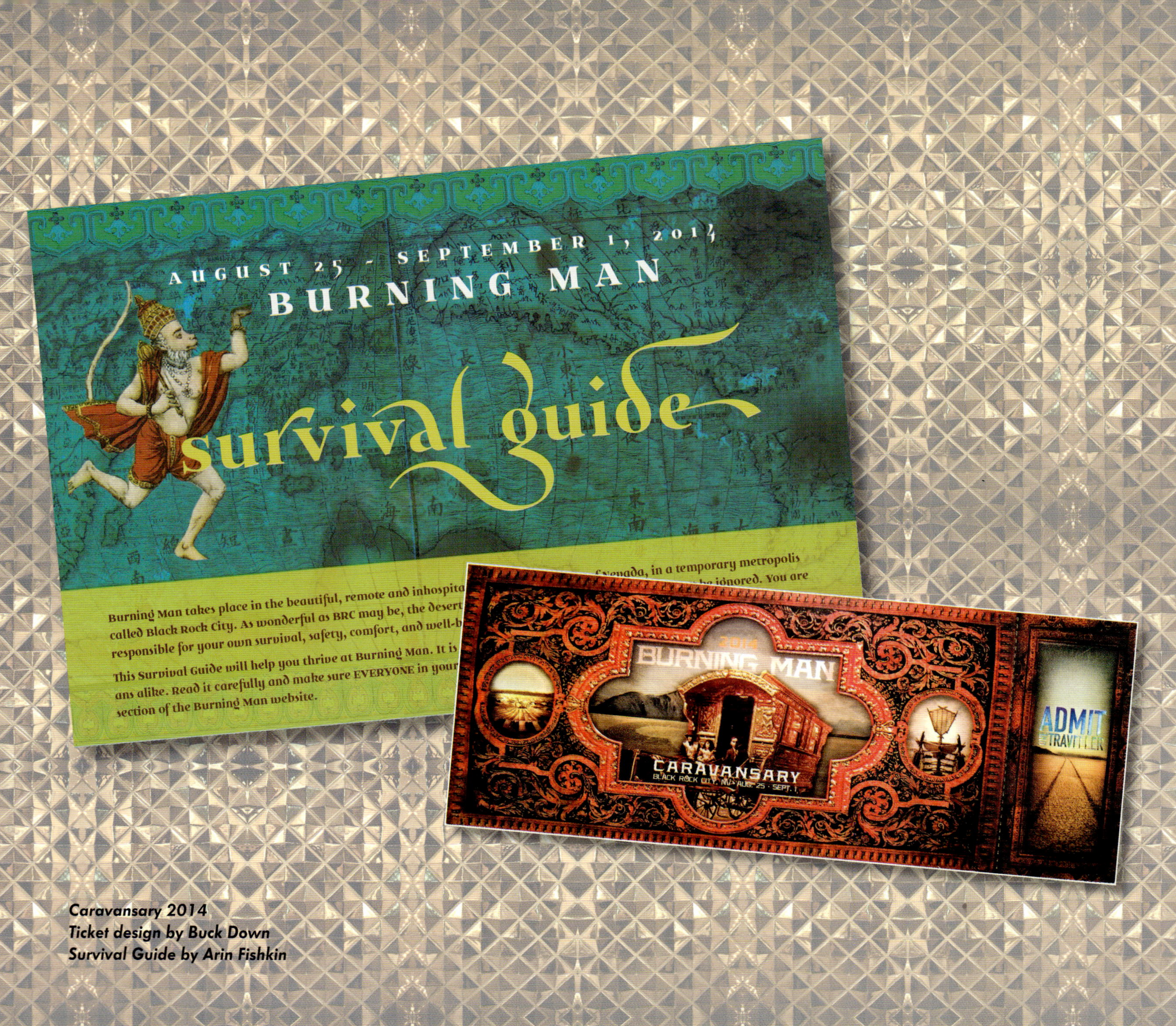

Caravansary 2014
Ticket design by Buck Down
Survival Guide by Arin Fishkin

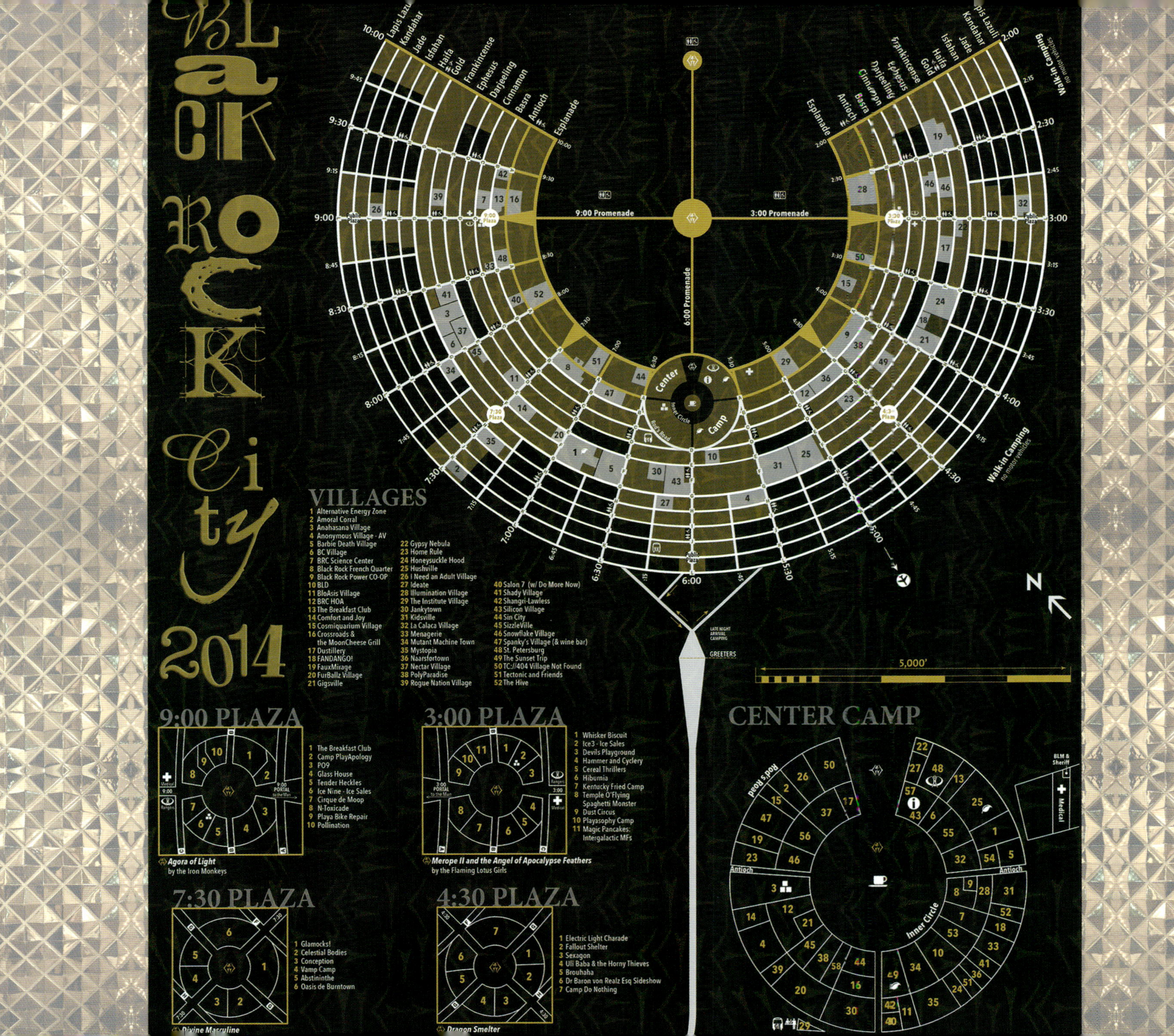

BLACK ROCK CITY 2014

VILLAGES
1 Alternative Energy Zone
2 Amoral Corral
3 Anahasana Village
4 Anonymous Village - AV
5 Barbie Death Village
6 BC Village
7 BRC Science Center
8 Black Rock French Quarter
9 Black Rock Power CO-OP
10 BLD
11 BioAxis Village
12 BRC HOA
13 The Breakfast Club
14 Comfort and Joy
15 Cosmiquarium Village
16 Crossroads &
   the MoonCheese Grill
17 Dustillery
18 FANDANGO!
19 FauxMirage
20 FurBallz Village
21 Gigsville
22 Gypsy Nebula
23 Home Rule
24 Honeysuckle Hood
25 Hushville
26 I Need an Adult Village
27 Ideate
28 Illumination Village
29 The Institute Village
30 Jankytown
31 Kidsville
32 La Calaca Village
33 Menagerie
34 Mutant Machine Town
35 Mystopia
36 Naarsfortown
37 Nectar Village
38 PolyParadise
39 Rogue Nation Village
40 Salon 7 (w/ Do More Now)
41 Shady Village
42 Shangri-Lawless
43 Silicon City
44 Sin City
45 SizzleVille
46 Snowflake Village
47 Spanky's Village (& wine bar)
48 St. Petersburg
49 The Sunset Trip
50 TC://404 Village Not Found
51 Tectonic and Friends
52 The Hive

9:00 PLAZA
1 The Breakfast Club
2 Camp PlayApology
3 PO9
4 Glass House
5 Tender Heckles
6 Ice Nine - Ice Sales
7 Cirque de Moop
8 N-Toxicade
9 Playa Bike Repair
10 Pollination
Agora of Light
by the Iron Monkeys

3:00 PLAZA
1 Whisker Biscuit
2 Ice3 - Ice Sales
3 Devils Playground
4 Hammer and Cyclery
5 Cereal Thrillers
6 Hibernia
7 Kentucky Fried Camp
8 Temple O'Flying
   Spaghetti Monster
9 Dust Circus
10 Playasophy Camp
11 Magic Pancakes:
   Intergalactic MFs
Merope II and the Angel of Apocalypse Feathers
by the Flaming Lotus Girls

7:30 PLAZA
1 Glamocks!
2 Celestial Bodies
3 Conception
4 Vamp Camp
5 Abstininthe
6 Oasis de Burntown
Divine Masculine

4:30 PLAZA
1 Electric Light Charade
2 Fallout Shelter
3 Sexagon
4 Uli Baba & the Horny Thieves
5 Brouhaha
6 Dr Baron von Realz Esq Sideshow
7 Camp Do Nothing
Dragon Smelter

CENTER CAMP

9:00 Promenade
3:00 Promenade
6:00 Promenade
Center Camp
Inner Circle
Rod's Road
GREETERS
Walk-in Camping
Late Night Arrival Camping
BLM & Sheriff
Medical
Antioch

5,000'

"Golden Night" photomontage by James Stanford

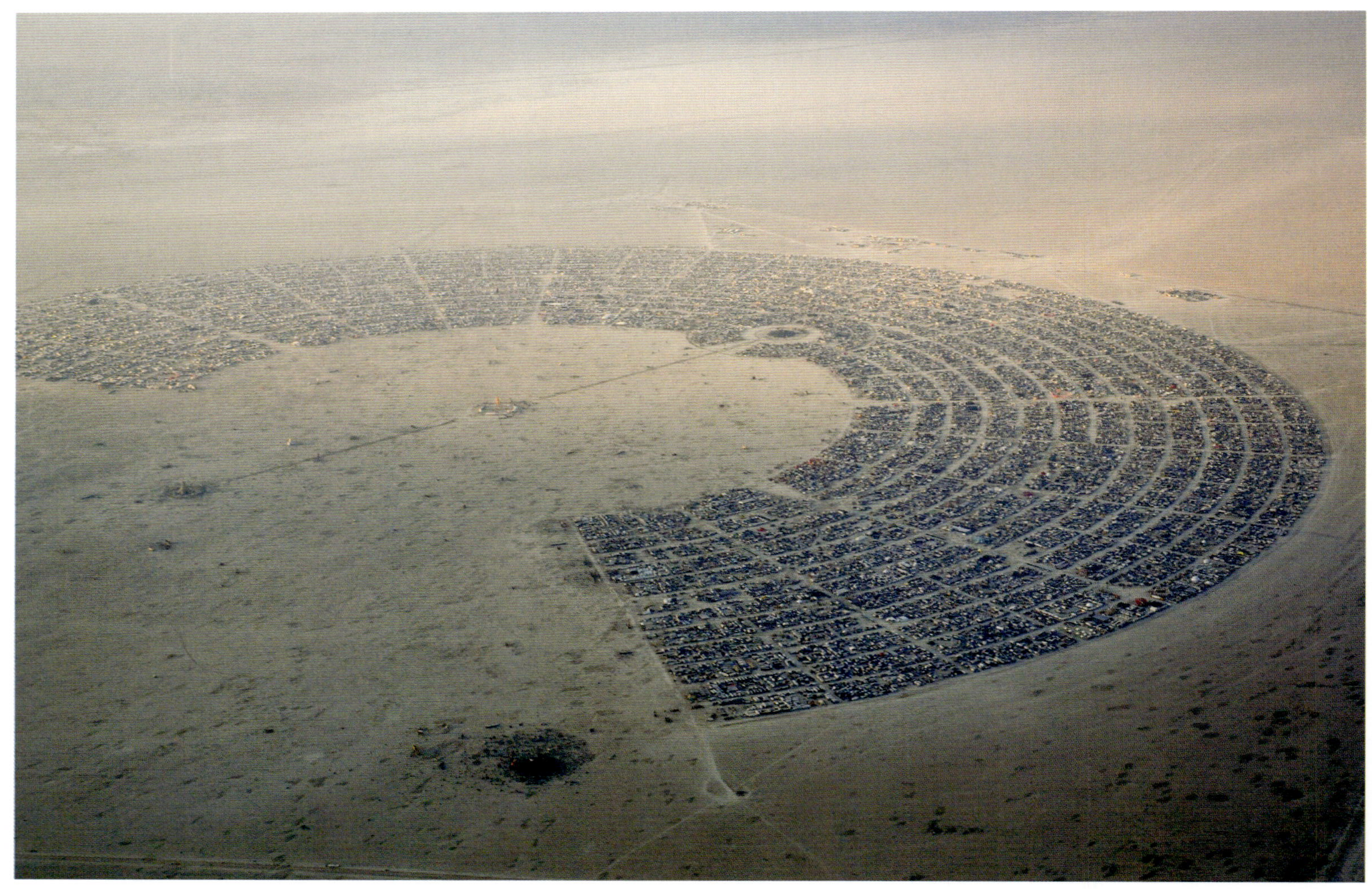

Right: *Vehicle tracks are revealed in the morning light, Population 65,922*

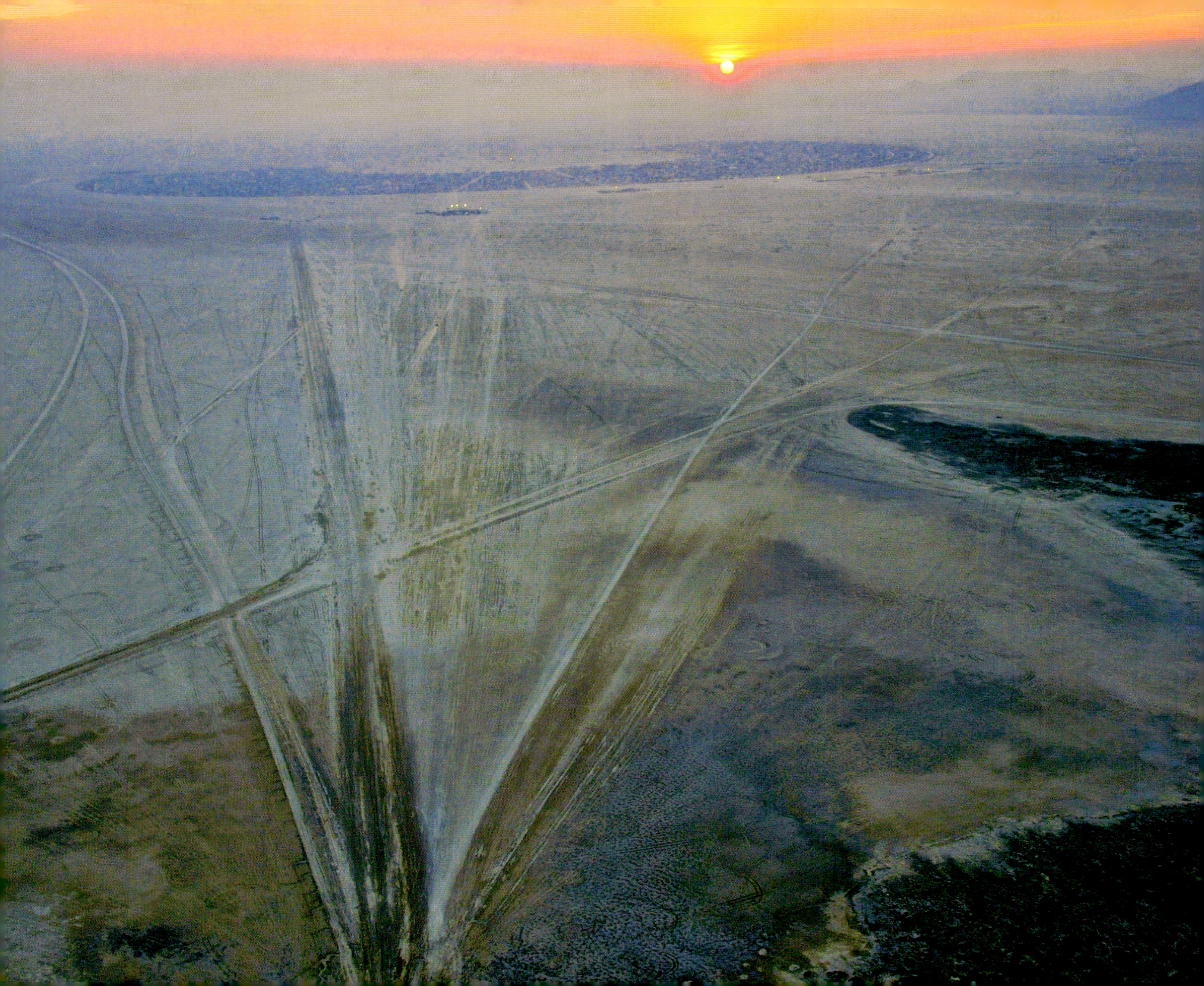

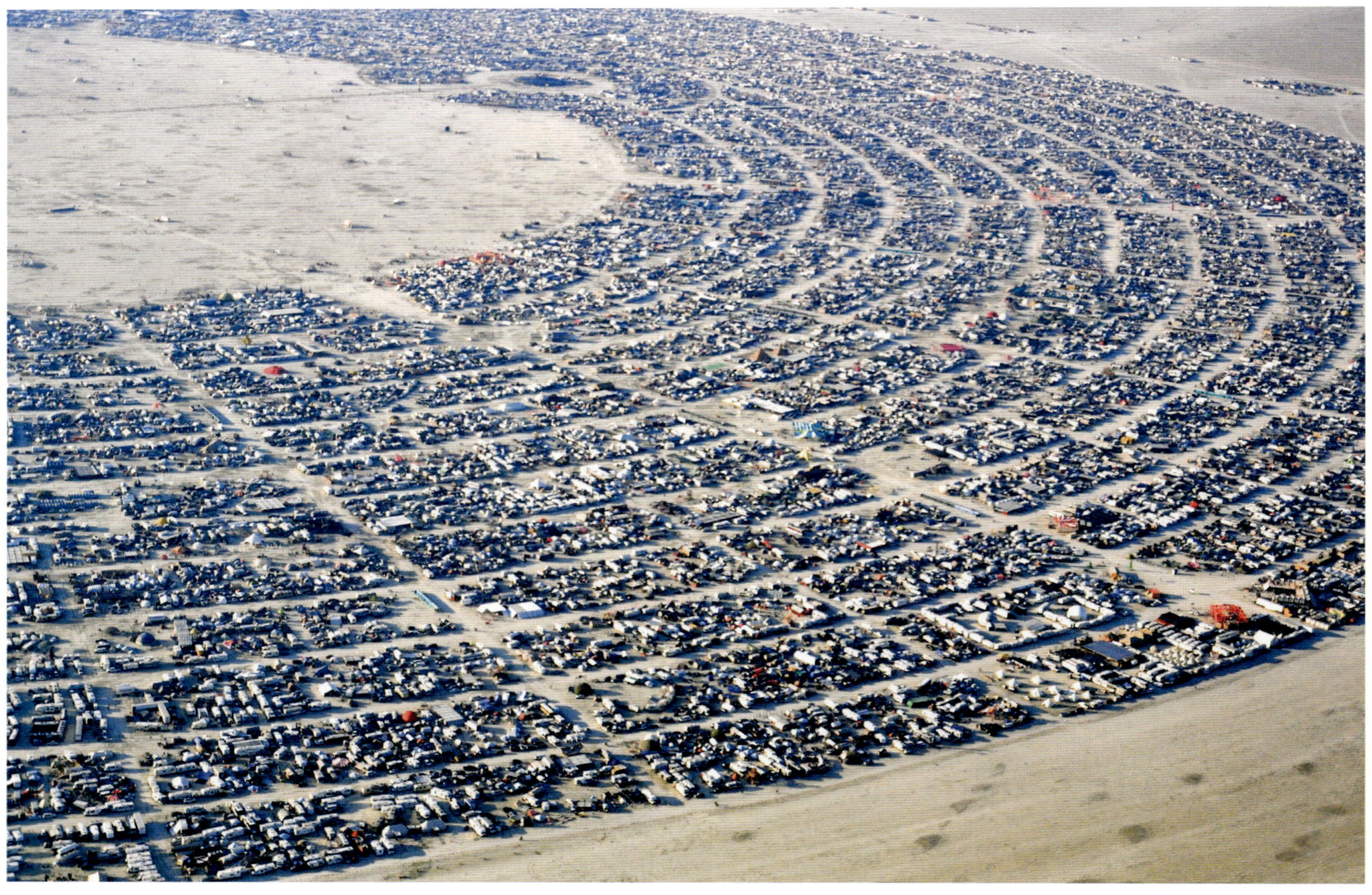

166

Right: *The desert awakens to the rising sun, torrential rainstorms shut the city down earlier in the week*

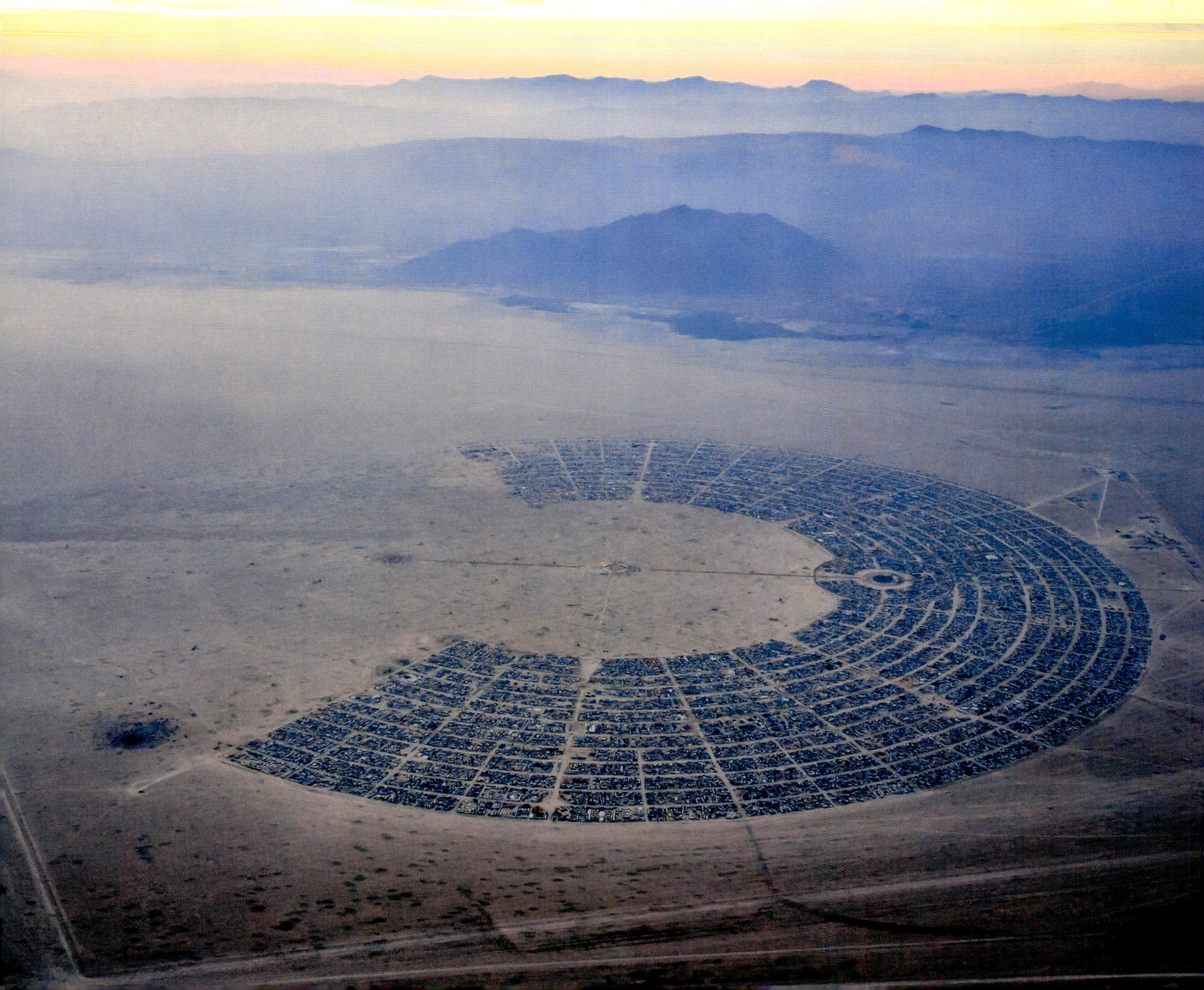

168

Black Rock City, 3,603 acres

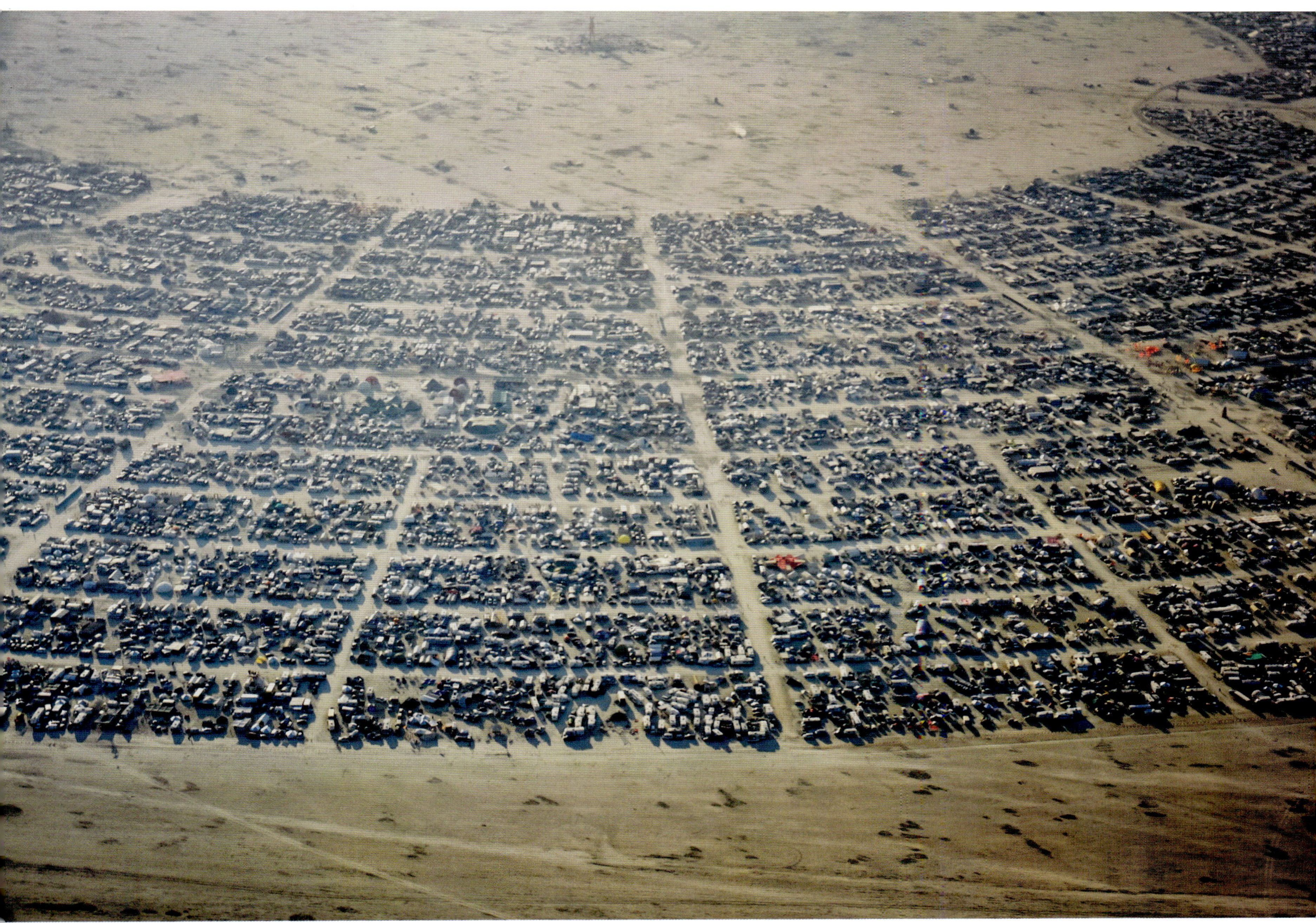

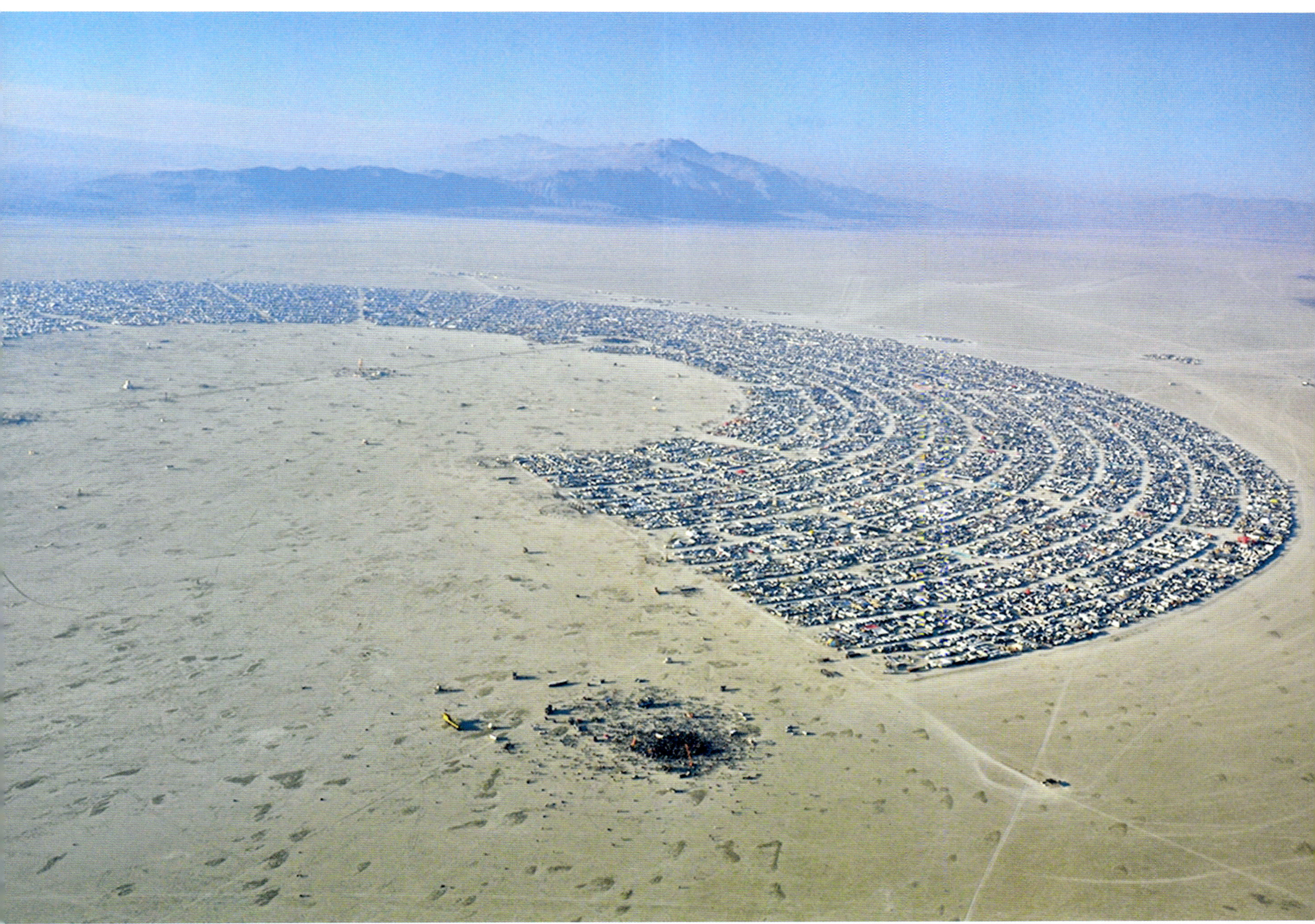

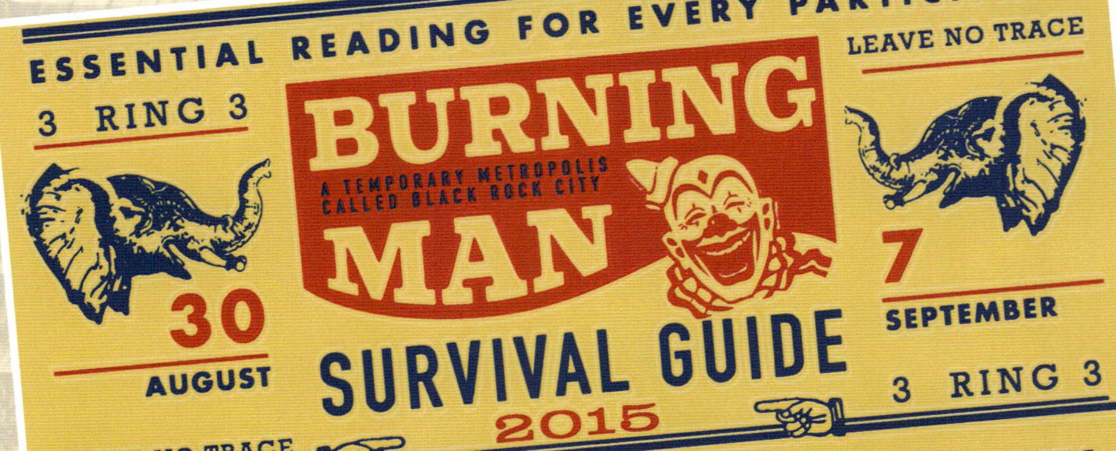

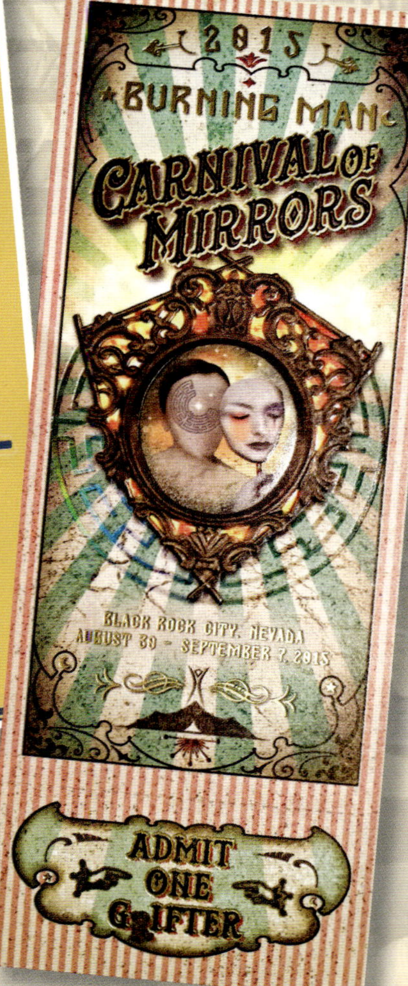

Carnival of Mirrors 2015
Survival Guide by Arin Fishkin
Ticket Design by Mark Harrison

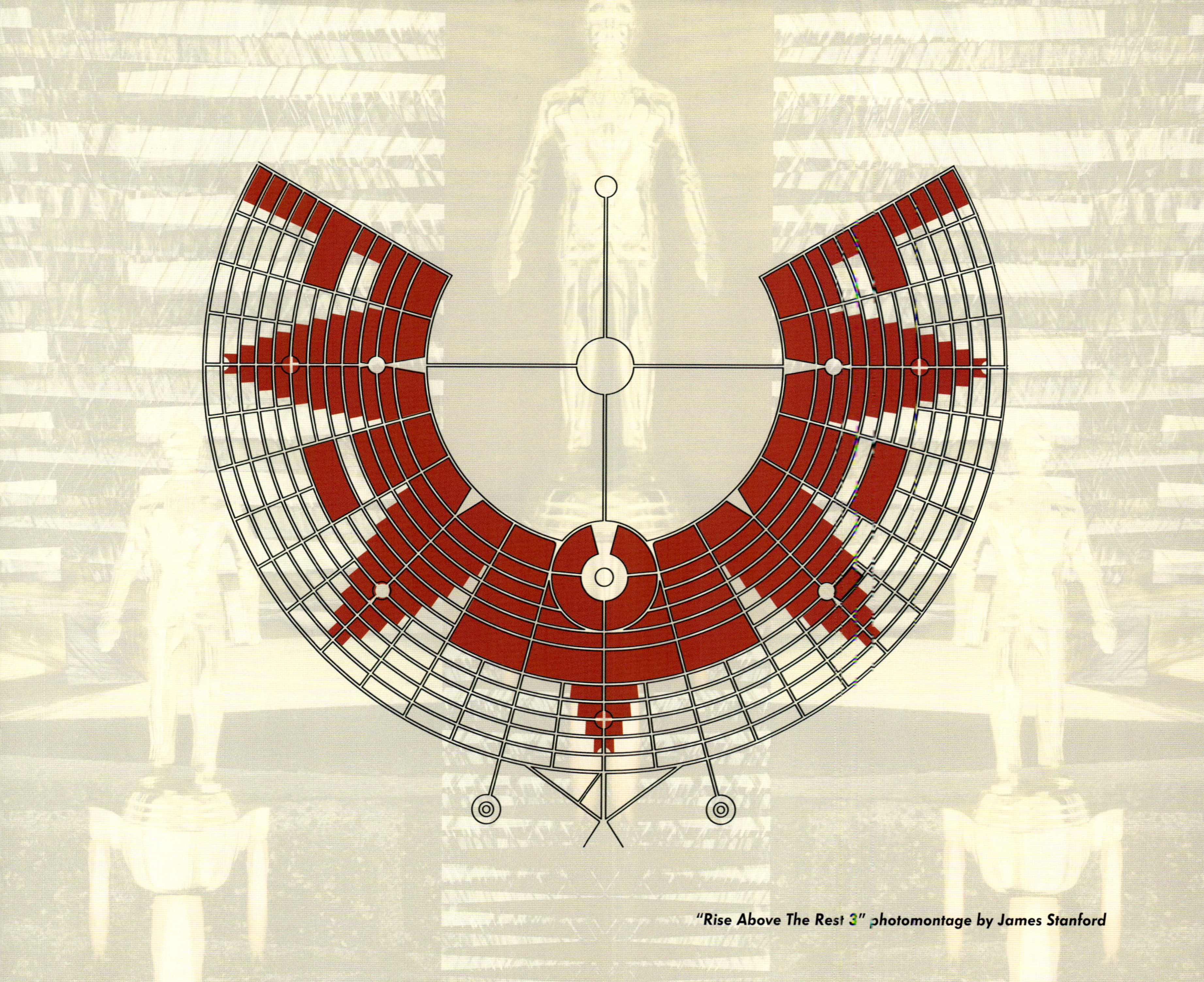

"Rise Above The Rest 3" photomontage by James Stanford

Facing north, far past the outer playa, is a range of short, small, dark mountains. Population 67,564

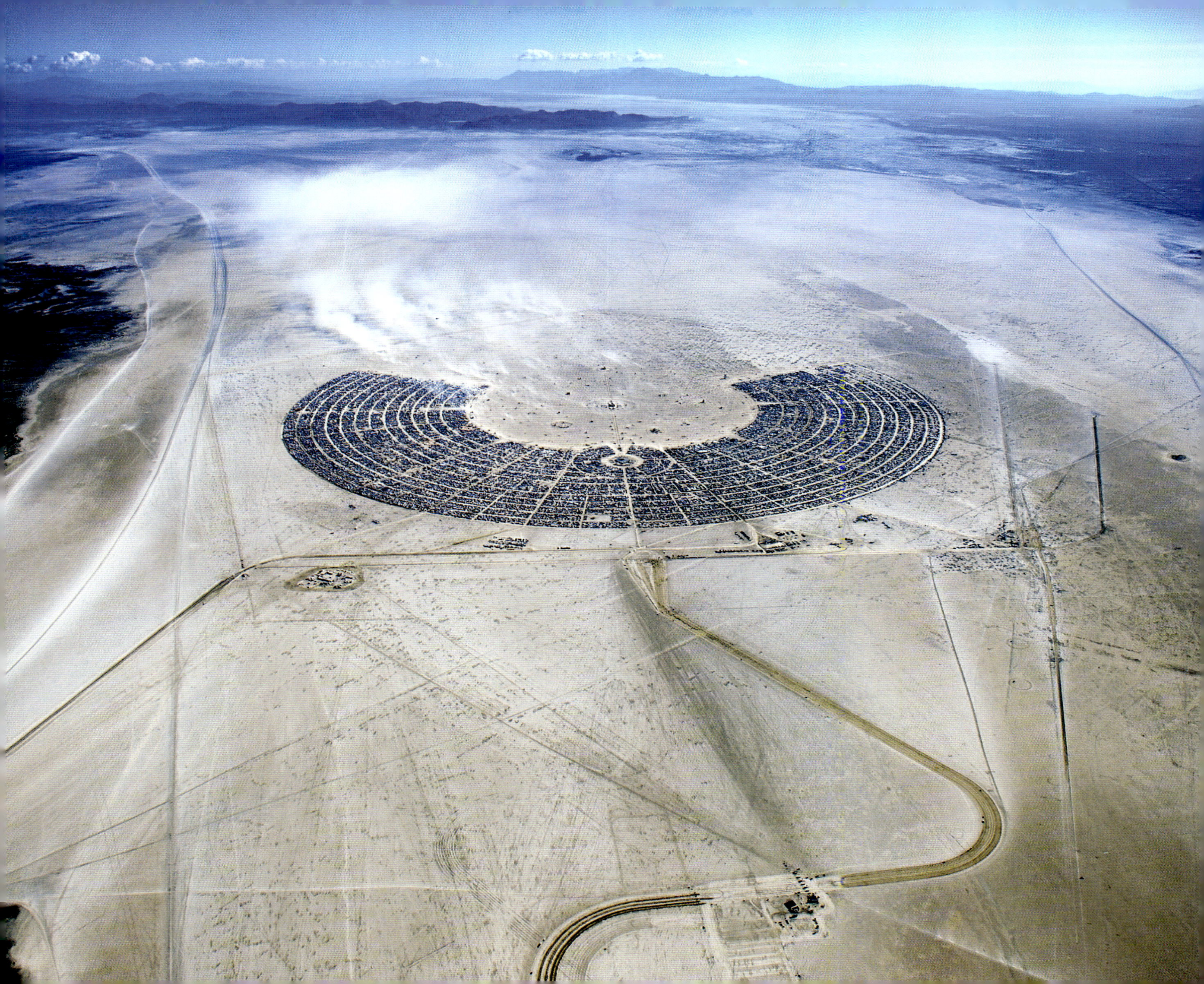

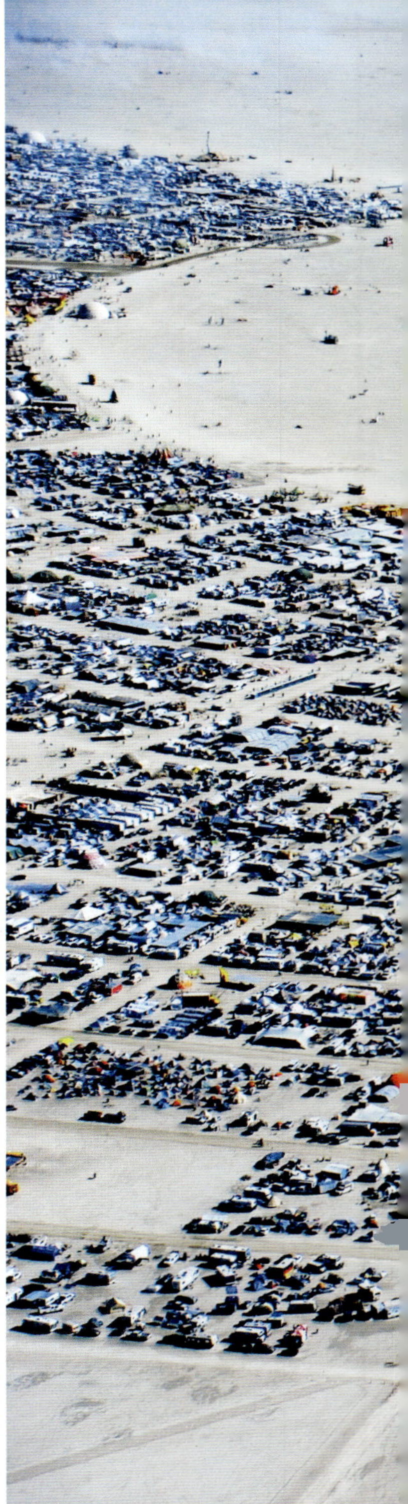

Center Camp is located along the mid-line of Black Rock City, facing the Man on the Esplanade. At 38,000 square feet, the structure is held up by two concentric wooden rings and secured to the earth by high-tension cable, capable of withstanding 120 mph winds, drastic temperature and weather changes

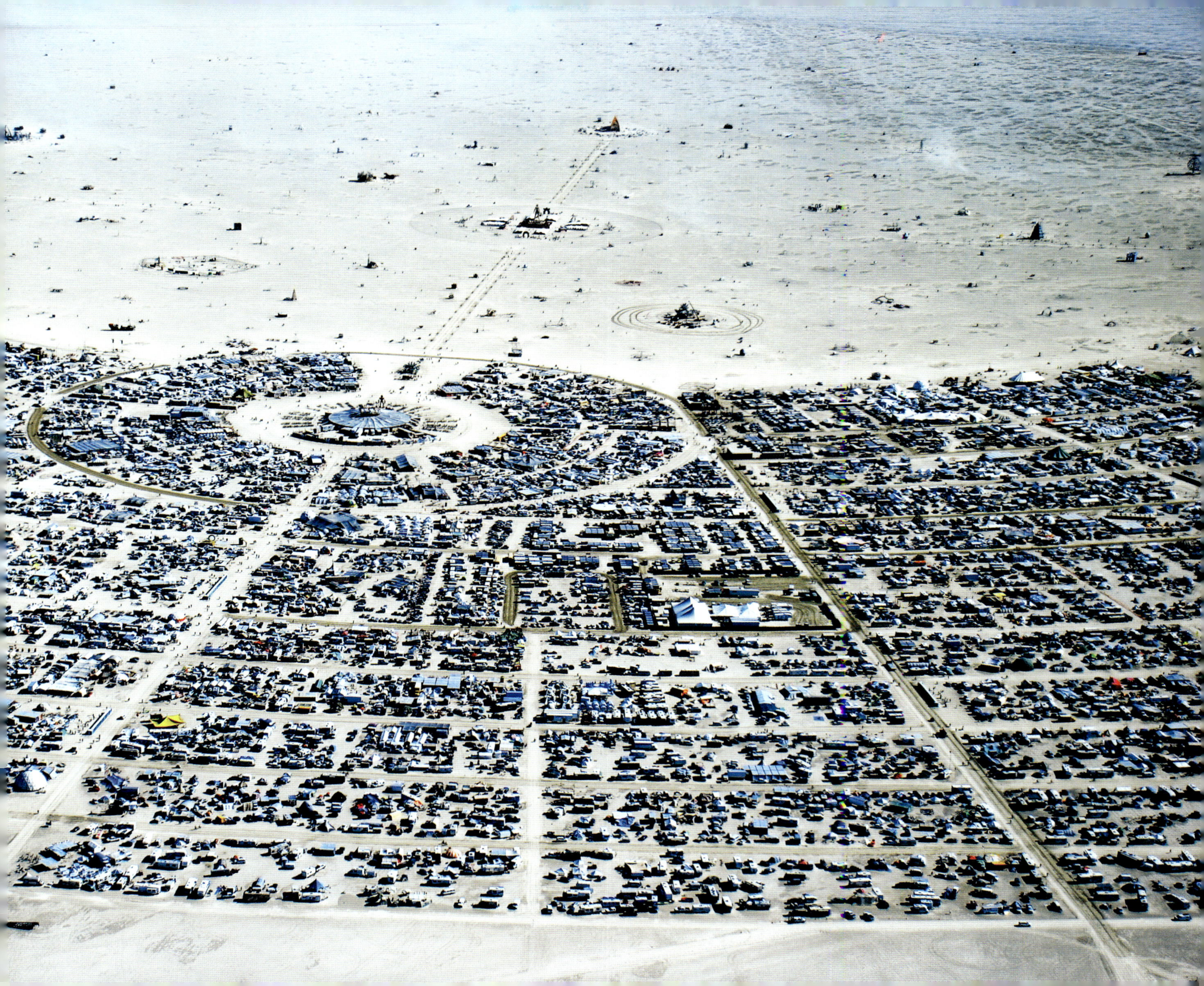

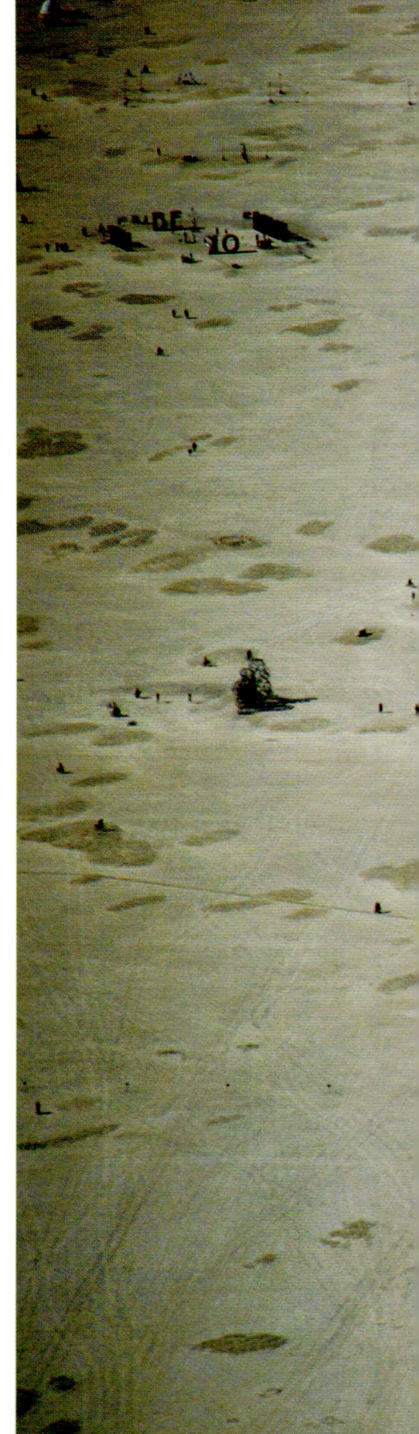

"Temple of Promise" by Jazz Tigan and The Dreamers Guild looking up the Promenade to the Man

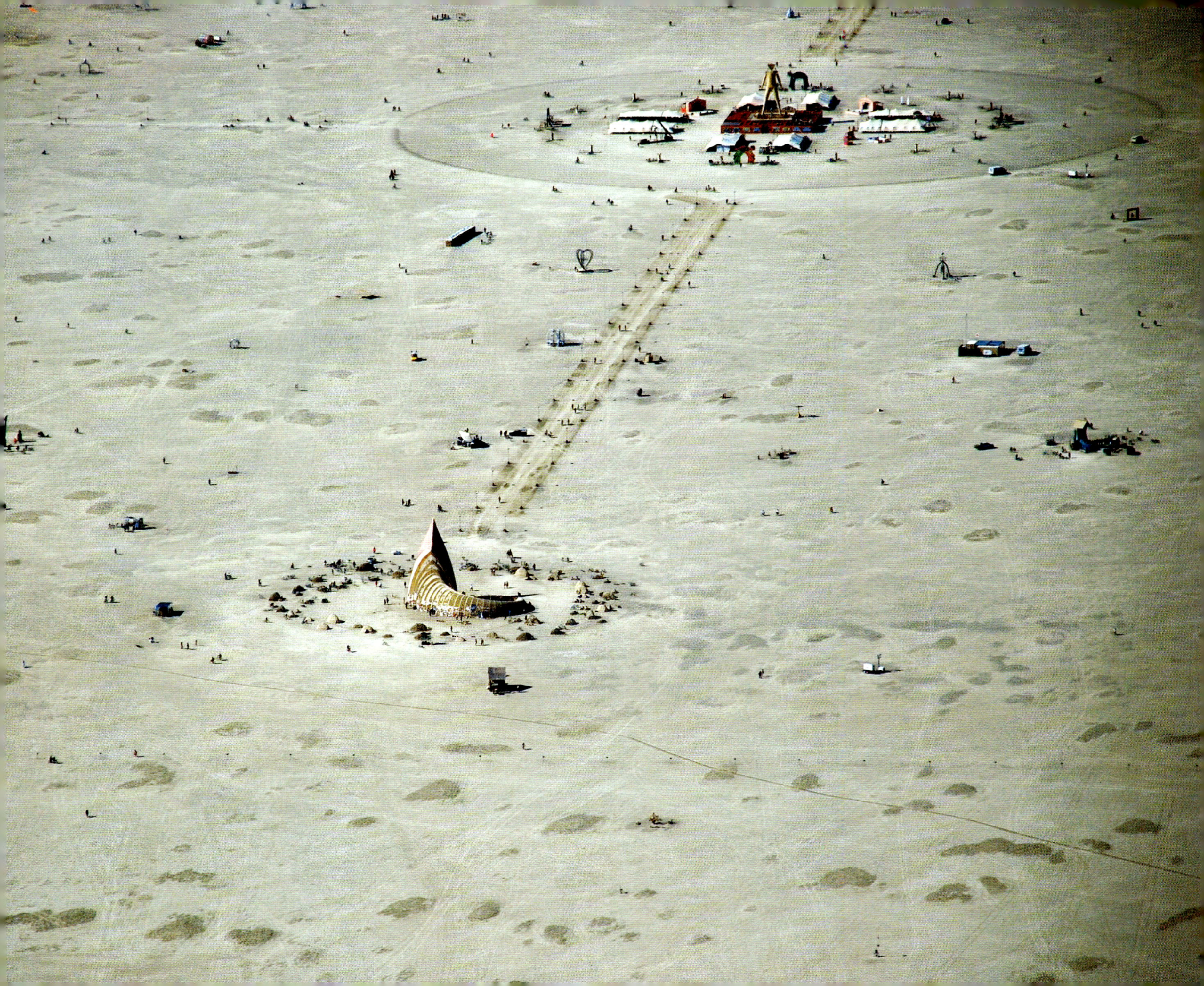

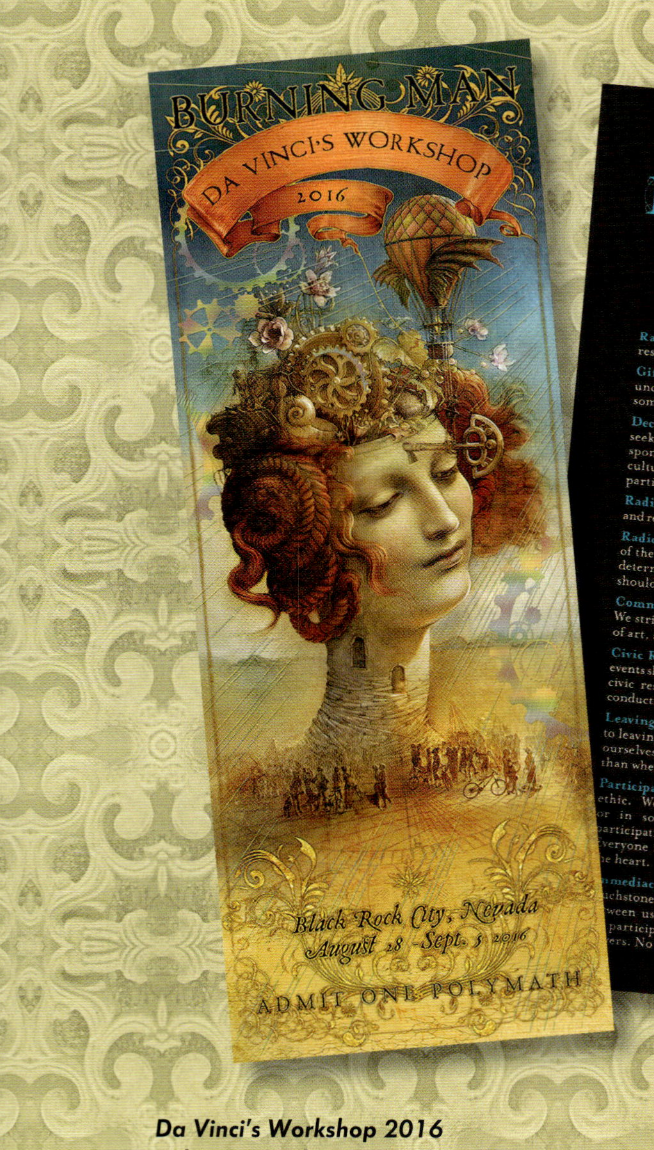

Da Vinci's Workshop 2016
Ticket Design by Cory and Catska Ench
Survival Guide by Arin Fishkin

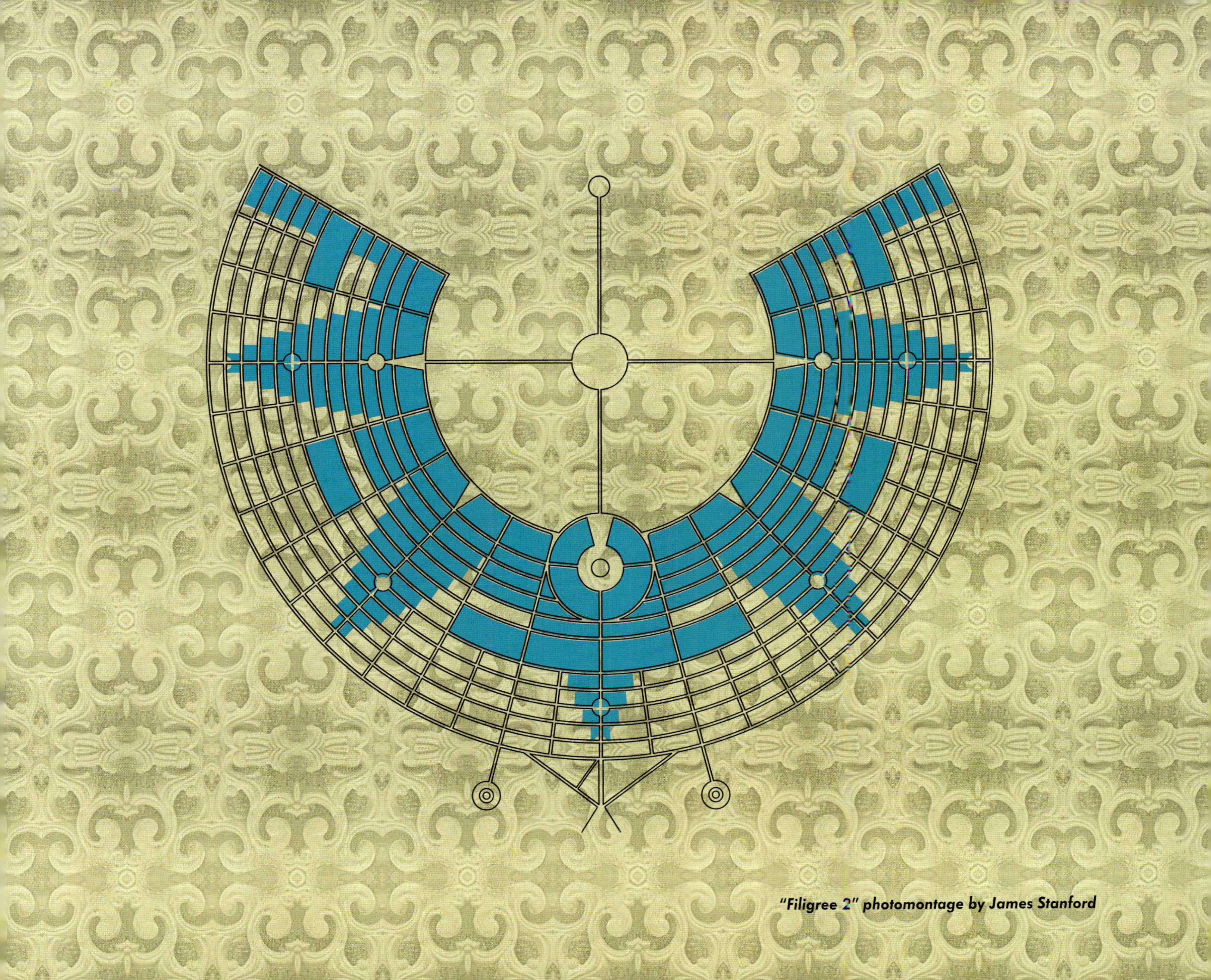

"Filigree 2" photomontage by James Stanford

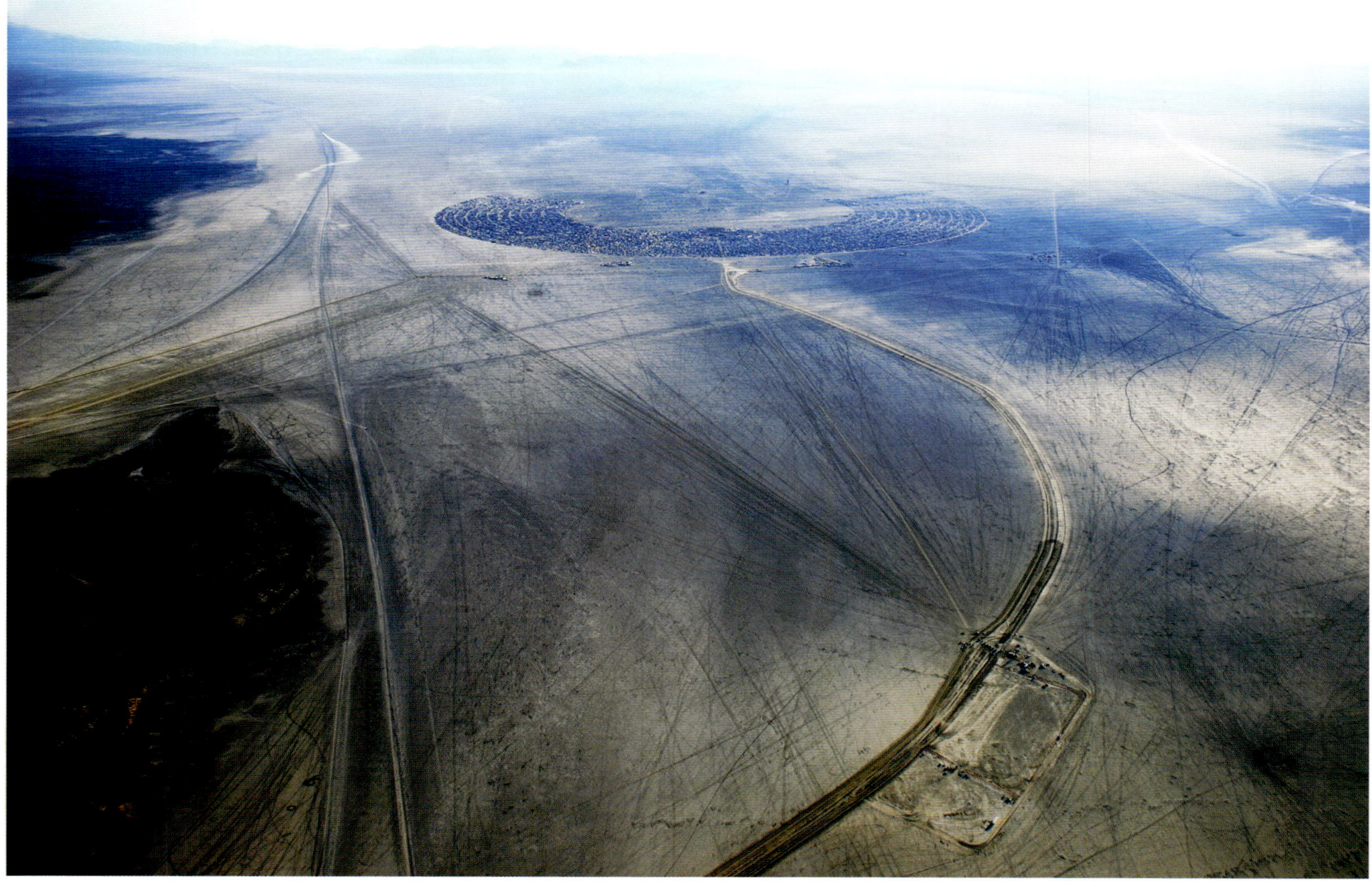

Above: *The playa after intense dust storms, high winds, freezing temperatures and rain*
Right: *This photograph exhibited in the "Home Means Nevada" and the "No Spectators: The Art of Burning Man" touring exhibitions.*
This photo serves as the cover of this book featuring a blue atmospheric condition called aerial perspective. Population 67,290

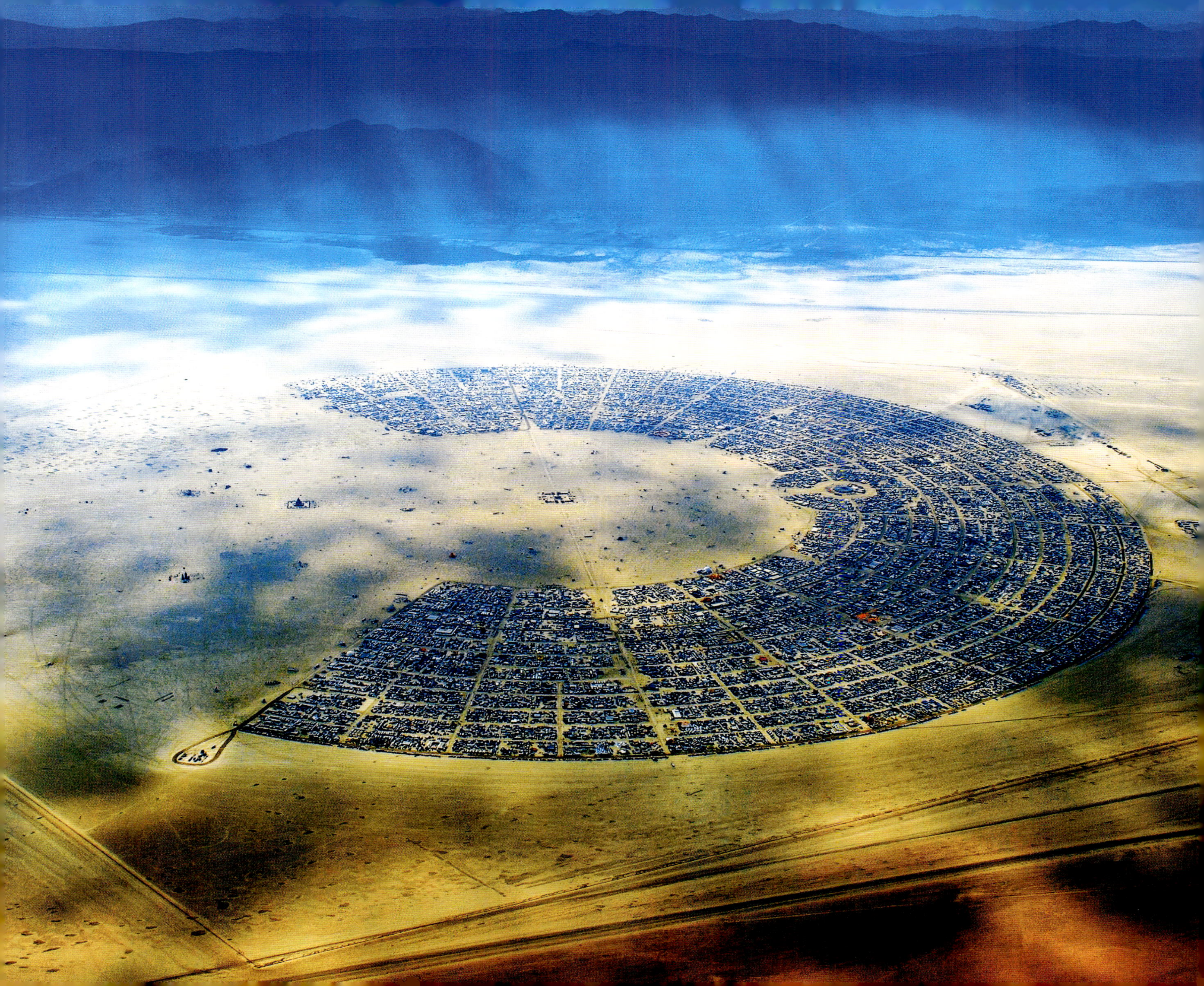

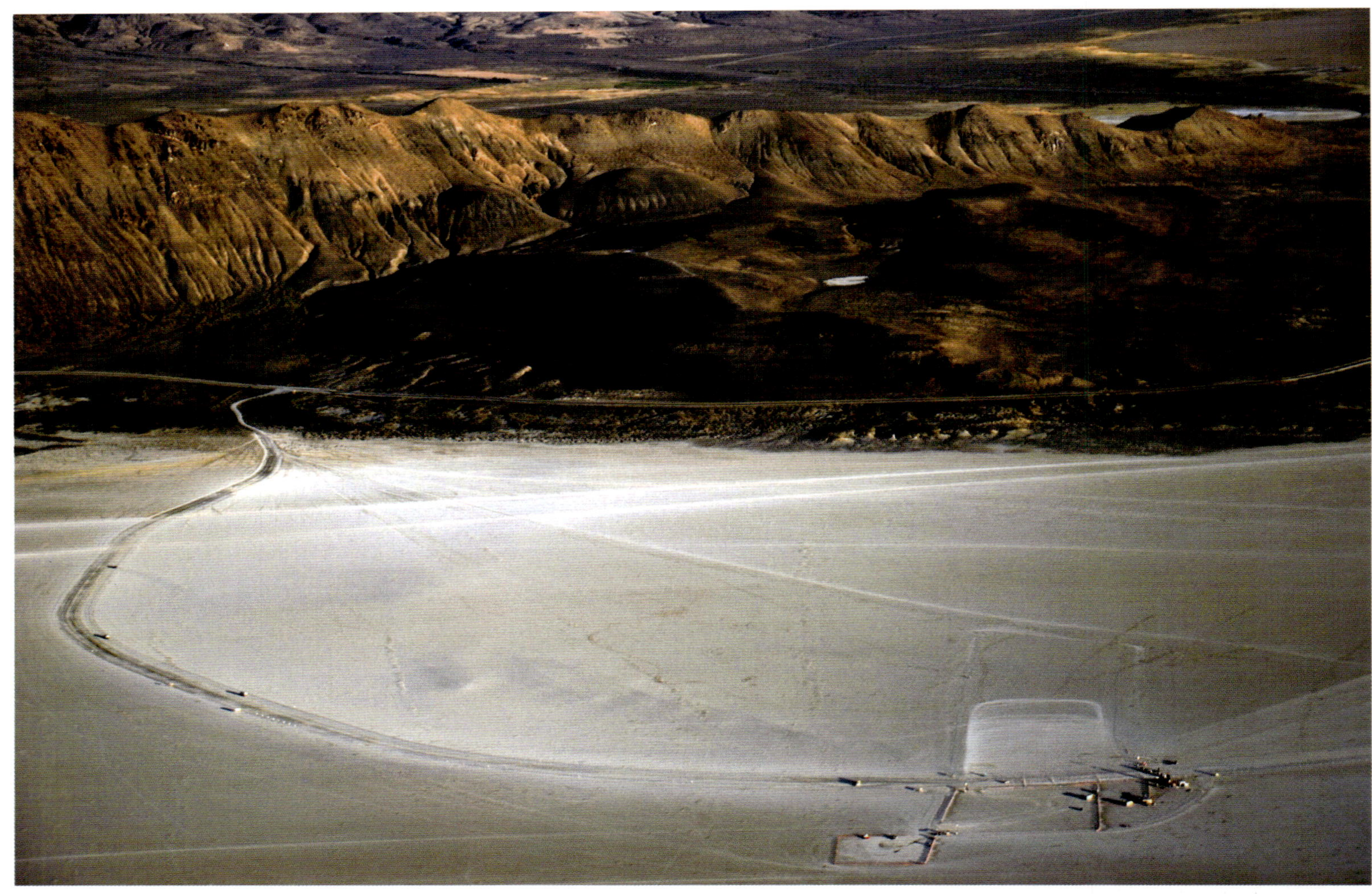

184

Above: *Highway 34 and Gate Road*
Right: *Law Enforcement Compound and DPW Depot. Population 67,290*

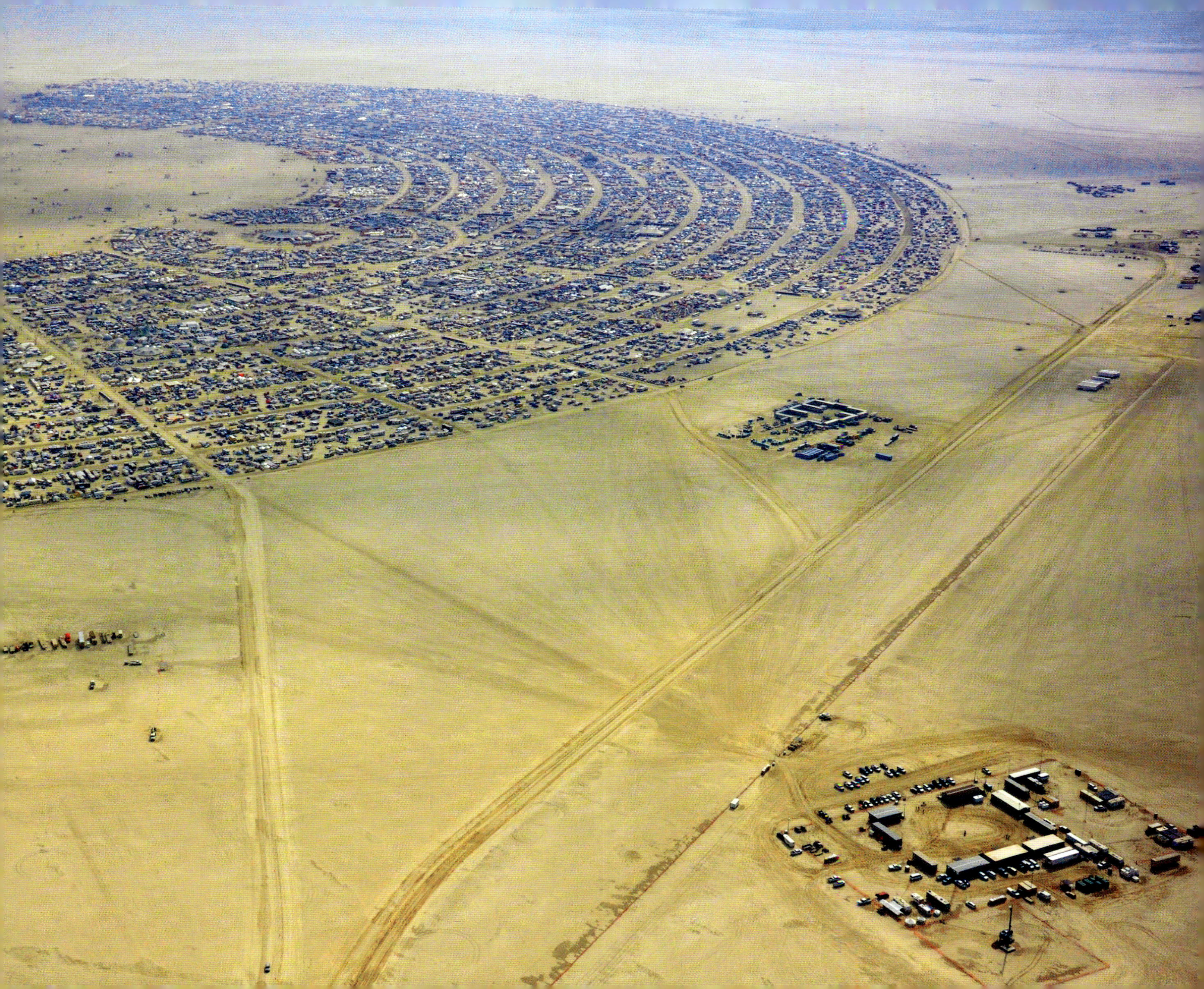

There were 316 total art installations on the playa, including 64 walk-in pieces, 58 honoraria and 29 Guild Workshops
Fire projects included: 18 open fire projects, 36 flame effects projects and 12 pyrotechnic projects

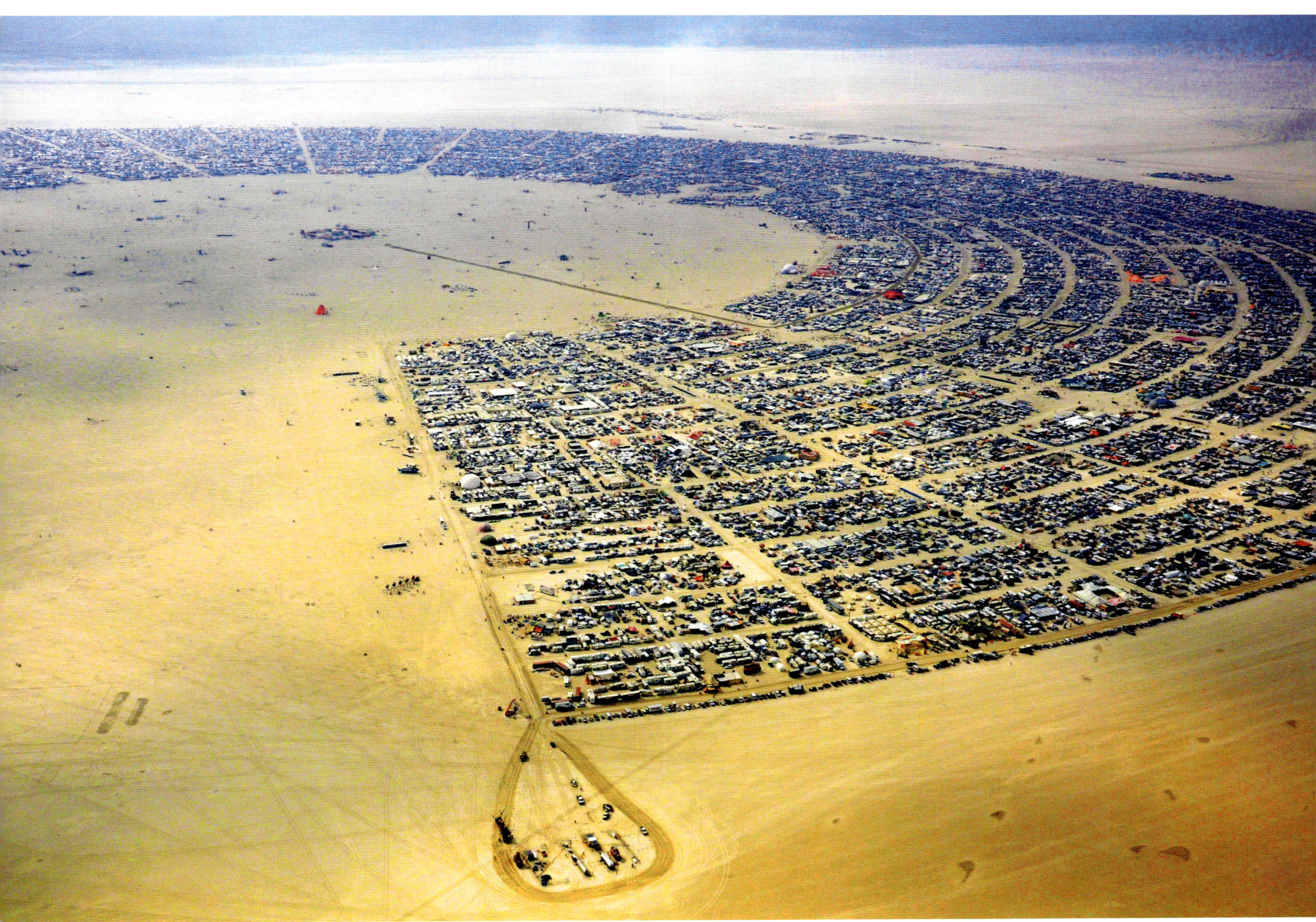

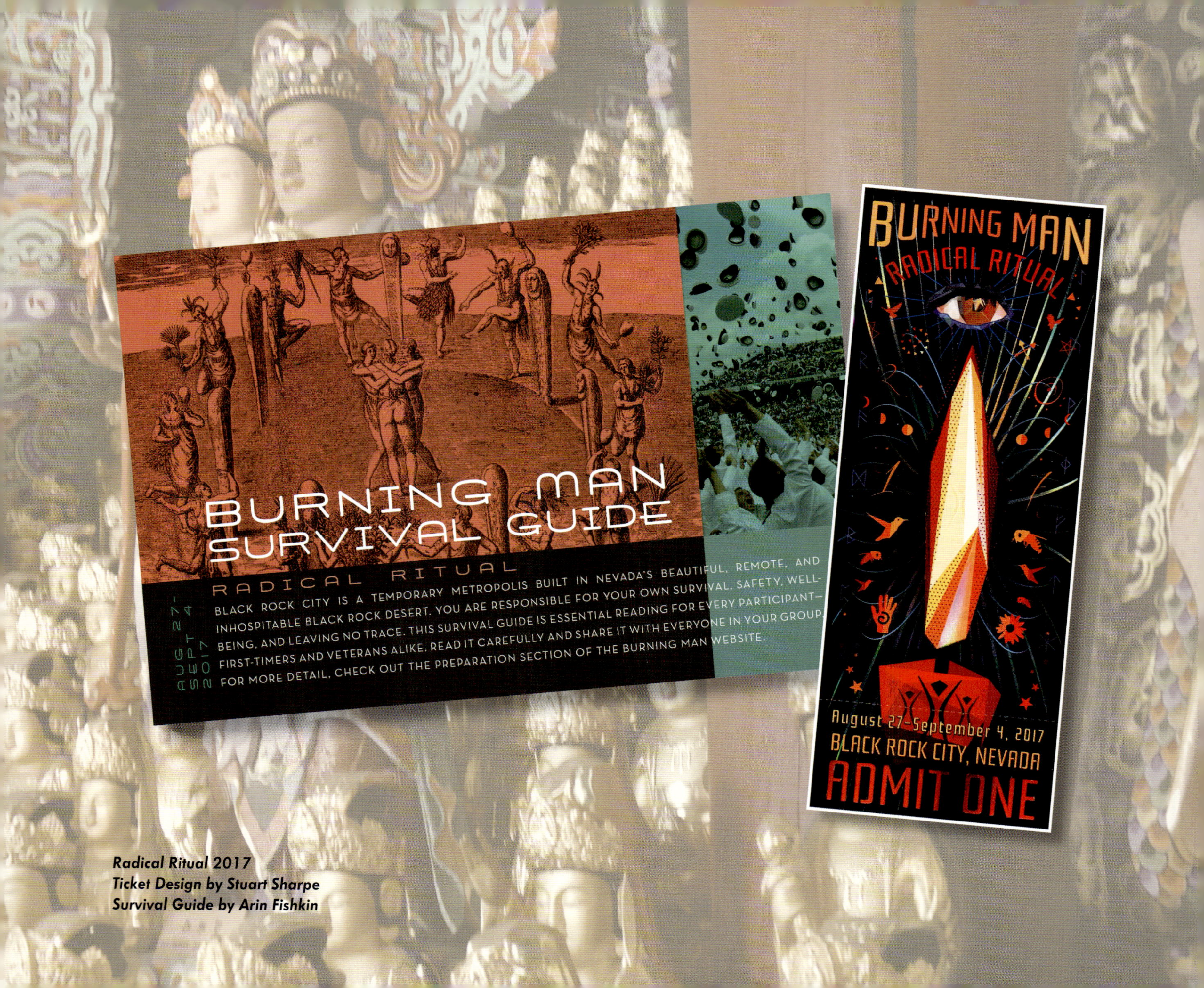

Radical Ritual 2017
Ticket Design by Stuart Sharpe
Survival Guide by Arin Fishkin

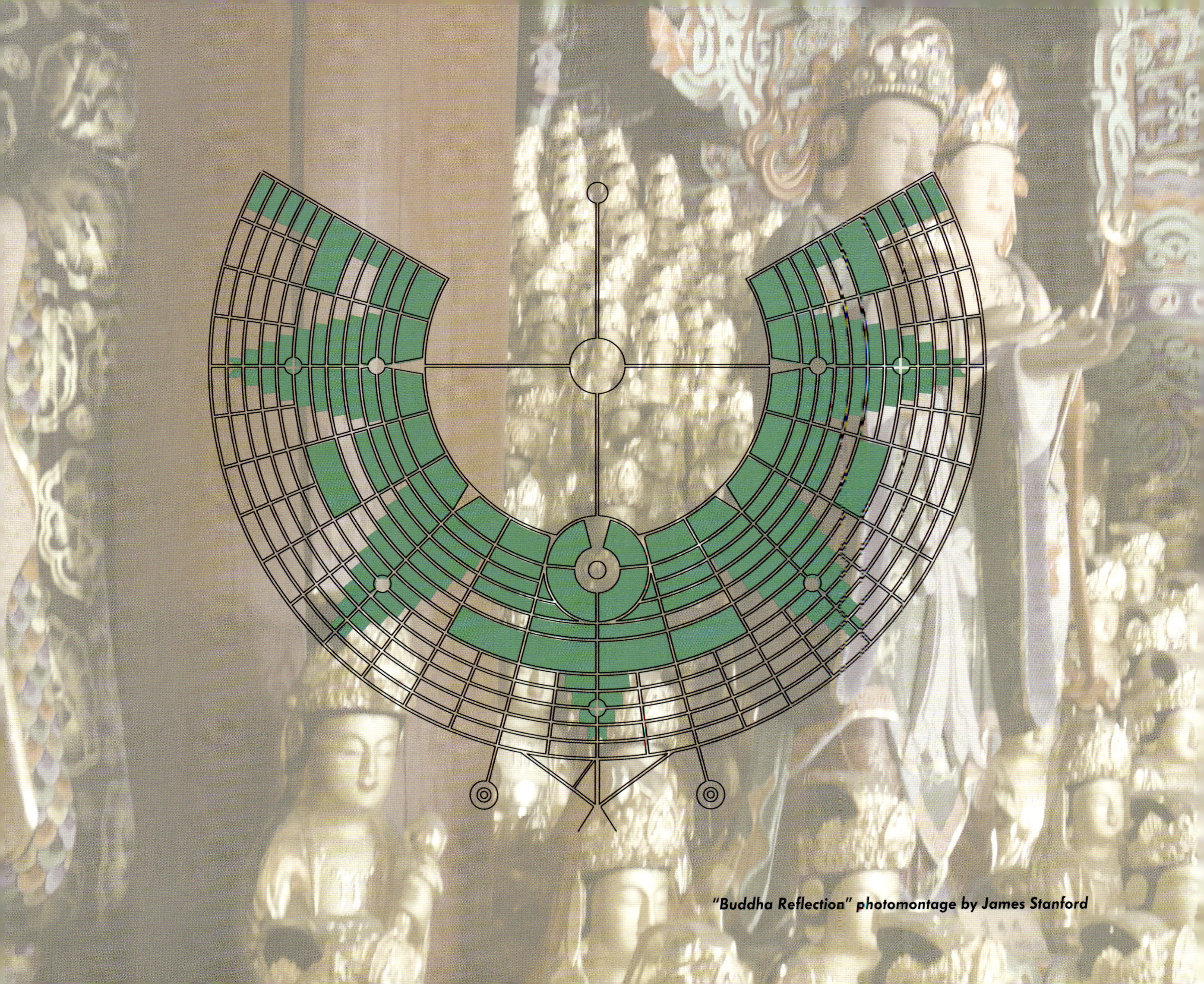

"Buddha Reflection" photomontage by James Stanford

Burning Man Information Radio (BMIR) broadcasts up-to-date info

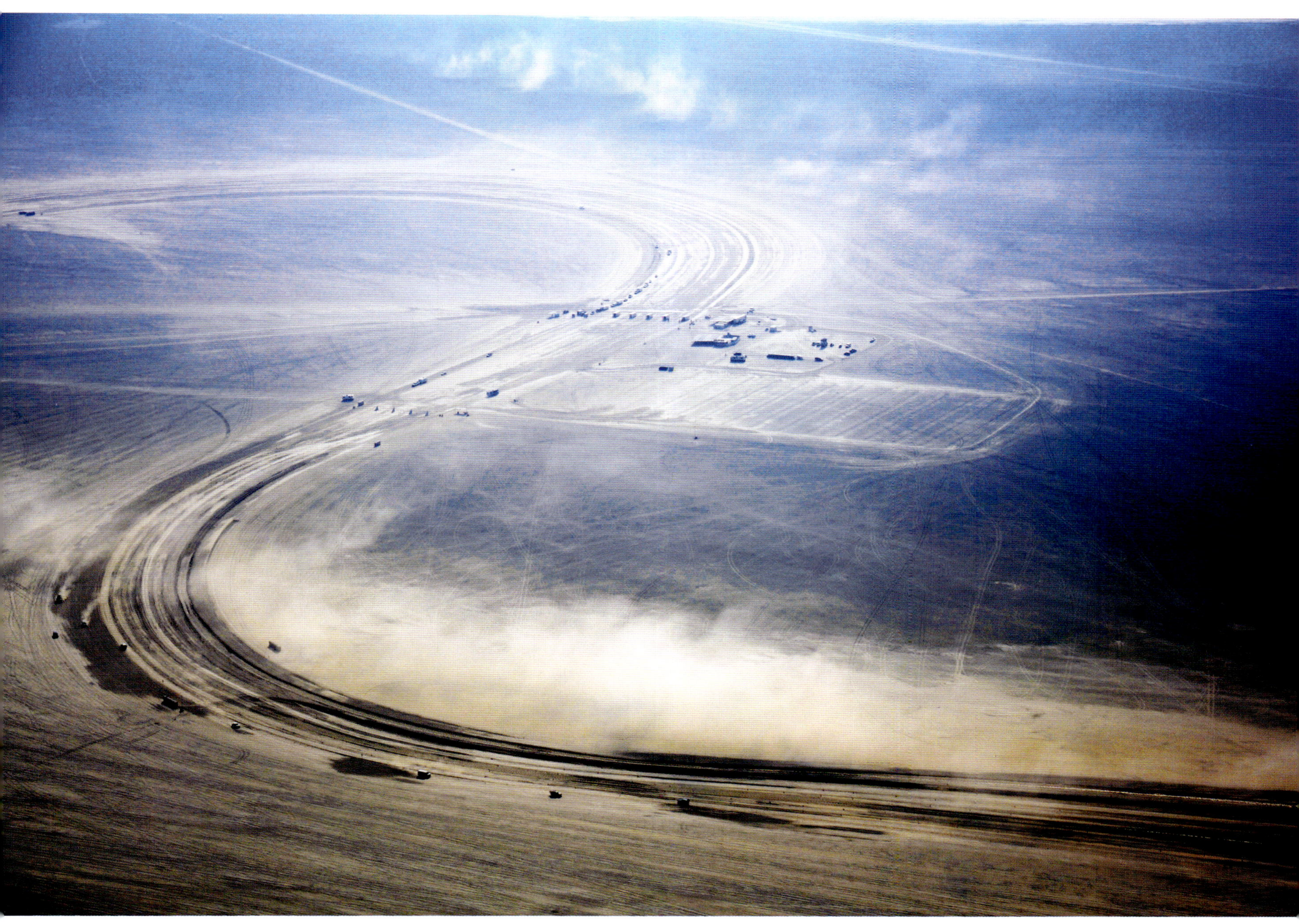

Dust storms, wildfires and other atmospheric conditions drastically affect sunrise and sunset on the playa, population 69,493

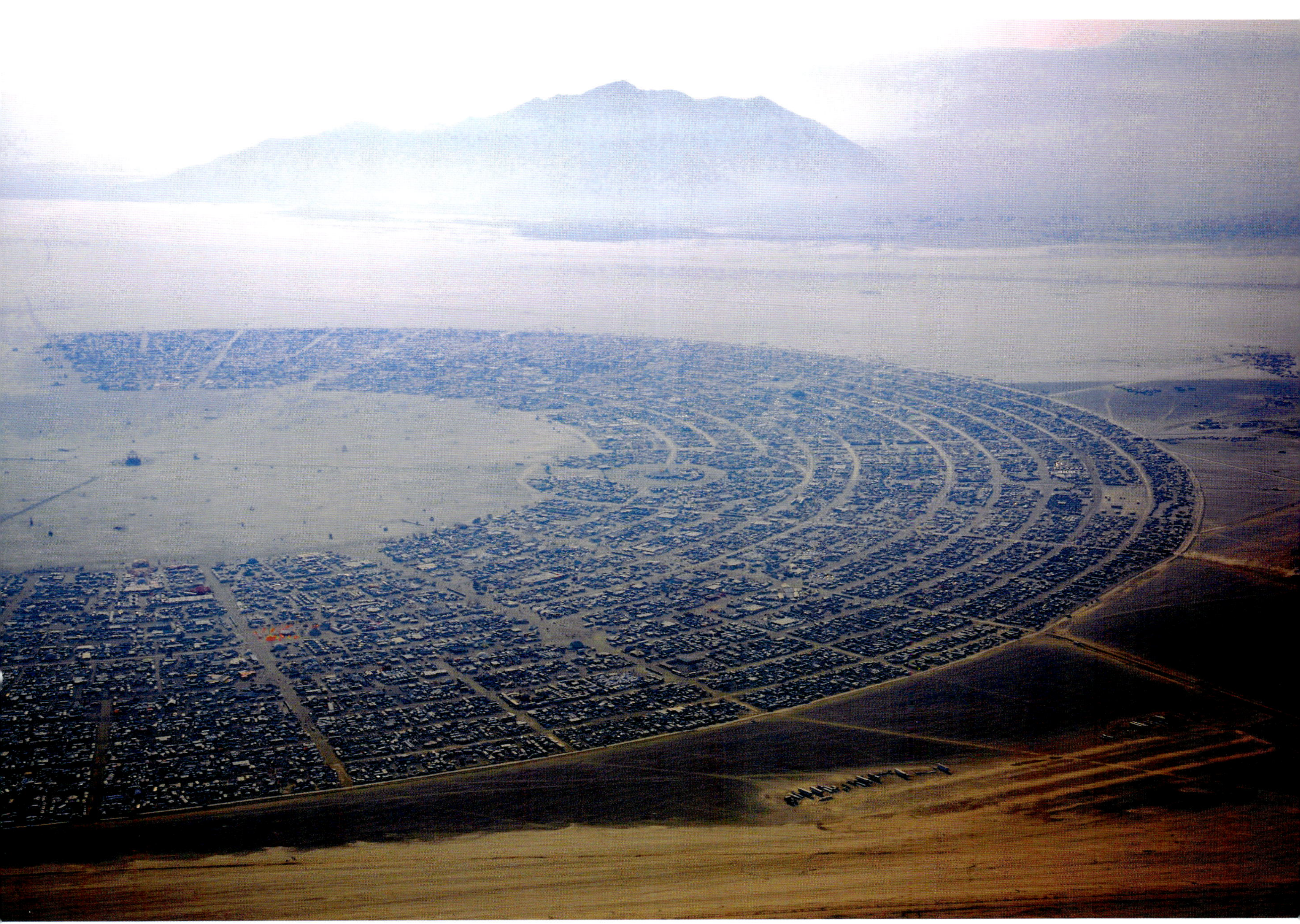

The Man housed inside the Pavilion, looking south towards Center Camp

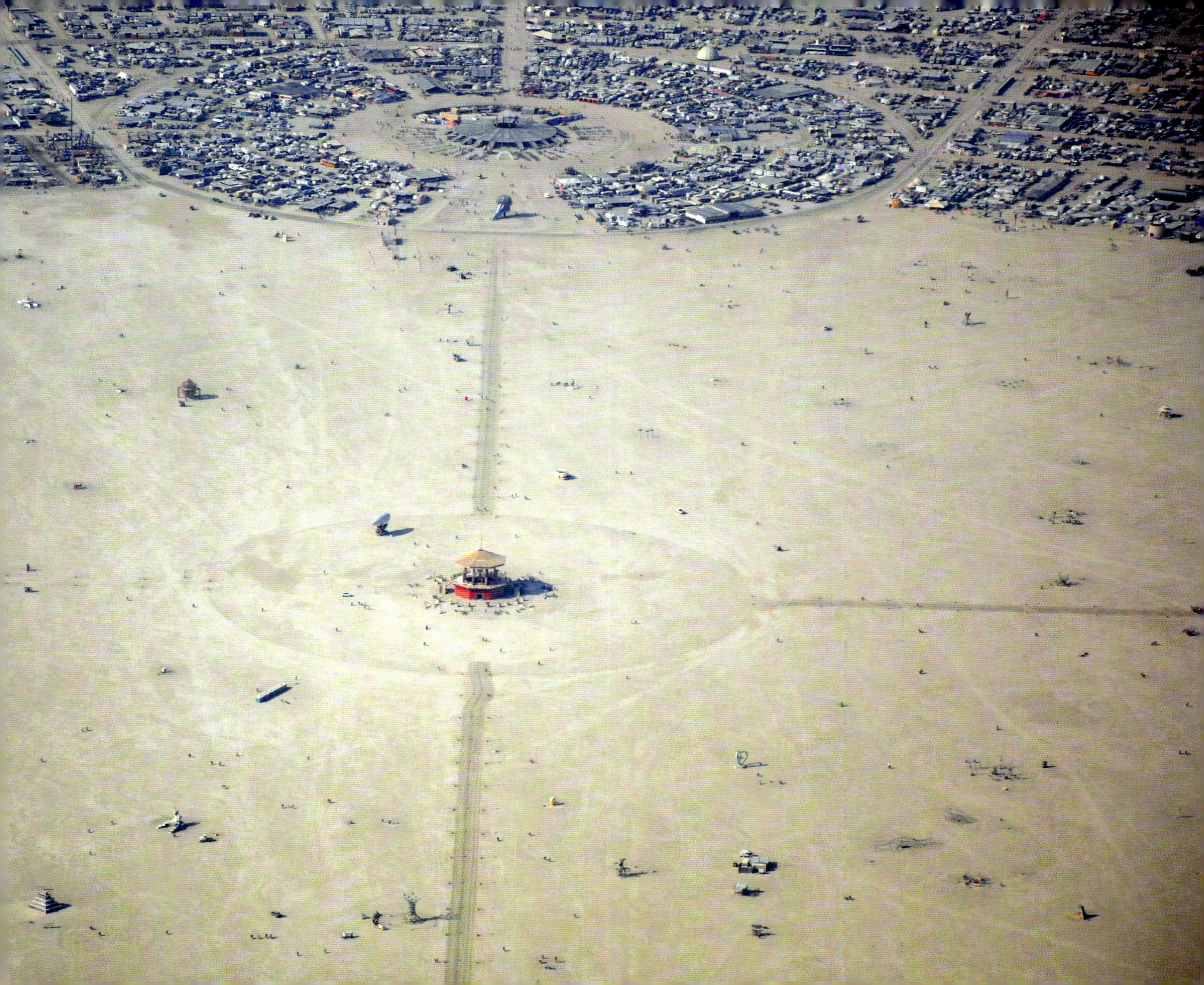

I, Robot 2018
Ticket design by Mark Harrison
Survival Guide by Arin Fishkin

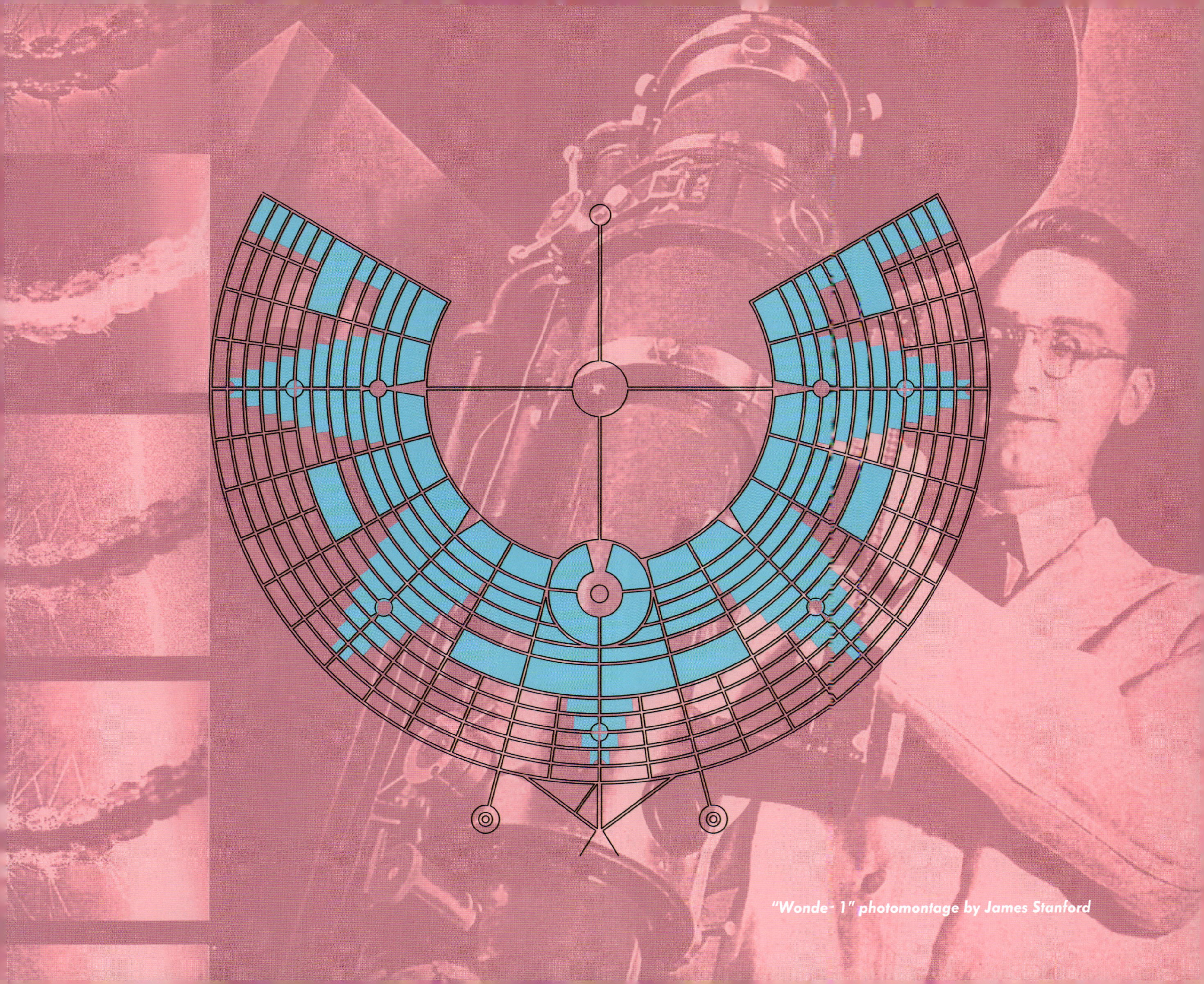

"Wonde- 1" photomontage by James Stanford

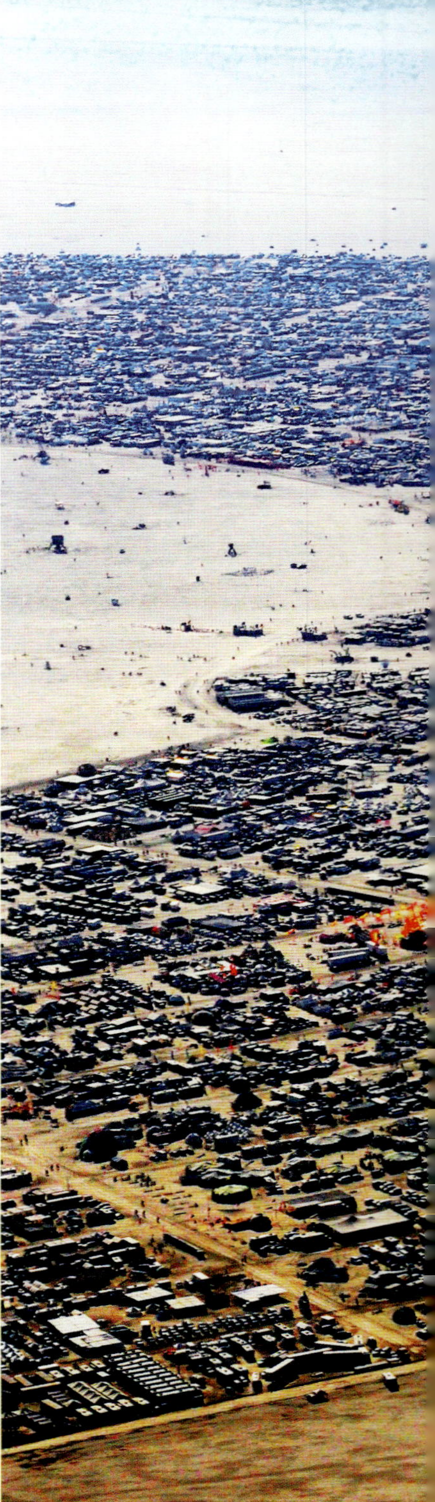

198

Black Rock City is Nevada's 5th largest city for a week. Population 70,248

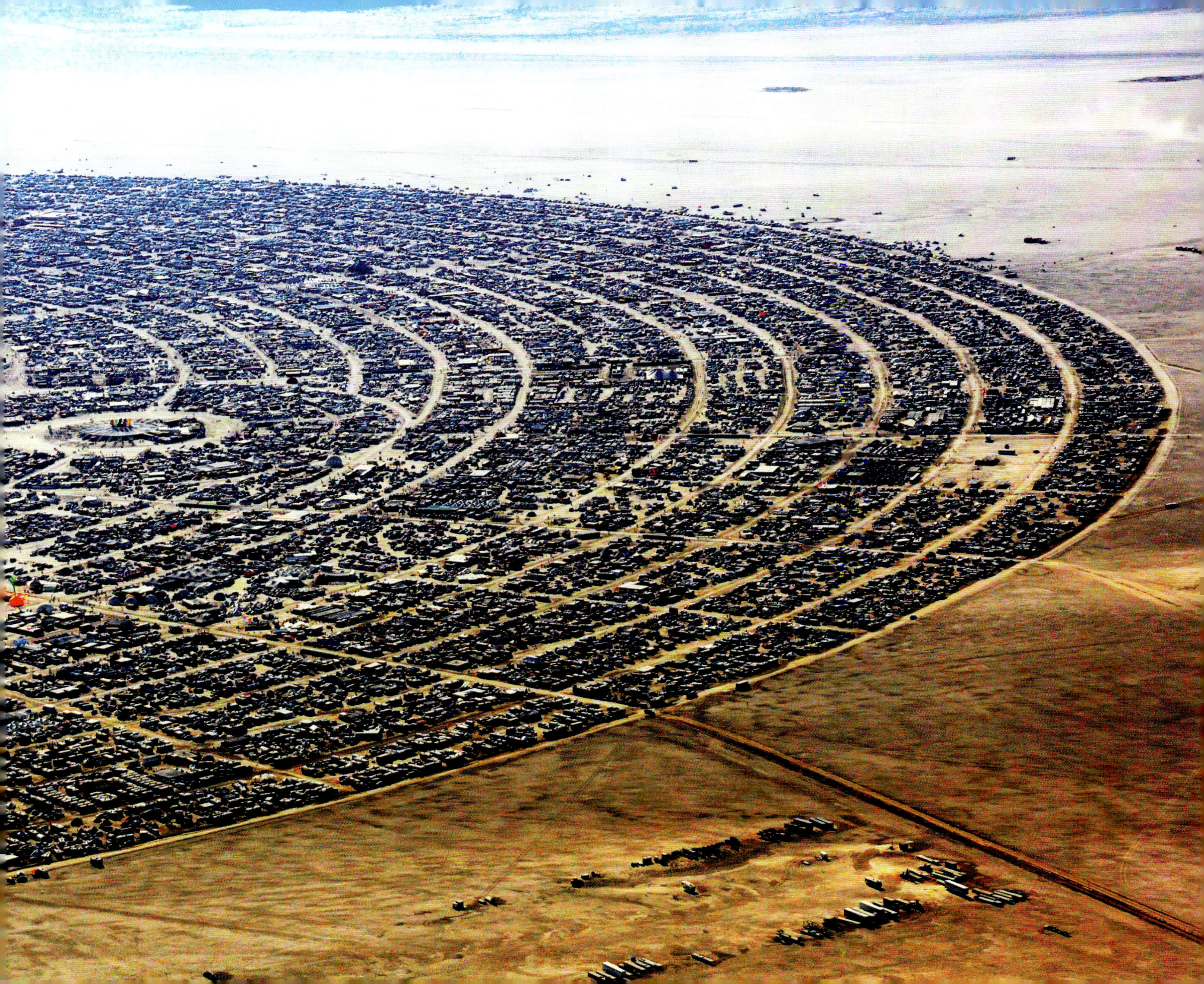

It took four weeks and hundreds of volunteers to build, operate and dismantle this hundred-acre airport

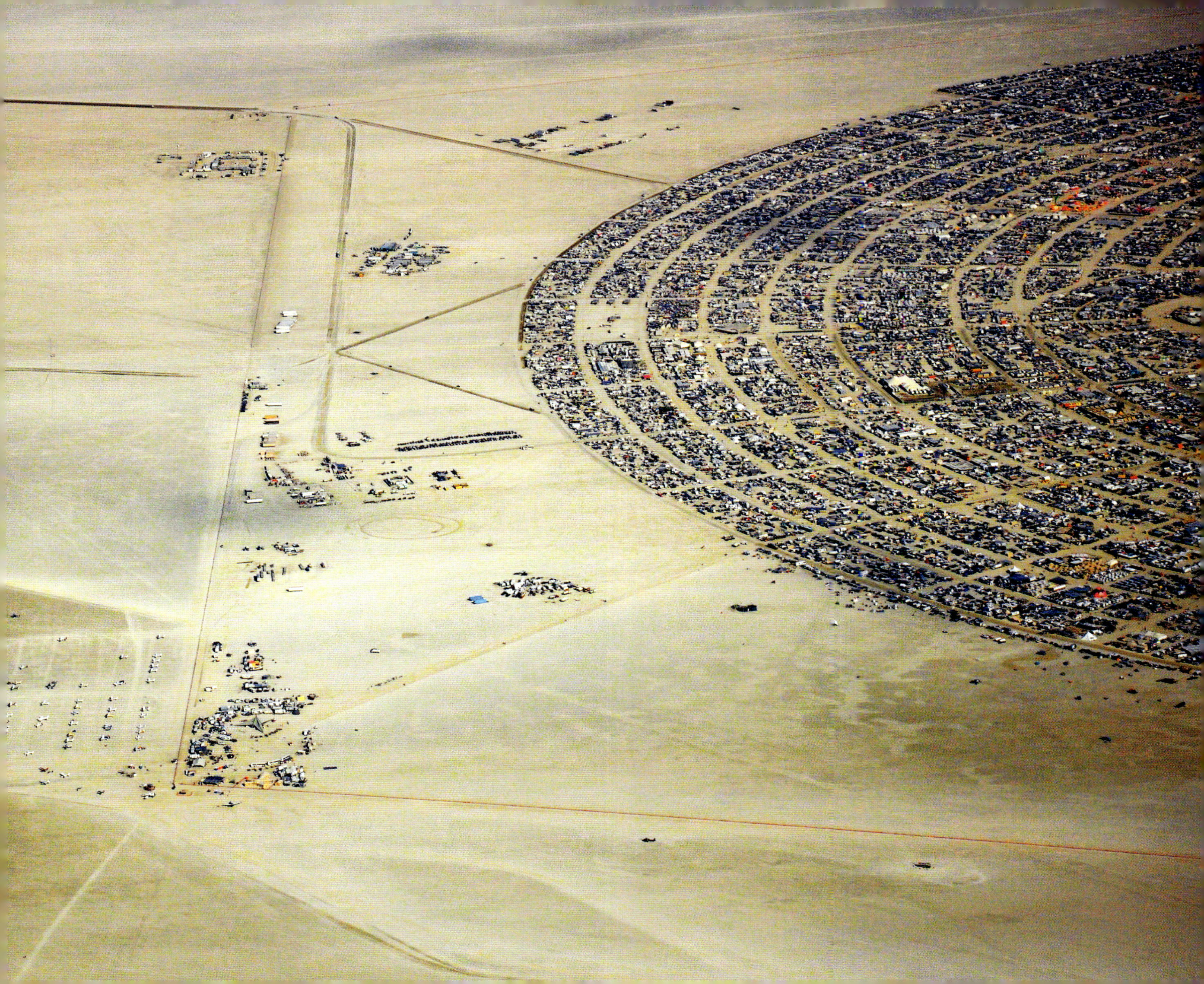

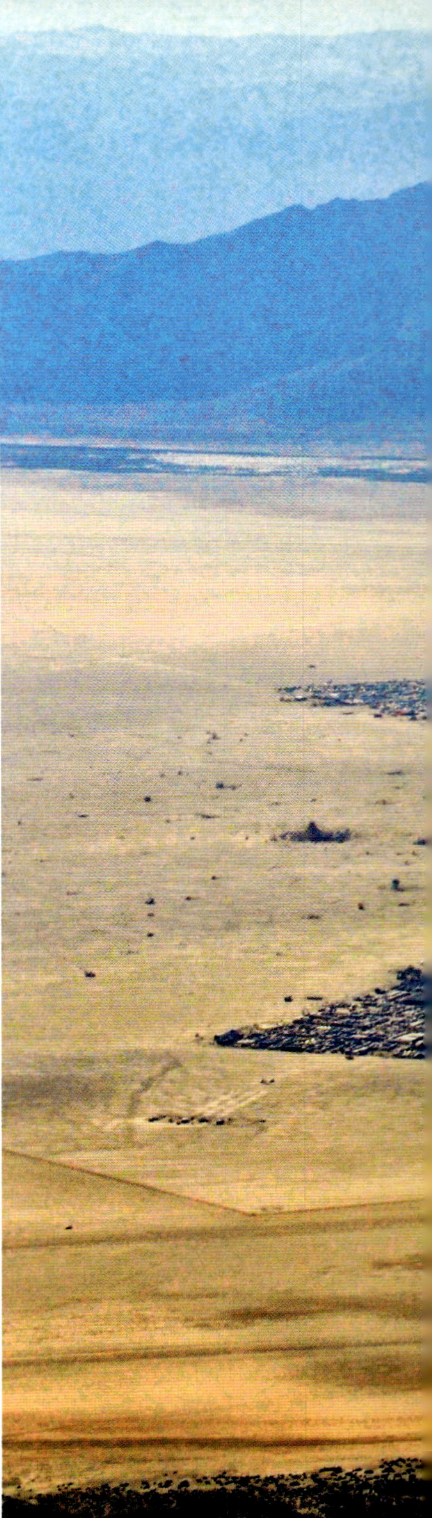

202

Black Rock City (2018)

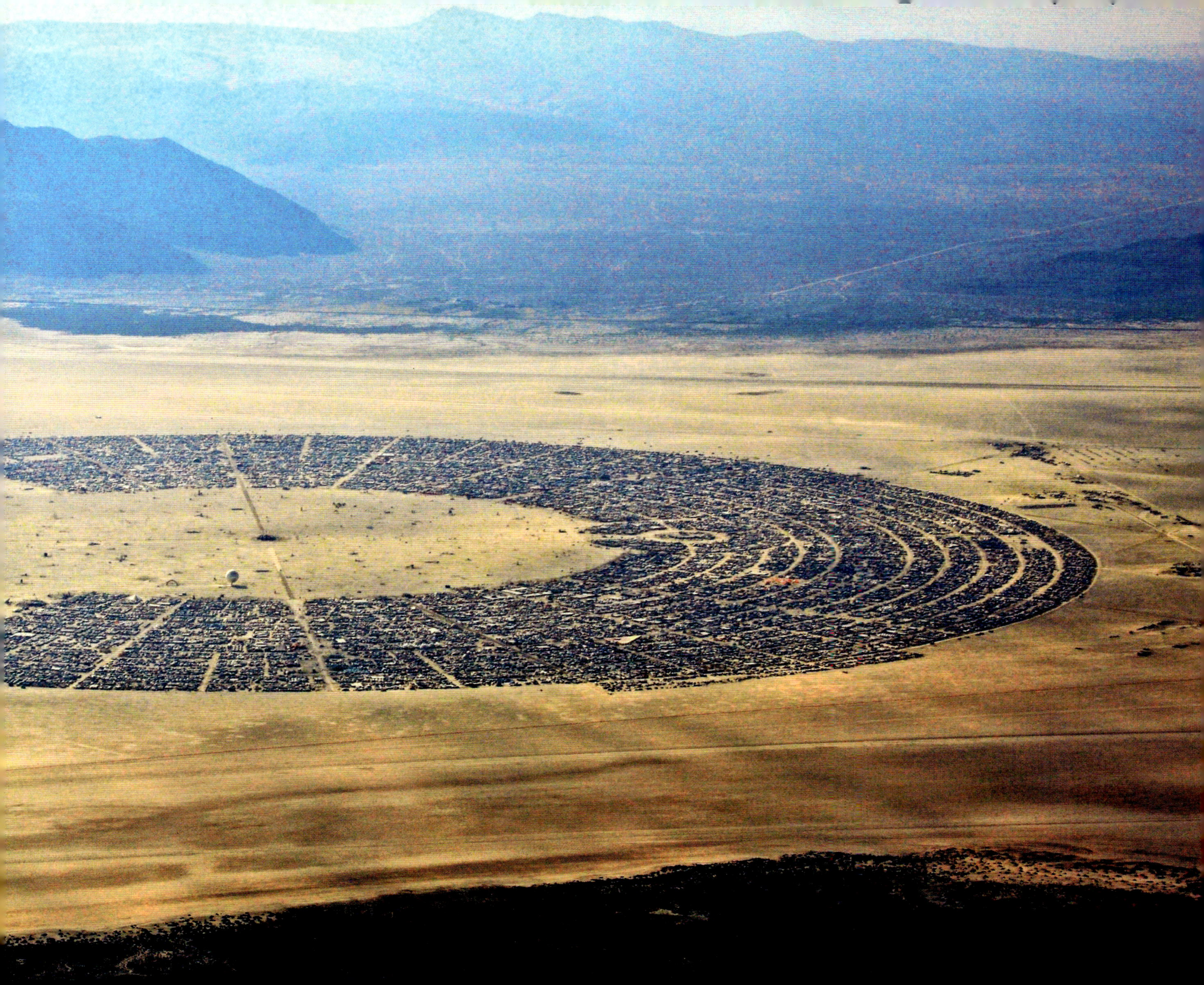

The Illusive Art Spirit

Crimson Rose

In those early years, there was no "how to" manual. We learned from our challenges and have grown to adapt our creative juices-the Art Spirit-in the vastness of the Black Rock Desert. This has taught us to be courageous and to not allow our fears to overtake us because we fear failure. Failure is in the NOT doing.

We were working to keep the event alive-the survival of Black Rock City-so there was no time to think about the items that would eventually become our archives. We were putting ourselves on the line for something that we believed in, even if we could not verbalize our inner feelings.

There were times when we were making it up as we went along. If something worked, we did it again. If not, then we changed it. This is still true today, and this is why Black Rock City continues to evolve. Our culture is a living, breathing organism that needs to be stimulated, disturbed, and set on fire.

Drawn to the Black Rock Desert, we were not trying to create a movement, change culture, or even create a business. Why would a place so barren and desolate seem to hold so much potential? Why would anyone go to the middle of what appears to be nowhere? Well, the vast limitless environment of the Black Rock Desert provokes possibilities. Their creative expression reflects the potential within and allows us to believe that anything is possible.

The city plans in this book eventually became part of

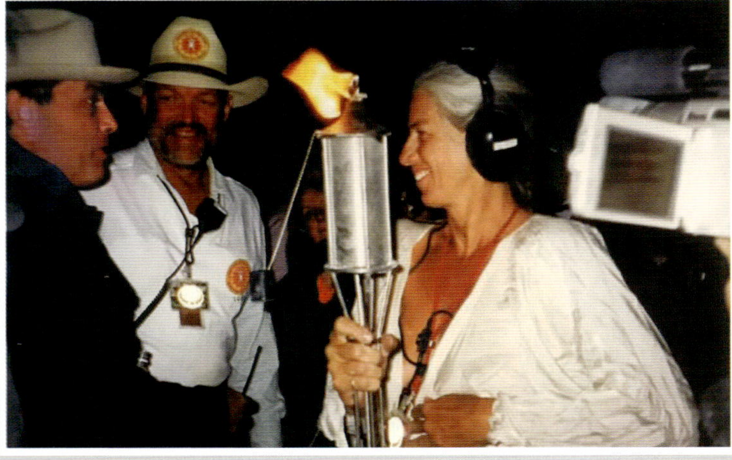

Top: *Will Roger, Crimson Rose, Maria Partridge, Larry Harvey. Photo (2015) by Eleanor Preger*
Bottom: *Larry Harvey, Will Roger, Crimson Rose on burn night. Photo (1998) by Eric Baron*

our archives, but during the time of creating the event, they were a "working design." As a starting point, each year, for bringing Black Rock City into reality, these designs were our North Star. From design to plan, concept to fruition. The city plans are a framework–a blank canvas. They're a dream of the future where participants, returning year after year, bring their energy and child-like enthusiasm to add to the effervescence of the culture in Black Rock City.

But how does one set an intention for culture to thrive? The designs would not have become the plans for the city without starting at a single point. Setting pencil to paper to create the design would then translate into cracking the surface of the playa to physically create the survey of Black Rock City.

What began as a starting point for the survey of the city became a ceremony of the Gold Spike, created by Will Roger and Tony "Coyote" for the Department of Public Works. Over the years, this gesture of appreciation shows those in attendance–those who take a swing at the Gold Spike–that the rewarding hard work ahead of them will promote creative inspiration. The Man that is released by fire gets burned will be positioned at the precise center from which the streets radiate outward, creating a context for creativity to blossom. This is how an idea can turn an environment into engagement.

The Burning Man idea became a means to evoke pas-sion and desire, to inspire vitality and curiosity. All this found its way into our archives. We saved all kinds of things: survival guides, tickets, ashes from the Man, photographs, and posters from different events we were producing during the off-season. These objects are our collective memory, a living testament of the creative spark. Since Black Rock City becomes dust every year, the archives allow us to hold onto that memory.

The archives have become more than a collection of things. They hold the stories that tell of our struggles, our delights, our evolution. And the stories are just as important as the physical items that are now finding their way into museums like: The Hermitage Museum in Norfolk, Virginia; Nevada Museum of Art in Reno, Nevada; Renwick Gallery of the Smithsonian American Art Museum in Washington, D.C.; and more museums to come.

We cherish the hope that what we created would matter –that maybe someone would be stimulated enough to take their own leap of faith.

Appendix: A Compass in the Wilderness

1. The ophiolite basement of California's Central Valley was made apparent in Nicola J. Godfrey's 1997 PhD dissertation in geophysics at Stanford, *"Crustal Structure of Northern California."*

2. A nice overview of the Black Rock's geology can be found in a paper by geologist Cathy Busby at the University of California Santa Barbara: Geol. ucsb.edu/faculty/busby/library/pdf/Burning%20 Man/20Geology/20Black/20Rock/20Desert.pdf

3. For an investigation into our inability to walk a straight line: Frissen I, Campos JL, Souman JL, Ernst M.O, *"Integration of vestibular and proprioceptive signals for spatial updating."* Experimental Brain Research 212(2): 163-176 (2011).

4. On visual expectation: Summerfield, Christopher and Tobias Egner, *"Expectation (and attention) in visual cognition."* Trends in Cognitive Sciences Vol.13 No.9: 403-409 (2009).

5. Rod Garrett's *"Designing Black Rock City"* was written for the Burning Man organization and can be found online at: www.Journal.burningman.org/2010/04/ black-rock-city/building-brc/designing-black-rock-city/

6. Larry Harvey's comments on the design of Black Rock City are from an interview conducted with him by Dezeen's founder and editor-in-chief, Marcus Fairs, on August 25, 2015: www.dezeen. com/2015/08/25/burning-man-needed-urban-design-because-its-a-city-says-founder-larry-harvey/

7. Gary Snyder's ruminations on wilderness and spirituality are complex, deeply informed, and nuanced. *"The Practice of the Wild"* (Berkeley: Counterpoint, 1990) is a collection of short essays that serve as an excellent introduction.

For more information about aerial cognition, photography, and the God's Eye, the following texts may be helpful:

8. Cosgrove, Denis. *"Apollo's Eye A Cartographic Genealogy of the Earth in the Western Imagination."* Baltimore: Johns Hopkins University Press, 2001.

9. Fox, William L. *"Aereality: On the World from Above."* Berkeley: Counterpoint, 2009.

10. Cosgrove, Dennis & William L. Fox. *"Photography and Flight."* London: Reaktion Books, 2010.

11. Gerster, Georg. *"The Past from Above: Aerial Photographs of Archaeological Sites."* Munich: Shirmer/Mosel, 2003.

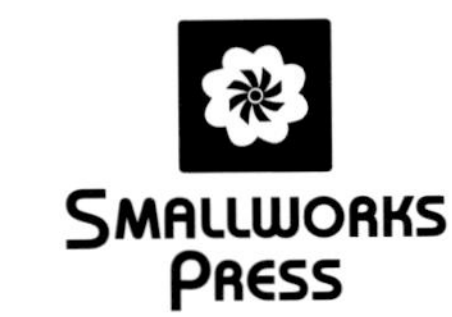

SMALLWORKS PRESS

3540 W. Sahara Avenue #464
Las Vegas, NV 89102, USA

Publication Date: June 18, 2019

ISBN-13: 978-0-9778806-5-2
ISBN-10: 0-977880656

I. Will Roger, II. Compass Of The Ephemeral: Aerial Photography of Black Rock City
through the Lens of Will Roger, III. Photography, IV. Burning Man

Printed in China

First Edition

Cover Photo: Will Roger
Editor: Phyllis Needham
Design & Typography: Milo Duffin
Design Consultant: Philip Lewis, Lewis Hallam Design
Project Management: Smallworks Press
Principle Photography: Will Roger

Special Thanks: Burning Man Project, Nevada Museum of Art, Center for Art + Environment Archive Collections,
Will Roger, Crimson Rose and Dr. Laura Henkel

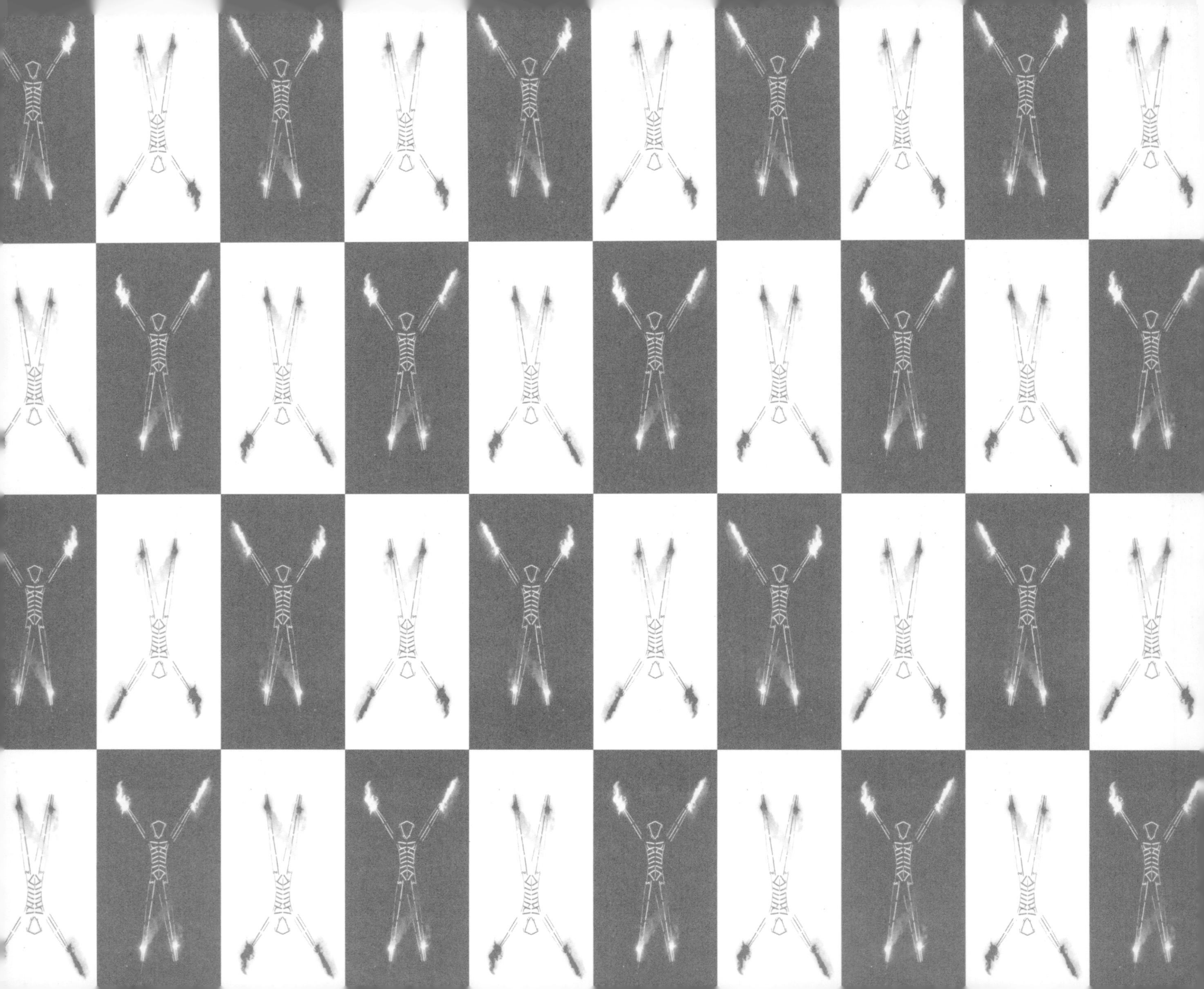